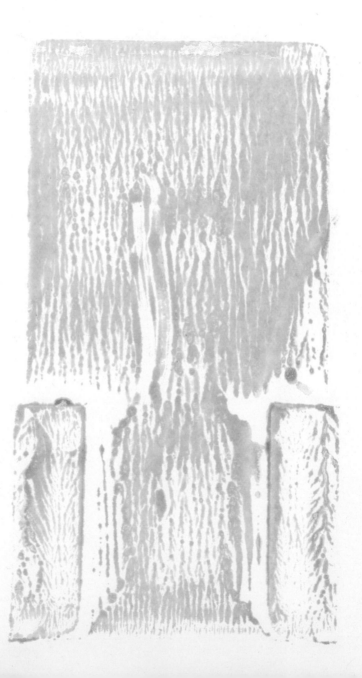

REFLECTIONS ON
GOVERNMENT

REFLECTIONS
ON
GOVERNMENT

BY

ERNEST BARKER

*Honorary Fellow of Merton College, Oxford
and of Peterhouse, Cambridge*

OXFORD UNIVERSITY PRESS

Oxford University Press, Amen House, London E.C.4

GLASGOW NEW YORK TORONTO MELBOURNE WELLINGTON
BOMBAY CALCUTTA MADRAS KARACHI KUALA LUMPUR
CAPE TOWN IBADAN NAIROBI ACCRA

FIRST PUBLISHED MAY 1942
REPRINTED OCTOBER 1942

REPRINTED LITHOGRAPHICALLY IN GREAT BRITAIN
AT THE UNIVERSITY PRESS, OXFORD
BY CHARLES BATEY, PRINTER TO THE UNIVERSITY
FROM CORRECTED SHEETS OF THE SECOND IMPRESSION
1945, 1948, 1953, 1958

PREFACE

THIS book has been written in times of trouble, and no doubt it bears some marks of the times. But I hope that I have risen above national and temporary animosities ; that I have not steeped myself unduly in the flood of the present; and that I have succeeded in looking at things, in some measure, *sub specie diuturnitatis*. I acknowledge, and indeed I am anxious to state, the limits of my outlook—limits deliberately imposed. The book is called by the name of *Reflections on Government*. But it does not include, nor is it intended to include, any reflections on international government. That theme goes beyond the area of government in the domestic sense in which I have understood the word ; and it belongs to the sphere of another inquiry. Nor, again, does the book include any reflections on government outside Europe. (For that matter it does not include any reference to some forms of government in Europe—for example the Swiss form—which deserve the closest attention.) This, again, is a limit deliberately imposed. I am far from being forgetful of the United States, of the overseas Dominions, or of the great Empire and the great problems of India. But I have not sought to write a text-book, or to take the world for my province. I have simply sought to set down thoughts, reflections, considerations, suggested to my mind by the main movement of ideas and forces in the continent to which I belong and of which I am, in some sense, a citizen.

These thoughts, or reflections, or considerations, may perhaps be said to fall within the scope of political science, a subject in which I was once a professor. But in another sense they can hardly be said to belong to any one branch of study or subject of inquiry. I am not a philosopher; but I could not refrain from some consideration of ethics, which must always be vitally connected with politics. I am not an economist; but I have been driven to think about economics, which can never be absent from any political inquiry. I am not a student of natural science; but I have found it impossible to refrain from reflecting on the methods and the achievements of natural science, which are deeply affecting the life of every political community. On the whole I seem to myself to have been engaged in moving about on the boundaries or marches of different subjects. Physical boundaries or marches are always exciting places— whether it be the Welsh border, from Chepstow to Shrewsbury, or the Scottish border that runs from Carlisle to the Cheviots. Perhaps the same is true of intellectual boundaries or marches. They are places of excitement, where discoveries may possibly be made.

The one merit which I can claim (but the claim may cause men of a younger generation to smile) is that I am well advanced in the sixties. A friend said to me the other day, *à propos* of nothing, and therefore, as I thought, candidly and impersonally, 'Any book about politics needs grey hairs'. I have now that qualification: indeed I have it abundantly. But I could wish that I had enjoyed more of that experience of practical affairs which should go along with grey hairs. My experience of life has almost entirely belonged to the field of education; and what I have seen of government and administration, in actual practice, has been limited to that field. I am aware that this experience is by no means of the first order. Such as it is, I have sought to use it, guessing from the small letters to the large, and arguing from what I have seen in small to the properties of government at large.

The argument of these *Reflections* is general, and perhaps

even abstract. I have attempted to see the pattern and design
of the wood rather than to examine the idiosyncrasy of each
tree : to consider the general movement of ideas and forces in
Europe rather than to investigate the particularity of each of its
parts. There is a defect in the method, but there may also be
some merit; at any rate, there is room for both methods. One
further thing may be added. The book, except for the last
chapter, was written before the outbreak of war. I waited
for two years to see whether the war had made it otiose
and superfluous. I ventured to decide, in the autumn of
last year, that it might still be of some service to the cause
of humanity and the humanities. I thank the Delegates of
the Clarendon Press for trusting the decision to which I came.
I hope that it may be endorsed by the judgment of my
readers. Of one thing I can assure them—a thing which was
at first a surprise to me, and then a comfort. There is no
judgment, and no expression of opinion (not even in regard
to Russia) which it has been necessary to alter in consequence of the movement of events during the last two years.
The only corrections made have been corrections of logic and
style.

*   *   *

There is a shortage of paper in these days. It affects many
things—not only the publication of the lucubrations of authors,
but also (when that is granted by grace and benignity) the
type and the form of their books. One of the things which it
affects is the ancient and honourable practice of dedication.
The edicts of war deny the use of a dedicatory page; and a
dedication without a memorial page on which it can be boldly
inscribed is a *dimidiatum quid*. But piety is not to be denied its
expression; and I venture to insert—in rounded Roman
capitals, if the printer will grant me that favour—some
dedicatory words in the conclusion of this preface.

These are the words :

TO THE
MOST NOBLE AND MOST EQUAL SISTERS
THE TWO FAMOUS UNIVERSITIES
FOR THEIR
LOVE AND ACCEPTANCE SHOWN

The words are those of Ben Jonson. They come in the
beginning of the Preface, written in 1607, to his play *Volpone,
or the Fox* ; and they are addressed to Oxford and Cambridge,
in which, as well as in London, the play had been performed.
I cannot but echo his words, over three hundred years afterwards (there is a continuity in English life, and things repeat
themselves naturally); but I echo them with some trepidation.
I fear that I may seem to claim too much in speaking of 'love
and acceptance shown'. Yet I cannot but feel that I have
had both from my pupils in the days, now past, of my teaching
and lecturing; and perhaps I am the best judge of what I
have had. In any case I have myself a love, and very much
more than acceptance, for the Universities of Oxford and
Cambridge, in one of which I spent twenty-seven years, and
in the other I have now spent over fourteen. I have written
this book in the one: it is being published in the other. Which
of the two I love best is a secret I must keep to myself. Indeed
I cannot do otherwise; for it is a secret even from myself.

There are also two other Universities—another pair of
sisters—to which I am bound to record my debt and express
my gratitude. One is the University of London, where I stayed
for a time (it was over seven years) on the journey that was
leading me, unknown to myself, from Oxford to Cambridge.
In King's College, London—*collegium amicum, collegium dilectum*
—I learned something of the difficult art of administration;
and as a member of the Senate of the University of London I
learned something of the even more difficult art of government
—the art of discussing and reconciling divergent opinions and

interests. But it is the University of Wales, and therein the University College of Wales at Aberystwyth, that I am more especially bound to remember. It was the University College at Aberystwyth which invited me, in 1933, to give a course of public lectures that might be eventually published. That invitation is the cause—now a far-distant cause—of this book. What is now published, at the long last, in literal obedience to the maxim of Horace (*nonum . . . prematur in annum*) is indeed a different thing, except for some passages in the last part, from the lectures originally given. But it has sprung from the lectures; and the original core of ideas remains, even if it has been developed and extended, by travel in Europe, and by study of the march of events in Europe, during the last nine years.

CAMBRIDGE,   E. B.
    January 1942.

CONTENTS

Part II

DEMOCRACY AND ITS EXTERNAL DIFFICULTIES

Part III

AMENDMENTS TO DEMOCRACY

A DEFINITION OF SOME TERMS

A NATION is a society or community of persons, whose unity is based

(1) primarily on space, or neighbourhood, issuing in the feeling of neighbourliness, and in that common love of the natal soil (or *patria*) which is called patriotism ;

(2) secondly on time, or the common tradition of centuries, issuing in the sense of a common participation in an inherited way of life, and in that common love for the inheritance which is called nationalism.

Physiologically, and in respect of the blood in their veins, the members of a nation are generally drawn from different races or stocks which have wandered into a contiguous territory during the course of human migrations. Psychologically, and in respect of the content of their minds, the members of a nation have been led by a life of contiguity and common historical experience to accumulate a common mental capital and to develop a common mental purpose for its maintenance and extension.

A STATE is ' a juridically organized nation, or a nation organized for action under legal rules ' (Vinogradoff, Historical Jurisprudence, Vol. I, p. 85). Expanding the definition, one may say that ' a modern State is generally a territorial nation, organized as a legal association by its own action in creating a constitution (such action being in some cases, as in Great Britain, a process along a line of time rather than an act at a point of time), and permanently acting as such an association, under that constitution, for the purpose of maintaining a scheme of legal rules defining and securing the rights and duties of its members '.

SOCIETY or COMMUNITY[1]—the national society or community—is not abolished by, or exhausted in, the emergence of the State. The State is a national society or community organized as a legal association under a ' deed ' called a constitution ; but the

---

[1] The two terms are here used as synonymous. A distinction is sometimes drawn between them—the term ' community ' being reserved for a disinterested group and for the feeling of fellowship which unites such a group, and the term ' society ' then being assigned to an interested group which is concerned to promote the particular interest or interests of its members. It is true, and it is a fact which may be cited in favour of this distinction, that in Roman Law *societas* signifies a company of partners formed for trading purposes. On the other hand it is also true that in general Latin usage the words *communitas* and *societas* are employed in an identical sense ; and it is also true that, in our English usage, the word ' society ' has been kept at the high level of meaning at which it is indistinguishable from the word ' community '. We thus speak, in a particular sense, of the Society of Friends,

national society or community continues to exist and act apart from the ' deed ' and as something distinct from the legal association. It exists and acts *for* a number of purposes (economic, religious, educational and the like), and *through* a number of contained unions, societies, and associations (such as Trade Unions, the Society of Friends, the British Association for the Advancement of Science, and the like), which collectively and in their aggregate constitute national society or community as a whole. Though State and Society are distinct, they are also connected and interdependent ; a Trade Union, for instance, acts for purposes for which the State is also acting, and thus acts in connection with the State, when it seeks to assert some control over the conduct of industry ; and again a Trade Union is affected and limited by the law of the State in conducting its activities, as the State is also affected and conditioned by the traditions and practices of Trade Unions in giving effect to its industrial policy. Connected and interdependent, but also distinct, State and Society play different parts in a system of co-operation—the State being the sole vehicle of law and legal regulation, but Society (through its contained unions, societies, and associations) continuing to act for a variety of purposes by the side of the State, in connection with the State, and on a system of interdependence between the State and itself.

SOCIALISM and COMMUNISM are terms connected with, and flowing from, the terms Society and Community. But while we may identify the words ' society ' and ' community ', it would be incorrect to identify the words ' socialism ' and ' communism '.

(1) Historically, the word ' socialism ' would appear to be the earlier, and to have come into use during the five years between the Reform Bill of 1832 and the accession of Queen Victoria in 1837. ' Communism ' followed a little later, in the early years of the next decade. The two terms seem to have had a difference of connotation from the first, though it is not clear that they were regarded as essentially different. Socialism implied the socialization (or rather, since the agent was to be the national State, the *nationalization*) of the means of production, distribution, and exchange, and the subsequent management of those means under a system of social (*i.e.* national) control. Communism had a similar implication ; but it added the special idea that payment for work should be made, not according to the quantity or quality of the work done, as the

---

which is obviously a disinterested group ; and in a general sense we use the word ' society ' for the sum total of all particular societies, including (and including particularly) the various disinterested societies. Society and community may therefore be treated as synonyms. It may be added that ' Association ' is a synonym for ' Society ' in its particular sense, with the one differentiation that it lays an especial emphasis on the act of forming the society and the activity of maintaining its life and purposes subsequently. It is for this reason (because of the *act* and the *activity* specially involved) that we speak of the State as a legal association rather than a legal society. But apart from this nuance there is no difference between an association and a society.

Socialists tended to think, but according to the wants or needs of the worker. (2) This original difference, however, began to be obscured, or succeeded, by another, which we may date from the growth and triumph of Socialism in Russia at the beginning of the present century. There had long been a divergence among the socialists between the reformist party, who sought to achieve the aim of nationalization by a gradual process and through the methods of parliamentary democracy, and the revolutionary party who sought to achieve the aim by a sudden *coup* and through the methods of a dictatorship of the proletariat. The first explosion of a revolutionary party had been the Parisian Commune of 1871 ; and in the twentieth century the term ' Communism ' began to be applied to the tenets of the Russian revolutionary party, led by Lenin, who followed Marx's interpretation of the lessons of the Parisian Commune. Here the essence of Communism would appear to be the method of achieving nationalization, and not the method of payment for work after nationalization has been achieved. (3) But a further reflection has now to be added, which complicates matters still further. The old idea that the special mark of Communism was its insistence on payment for work according to needs returns. When that idea returns, it begins to be held that a revolutionary dictatorship of the proletariat is not Communism, however revolutionary it may be, unless and until it inaugurates a system of payment for work according to needs. It is only Socialism ; and it will not be Communism until it has achieved the communist system of payment. . . . The result of the whole development is that most of us nowadays speak of Russian or Soviet Communism, on the ground of its revolutionary character, but the Russian leaders themselves (Lenin, followed by Stalin) deny that Communism as yet exists in Russia, and speak of Russia as passing through a socialist phase on the way to Communism. In this book the term has been used, not in this later refined sense, but in the ordinary sense in which it denotes the policy of a revolutionary socialist party.

PART I

DEMOCRATIC GOVERNMENT AND ITS INTERNAL DIFFICULTIES

I

THE NAME AND THE NATURE OF LIBERTY

§ 1. GOODNESS AND LIBERTY

THERE are many words, of the sort we call abstract, which sound in men's ears with the sound of a trumpet. They denote things which we cannot see, but in the existence of which we none the less deeply believe : things which are ideas of our inward mind, but are also the moving ideals of our outward and visible life. Such are the three great words truth, beauty, and goodness—the names of the values we recognize, or the ultimate ends we seek to achieve, in the sphere of knowledge, the sphere of art, and the sphere of action.

Within the sphere of action, and as parts or elements of goodness, there are other values or ends (we may call them derivative values or consequential ends) which we recognize and seek to achieve. Looking only at the social aspect of goodness, and confining our attention, therefore, to the social side of the sphere of action—the side which appears in our community life, of which our life in the State is only one, if a great and peculiar example—we find the idea and ideal of justice : we find, again, the ideas and ideals—proclaimed in 1789, but long anterior to the French Revolution, and indeed as old as the first beginnings of Stoic philosophy—of liberty, equality, and fraternity. We must not pause to discuss the relation of justice to these three sisters : we must not even pause to discuss the relation between the three, or to inquire whether equality, and still more fraternity, can properly be called a full sister of liberty. These are questions which may recur, at a later stage of the argument ; but for the moment our concern is simply with liberty, and with liberty as a part or element of the social aspect of goodness.

Words are living things, and their meaning is best understood if we consider them in their growth. Originally liberty signified the quality or status of the free man, or free producer,

4113　　　　　　　B

in contradistinction to the slave. It thus implied, in its elementary sense, a power of original action, or in other words self-determination, resident in the individual, and relative to the area of economic activity. The primary liberty was that of individual producer ; but if it was confined to individuals, and to one aspect of individuals, it could readily be extended to other and wider spheres, as soon as they attracted attention and raised new problems of status. The subsequent history of liberty has been a history of such extension, not only to areas of action other than the economic, but also to agents other than the individual. Men have learned to think of civil, religious, and political liberty, as well as of economic liberty : they have learned to think of the liberty of groups as well as of individuals. Liberty has grown from its original root to a great and branching tree, and some of its branches chafe and jar against others.

§ 2. THE VARIOUS PARTIES OF LIBERTY

We shall understand the multiplicity—and incidentally the contradictions—of modern liberty if we look at the various causes which its name is used to cover. The ardent Nationalist himself invokes the name and cover of liberty, which can be used no less by parties of the Right than by parties of the Centre and Left. To the Nationalist liberty is not a matter of the individual, or of any voluntary association of individuals : it is a matter of the divinely or naturally given fact of the Nation, organized as a State, and claiming an absolute autonomy for all its works and ways. In the nationalist philosophy the freedom of the national State is the supreme freedom, which absorbs and engulfs—or, as the Nationalist himself prefers to say, includes and realizes—the freedom of the individual. Whether the Nation be conceived, as it is in the new philosophy of modern Germany, as a racial unit resting upon a physical basis, or whether it be regarded, as it is in the philosophy developed by Italian Fascism, as a transcendental metaphysical organism, with a higher existence and with higher ends and means of action, the national State must above all be free—free within, from the conflict of sectional parties and the collision of local or provincial interests : free without, from the presence of any ' foreign ' constraint or would-be international limit which impedes the flow of national political control over the whole of the area assumed to belong to the national stock and the national interest. This is the freedom of a colossus ; but liberty has become a wide enough term to cover even the colossus of Nationalism.

There was a time when Liberalism might be described as the party of the Left. To-day it has moved to the centre ; and it leads a precarious life, under a constant threat of elision, between the Nationalism of the Right and the Socialism which now occupies its old station on the Left. By its very name it vindicates, or seeks to vindicate, a peculiar interest in the cause of liberty. Originally, and primarily, the interest of Liberalism was an interest in what our Whig forefathers called, and we may continue to call, the cause of civil liberty. It was a passion for the right of the individual citizen to pursue his own life according to his own views, at once protected and respected by the State of which he was a member. It was a protest, as old as Magna Carta, against arbitrary imprisonment and arbitrary taxation : it was also a claim (which is already advanced in the great argument of Milton's *Areopagitica*), for liberty of speech, liberty of meeting, and that general liberty of discussion which is the life-breath of every society. This original attitude of Liberalism may seem to be negative, the attitude of the spirit *der stets verneint*, the attitude of a constant ' No ' to the claims of the organized State. But it is negative only to those who regard the spirit of man, in its own intrinsic individuality, as itself a negative quantity ; and in any case the primary protest of Liberalism soon came to be transcended. Liberty of discussion was widened, until it came to mean the right of the members of a State to constitute its government and to determine its policy by free debate and vote. Political was added to civil liberty ; and the cause of Liberalism, by a natural extension, became the positive course of affirmative and active Democracy.

It has become the fashion, among many Continental writers —who none the less include both causes in a common condemnation—to distinguish the cause of Liberalism from that of Democracy, and to treat them as diametrical opposites. The Liberal, in their view, is a man who would limit, and even, if it were possible, abolish, any control which the State seeks to exercise over its members. The Democrat, on the contrary, is one who believes in the right of the majority, or in other words of mere number or mass, and is ready to subject the members of the State, at every point and on every issue, to the arbitrary and incalculable play of the brute power of mass-decision. Better, it is argued, than either of these extreme philosophies is the philosophy of a real national will, disengaged and expressed by a genuine leader of the nation ; a will which readily and naturally controls every member of the nation who feels its call in his blood, and thus transcends the negativism of the mere Liberal ; but also a will which never sinks to the depths of brute decision by a mass-vote, and thereby transcends the mere democrat's idolatry of number.

We need not pronounce, at any rate here, upon this alternative philosophy. It will occupy us later, in its proper place. But we may protest, *ab initio*, against this disjunction of the cause of Liberalism from that of Democracy. They are only opposed because they have first been misrepresented. Liberalism is not negativism. It is a positive doctrine of the free man, freely holding his own position in the community, not in the teeth of the State, but by the aid and the guarantee of the State, which secures to him the rights—and not least the rights of free speech and free discussion—which are the conditions of his holding any position at all. Nor is the cause of Democracy a cause of number. It is not the worship of quantity : it is the worship of a quality—that quality of the thinking and discoursing mind which can dare to raise and to face conflicting views of the Good, and to seek by the way of discussion some agreed and accepted compromise whereby a true (because general) national will is attained, as it cannot otherwise be, and a national Good is secured which is really good because it is freely willed.

The freedom of the mind which issues in free discussion is the bridge, if one were needed, between the cause of Liberalism and that of Democracy. But there is no bridge needed, because there is no gulf to be spanned. We may say, if we will, that when Mill wrote his essay *On Liberty* in 1859 he was vindicating the cause of Liberalism, and that when he wrote his *Considerations on Representative Government* in 1861 he was vindicating the cause of Democracy. But he would have been amazed to hear that he was vindicating different and discrepant causes ; and indeed he uses just the same argument—the argument that individuality of character is encouraged and enriched by freedom of expression—in defence of both causes. In truth there is only one cause at stake, and Milton put its essence in a nutshell when he wrote, at the end of his *Areopagitica*, 'Give me the liberty to know, to utter, and to argue freely according to conscience, above all liberties'.

There is more than one party of the Left. But the greatest party of the Left, in our days, is the Socialist. That, too, is a party of liberty ; but the liberty which it seeks is primarily economic liberty, and it seeks that liberty primarily for a class, which it calls by the name of the proletariat. Socialism in general, in so far as it vindicates liberty for a particular class (however large that class may be), may be argued to be partial in its conception—at any rate so long as other classes remain, and until the socialistic idea of an ultimate society without any classes is finally realized. The liberty of classes other than the proletariat would seem to be left unregarded, or even consciously, sacrificed, in the reckoning of the present, and only to be included in the calculation of the future for the distant day when they shall have suffered a total change and undergone a process of total assimilation to the victorious class.

But it is difficult to speak of socialism in general, or as a whole. If it belongs to the Left, Socialism has now its own Centre (and even its Right), as well as its own Left Wing. The old Social Democrats of the Continent, and the Labour Party in England, have shown themselves in many respects to be a new and more advanced form of Liberalism, anxious for what their own Left Wing would call the 'bourgeois' ideals of liberty of speech, liberty of meeting, and liberty of association for *all*, and concerned to maintain, and even to extend, the old Liberal idea of a system of representative government based on the *whole* community. On the other hand the Socialists of the Left, pursuing their creed to a more extreme conclusion, are willing to purchase economic liberty at the cost of both civil and political freedom. They are ready to embrace the political ideal of a revolutionary dictatorship wielded by (perhaps we should rather say *for*) the proletariat : they are ready to substitute for civil liberty, with its guarantee of personal security and other personal rights, a régime of 'revolutionary legality' which subordinates personal security and other personal rights to the needs of the institution of that ideal. Yet it can hardly be said, in the last analysis, that the payment of this great price will really secure economic liberty itself in the true sense of that term. Liberty should surely imply, in the economic field as elsewhere, some power of initiative and play of individuality, and some of that variety of experiment (or as Mill, quoting Humboldt, said, that 'variety of situations') which is the result of initiative and individuality. An economic régime which was entirely State-planned, or in other words dictatorially controlled, would not square with the requirements of true economic liberty any more than does a régime of great and monopolist capitalism.

There is a Left which lies to the left even of the Socialism of the Left; and this extreme Left has its own conception of liberty. In its Russian form, and as preached by Bakunin and Kropotkin, the philosophy of the extreme Left is a philosophy of Anarchism. Its ideal is the absolutely free individual who lives by his own free will in a spontaneous adjustment to some self-acting society which needs and imposes no rules. For the Anarchist there is no civil liberty, because such liberty implies law, and law, in any form and under whatever limits, is a coercive thing : there is no political liberty, because such liberty implies organization, and organization, in any form and however democratic, is compulsion : there is only liberty in itself, pure, absolute, and unqualified. This was the liberty of which Shelley dreamed in the *Prometheus Unbound*.

> The man remains—
> Sceptreless, free, uncircumscribed, but man ;
> Equal, unclassed, tribeless and nationless,
> Exempt from awe, worship, degree, the king
> Over himself ; just, gentle, wise : but man.

It was also the ultimate liberty of which Lenin dreamed, when the State, even in its proletarian form, should have 'withered away', and when, in their final consummation, 'people would *grow accustomed* to observing the elementary conditions of social existence *without force and without subjection*'.[1]

Anarchism, in its proper form, is an absolute cult of the free individual, who somehow lives in a group, but is under

---

[1] *The State and Revolution*, Chapter IV, *ad finem*. The same idea is repeated in the course of Chapter V. The italics appear in the text of the translation.

no obligation to the group in which he lives. Its basis is economic, and its conclusion is economic : it starts by rejecting the whole of the present economic system, with its legal and political concomitants : it ends by proclaiming a new economic order in which each man voluntarily works according to his abilities and is freely allowed a reward according to his needs. It has the glow of an ' uneffectual fire ', burning in a lonely void ; but it belongs to the kingdom of the void. More fruitful than Anarchism, in its influence and consequences, has been the cognate doctrine of Syndicalism. Syndicalism is an absolute cult not of the free individual, but rather of the free group. The group which it enthrones, and for which it vindicates liberty, is an economic group. It is a group composed of all those who follow the same occupation or are engaged in the same branch of production. The syndicalist claim for such a group is that it should freely own the means of production, freely control its processes, and freely market its product for that of other groups. The free economic group thus moves into the centre of life : the individual passes into its service : the State disappears, or recedes, to leave free scope for the group. The doctrine of Syndicalism is new ; but the practice of the ideas which it enunciates is about as old as man. Guilds, professions, and associations generally—even religious and educational associations—have often sought, by a natural if dubious instinct, to control their own members and to escape, so far as they could, from being controlled themselves. They have felt, if they not always said, that the one liberty which mattered was their own liberty. They have in their day done service, by their policies and their claims, in restraining the encroachments of an authoritarian State. It is not clear that their emancipation, in the days of the liberal State, would increase the sum of human liberty. Guilds and syndicates may vindicate their freedom against the State ; but their freedom is not always the freedom even of their own members, whom they may seek to discipline as well as to defend. The State can also be a vindicator of freedom, for all of its members equally. It may co-operate with groups in this service (as it has co-operated, in England for instance, with trade unions) ; but it may also find itself forced to vindicate freedom against them in the name of the general body of its citizens—and even of their own members.

§ 3. THE VARIOUS CLAIMANTS FOR LIBERTY

We have seen the idea of liberty spread and deployed, in a large semicircle, from Right to extreme Left. It has assumed many forms, which seem, *prima facie*, to quarrel with one another. The Nationalist starts from the nation, and proclaims the primary need of *its* liberty. The Liberal starts from the individual, and vindicates for him a civil liberty of managing his own life and a political liberty of participating in the management of the common life. The parties of the Left, all sharing a passion for economic liberty, expend their passion differently : some desire the emancipation of the whole proletariat (either by means of, or at the expense of, the Liberal system of political liberty) : some desire the liberation of the individual from every form of social fetter : some desire the new liberty of the autonomous syndicate or occupation. Nor is it only political and economic parties which have their versions of liberty. Churches claim ' spiritual independence ', and profess the cause of ' life and liberty ' : professions as well as occupations—and not least the professions of medicine, law, and teaching—have all their own claims to advance. We seem to have a chaos of different claimants for the same thing, which dissolves, as we look at its manifestations, from one thing into many.

Is it possible to introduce system into the chaos ? We may begin by saying that there seem to be three main different claimants for liberty. In the first place, there is the claim of the Nation, or State. (In these days of national States, we may identify Nation and State. In the act of doing so we have to confess that a nation may be conceivably, and indeed has often been actually, something different from a State, and that it may seek, under such conditions, to vindicate its liberty against the State in which it is included. But its effort, in such a case, is directed, after all, to the achieving of an identity between Nation and State—primarily for itself, but secondarily, and in consequence, for the State from which it secedes, and which it reduces, by its secession, to a basis more purely national.) The national State may claim that it is, or should be, a place of liberty in a variety of ways. It may claim freedom from any ' foreign ' control or any external or international limit on the development of its own particular polity and policy. This is a claim for plenary national sovereignty rather than for liberty ; but there may be countries and times in which (as in Germany recently) the exercise of a plenary national sovereignty may seem to be the essence and the whole of liberty itself. Again, the national State may claim freedom from any internal check or impediment upon its unity : it may revolt, in the name of its own freedom of action, against the sectionalism of political parties and the particularism of local provinces or territories. This is a claim for unity rather than for liberty ; but here again there may be countries and times (and once more we may cite the example of modern Germany, and also of modern Italy), in which the cause of *Einheit* is passionately identified with that of *Freiheit*. Finally, a national State may claim to be a place of liberty in still another sense— not in the negative sense of being free from external control or from internal impediments, but in the more positive sense of having the issues of its common life determined by the common thought and the general will of all its members. This is a liberty of the sort which we call by the name of political or constitutional liberty. It is what France has understood, since 1789, by the name of *Souveraineté nationale* : it is what is also called parliamentary democracy or representative government.

A second claimant for liberty is the group—some form of group other than the State : generally, in our days, the economic group, claiming a liberty which is primarily econo-mic. This, again, is a claim which assumes a variety of forms. Sometimes the group may be the whole body of the working classes—either organized (or assumed to be organized) as a single political party within the sphere of the democratic national State, and therefore seeking to achieve its aim of economic liberty within the scheme, and as part of the scheme, of political liberty ; or embodied as a revolutionary pro-letariat, in hostility to any form of existing State, and therefore seeking to achieve its aim by the new economic and political system of a proletarian democracy. Sometimes, again, the group may be the organized occupation or syndicate, resolved to overthrow, or at any rate to attenuate to the barest possible minimum, any form of State whatsoever, whether bourgeois or proletarian, and to leave free room for the liberty of each separate group of producers to regulate its production and its general activities. The logic of absolute syndicalism may,

however, be qualified by some regard, greater or less, for the
practical necessities of life.   In that case we may have a
doctrine of ' guilds ', such as was once professed by the English
Guild Socialists—guilds united in a guild parliament, and not
obstinately independent in their own isolation : guilds consenting to admit a modified parliament of the State side by
side with their own parliament, and thus acting as partners,
rather than enemies, of the system of political liberty.   Short
of this, we may have a simple doctrine of the liberty of existing
trade unions, within the sphere of the existing system of the
ordinary parliamentary State ;   and this will involve their
freedom to recruit their members without limitation, to control
them (by levy and otherwise) without qualification, and to
throw them *en masse* into the struggle against their employers
with the minimum of legal obstacles.

In any case, and under all these forms of the claim of the
economic group, the liberty which is demanded is the economic
liberty of the worker to control, to a greater or less degree, the
process of his production.   But, as we have seen already, there
may also be groups other than economic, demanding a liberty
of their own appropriate to their nature.   Churches have
fought through the ages for ecclesiastical liberty ;   and any
group that strikes its roots deep in the convictions, or the
affections, or the interests of its members—be it a rationalist
society, or an educational association for the maintenance of
a particular type of school, or an association of vine-growers
in France or of tithe-payers in England—will proclaim the
cause of its own particular liberty.

The individual himself seems a simple claimant when he
enters the lists in succession to these great figures of Nations
and States and groups ;   and yet, as we shall see in the issue,
he is really the root of the matter, and the ultimate home and
residence of every form of liberty.   It is only in appearance,
and not in reality, that he is a claimant for liberty by the
side of the other claimants, or that these other claimants loom
larger than he does.   But if we confine ourselves, for the
moment, to the plane of appearances, we may say that the
individual asserts a concurrent claim to the enjoyment of
liberty.   He asserts, in the first place, a claim to personal or
civil liberty.   He demands, in other words, that—subject to the
proviso that others shall equally enjoy what he enjoys, and

subject therefore to the system of law which is intended to realize this proviso—he shall enjoy the right to think and advocate his own thoughts, to form and pursue his own tastes, and to associate himself with others for the common advocacy and the common pursuit of the thoughts and tastes which he and they share. This is a fundamental liberty ; and indeed we may find, in the issue, that it is the basis of all others. If we call it by the name of personal or civil liberty, we must not unduly restrict the meaning of this term. Religious liberty, so far as it means a liberty of individuals (and not of ecclesiastical groups as distinguished, or supposed to be distinguished, from individuals) is included in it ; and one of the toasts of our Whig forefathers was accordingly that of ' civil and religious liberty '. Economic liberty—again in so far as it means a liberty of individuals, and not of economic groups as distinguished, or supposed to be distinguished, from individuals —is equally included : a man is free in the sphere of his work by the same title, under the same conditions, and by the same means, as he is also free in the sphere of his thoughts and tastes and the general conduct of the rest of his life.

In the second place, the individual asserts a claim to political or constitutional liberty. This is a natural extension, as we have already had reason to notice, of the claim to personal or civil liberty. If a man is free to advocate his own thoughts, and to associate himself with others for their common advocacy, he must be free to advocate personally thoughts of his own about the affairs of the commonwealth, and not only so, but also to form or join political parties by which such or similar thoughts are generally advocated. Any advocacy of opinions in regard to practical affairs which stops short at the act of advocacy, and does not seek to translate those opinions into actual and living practice, is sounding brass and a tinkling cymbal. That is why a party, which not only advocates a set of opinions and gains a general adhesion for it, but also seeks to give it actual and practical effect, is a necessary development and logical outcome of personal freedom of forming and advocating opinion. On this basis there was developed, in our own country, a system of government by party-leaders who had gained a general adhesion for their set of opinions from the generality of a parliament representing, or accepted as representing, the general trend of opinion in the country. Free discussion among individuals was the source and origin of this system : free discussion among individuals continues to be its method and its essence. Personal or civil liberty has thus issued in political or constitutional liberty ; and both of these liberties are liberties of the individual, even if we speak of the State in which political or constitutional liberty is realized as itself being free, and as itself possessing the attribute or character of freedom.

§ 4.   THE DIFFERENT LIBERTIES CLAIMED

If the claimants for liberty are many, we may also say that the thing claimed is many and various. We have seen that there is a liberty which is national, and which may also be called by the name of national independence or national sovereignty. We have seen that there is a liberty which is political or constitutional—the liberty of the free citizen to participate in the discussion and direction of the common affairs of the free State. We have seen that there is a liberty which is personal or civil—the liberty of individuals, either by themselves or in association with one another, to choose and pursue objects which they deem good, subject to the proviso that all shall enjoy that liberty equally. We have also spoken of a liberty which is economic, and again of a liberty which may be called religious, or 'spiritual', or ecclesiastical.

We may pause here to note that these last two are forms of liberty which raise some difficult problems. From one point of view both economic and religious liberty are liberties of the individual, and as such they are aspects or elements of his general civil or personal liberty. From another point of view they may be regarded as the liberties of the groups—economic and religious—which form the contractually 'gathered', or (in the theory of some of the churches) the divinely appointed, organs for their vindication and enjoyment. From this latter point of view we begin to see possibilities of conflict. Other liberties (civil liberty and political liberty) are enjoyed in the single group which constitutes the national State. *These* liberties, upon the view which assigns them to the group, must be enjoyed in, and they must be enjoyed by, groups which may indeed be contained in the national State, but yet are distinct from the group which constitutes that State. This raises a problem of the 'separation of liberties', analogous, in its way, to the problem of the 'separation of powers'; and that problem raises, in its turn, the issue of the demarcation of boundaries.

The idea of separation, and of demarcation of boundaries, between the sphere of ecclesiastical and that of civil and political liberty is old; but the problem and the issue which it involves cannot yet be said to be solved. The idea of separation and demarcation between the sphere of economic and that of other forms of liberty is new; and it involves issues which are even more acute than the issue of 'Church and State'.[1] Churches, whether we regard them as human institutions or as divinely appointed societies, are obvious facts of experience, and facts of the same general pattern. But what is the actual and obvious organ for the vindication and enjoyment of economic liberty? Is it the whole body of the proletariat, or is it each separate occupation? The doubt itself proves that there is no single or obvious organ. If, however, we create one—if, for example, we install the industrial proletariat as the organ of economic liberty—what is the ultimate issue? The organ of economic liberty engulfs other liberties—civil, political, and religious. We are left with a single liberty—that of a class, or rather of a party which organizes that class, or rather, in the ultimate issue, of the leaders who control that party; and liberty is thus reduced, in effect, to a single plane, and even to a single point on that plane. The attempt at separation has only resulted, after all, in a new integration—an integration so violently achieved that it omits or excludes vital elements of the whole.

[1] In many respects, the new issue between economics and politics is parallel to the old issue between Church and State. The papalists who denounced the State as a *régime* of power, and even conceived it, in hot moments, as diabolical, have their analogy in the Marxists who denounce the State as a *régime* of capitalistic force and an organ of selfish class-interest. But the papalists generally regarded the State, no less than the Church, as a divinely appointed society, with its own rights and liberty. If they claimed a separate liberty for the Church in this world, the liberty which they claimed was spiritual and not material; and they claimed it, in the last resort, because their eyes were fixed on another world, and because the liberty of the Church in this world was, in their view, the condition of all men's entering into the inheritance of the next. There are thus profound differences as well as analogies. Even so, the claim of the Church was a cause of war; and the claim of economic society, if it be pressed, can only tend in the same direction. But the analogies, and the differences, between the two issues demand a far deeper consideration than is possible here. It is, in any case, a gloomy view which would expect a period of Wars of Economics in the future, analogous to the old Wars of Religion in the past. The democratic State, in its relation to fluid and uncertain economic groups, is in a different position from the old monarchical State, in its relation to clearly defined and closely organized Churches.

This is not to suggest that there is no such thing as economic liberty, or that such liberty does not need vindication—vindication not only by the State, but also by associations of individuals formed specifically for that purpose. Our only contention is that the conception of economic liberty as something *sui generis*, which essentially and exclusively belongs to some special group, can only lead us astray. Economic liberty is also a part of civil or personal liberty, and like all civil liberty it is the right of all and every one. It is a part which is, in large measure and for many persons, imperfect and unrealized ; and its very imperfection is the justification for making it a separate category and giving it a separate name. But it must be realized within the framework of civil liberty, by the same means as the rest of civil liberty, and for the same persons who enjoy the rest of civil liberty. At the present moment the idea of economic liberty may well seem to stand contrasted, and even opposed, to the ideas of civil and political liberty. It is imperfect : they are developed. It is an idea which inspires the working classes : they are ideas which are strongest in the middle and professional classes, who are best able to enjoy their benefits. The contrast between the economic status of dependence (not to term it slavery) in which the majority live, and the civil and political status of liberty which all, but pre-eminently the secure and settled classes enjoy, is a contrast which has to be emphasized—and removed. But the contrast is not removed by any secession or ' swarming ' into a new economic world in which men are called to enjoy a new economic liberty, like so many bees, as a group. That way there only lies the dubious liberty of the hive, purchased, it may be, at the price of the certain liberties we now enjoy. The true way to remove the contrast is to continue to live in the world of civil and political liberty which we already inhabit, but to make it a better and a more consistent world by carrying its principle of liberty into the economic field and among the body of the workers.

§ 5. THE ULTIMATE LIBERTY OF INDIVIDUAL PERSONALITY

After this picture of differences and disharmonies—of different claimants for liberty, and the different liberties claimed—it remains to attempt some scheme of unity. Quarrels and contradictions, or what seem to be quarrels and contradictions, have appeared in our survey. There are some who argue that political liberty contradicts and suppresses civil ; that the democratic principle of the absolute right of Number overbears the liberal principle of the personal rights of the individual. There are others who believe that the economic liberty of the working masses is contradicted and abrogated not only by civil liberty, with its doctrine of freedom of contract which is never free for the worker, but also by a so-called political liberty which means in effect the liberty of capitalism to manipulate democracy for its own particular and sectional ends. There are some who contend that the liberty of the State, as something superior to the liberty of any of its members or any group of its members, must assert itself at the expense of that licence of political parties which, in their view, lies at the core of the specious conception of political or constitutional liberty : there are others who feel that the liberty of the State is itself the great enemy of general human liberty—the ultimate obstacle, by its ' autarcic ' policy of economic and general isolation, to the freedom of humanity at large to organize itself in an international system of mutual intercourse and inter-dependence. In this battle of liberties the very liberty of religion itself, once thought to be guaranteed by the doctrine and practice of toleration, seems to be again engaged. In one country, civil and political liberty contends against religious ; and French democracy has sought to ensure that religious society shall only exist, in the eye of the State, in the particular form of registered contractual ' association ' which is recognized in the system of civil liberty. In another, economic liberty is the enemy of an ancient Church, as being an element and a support of the system of capitalism ; and religious liberty is accordingly reduced, in Russia, to the dimensions of liberty to perform religious rites, which is balanced and corrected by an equal (or greater) liberty of anti-religious propaganda.

In spite of these differences—and they are deep—we cannot but feel that there must be some single and ultimate claimant for liberty, and some single and essential liberty which that ultimate claimant demands. What is this ultimate claimant, and what is this essential liberty ? We may make an assumption, and we shall find an answer. The assumption is that in our human world, and under God, the individual personality of man alone has intrinsic and ultimate worth, and having also the capacity of development has also an intrinsic and ultimate claim to the essential condition of its development. Liberty will then be that essential condition ; and the essence of liberty will be that it is a condition, or status, or quality, which individual personality must possess in order that it may translate itself from what it is to what it has the capacity of becoming.

The personality which has this capacity of development, of translating itself from its present self to a future and higher self, is moral personality. It is something more than psychological personality—the personality which consists in being aware of sensations, and in determining action thereby. It is a moral personality which consists in being conscious of conceptions—conceptions of some possible good—and in determining action in the light of such conceptions. The liberty which such a personality claims is therefore a moral liberty. It is a liberty which consists in possessing the status or condition or quality of determining one's own action by one's own conception of the good. The essential ground for claiming such liberty is that personality only develops, and disengages its intrinsic worth, if it determines itself by its own conceptions in the process of that development. If it were not self-determined, but other-determined, it would simply stay, in itself, on its own existing level, even if its acts, considered simply as acts, were raised to another level. Moral personality can only develop through the moral liberty of a personal will which wills for itself the conceptions which it has itself embraced.

But no moral personality exists *in vacuo*. A moral personality could not exist or act unless it existed and acted in a society of other such personalities. It lives by acting upon those who are like itself and of the same substance as itself, and by being acted upon by them in turn. If we abolish the notion of this interplay of like agents, we abolish the very idea of moral action, and we thus extinguish moral personality, which exists in and by such action. Two consequences follow from this fact that the existence of moral personality implies a society of such personalities. The first conclusion is formal. Because the personalities are like in their nature—of the same substance and the same worth—each must respect in the others what it values in itself, and each must allow, and indeed claim, for the others the same liberty of self-determination which it also claims for itself. Each being an end in himself, and for himself, the society of all must be necessarily based on the formal rule that each shall be treated by all as a free moral agent ; and any social control—any adjustment of personal relations intended to ease their possible friction—must be compatible with this rule. In other words, such control or adjustment must be intended in the interest of moral liberty ; must seek to remove obstacles to that liberty ; must serve, not to diminish, but to defend and extend, the area of self-control.

The second conclusion is more substantial. If all are beings of the like nature, seeking alike to determine their action by a like conception of the good, we must not conceive them merely as existing in juxtaposition : we must also conceive them as acting in collaboration. They will exchange ideas, and thus clarify their conception of the good : they will borrow impulses, and thus corroborate their will for its attainment. The process of moral life, as it unfolds itself in a society, is thus a process by which the idea of the good becomes an idea of social thought, and the will for the good becomes a matter of social volition. We must indeed, each of us severally, *appropriate* the idea : we must make it our own, and will it, as our own, with an effort of our own will ; we must even, if we can, go beyond the idea as it stands at any given moment, adding some new thought of our own, seeking to realize it in our own lives, and offering it for incorporation in the general social stock. But always, behind ourselves, stands the society of ourselves—the general bank and capital of common thought and common will, to which we have all contributed and on which we can all draw, but which never absolves us from the duty of keeping our own account.

This society, and its great inherited deposit, are facts which we must never ignore. Equally, they are facts which we must never exaggerate. It is easy to fall into the idea that the society of ourselves, being so majestical, is something other than ourselves—higher, transcendent, a being beyond our beings. But the common thought and will which the society of ourselves precipitates is not a something above us, or in any way separate from us. We ourselves have made it, and are making it still : it is our own creation, and the work of our own minds. So far as it controls us, consistently with our

C

nature as moral persons, it controls us from within, and not with the force of an external presence ; it controls us as freely accepted and genuinely appropriated thought, which is part of our own personality.   And as we must freely accept it if we are ourselves to be free, so we may also be bound, in hours of crisis and ultimate decision, to reject it freely for just the same reason.   There are times and seasons when we may feel it our duty, and our true liberty, to guide ourselves by a conception of good which is beyond social thought and social will, and proceeds immediately from our own deepest self. Resistance is part of liberty, as well as acceptance.   But the ground and the source of resistance is the same as that of acceptance.

Upon this basis we may attain some conception of the relation of man and the State, and of the place of liberty in that conception.   The moral personality of the individual, determining itself by its own conception of a good, is the beginning from which we start and the end with which we conclude.   But this is not all.   There is a middle, as well as a beginning and an end.   If we made the beginning and the end everything—if we refused to interpose a middle term, and to recognize that society intervenes between the beginning and the end—we should be compelled to embrace the gospel of Anarchism.   But the middle exists ; and we need not embrace that gospel.   The society of selves is a fact as well as the self ; and the two are not independent but interdependent facts. We may even say that the society of selves exists with a double existence—existence by formal rule, and existence by dynamic process which produces a substance or content.

So far as the society of selves exists by formal rule, it exists as a scheme for the adjustment of relations.   Under this scheme all alike are recognized as free agents ; the conditions of their free agency are guaranteed ; and while each is thereby limited for the sake of the freedom of all, each is also secured in a guaranteed freedom of action which he would not otherwise possess.   This involves a system of law, intended to secure free agency and the conditions of such agency ; and thus liberty—of the sort which we have termed by the name of personal or civil—is the end (as it is also the source) of the system of law which expresses the existence of the society by the method of formal rule.

So far as the society exists by dynamic process, it exists for and by the mutual interchange of conceptions and convictions about the good to be attained in human life and the methods of its attainment. It thus exists for and by a system of social discussion, under which each is free to give and receive, and all can freely join in determining the content or substance of social thought—the good to be sought, and the way of life in which it issues. Now such discussion is also, as we have seen, the essence of democracy. It is the core of that political, or constitutional, liberty which exists under a system of democracy. Social discussion may indeed be something broader than political discussion, both in the area which it covers and the methods by which it acts. That is a question to which we must ultimately turn. But at any rate we are already entitled to say that political discussion, even if it be only a part, *is* a part, and a necessary part, of the general process of social discussion. The argument which we have followed thus brings us to the conclusion that a régime of political or constitutional liberty is a necessary part of the development of human personality in and through a society of selves.

§ 6. LIBERTY IN REGARD TO THE IDEAS OF SOCIETY AND THE STATE

We now turn to a further question which has already begun to emerge. So far, we have spoken mainly of man and society ; only once, and almost in passing, have we spoken of man and the State. Man is related to, and exists in, both society and the State ; but what is *their* relation to one another ? Are society and the State identical, or do they differ ; and if they differ, what is the nature of their difference ? Society, in our days, takes the form of national society. Coterminous with it, in the general scheme of national boundaries to which we are tending, is the national State. Is national society exhausted, or totally comprehended, in the national State ? We cannot say that it is. A national society is a community (itself composed of many communities, each formed for its own specific purpose) which exists for the general promotion of the whole of national culture, in all its ranges and aspects. It is a society of selves which exists for the general development of every self, in every sphere of self-development. A national State is a particular aspect—or rather, we may say, a particular organization—of a national society, intended for a particular purpose. It includes the same members as a national society ; but it includes them in a particular way, and under a particular scheme. A national State is a national society organized as a political association, and acting, as such an association, in terms of civil and constitutional law, for the purpose of securing the values of civil and constitutional liberty and other political values. But the fact that a national society has assumed this form of organization, for this particular purpose, does not preclude it from still existing in its own general social life, for its own general social purposes. The French Republic is France, and yet it is not all France ; any State may be, and every State is now tending to be, a nation, and yet no State is ever the whole of a nation or expresses the whole of its life. Behind the political association there always stands the society of which it is the legal expression—but not the only expression.

There is thus the State ; and civil and political liberty are liberties within the State—the liberty of the formal rule, and the liberty of the dynamic process, as they exist within that area and under the scheme of that association. But there is also society—the People, the Folk, the general community ; and there is a liberty, or there are liberties, in that area. Legal system, and the play of liberty in that system : social life, and the play of liberty in that life—these are two things which we have to distinguish, and yet, at the same time, to connect and to harmonize with one another.

The first necessity is that of distinction. There is a vision which has often haunted human thought—the vision of the one and only organization : the vision of the total State which is all and everything, and includes all and every purpose. This was the theory of the Greek city-State, as it appeared to Plato : it was also the theory of the modern nation-State, as it appeared to Burke.[1] But if we adopt this vision of unity, we only achieve a deep disunity. It is not only that the individual may rise insurgent against an excessive claim. It is also a matter of other and rival societies arising, based on some

---

[1] ' The State ought not to be considered nothing better than a partnership agreement in a trade . . . it is a partnership in all science ; a partnership in all art ; a partnership in every virtue, and in all perfection.' (*Reflections on the Revolution in France*, Vol. IV, pp. 105-6, of the edition in the ' World's Classics', Oxford.)

rival principle, whether of religious faith or of economic doctrine, which either claim to be franchises or immunities, exempt from the State, or aspire to dethrone it and take its place as the one total organization. The State which is all and everything is a State which always invites negation.

We must therefore distinguish between society and the State—between the sphere of social life and the sphere of legal system. Our distinction will never be clear and absolute. We can never say, of any given matter, that it belongs exclusively to the sphere of social life or to that of legal system. Artistic creation, for example, may seem to lie entirely outside the legal system ; but an obscene picture is not exempt from the rules of the system. Nor can we say, of any given group, that it is purely a social group, or purely a legal group. It may now act as one, and now as another : it may even be both at once. A political party, for example, is a group which is formed in the social area but seeks to act in the political. There is no precise line to be drawn ; and yet there are two different spheres. One is the sphere of the social activity of general national society, acting through all the social groups of which it is constituted : the other is that of the legal and political activity of the organized national State. The general national society—as such, and apart from the national State—has no formal organization. The fact of community is there ; but the form which that fact assumes is a community of ideas— a community of the spirit—the community of a common culture. Within this community of ideas—within this genuine, and yet, in itself, unorganized society—there exists, however, a rich variety of organized social groups. We must admit, indeed, that there are some social groups—for example, classes—which are generally themselves unorganized, like the national society to which they belong. A social class is a community of ideas, and even of interests, and its members will tend to act together under the influence of those ideas and interests ; but if the fact of social class expresses itself in this way, it seldom assumes the form of a definite organization. Class, however, is exceptional. Most social groups *are* organizations, consciously formed for some specific purpose—religious, educational, charitable, economic, or even purely ' social ', in the more restricted sense of that word. Taken together they have always formed, and they will always continue to form, a large territory of human activity. They form, too, in their aggregate the substance and content of what we have called by the name of society.

The development of man thus expresses itself not only in the State, but also in the social groups which constitute the substance of society. If there must be liberty in the State, on the basis on which we have argued, there must also, and on the same basis, be liberty in these groups. They, too, must respect the personality of their members : they, too, must act by the method of free discussion between their members. But this is not the whole of the matter. There are further questions of liberty which immediately arise when we begin to consider the action of social groups. There is, above all, the great question of the relation of the State and liberty in the State to the social group and liberty in the social group. On the one hand we may lay it down that the State must respect the liberty of the members of a social group to combine and to act for their own specific purpose. The State is not the agent of all the purposes of man ; and provided that the purpose of a social group does not contravene, or injuriously affect, the State's achievement of its own purposes, the group should be free to pursue its own particular purpose. On the other hand the proviso which has just been stated involves us in the conclusion that a social group must equally respect the liberty of the members of the State. A group must not offend against the principles of civil liberty, either in its treatment of its own members or in its treatment of non-members. It must not offend against the principles of political liberty, either within itself, or by opposing itself from without as a rival and enemy to the system of self-government in the State.

A problem which agitates the minds of men to-day is the problem of divided loyalties. There are so many groups which vindicate loyalty, and each tends to claim for itself an exclusive loyalty. There is the claim of the Nation. There is that of the State. There is the claim of the Party, which may be felt so strongly by a convinced partisan, zealous for some 'general line', or *dottrina*, or *Weltanschauung*, that he will consent to recognize the claim of the State only when the State accepts and serves the principles of his Party. There is the claim of Class, especially for those who are full of the zeal of the international and revolutionary proletariat. There is the claim of the Occupation, with its appeal to the Syndicalist. There is the claim of the Church, still the final claim to the millions of faithful who set loyalty to their religion in the forefront of their loyalties. No arbiter can determine our loyalties for us. They are too much the product of our emotions. But so far as we submit our emotions, and with them our loyalties, to the test of reason, we may find some clue for our guidance in the conception of State and society, and of their relation to the individual, which has just been tentatively sketched.

We owe our loyalty to the national society to which we belong ; and we enjoy the liberty and unfolding of ourselves which is the other side of that loyalty. We owe our loyalty also to the national State to which we belong ; and we enjoy the liberty and unfolding of ourselves which, again, is the other side of that loyalty. We have to distinguish these loyalties and liberties ; we have also to reconcile them. It is a difficult problem, which becomes even more acute when we notice that social loyalty may assume different forms, according to the social group on which men set their emotions and their hopes. Some may pin their faith to the whole national society, and not to any particular group. They become nationalists ; and proceeding not so much to reconcile, as to confuse, national society and the national State, they first make the national State the ultimate and only group, and they then sacrifice the individual himself to the greater glory of that group. But others—and they are many—give their loyalty to, and expect their liberty from, some particular social group— party or class, occupation or profession. They, too, may tend to confuse, rather than to reconcile, the social group of their allegiance and the national State of their residence. They may wish to constitute a pure party-State or a pure class-State, abrogating the general or national character of the State, and abrogating with it its principle of general liberty for all. Or again, they may wish to substitute their group for the State, dismissing the political association to limbo or some poor residuary function, and enthroning instead the autonomous group in some form or version of Syndicalism. So difficult is the problem of loyalties : so easy is it to solve the problem by enthroning one loyalty, and by purchasing unity at the cost of confusion.

It is all the more important to distinguish justly, and to

reconcile truly (not by abolishing the one or the other, but by leaving room for the existence and the collaboration of both), national society and the national State, the loyalties due to both, the liberties flowing from both. There is a liberty belonging to the members of a social group : there is also a liberty belonging to the members of a State ; and both of these liberties have their reason and their place. There are purposes which are best served by social groups and not by the State ; and it is therefore best that groups formed for these purposes should be left free, so far as the State is concerned, in the action which they take for their attainment. But their being left free by the State does not mean their being left entirely alone by the State. On the contrary, the State will leave groups free only if, in the first place, they respect freedom in themselves, and if, in the second place, they respect it in the State. The freedom of the social group is not an absolute freedom. It exists in conjunction with, and it must act in relation to, the liberty which exists in the area of the State. Nor, again, is the liberty of the social group identical in kind with the system of civil and political liberty which belongs to the State. It is a different liberty. It is a liberty of voluntary co-operation for the attainment of some particular social purpose. It does not involve or imply the existence of a second State which is the parallel and therefore the rival of the existing State ; it only implies the existence of a social group which is different from the State and can thus be com-plementary to it. If social groups be thus regarded, not as alternative or opposing States of equal dimensions and like claims, but as voluntary societies in another dimension and with different claims, we shall escape that problem of the separation and demarcation of liberties to which we have already referred. We shall not speak, for example, of an economic liberty which is peculiar to some one particular economic group, and of a civil and political liberty which is peculiar to a parallel but separate political group. We shall rather speak of a number of groups voluntarily formed for particular economic purposes, and seeking to achieve those objects by the methods of voluntary co-operation in the area of society (in the form of a Labour Party or of various Labour parties, of Trade Unions and a Congress of Trade Unions, and the like) ; we shall speak of a State formed for the general purpose of easing the friction of human relations, and of promoting the common discussion and realization of the common good, by its own methods and in its own area of civil law and political institutions ; and we shall regard both as pursuing, in collaboration and not in antagonism, the same end of human liberty—of free human development—by their different methods and in their different areas. The economic liberty which has still to be fully achieved will thus be the joint work of both, and not the monopoly of either.[1]

§ 7. THE DISTINCTION AND CO-OPERATION OF SOCIETY
AND THE STATE

The collaboration of the free State, based on civil and political liberty, with the free play of voluntary co-operation, acting in the area of society, is the sum and substance of modern liberty. That collaboration may be threatened in opposite ways and from opposite angles. On the one hand there are those who would reduce human life to terms of pure society ; who refuse to recognize any liberty other than social liberty, and would therefore abolish the State in the name and cause of liberty. The Anarchist holds that the individual is only free when he has escaped from the bonds of the State, and lives as a member of a self-acting *general* society (however formed, and on whatever basis it may cohere) by the one pure method of voluntary co-operation. The Syndicalists hold that the individual worker, to whom they limit their view, can only be free when the State is abolished or reduced to its absolute minimum, and when each worker lives as a member of a self-acting *particular* society (that of his occupation) which is somehow united with other similar societies in a general self-acting federation. The Communists admit that there must be a State ; but they add two quali-fications. It must not be a State of all : it must be the State of a particular social class, which will dominate and assimilate the members of other classes until they have adopted its

---

[1] Mr. Sidney Webb, in a chapter in the last volume of the *Cambridge Modern History*, published in 1910, has emphasized this idea. ' Trade Unionism and factory legislation share the field between them ' (p. 749). ' An increase of governmental action has been invariably accompanied, at a slightly later date, by an increase also in voluntary co-operation in the same sphere. . . . We see here no sign that governmental collective action is inimical to voluntary co-opera-tion in supplement and support of what is done by the State and by the law ' (p. 764).

opinions and way of life. It must not be a permanent State : it must be a temporary State, necessary for the transitional purpose of assimilation, but destined to wither away when the purpose has been achieved, and to leave room for a pure self-acting society in which men have grown ' accustomed to observing the elementary conditions of social existence without force and without subjection '.[1]

On the other hand, and at the opposite end of the scale, we find the Nationalist. In spite of his name, and in spite of the philosophy of nationalism which he professes, he owes his loyalty not to the Nation, but to the State. It is not national society, in the sense in which we have used that term, but the national State, which is the basis of his belief. He may term the nation an organism which is superior to its members : he may even term it a personality, higher than the personalities of individuals ; but since he regards the nation as created and ' actuated ' by the State, the benefit of these terms enures to the creating and ' actuating ' State.[2] In his essential belief, national society is engulfed and absorbed in the State ; and since the individual has already been engulfed and included in the superior organism or higher personality of the nation, he too is engulfed with it and absorbed in its absorption. The ultimate end of life becomes not the development of individual personality, but the exaltation of the super-personality of the State ; and the cult of power is substituted for that of liberty.[3]

---

[1] Lenin, *The State and Revolution*, Chap. IV, *ad finem* ; cf. *supra*, p. 6.

[2] (*a*) The conception of the nation as an organism is expressed in the first article of the Italian Charter of Labour of 1927. ' The Italian nation, by its power and its duration, is an organism, with a being, ends, and means of action, superior to those of the individuals, separate or grouped, of whom it is composed '. (*b*) The conception of the nation as a personality, and a higher personality, is expressed at the end of part I, §§ 9-10, of *La Dottrina del Fascismo*, published in 1932. Nation is ' not race, nor a region geographically specified, but a stock (*schiatta*) perpetuating itself historically, a multitude unified by one idea, which is a will for existence and power : consciousness of self, personality . . . higher personality '. (*c*) The conception of the nation as created and actuated by the State is expressed in the same passage. ' This higher personality is a nation only in so far as it is a State. The nation does not exist to generate the State. On the contrary the nation is created by the State, which gives to the people, conscious of its own moral unity, a will, and thus an effective existence '. In the same sense the concluding sentence of the first article of the Charter of Labour adds to the conception of the nation as an organism the further conception that the nation ' is a moral, political and economic unity *which is integrally realized in the Fascist State*'.

[3] ' The nation as State is an ethical reality which exists and lives in so far as it develops. Its arrest is its death. For the State is not only an authority which governs . . . but also a power which makes its will prevail externally.' *La Dottrina del Fascismo*, I, §11.

We have thus, on the one hand, a philosophy of society and nothing but society, and, on the other, one of the State and nothing but the State. Perhaps the latter is the more dangerous of the two. The philosophy of the State and nothing but the State not only eliminates society, but also the individual : it leaves us in a realm of ghosts, who have lost the quality of personality and, ceasing to possess intrinsic worth, have become mere means to the higher value of the State. The philosophy of society and nothing but society neglects and rejects the system of civil and political liberty contained in the State, and thereby seeks to eliminate a necessary and indispensable condition of the free play of individual personality ; but while it thus refuses to accept a necessary means, it still recognizes—and indeed, by that refusal, it may even be said to over-emphasize—the truth that the free development of human personality is the ultimate end of human life. It is a philosophy, we may say, which is least dangerous when it is most anarchistic. When it seeks to recognize the claim of society in the particular form of a workers' society, and when it proceeds to enthrone such a society as a workers' republic for a transitional period of drastic reorganization (which may well be permanent), it approaches, and it may even transcend, the excesses of nationalism. Instead of dethroning the State in favour of a workers' society, it merely enthrones a workers' society (which, after all, is only a part of society) as a new and more terrible State.

If there is any lesson of our times, it is that we need simultaneously both society and the State. So long as men think and feel in terms of nations, society will be national society and the State will be a national State.[1] Both in national society and in the national State, and in both simultaneously, men find their free fulfilment. Both exist for that purpose : both are necessary for that purpose. If we imagine a State which is all in all, and leaves no room for voluntary social co-operation, we imagine something which instead of promoting will tend to defeat the free fulfilment of individuals.

[1] The Russian Revolution itself, starting in 1917 on the basis of the international solidarity of the workers' society in all nations and States indifferently, and still dreaming in 1924 that the new federal union of that year would be a new and decisive step towards the union of the workers of all countries in a socialist Soviet Republic of the world, has now settled down, under the constitution of 1936, on the basis of national society and a national State.

If we imagine a society which is all in all, and leaves no room for the action of the State, we imagine something which will also tend to defeat that fulfilment—whether the State be really abolished, and its necessary services of securing civil and political liberty really cease to be rendered ; or whether the State be only nominally abolished, and the society which professes to take its place be simply a new and illiberal State. The variety of man, with his many purposes and his different methods, must flow in more than one channel if it is to flow at all.

But what must flow freely, and what must be free, is always man himself—the individual man—the human personality. Thinking of the multiplicity of channels, and of the possibility that one channel may steal the waters of others, we sometimes talk of the freedom of the channel. We speak of the freedom of the State : the freedom of the Church : the freedom of this or that other group—class, occupation, profession, or party. But a free State, or Church, or party, or class, is simply a channel along which individuals can flow freely. It is simply a group in and by which they can attain *their* freedom—the only true and ultimate freedom. Ultimately, as also originally, the only freedom is that of the individual ; and if we speak of the freedom of groups, it is only derivatively and secondarily that we so speak. Their freedom exists, or should exist, in so far as they promote individual freedom, and in consequence of their promoting that freedom. A group can proclaim the cause of its liberty only in so far as it is a condition of the liberty of its members.

Organizations always tend to be regarded, especially by their organizers, as ends in themselves. No organization is ever that. Any organization is a means to the freedom of its members. But no organization is absolutely justified even if it promotes the freedom of all its members—but promotes *their* freedom only. It may do that, and yet be inimical to a broader liberty. That is why each partial organization needs the criticism of some higher organization, and why, ultimately, all other organizations of men must come to the bar of the organization of all men, if that can ever come to pass. We can imagine a high measure of general liberty under a system of national societies and national States. We can imagine a perfect liberty only in a world society and a world State.

Meanwhile, so long as we think and feel in terms of the nation, we may well accept the criticism of the national State, with its general scope and concern, as a criticism which is a necessary service to the general cause of liberty in the nation—provided always that the criticizing State is so built and so constituted (by its system of civil and political liberty) as to be a servant of that cause. For the national State is the most general and the most comprehensive, if it is not, and should not be, the only organization of the nation.

II

THE SYSTEM OF CIVIL AND POLITICAL LIBERTY

§ 1. CIVIL LIBERTY, THE CIVIL CODE, AND DECLARATIONS OF RIGHTS

WE shall be concerned, for the future, with liberty as it appears in the State. Our theme will be twofold. It will include, in the first place,. some consideration of the general rights of private action which are guaranteed, under civil law, on the one hand to individuals, and on the other hand to groups or associations of individuals, in so far as such groups or associations are acting in the sphere of civil law, and in so far, therefore, as they become the claimants of rights in that sphere. It will include, in the second place, some examination of the general system of institutions which is established, under the law of the constitution, in order to secure rights of public action, or of co-operation in public action, to individuals and groups of individuals. Of these two themes it will be the latter—or, in other words, the theme of political liberty—which will mainly engage our attention.

Civil liberty will be at its greatest when two conditions are established : when rights of private action are clearly defined in ample terms, to cover the widest possible range of such action, and when these rights, so defined, are strictly enforced by definite remedies which can be applied as speedily and effectively as possible. It is the second of these two conditions which has been particularly satisfied in our English system of civil law. Our definitions of civil rights are scanty or at any rate scattered : our remedies for the enforcement of rights are numerous and, above all, effective. On the Continent definition has played a far larger part ; and codes have been issued, such as the Civil and the other codes of Napoleon, or the German Civil Code of 1898, which have stated the range of civil liberty in exact proportions and in orderly sequence.

Nor is this all. In other countries a definition of civil rights has often been incorporated in, or connected with, the Constitution itself. It has not been left entirely to the sphere of ordinary or secondary law : it has also been included in the sphere of that primary law which constitutes and controls the State. The example was set by the North American Colonies, in 1776, when in seceding from England they gave themselves not only new ' frames of government ', but also ' declarations of rights ', which were sometimes anterior to, and sometimes included in, the statement of the ' frame of government ' or form of the constitution.[1] There was a double reason for this connection of a declaration of rights with the constitution. In the first place, so far as the rights declared were rights of private action, they were made to precede, or at any rate to accompany, the establishment of government, and thus to limit, in advance, the scope of the future action of government. In the second place, some of the rights declared were more than rights of private action : they were rights of public action, expressed in the form of general rules[2] ; and as such they were naturally linked with the creation of public institutions which followed in the actual frame of government. The American example was imitated in the French Revolution : a *declaration des droits de l'homme et du citoyen* was issued in 1789, and afterwards prefixed to the constitution of 1791 ; and this declaration, as its title indicates, mingled together the rights of private and the rights of public action. New declarations, of a similar nature, were prefixed to the new French constitutions of 1793 and 1795 ; and the constitution of 1848, if it was not furnished with a declaration, was at any rate preceded by a brief preamble which recited some of the principal articles of the revolutionary doctrine of civil and political rights. Germany, too, in the Weimar constitution of 1919, followed a somewhat similar method. The Constitution included two parts—a first part entitled *Aufbau und Aufgaben des Reichs* (or, roughly, ' The frame and functions of government '), and a second part entitled *Grundrechte und Grundpflichten der Deutschen* (or, roughly again, ' A declaration of fundamental rights and duties ').[3] It is perhaps significant that the

[1] In Virginia the declaration (of 12 June 1776) is a separate document, anterior to the constitution of 29 June 1776. In Pennsylvania it is a part of the same document, forming Chapter I ; and it is subsequently declared in section 46 to be ' a part of the Constitution '.

[2] An example of such a rule is contained in article 2 of the Virginia Declaration —' that all power is vested in, and consequently derived from, the people : that magistrates are their trustees and servants, and at all times amenable to them.'

[3] The word *devoirs* had been already added to the word *droits* in the French constitution of 1795. It may be added that in the Russian constitution of 1936 there is a chapter (the tenth) on ' the basic rights and duties of citizens ', as well as a first and preliminary chapter on ' the structure of society '. That constitution thus begins with a definition of society ; proceeds to define the form of government of the State ; and ends with a declaration of the rights and duties of the individual citizen.

declaration here follows, and does not precede, the constitution proper, and that it is confined, on the whole, to the rights of civil liberty. (But it is also perhaps significant, on a wider view, that groups and group-life play a large part in the German declaration, and that while only the first section is devoted to the individual, four whole sections are devoted to groups and general group-interests.)[1]

Two problems here emerge—that of the value of the civil code, and that of the value of the solemn declaration of rights annexed to, or contained in, the constitution. The question whether the cause of civil liberty is best served by the definition and order of a civil code, or by the system of remedies provided in legal procedure, lies beyond our scope. Bentham believed that a civil code would emancipate the layman from the lawyer, by giving him a clear and intelligible scheme which he could understand for himself. It is perhaps a better argument that codification might emancipate the lawyer from himself, by giving him a clean sheet and a quittance from accumulated lumber. But the problem of the relation of a civil code to the cause of civil liberty is a technical and professional problem. More serious, in its general bearing, is the problem of the relation of the solemn declaration of first principles (included in or connected with the constitution) to the general cause of civil, and also of political, liberty.

The English temper is apt to mistrust enunciations of legal and political principle, as being but sounding words and abstract propositions, which may distract attention from the real necessity of actual legal remedies and concrete political institutions. We have, or we think that we have, an unwritten constitution ; and if we have left our constitution unwritten, how (we may well inquire) can we write declarations of rights, which seem to be logically connected with the written constitution ? But there is something to be said, none the less, in favour of declarations of rights. Even in our own country, and even if our constitution is unwritten, Magna Carta, the Petition of Right, and the Bill of Rights are all declarations of rights. A declaration issued in a grave moment of national history, when the minds of men are stirred to the depths, may become the tradition and inspiration of succeeding

---

[1] These four sections are concerned with the life of the community, religion and religious associations, education and schools, and economic life.

generations. The French Declaration of 1789 did not cease to operate when the particular constitution in which it was incorporated passed away. It is still the inspiration of Republican France ; and great French jurists have even contended that any legislation contrary to its principles is unconstitutional and should be regarded as invalid.[1] Their contention, in the particular case, is hardly warranted. The Declaration of 1789 is not a part of the modern constitution established in 1875 ; and even if it were, there is no constitutional court in France which could declare that a law conflicting with it was unconstitutional and invalid.

But let us suppose that we have a written constitution containing a declaration of rights as one of its integral elements, and that, in addition, a constitutional court is established under that constitution, with the power of pronouncing that laws which are contrary to it, or to any of its elements, are *eo ipso* unconstitutional, and thereby null and void. In that case two conclusions will follow. In the first place, the constitutional court will have the power of protecting the liberties enunciated in the declaration against any infraction by any of the authorities—including the legislature—which are established by and bound to act under the constitution. In the second place, since the legislature is thus debarred from infringing or altering those liberties, it follows that they can only be modified by the body which is able to modify the whole constitution of which they are part. Now the body which is able to modify a written constitution and any declaration of rights which it may contain is generally required to act by a special majority. This means that a minority which objects to a modification of any declared right will have a reasonable chance of sustaining its objection. In this way the system of the fixed constitution, with a constitutional court and a special system of constitutional amendment which requires a special majority, not only protects the rights declared in the constitution from invasion by any of the ordinary authorities ; it also protects the rights of minorities. It thus serves to qualify and to restrict that pressure of the rule of the majority, and that mere weight of number, which is often alleged as an argument against democratic institutions.

Of course, the gain may be purchased at the price of a loss ;

[1] Cf. Esmein, *Éléments de Droit Constitutionnel* (ed. 1927), Vol. I, pp. 646ff.

D

and the loss involved may be even greater than the gain. We have to think of the cause of progress, as well as of the causes of liberty and of minority-rights. The cause of social progress may be defeated if an obstinate minority, clinging to some obsolescent principle enunciated in a declaration of rights, is able to defeat constitutional amendment, and to influence the constitutional court to disallow legislation which runs contrary to that principle. This is a genuine danger. But it may be worth incurring for the sake of the possible gain ; and the danger may well be diminished if the declaration is not too tightly and specifically drawn (it is not everything that deserves to be written in letters of brass), and if the special majority required is not too large. To require a majority of three quarters is really to enthrone a minority which just exceeds one quarter.

§ 2. POLITICAL LIBERTY : ITS METHOD OF DISCUSSION ; THE AREA OF THAT METHOD ; ITS STAGES AND ORGANS

The cause of civil liberty, we have argued, may conceivably gain by the formal codification of civil law ; it may also gain by a formal declaration of rights (which is really a declaration not so much of actual rights as of general theorems in regard to rights) which is contained in, or associated with, the constitution. But the reality of civil liberty must always depend not upon forms, but upon the detail and substance of actual rules, and, no less, on the actual methods of legal procedure by which those rules are enforced in practice. Much the same is true of the cause of political liberty. It stands to gain, at any rate in theory, from the form of a written constitution, accompanied by a declaration of rights, safeguarded by a constitutional court, and protected by a special organ and methods of constitutional amendment. But, here again, the reality of political liberty consists in the detail and substance of actual institutions, and—even more—in the working of these institutions, in the methods of political procedure, in the tone and temper of action. Institutions are one thing, and the actual working of institutions is another thing. It is possible that good institutions may work badly, if wrong methods of procedure are applied, or a proper tone and temper of action are not forthcoming. It is not so easy for bad institutions to work well ; but at any rate they may be made to work better than good institutions used wrongly.

To speak in advance of good and bad political institutions may seem a *petitio principii*. But upon the basis of our previous argument we are justified in assuming that institutions which are consonant with, and tend to promote, the general development of personality in all the members of a State are to that extent, and in that respect, right, and that those which are of an opposite nature and tendency are similarly wrong. Are we justified, however, in making a further assumption—that the institutions which are consonant with, and tend to promote, the general development of personality are democratic institutions, and democratic institutions only, and that democratic institutions are therefore right, and the only institutions which are right ? We must pause before we can give an answer.

The word democracy, in its etymological significance, means government by the people. It is thus synonymous with Popular Government. The principle which underlies such government is often stated in the words, ' The will of the people must prevail '. Without, for the moment, challenging that principle, we have to remark that the will of the people is not a single will. There are some who will one thing, and some who will another. ' In that case ', the answer comes, ' let us count heads : let us discover the majority ; and let us say that its will is the will of the people, and must prevail.' But why, we may ask, should the will of a part, however numerous, be identified with the will of the whole ? The answer generally given to that question is an answer which rests on the argument of force. ' We count heads instead of breaking them : the majority would win the day if it came to an actual struggle ; the minority consents to be beaten in advance, and thus counted as part of the whole, rather than force the issue to the point of actual struggle.' This reduces the proposition that ' the will of the people must prevail ' to the simpler but less attractive proposition that ' the force of the majority of the people must prevail, because, if it were challenged, it would prevail.' In a word, the basis of democracy becomes force—not actual force, but hypothetical force ; not force actually employed, but the force which could and would be applied if there were any resistance. This is a qualification of some importance. On the one hand it may seem, if not to justify, at any rate to excuse democratic government. Such government does not proceed to the actual employment of force. On the other hand the qualification seems to endanger democracy even more than to justify or excuse it. If democracy possesses only hypothetical force, what is to happen when its hypothesis is challenged by a resolute and organized minority ? The bluff may be called, and the stakes may be lost.

Democracy which rests merely on the will of number rests merely on force. If we keep the name and the idea of democracy, we must find some other basis. The force which democracy can employ, being hypothetical, is inadequate merely as force ; and above and beyond that, the very idea of force, whether adequate or inadequate, has no place in our argument. We have to discover a system of government which squares with, and is based upon, the free and full development of human personality—not in some, or even in many, but in all. From this point of view it is not the people, as a people, that matters. It is not the majority, as a majority, that matters. It is each human being, as such. The form of government we have to find is one which elicits and enlists—or at any rate is calculated to elicit and enlist, so far as is humanly possible— the thought, the will, and the general capacity of every member. It must be a government depending on mutual interchange of ideas, on mutual criticism of the ideas interchanged, and on the common and agreed choice of the idea which emerges triumphant from the ordeal of interchange and criticism. A government depending on such a process can enlist in itself and its own operation the self of every member. It will be self-government : it will square with, and be based upon, the development of personality and individuality in every self. It will be government by the people not as a mass, or as a majority, but as a society of living selves. In that sense it will be a democracy. But it will be a democracy which does not rest on number or mass or quantity. It will be a democracy which rests on the spiritual quality of the process which it disengages, and on the value of the process for every participant.

That process is, in a word, discussion—discussion of competing ideas, leading to a compromise in which all the ideas are reconciled and which can be accepted by all because it bears the imprint of all. It is a process which raises two problems. The first is the problem of the area, the organs and the methods of discussion. The second is the problem of the conditions of a true reconciliation between the conflicting views which emerge in the course of discussion.

The great States of our modern world, with populations which run to tens and even hundreds of millions, seem precluded by their very size from acting as circles of discussion. Looking at their magnitude, we might despair of our principles and succumb to the idea that some guiding authority must somehow emerge, from above, to manage and dominate what seems to be only a great and inert mass. But we need despair only if we make the assumption that discussion must proceed immediately and solely from the whole civic body. That is an assumption at once unnecessary and untrue to life. Discussion, as we see it actually at work in modern States which are governed upon that basis, proceeds in a number of stages and moves in a series of concentric circles. It begins on the circumference, with general issues : it moves inwards toward the centre, and ends in concrete decision. Each circle or stage has a function of its own ; and each stage has its own organ. We may see these stages emerging if we merely look at popular nomenclature. We speak of democracy or popular government. But we also speak of the parliamentary system or representative institutions. That implies a further stage. We also speak of responsible government or the cabinet system. That implies a still further stage. What is the order of the stages which are thus implied in our current speech, and what is the function and the organ of each stage ?

A system of government by discussion proceeds through four main stages—first of party, next of the electorate, then of parliament, and finally of cabinet. These stages have not developed historically in that sequence. In our own country there were parliaments (organs for ' parley ' and discussion of affairs, convoked by the king from his tenants-in-chief) before there was an electorate ; and both parliament and the electorate had existed for centuries before a party system began to appear in the reign of Charles II. But if we look at the logic of modern life rather than the sequence of history, we may say that the process of political discussion begins originally with the action of political parties, which debate and formulate their programmes as the issues for electoral discussion, and then proceed to select and propose their candidates as the exponents of those programmes. Discussion is then carried forward to the electorate, which chooses between the programmes, after the grand debate of a general election, by the simple act of choosing between the candidates and thus constituting a majority in favour of one of the programmes. It is next carried forward to parliament, in which the majority, subject to the condition of constant debate with the minority, seeks to give legislative force to the measures, prepared by its leaders, which issue from its programme, and to sustain and support, again in constant debate with the minority, the general conduct of administration undertaken by its leaders in the spirit of its programme. Finally, the process of discussion is carried forward to the cabinet, a body of colleagues, selected by the accredited leader of the majority, who discuss and settle, under his presidency, the legislative measures to be submitted to parliament and the general lines of administrative action to be taken. The whole process is homogeneous, in so far as it is a process of discussion and debate at each stage. But it is also, in another sense, heterogeneous. Each of the organs has a specific function in the process. The function of each is indeed a function complementary to those of the rest ; but it is, considered in itself, a function which is *sui generis*. If any of the organs is ambitious, and seeks to transcend its function, it will interfere with another organ, and it will also interfere with the general working of the whole system. Any of the four organs (and not least the organ of party) may thus throw itself out of gear, and the whole system along with itself. The difficulty of the democratic system of government by discussion, conducted in successive stages, is to achieve respect for what we may call the principle of division of labour—division between the stages, and division between their organs.

§ 3. PARTY AS A STAGE AND ORGAN IN THE METHOD OF DISCUSSION

The first stage is the formulation of the general issues of discussion. This is itself achieved by a process of discussion within, and also between, political parties, which results in the construction, and also the ventilation, of different party programmes. Parties, in their origin and their nature, are voluntary groups which are freely formed in the area of social life ; but since, in their ultimate issue, they present programmes and candidates to the electorate, which is part of the political scheme, they also enter the area of political organization. A party has thus a double nature or quality. It is, we may say, a bridge, which rests at the one end on society and at the other on the State. It is, we may also say in another metaphor, a conduit or sluice, by which the waters of social thought and discussion are brought to the wheels of political machinery and set to turn those wheels. It is one of the problems of modern politics whether parties should be left entirely in the voluntary area of society, unregulated by the State, or whether, on the ground that they act as factors in the political scheme, they should be made the objects of State regulation. If the latter policy be adopted, we may have laws passed, as has been done in the states of the U.S.A., to regulate the conditions under which parties may hold their meetings and propose their candidates[1] ; or, with a different purpose, and from a diffcrent point of view, we may have laws passed, as has been done in some of the states of the Continent, to recognize the party lists prepared by the different parties, to compel the voter to vote for the whole party list (and not for a particular person or persons), and to assign seats to each party, as such, in proportion to the number of votes which has been cast for its list.

Whatever view we may adopt in regard to this problem, and whichever policy we may approve, there is one rule which we may lay down in regard to parties, a rule entailed by the general process of discussion to which they belong and which they are intended to serve. There must necessarily be a plurality of parties. A single party cannot provide the basis of a system of government by discussion. Discussion is ended at once if only a single issue is formulated and a single programme enunciated. When the State not only regulates parties, but so regulates them that it abolishes all parties other than the single party of the ' people ' or ' nation ' or ' proletariat ', it really abrogates the essence of party, and in that act it also abolishes any real activity of the other stages and organs of democracy. Party ceases to be an organ of

---

[1] Lord Bryce, referring to these laws, speaks of ' this legal recognition of Party as a public political institution . . . this application of statutory regulation to what had heretofore been purely voluntary and extra-legal associations ' (*Modern Democracies*, II, p. 142).

discussion in itself ; it equally ceases to be a stage in a movement of discussion which goes progressively through other
stages. Changed in itself, it changes the whole process. Ceasing
to be a part, it becomes the whole. Ceasing to be a means, it
becomes the end.

The function of party—as a part or means of a general
system of discussion which acts on the principle of what may
be called political division of labour—is to formulate issues,
and to provide representatives of the issues formulated, for
the discussion and choice of the electorate. Since the issues
are to be submitted to the general electorate, they must be
issues capable of interesting the general electorate. They
cannot be limited issues which affect only a section of electors :
they cannot be issues of a purely particular interest—the
interest of a particular branch of production, or a particular
grade of employment, or a particular shade of religious
opinion. Such interests would not be comparable with one
another : each of them would live in its own little separate
world : they could not be pitted against one another for the
purpose of general discussion. Discussion implies similarity,
as well as difference, in the things discussed.

This general reflection may lead us to another conclusion, of
even greater importance. Not only must the issues formulated
and presented be similar in the sense of having the same sort of
power of exciting *general* or widespread interest. They must be
similar in a deeper sense. They must all alike suppose, and all
alike be addressed to, a *common* or identical interest. It is impossible to debate or discuss if there is no common ground between
the disputants. If the issues formulated by parties, while alike
in being general, are absolutely different in the assumptions
on which they proceed, and mutually exclusive in the purposes to which they are directed, they cannot be debated, and
the decision between such issues cannot be attained by discussion. The only way will be the way of force. This is why
the logical or extreme socialist, who feels that his programme
differs with a fundamental difference from that of other
parties, is driven to confess that he cannot adapt himself to a
system of discussion. When a party becomes a separate ' view
of the world ' (*Weltanschauung*), it sheds the character of a
political party, capable of debating and compromising with
other similar parties, and it assumes the quality of an exclusive

faith or doctrine which stands by itself in a world of its own. To say this of such a party (for example, a communist party) is not to condemn it *in toto*. It is only to say of it (what many of its own adherents also say) that it is not qualified to be a part, or a means, in the system of government by discussion.

§ 4. THE ELECTORATE : ITS SELECTIVE AND INSTRUCTIVE
POWERS

The second stage of discussion is the choice between party programmes, and between the representatives of those programmes, which is made by the electorate. When a party system, with a plurality of parties, has done its work, the electorate is presented with different and yet similar issues— different, in that different lines of policy, in each of the various areas of the State's activity, are necessarily involved : similar, in that the issues are of a similar general character, and in that they suppose a similar common interest. Along with these issues, the electorate is presented with their exponents. Its function, in the position in which it stands, is determined partly by the activity of party which has gone before, and partly by the activity of parliament and cabinet which has to come afterwards. The electorate cannot be regarded by itself, or in isolation, or as if it were a sovereign which was the beginning and the end, initiating everything and concluding everything. It is a part of the system of discussion, which has both to take over and to hand on the torch in such a way as will best keep it burning and bright. Its function is thus twofold. First, in the act of ' taking over ' from party, it discharges a selective function. It discusses and decides, at the moment of its choice, the selection of the representatives of programmes ; and therein and thereby, according to the selection of representatives which it makes, it also discusses and decides the selection of a programme. In a word, it primarily selects men ; but by doing so it also selects a policy. Secondly, in the act of ' handing on ' to parliament, it discharges what we may call an instructive function. It instructs the men, whom it has elected, to carry discussion to a further and finer point in a legislative assembly ; it instructs them to discuss the translation of the programme, for which they stand and on which they have been elected, into a body of general rules, or laws, and thus to attain a further stage in the system of division of labour on which the whole process of discussion is based.

The selective function of the electorate is a function which is primarily concerned with men and the selection of men. It is true that the men who present themselves to the electorate for election have been pre-elected, as it were, by parties, and thus appear before the electorate less in themselves, or as themselves, than as representatives of parties : it is also true that the electorate, in exercising its selective function, not only chooses between men, but also between parties and the programmes of those parties. But it is also true that the essence of the selective function of the electorate consists in the choice of men who, in their personal capacity, and in virtue of their character, are fitted to discharge the task of deliberation and discussion at the parliamentary stage. In choosing such men the electorate needs the preliminary service and the general guidance of party ; but it must also be free to make a real choice, and to exercise a real judgment. Otherwise it will not be a new and separate organ which represents a new and separate stage of discussion ; it will be only an appendage and instrument of party. A free electorate, guided by party, but not enslaved by party, is a thing difficult to attain.

It is obvious enough that a free electorate requires a system of universal suffrage and secret ballot. It is almost equally obvious, though it is not an uncontested proposition, that a free electorate requires a system of geographical divisions or constituencies, each general enough in its composition to serve as a microcosm and mirror of the whole. If we pursued another policy, and if we divided the electorate into occupations or 'functions', each returning its quota of members, we should have sectional and disparate constituencies which not only failed to square with the character of the general political parties, or to produce a general political parliament capable of debating on a common ground, but also were calculated to paralyse the general freedom of the electorate by making it a mere congeries of different sectional interests. But while these things are obvious, or tolerably obvious, it is much less clear how the guidance of party can be reconciled with the freedom of the electorate. There are many who, consumed by an honest zeal for party, would accommodate the electorate to its exigencies. They demand systems of proportional representation which will give to each party, as such, a proportion of seats exactly equivalent to its voting strength. They demand, for this purpose, larger constituencies, each returning a number of members, with the result that the electorate will rather decide how many seats each party shall have than who is the person to be selected for a seat ; and sometimes they may even demand, in the extreme of their logic, that the electorate shall not vote for persons at all, but only for party lists. But there is another point of view, which would seem to be better accommodated to the general process of government by discussion, and to the necessary independence (which, it is true, has to be combined with interdependence) of each stage and organ of that process. It may be argued, and argued with justice, that when the electorate is acting as an electorate, it should be actually free to elect. Those who hold this view will seek to accommodate party to the freedom of the electorate. They will hold that elections are elections of men, and that the electorate must be left free to choose the men it desires ; and they will advocate accordingly the small or single-member constituency in which the personality of candidates can make itself felt and the electors can pick the best man for deliberative office in parliament.

When we turn to what we have called the instructive office of the electorate a similar difficulty emerges. Just as, in the act of selection, or, as it may also be termed, the moment of 'taking over' from party, the electorate has at once to follow the guidance of party and to exercise its own judgment, so in the act of instruction, or the moment of 'handing over' to parliament, the electorate has both to guide parliament and to vest it with the exercise of its own deliberative discretion. Unless parliament consents to be guided, it will not be a further stage in discussion, but a totally new and entirely disconnected stage ; but unless it also exercises its own deliberative discretion, it will fail to carry discussion further, or to be a genuine further stage, and it will be only an appendage and instrument of the electorate. From this latter point of view it is perhaps dangerous to speak of an instructive function. In a general sense, it is true, the electorate instructs or authorizes parliament to proceed to the discharge of that particular function which, on the principle of division of labour in the general conduct of discussion, belongs to the parliamentary stage. In other words, it instructs or authorizes parliament, in the light of the general result of the previous process of selection, and according to the majority which it has given, to discuss and enact legislation and to control administration. But, in a more particular sense, the electorate does not give detailed instructions or specific mandates. It creates a legislature ; but it does not dictate legislation or participate in legislation. It elects a body for the purpose of doing something beyond what it does itself, and something different from what it can do itself.

This, at any rate, is the current doctrine ; but it is not an indisputable or an undisputed doctrine. Here, again, as in the previous case of party, there are two factors which must always be present ; and different views may be taken of their balance. On the one hand, the verdict of the electorate and the result of elections must guide the action of parliament : on the other hand, parliament must freely discuss, and freely decide by its own honest light, the emergent problems of national life. With such a delicate balance, it is difficult to lay down precise rules of ' Thus far, and no farther '. We must respect the idea of division of labour ; but we must not respect it idolatrously. There may be cases in which the electorate, after an election fought on a specific issue, actually and properly gives a mandate which dictates the legislation on that issue ; there may even be cases in which the electorate may properly decide, by a referendum, the final fate of a law which, though duly passed by the legislature, still hangs in the wind of national opinion. It would be wrong, indeed, to exaggerate the guidance of the electorate into a universal system of mandate, referendum, initiative, and recall. But it would equally be wrong to exaggerate the independent function of parliament into its total and absolute independence of the electorate. We have to think of the whole general process of discussion, in which each stage and each organ has its own business, and yet all the stages and organs are interconnected and interdependent. It is easy to take one stage and its organ, to isolate that organ from the process of stages and the nexus of organs in which it is engaged, and to proclaim that, so isolated, it must be free and even sovereign. We can thus worship the free and sovereign Party (as many do, in fact if not in name), or the free and sovereign Electorate, or the free and sovereign Parliament, or even the free and sovereign Government. Really none of these is free and sovereign— by itself alone. The free and sovereign thing is the whole process of discussion. Each of its stages and organs is indeed free ; but only within the limits of the process, and as a part of the process. The electorate and the parliament, for example, must each discuss and decide freely, as if everything hung upon their discussion and decision ; and yet each must also, because there is a stage or stages precedent and a stage or stages subsequent, adapt and adjust itself to those stages and their organs. There is a necessary ' give and take ' in the whole connected process. And the process is all the more delicate, and all the more difficult of operation, because we cannot define exactly what must be taken and exactly what must be given. The method of government by discussion, when it is translated into institutions and the attributes of institutions, is not the easiest, but the most difficult, of methods of government. Discussion is a high faculty, and it requires a high temper of the mind. Its instruments are only instruments ; but each of them tends to be worshipped as an end. The zeal of each instrument eats up those who use it.

§ 5.   PARLIAMENT :   ITS SOVEREIGNTY AND ITS PLURALITY

The third stage of discussion is parliament. In the first stage, the programmes have been formulated by debate in each party. In the second, representatives of programmes have been selected after debate by the electorate, and authorized by it to form a parliament for further debate, to be conducted in a particular form and for a particular purpose. In the third stage this parliament is assembled and sets to work at its function. That function is so important that the whole process of government by discussion is often called by the name of parliamentarianism. The name is not inappropriate : the idea of ' parley ', which is suggested by its etymology, is the same as the idea of discussion. On the other hand the name of parliamentarianism also tends to identify the whole of the process of discussion with one of its stages or organs ; and the magnification of parliament into a total and absolute sovereign may thus be connected with the use of the name. In England we find the sovereignty of parliament currently proclaimed in theory : in France we find it definitely asserted in practice—

and that though the sovereignty proclaimed for lip-service in France is the sovereignty of the nation, and not that of its parliament. There is indeed a sense in which parliament is sovereign ; but it is in a qualified sense—and indeed, we may even say, a doubly qualified sense.

In the first place parliament is sovereign, or competent, or free (whatever the word we use), in its own particular sphere, and for its own particular function, under the general system of division of labour on which government by discussion necessarily proceeds. Selected by the electorate, and authorized or instructed by it, in general terms, for a particular purpose, it exists for the due discharge of its purpose. The purpose is that of translating the programme endorsed by the electorate into rules of law, so far as it can be run into the mould of law, and, for the rest, of controlling the spirit in which the executive government acts (whether in enforcing rules of law, or in exercising the discretionary authority which lies outside the area of rules) in order that it may conform with the general trend of the programme. A parliament exists in order to discuss and enact laws, and in order to discuss and guide the general conduct of executive government ; but it does not exist in order to govern, and if it assumes the character of a government, it will be going beyond the generality which is its nature and trespassing on the sphere of the particular.

In the second place a parliament, even in the area of its particular purpose or function, does not stand in isolation and cannot act alone. It is part of a general system of discussion, connected with other parts ; and it must look before and after—before, to the electorate ; after, to the executive government. If we speak of the sovereignty of parliament, we have to remember that it is exercised in conjunction with two colleagues. On the one hand parliament must maintain some sort of harmony, and act in some sort of contact, with the electorate. A parliament which has lost contact with the electorate is a parliament which is virtually *functus officio* : it has dropped out of the general current of national discussion into a backwater ; and it must be brought back into the current, by the machinery of dissolution and a new election, before it can act in its proper office and perform its proper function. On the other hand, and equally, parliament must necessarily act in conjunction with the executive government.

In our English form the sovereignty of parliament is more truly described as that of the King in Parliament. In other words, it is the sovereignty of the executive government acting in, and surrounded by, parliament ; it is the sovereignty of the two in one, but not that of either without the other. There is a deep truth involved in this formal description. Parliament cannot properly legislate without the guidance of those who are responsible for the execution of its legislation. If it needs the guidance of the general programme which comes from the electorate, it also needs the guidance of detail which can only come from the executive government. Similarly the executive government cannot properly administer without the guidance of a parliament which is responsible for the general conduct of administration in the spirit of its own instructions and its own authorization from the electorate. The executive needs the guidance of that spirit, as well as the guidance of the expert knowledge which it either possesses itself or can draw from its agents and officers.

It is natural to speak of parliament as one ; but we shall altogether misconceive its nature unless we remember that it is also two, or even more. It is a body composed of representatives of parties and party programmes ; and by that very fact it is plural. It could not be a body for the further conduct of debate and discussion unless it were organized on that basis. It is true that there will always be a majority party or combination of parties. But it is also true that there will also be a minority party or combination of parties ; and it is no less true that the minority party or combination of parties is not extinguished by being in a minority. If it were extinguished, it would be idle to talk of discussion, or even to use the word parliament. We should simply have a registering body, and not a debating assembly. In all that it does itself, and in all the relations in which it stands to other bodies, parliament proceeds by way of debate ; and it therefore proceeds as a body which in order to be itself is divided against itself. If there is a majority in contact with the electorate, there is also a minority in similar contact. If there is a majority in touch with the cabinet or executive government, there is also a minority in similar touch with an anti-cabinet, composed of the leaders of the opposition to that government. If the majority seek to translate their party programme into general rules of law, the minority seek to incorporate elements from their programme into the translation. If the majority seek to bring the general spirit of administration into harmony with their programme, the minority also seek to qualify that spirit in order that it may have some degree of harmony with *their* programme. The existence of differences at every stage, and above all at the parliamentary stage, is the necessary condition of the continuance of discussion.

These differences and this division of parliament must necessarily be organized : they would defeat discussion if they ran wild : indeed we may even say that, for purposes of real debate, they must be organized in two sides, and two sides only—the side of the Ayes and the side of the Noes. When we have more than two parties, as we in this country have had for many years, such an organization into two sides may seem difficult, or impossible. Actually, if it is difficult, it is never impossible. On the contrary—granted a cabinet, which attracts one set of parties to its side, and repels the rest to the other side—it always happens. On that condition there is always a side of the Ayes and a side of the Noes—a side of the Ins, and a side of the Outs—even if either of the sides contains a number of parties. The difficulty (and it is a genuine difficulty) is the fluidity of the two sides when each of them is an amalgam of parties. Each tends to dissolve and reconstitute itself, for more or less personal reasons ; and thus a process of sustained debate based on genuine differences of principle may be turned into temporary passages of arms determined largely by differences of personal interest. Debate and discussion suffer if there are not two permanent groups in parliament divided by permanent and impersonal differences. But if they suffer under a system of impermanent and variable groups, they do not disappear. They disappear only when a single group acquires a monopoly of parliament. Better two permanent groups than two which are shifting and kaleidoscopic. But better two groups, however shifting, than one single and solitary group.

§ 6. THE CABINET : ITS RELATIONS TO PARLIAMENT AND THE ELECTORATE

The furthest and last stage of discussion is the stage of the Cabinet, or executive government. Here discussion passes from speech into action—or rather (since parliament already acts, but only in the form of making general rules and exercising a general control of administration) it passes from the area of generalities into that of the particular and concrete. First the formulation of general programmes by parties : then the choice of representatives of these general programmes by the electorate, with a majority chosen in favour of one of the programmes : then the translation of the general programme of the majority into general rules of law and a general spirit of administration : then the final translation of all that has preceded into the particular act. On the principle of division of labour which runs through the system of discussion the cabinet has thus its specific function—the function of turning a general programme into a series of particular and separate acts, which are yet connected together by a common fidelity to the principles of the programme.

But the stages of discussion are from first to last connected, as well as distinct ; and the connection between the parliamentary and the cabinet stage is particularly close. If the cabinet has the function of administration, parliament has the function of general control of the spirit of administration. If parliament has the function of legislation, the cabinet has the function of drafting legislative measures for parliament and of guiding their passage through parliament. We may distinguish in idea between legislation and administration ; but in practice they are so intimately interconnected that their organs will also be similarly interconnected. The bond between parliament and cabinet is thus closer than that between the electorate and parliament. When the electorate has selected and generally instructed a parliament, the parliament so selected and instructed will henceforth sit and act as a separate body. When a parliament has constituted a cabinet (we can hardly apply the word 'selection' to the informal and mainly indirect methods by which cabinets come into existence), the cabinet sits in the parliament, and a large part of its activity will be its activity in parliament. It will be instructed or guided by parliament : it will equally, or even more, give instruction or guidance to parliament. Under these conditions a system of reciprocal control emerges. Where the control is genuinely reciprocal, either of the parties to the system may, in the last resort, dismiss the other. Parliament may push its power of guidance to the point of evicting a cabinet which does not agree with its views of the general spirit in which administration should be conducted. Cabinet may push its power of guidance to the point of dissolving a parliament which will not accept its views in regard to some urgent problem of administration or some pressing need of legislation.

This system of reciprocal control between cabinet and parliament is not universally, or perhaps even generally, accepted as a necessary element in the operation of parliamentary institutions. On the contrary, a total or one-sided subordination of the executive to parliament, which in turn implies a similar subordination of parliament to the electorate, is often held to be the essence of true democracy. By a natural and attractive logic, which makes the authority of each stage derivative from that of the preceding stage, and therefore subordinate to it, it is argued that just as parliament is the nominee and delegate of the electorate, so the cabinet is the nominee and delegate of parliament. Authority is thus conceived as a waterfall, which descends in a series of cascades; and it is assumed, on the strength of this conception, that whatever exists below must necessarily have come from above, and that whatever is done below must necessarily be done by virtue of a power delegated or derived from above. If we accept this conception, which has the merit of an apparent simplicity, we shall hold that all authority, both legislative and executive, belongs to the electorate : that it is then devolved or delegated by the electorate to a subordinate parliament—not without reservations in favour of the continued exercise of some sort of 'direct' legislative power by the electorate ; and that it is then further devolved or delegated by this subordinate parliament to a still more subordinate cabinet— but, once more, not without reservations and the imposition of conditions.

We must challenge, however, the whole of this picture of the descending waterfall, the series of cascades, and the hierarchy of superior and subordinate powers. We must think in terms of ascending rather than of descending. Discussion climbs to new heights : at each new height a fresh function and a more intensive quality of discussion emerge ; with each fresh function and each increase of intensity a fresh organ is required. The principle at work is that of a complex division of labour among new and developing organs, for purposes of growth and ascent—not that of the mere delegation of a single and simple unchanging authority in successive phases of descent. It is true that in the process of ascent, on this principle of division of labour, each stage is linked to the next, and each must prepare the way for the next. Parliament does not merely emerge : it is created by the electorate. Cabinets do not merely emerge : they are created by parliaments. But the creator does not create a mere creature. It brings into being an organ which has its own function, and which must be competent for its own purposes. Just as the electorate creates, by its formal and regular selective activity, a legislature which is then its own master and competent for its own function within the range of the general instructions involved in the act of selection, so the legislature creates, by its more informal activity of appointment, a cabinet which is then equally its own master and competent for its own function within the range of the general instructions involved in the act of appointment. Either of the creating bodies may feel, with surprise and even annoyance, that in spite of being a creator it is face to face with a master. But in either case the new master is only master in his own sphere, and for his own function. And in either case it would have been better for the creator never to have created at all than to deny to what he has created that mastery over function which is necessary to its discharge.

Parliament, then, does not dominate the cabinet, any more that the electorate dominates parliament. As the electorate creates a parliament, and leaves it to make general rules of law, so parliament creates a cabinet, and leaves it to determine the conduct of particular acts of administration. By the same logic by which parliament vindicates freedom for itself, even against the electorate, in the discharge of its legislative function, it must acknowledge the freedom of the cabinet, even against itself, in the discharge of the function of administration. It creates, and in general terms it instructs, an administration ; but it does not itself administer, or interfere in administration. It is not, by its nature and function, the master of the particular acts which are the essence of administration. It will, therefore, leave to the cabinet the proposal of all particular items of expenditure, as the English Parliament has done for over two hundred years[1] : it will not allow its members to make such proposals themselves, and thus to encroach on the domain of particular acts which does not belong to their sphere. Finance is the key of administration : and if the cabinet is deprived of the key of its function, it is deprived of its function. Similarly, parliament will leave cabinet free to act as the one organ and only committee of administration. It will not erect a system of organized special committees, each concerned with a sphere of administration, and each tending to push its right of enquiry and report in that sphere to the point at which it becomes an ' executive committee ' rivalling and enfeebling the administrative authority of cabinet. The creator, when once it has exercised its power of creation, will refrain from playing with that power by such acts of sub-creation.

There is another way in which parliament may play with its power of creation. It may not only indulge in acts of sub-creation : it may also kill, with a rapid impatience, the cabinets which it has created, and seek to enjoy the sport of repeated acts of creation. On general principles, and apart from the merits of any particular case, this is a procedure which is fatal to the proper discharge of the function of administration. If legislation is an *oeuvre de longue haleine*, which requires the continuation of a parliament for a life of four or five years, administration, in order to acquire momentum and to achieve a considered policy, also (we may even say, equally) requires some length of life. Granted that parliament has a right of evicting cabinets, cabinet must thus exercise a similar right of dissolving parliament. The system of reciprocal control, of which we have already spoken, is not only based, as it primarily is, on the peculiar intimacy of the connection between parliament and the cabinet. It is also, and secondarily, necessary in order to maintain the integrity of the separate function of either body. Parliament cannot discharge its function of general legislation, and of general control of the spirit of administration, without the power of dismissing the executive government, which enforces in action (and even supplements by its orders) all parliamentary legislation, and also determines the

---

1 ' This house will receive no petition for any sum relating to public service, or proceed upon any motion for a grant or charge upon the public revenue, . . . unless recommended from the Crown' (i.e. from a minister). Standing Orders of the House of Commons for Public Business, No. 66, passed in 1713, and amended in 1852 and 1866.

conduct of day-to-day administration. Equally the cabinet cannot discharge its function of administration without the power of dissolving a parliament which might otherwise be tempted, and might succumb to the temptation, to encroach upon its sphere. A parliament which was itself immune from eviction, but could freely evict the cabinet, would inevitably usurp administrative functions by seeking to control the details of finance and to bring each sphere of administration under the purview and the direction of its committees.

But there is also a third and further reason for the exercise of the power of dissolution by cabinet. Such a power is necessary to maintain the free flow of the whole current of discussion through all its stages and organs. The cabinet's power of dissolution is not merely a matter of its own relations to parliament. It is also a matter of the relations of both cabinet and parliament to the electorate. Parliament, as we have seen, must maintain some permanent contact and harmony with the electorate, in order that discussion may circulate freely from stage to stage of its process. If parliament drops out of contact with the electorate and becomes a body which is stagnant and land-locked, its dissolution becomes a necessity in order to restore the contact and renew the flow. That the cabinet should freely decide whether the contact of parliament and the electorate has been broken, and that, if it so decides, it should send parliament back to the electorate, may well seem a very large thing. Created a master for its own function, it turns upon its creator, and, ending its life, it ends—at any rate for the time being—its power of performing its function. But this sweeping action of cabinet has its own large justification. The cabinet, too, has its contact with the electorate : indeed we may say that it must have direct and constant contact with the electorate, in order to draw the strength and support which it needs for its work. It depends upon parliament ; but it also depends on the stages and organs of discussion which precede parliament. It depends, in a word, upon the whole system, and not upon any one part. It is its business, as the last stage and organ of the system, to assure itself that there is a free course through the whole. A cabinet cannot be fully competent for its work unless it is in touch with a parliament which in turn is in touch with an electorate which, in turn, is in touch with the life and the thought of parties. In this interconnected system, the first stage runs through till it reaches the last, and the last runs back till it reaches the first. Party is operative not only in the stage of making programmes and selecting candidates, but also in the subsequent stages of electorate, parliament, and cabinet ; and conversely the cabinet is operative not only in the final stage of active administration, but also in all the preceding stages. There is thus a sense in which we may say that the final stage resumes, and recapitulates in itself, the characteristics of those which have gone before. It is this ' recapitulatory ' character of cabinet which explains its importance and justifies its power.

As one of the stages and organs in the system of government by discussion, the cabinet acts and administers by the method of discussion. There is a famous French phrase (it may almost be called a Cæsarian phrase) of the year 1800 : *administrer est le fait d'un seul ; délibérer est le fait de plusieurs*. The cabinet system, following an opposite line (because it springs from an inspiration which is the opposite of Cæsarism), makes administration depend on the deliberation and the discussion of a body of colleagues. But the cabinet is not merely immersed in its own interior discussions : it has to play its part in a far wider area of discussion. Just as there is a sense in which parliament is not singular, but plural—not one body, but two—and just as this sense explains the capacity of parliament for debate, so there is a sense in which the cabinet also is not one, but two. Every cabinet, under the working of the party system, is confronted by some sort of anti-cabinet of the leaders of the Opposition. It depends on the particular formation of the party system in each country how definite is the organization, and how strong is the influence, of this anti-cabinet. But it will always be there ; and it will always sit, equally with the cabinet itself, in parliament. A cabinet is thus committed to a constant duel of discussion with a constant rival ; and every cabinet *in esse* is confronted and criticized by (and, as we shall have reason to observe in a later stage of our argument, it will tend to seek a compromise with) a cabinet *in posse*. We need not fear the tyranny of cabinet, which may seem to be involved in the idea of its recapitulatory character, so long as the tyrant has always an anti-tyrant at his side. Nor can we desire any better guarantee for the future of government by discussion than is furnished by the co-existence of a strong government and a strong opposition—two things which are generally corollaries and companions.

But it remains true—and it is a truth which deserves to be emphasized in any consideration of the nature of cabinet—that a democratic executive, in the sense of an executive duly qualified for its place in a system of government by discussion, is necessarily a strong and, we may even say, an independent executive. It is not an executive which is at the beck and call of parliamentary groups, and is liable to processes oı distraint and eviction at their hands which it can never inflict upon them : still less is it an executive which is bound to satisfy local constituencies and their interests, or to act by the directions of party conventions and their votes. A cabinet has to be in touch with parliament, electorate and party ; but there is an independence which it may, and indeed must, demand from all three. It must be independent for the purposes of its work : it must be master within the area of its function : it must govern, as well as reign, in the sphere of all particular acts. Its independence, its mastery, its government —within its own sphere—are the necessary conditions of the translation of the result of *general* discussion into a series of particular acts congruous with that result. It is one thing to say that a cabinet must act in general agreement with the general programme of a party or group of parties ; with the general instructions of the electorate ; with the general control of the spirit of its administration by parliament. It is another thing to say that it should allow the tenor and policy of its administration to be deflected, upon particular issues, by the vote of a party convention or party caucus ; by the pressure of a group of constituencies ; or by the solicitations óf a parliamentary combination of interests. The whole general process of discussion is falsified, in the last and not the least crucial of its stages, if the organ of that stage, instead of being left free to play its own part in the process, is made a mere instrument—an instrument, too, not of this or that preceding stage as a whole, but of some section or fraction in the stage concerned, which presses, in effect, a particular claim, though it may allege the general right of party or electorate or parliament. The principle of division of labour which applies to each stage applies to the stage of cabinet no less than to the previous stages ; and we may even argue that it is in the interest of the electorate and of parliament, if we regard each of them as a whole, that the cabinet should have and should exercise its own independent function. In order that the electorate in general, and parliament in general, may be assured of an administration which will carry further, and carry into action, the previous process of discussion in which they have played their part, the body which is charged with the function of administration must be free to discuss and determine the lines of its action in the light of the previous process. The fundamental obligation of cabinet is an obligation to the whole system of discussion in which it is set.   That obligation demands that cabinet should take into account the results of each previous stage of discussion. It equally demands that cabinet should itself carry on discussion freely to a further and final point.   What it does not demand—what, on the contrary, it prohibits—is that cabinet should ever remove the conduct of affairs with which it is charged from the area of free discussion to that of obedient accommodation.

§ 7. THE TWO PRINCIPLES OF DIVISION AND CO-OPERATION IN THE
ACTION OF THE STAGES AND ORGANS

We have traversed the four stages of discussion which we started by distinguishing. They are not the only phases or forms which discussion assumes in a community based on that principle. There is, for example, the whole province of juris-diction—the whole system of the courts of law, with their highly developed methods of discussion for discovering both the facts of a case and the law which bears on the facts. We may almost say that the lawyers, at any rate in our own country, were the first to organize discussion—among the judges ; between judges and barristers ; and also among the jury—for the purposes of their own procedure ; and we may even add that the procedure of legal discussion in the courts prepared the way for a system of political discussion.   Our parliament began as a High Court, and it still has something of that nature. Apart from and beyond the area of the State, there are also great fields and systems of discussion in the area of society—churches ; trade unions ; educational associations ; associations of every sort for the discussion and promotion of

every sort of social object. Behind political parties, or rather
by their side (for political parties, as we have seen, are themselves groups freely formed in the area of society), there stand
a multitude of social organizations ; and each of these is
occupied not only in discussing and advocating its own particular purpose—charitable, religious, educational, economic,
or whatever it may be—but also in discussing the relation of
that purpose to the general life of the community and the
political activity of the State. The activity of discussion which
animates a self-governing State is fed from many fountains.
It is not only a matter of parties and parliaments ; it is also
a matter of religious societies and church congresses, of educational bodies and conferences, of trade unions and their general
congress—of every gathering-ground of thought which, collecting its own immediate waters, can pour them ultimately
as a tributary into the general current of national discussion.

Confining ourselves to the four stages of discussion which
are pre-eminently political—party, electorate, parliament, and
cabinet—we may notice that two principles are involved in
the general system which moves through these stages. One is
the principle of division of labour, or differentiation of function.
Each organ, in each stage, has its own particular work to do ;
and it must neither abnegate its duty nor seek to extend its
province. It is a necessity of the system that each of the organs
should value its function highly, and should act as if it were
cardinal ; but it is also a danger of the system that each of the
organs should magnify its function unduly, and should act as
if it were supreme. Party, because it is the beginning, may
claim to be also the end ; it may turn itself from being a part
into something of the nature of a whole, something totalitarian,
which seeks to dominate and determine the action of the other
organs. But party, though it is perhaps the most powerful, is
not the only encroacher. The zeal of its house may eat up a
parliament ; and a passion for the rights of the people may
consume an electorate. There is all the more need for remembering the principle of division of labour. We may even say
that the old idea of ‘ separation of powers ’ has again to be
enunciated, in a new form and with a new application. It is
not only necessary to distinguish the judicial from the executive
and the legislative power. It is also necessary to distinguish
the power of party from that of the electorate, the powers of

both from that of parliament, and the powers of all three from that of the cabinet.

But separation of powers, or division of labour, is only one side of the matter. There is also another side, or another principle. This is the principle of co-operation and inter-connection. The different organs and their functions must necessarily be interlocked as well as differentiated. Each has to act as part of a system ; and each has therefore to act with reference to, and in harmony with, the other parts. Each must stay within its own borders ; and yet each must also go outside its borders into those of the others, in order to give and to take. Parliament, for example, has a specific function of making general rules of law. It is specifically responsible for legislation ; and it must take that responsibility seriously, as the essential core of its own determinate province of activity. But parliament has to remember the general instructions which it has received from the electorate ; and it has to remember equally the guidance which it needs from the executive government. Parliament is the giver of laws ; but it is, in a sense, also a taker of the laws it gives. Legislation is not the result of its unaided activity : it is the result of a joint activity in which the electorate and the cabinet are also necessarily concerned.

The delicacy of the balance between the two principles of differentiation and co-operation will serve to explain some of the difficulties of the system of government by discussion. It is necessary to divide : it is equally necessary to combine. If we think only in terms of division, we shall emphasize the exclusive right of parliament in legislation ; we shall speak of the ' encroachments ' of the executive or the electorate ; we shall denounce the system of the ' new despotism ' under which the executive co-operates with parliament in the making of law ; we shall equally condemn the method of new and direct democracy by which the electorate seeks to co-operate, whether in the way of suggestion (initiative), or in the way of ratifica-tion (referendum), or in both ways. If, on the other hand, we think only in terms of co-operation, we may be tempted to deny any real differentiation of function. We may say (like the earlier Russian theorists of the Soviet State) that the idea of separation of powers, in any form, is a myth ; and then, according to our predilection, we shall install some one of the

organs (for we cannot really have all the organs doing all
things simultaneously) as the one general and omnicompetent
authority. We shall, in a word, end in the autocracy either of
party, or of parliament, or of the cabinet.

It is better, and indeed it is essential, to think simultaneously
in terms both of division and of co-operation. We may be
plunged in some logical difficulties. We may seem first to
enunciate, and then to deny, the doctrine of separate functions.
In particular, we may seem to be guilty of first saying that
general rules of legislation belong to one stage and organ, and
particular acts of administration to another organ and stage,
and then of confessing that the dikes are down and the waters
interfused. But these logical difficulties are more apparent
than real. They only arise if we may make the assumption
that each stage must be exclusively concerned with a separate
thing, or a separate set of things, which is then altogether
excluded from the province of other stages. That is not the
assumption which underlies the system of stages. Each is
concerned with the same fundamental issues ; and the real
assumption which we have to make about the difference of the
stages is that each is concerned with the same issues in a
different form, and each discusses them from a different point
of view. Just because the forms and the points of view are
different, and because each is necessary to the solution of the
issues, they must necessarily be combined. Electorate, parliament, cabinet—all three can bring discussion to bear in a
different form and from different points of view, and all three
should do so separately ; but since they are all discussing the
same issues, they must all be interconnected. The electorate,
on the one hand, will discuss general programmes of legislation : the cabinet, on the other, will discuss a specific draft
of particular legislation, with a special reference to practical
detail and administrative considerations : parliament, as a
middle term, will discuss and decide the actual enactment
of a law, with special reference to its general form as a set of
rules or norms, but also with some reference both to its place
in the whole programme which has been endorsed by the
electorate and to its administrative effects and consequences
as they are presented by the cabinet. The difference involved
is not so much a difference between election, legislation, and
administration, considered as separate spheres of action : it is

a difference between the electoral, the parliamentary, and the cabinet forms of discussion—the electoral, the parliamentary, and the cabinet points of view—in contributing to the total solution of the same fundamental issues.

§ 8. THE RECONCILIATION OF DIFFERENCES IN A SYSTEM OF GOVERNMENT BY DISCUSSION, AND ITS MATERIAL CONDITIONS

We have dealt with the problem of the area, the method, and the organs and stages of discussion. It remains to turn to the other problem which still confronts us—that of the conditions of a true reconciliation between the opposing views which emerge in the course of discussion.[1] It may seem as if we had already dealt with this problem of reconciliation. We have already seen, in dealing with the relations of the different organs of discussion, that these organs have not only to be differentiated, but also to be connected and reconciled with one another. But there is a deeper sense of the idea of reconciliation, which has still to be elicited. The system of government by discussion not only implies separate organs and functions, divided and yet united : it also implies a whole community, divided against itself by different and conflicting points of view, and yet—if it is a community and is to remain a community—united none the less. Division emerges at each stage and in each organ of the process of discussion. We begin with the division of parties, which may vary indeed from country to country in depth and trenchancy, but always remains a division. We pass to the division of the electorate among the adherents of the different parties—a division which sometimes may be easy and tolerant ; a division which, at other times (when the grouping of constituencies and the methods of voting are such as to exacerbate the claims of party, and still more when parties become rival religions of a new millenium rather than different schemes for adorning the Sparta we actually inhabit), may become accentuated and bitter ; but a division which, in some form and to some extent, must always and everywhere be present. We proceed to the division of parliament among the members chosen to represent the divisions of the electorate and the parties behind the divisions. Parliaments differ from country to country : some have more of the sense of their own corporate unity, and

[1] See above, p. 37, *ad initium.*

some are houses radically divided against themselves ; but every parliament is in its nature a house of dispute. When we come to the cabinet, we seem to arrive at homogeneity and solidarity ; but the homogeneity of cabinets is sometimes only the homogeneity of a mosaic, and in any case every cabinet has to face an anti-cabinet—if not (as in France) a number of anti-cabinets entrenched in a number of powerful parliamentary committees. Division seems rampant ; and it seems equally natural, *prima facie*, that a sigh should go up for the One behind the Many—for the unitary State, non-party or super-party, which will fuse the differences in some single crucible, and reduce the nation to its ' first intention '.

Yet division is a necessity of discussion ; to abolish division is to abolish discussion ; and to abolish discussion is to end that play of the mind, and to banish that liberty of thought, which are the core and essence of all liberty. We may even say, without any paradox, that to abolish discussion is to abolish the true unity of a society, which can only be attained when the minds of its members have been led, by a free process of thought (and not by a process of induced emotion), to be of one mind and to hold the same ideas. On the other hand division which is mere division, and obstinately stays at the level of difference, can never lead to any sort of unity. It cannot even lead to discussion, which must always imply some common ground ; it can only end in unending dispute. The fundamental threat to government by discussion arises from a disposition to stand on differences—unreconciled differences, which are even alleged, by those who stand on them, to be irreconcilable. It is the emphasis on difference at the expense of any eventual unity which has led to a counter-emphasis on unity at the expense of all difference. Fascism, in all its forms, is an assertion that some sort of unity, however it may be attained (by applying force, or by evoking emotion, or by both methods), is a necessity of national existence. We can only meet the assertion by admitting that it contains its measure of truth. A country in which differences are obstinately different *may* need to pass through a purgatorial period of compulsory or emotional unification. It may be a ' cruel necessity '—a necessity of transition—a necessary preparation of the basis on which men may ultimately wage the war of ideas in peace, and agree to differ in unity.

What are the conditions which are necessary, in a normal and settled community which governs itself on the basis of discussion, in order that it may be one as well as many—one behind its parties ; one behind the divisions of its electorate ; one behind the groups of its parliament ; one behind the difference between Government and Opposition ? There are some conditions which we may call, in a sense, material.[1] National homogeneity is such a condition. There must be some accepted language of intercourse, and some common stock of historical tradition, before there can be any discussion which is conducted in common terms. ' Free institutions ', as J. S. Mill said long ago, ' are next to impossible in a country made up of different nationalities.' Some measure of social homogeneity is another condition of the material order. If a country made up of different nationalities has no common medium of discussion, the same is true of a country made up of two different nations of rich and poor, unable to comprehend one another, or to speak to one another across a gulf of difference. The ideal discussion is that between equals ; and a community in which discussion moves easily must also be a community animated by a spirit of social equality. How far equality should go—whether democracy, for its full play, requires the socialization of wealth, in order that all may debate on a level field, free from the adventitious handicaps of poverty and riches ; or whether it only demands a more equal distribution of private property and a more diffused system of private ownership ; or whether, again, it can work under *any* scheme of economics, provided only that equal opportunities of education are open to all, and all classes can equally express their thoughts and their aspirations—these are questions which are vital, and to which, at a later stage, we must address our argument. Here we can only note that, in the present stage of our general social thought, it is impossible to give any agreed answer. Men are still divided on the fundamental issue which is involved in these questions. Is economics the moving finger of destiny, and are human beings

---

[1] Material, that is to say, in the sense that they (i.e. national homogeneity and social homogeneity) imply a definite matter—the matter of a common language, or the matter of a common standard of living. It is in this sense that I have distinguished them from the more formal and less material (but even more essential) conditions of Agreement to Differ and acceptance of the Majority Principle.

subject to a law of economic determination which makes even what they call 'liberty' a form of economic determination? In that case there will be no liberty in the absence of the appropriate economic factors which produce and determine liberty; indeed, in any strict sense, there will be no liberty even then, since these factors will themselves have been economically caused, and will economically cause in turn the so-called liberty which they produce. Or is man the master of his fate, and only an underling by his own fault: is he more than a factor of class and property and economic conditions, and can he be a free agent in a free state by virtue of what he is in himself? Perhaps it is impossible to answer 'Yes' to either alternative, because they are both pure extremes of logic. But they remain suspended before us; and until we have found some sort of answer, we have to leave indeterminate the nature of the social homogeneity which is one of the conditions, and one of the greatest of the conditions, of a system of government by discussion.

§ 9. THE SPIRITUAL CONDITIONS OF THE RECONCILIATION OF DIFFERENCES

National and social homogeneity are conditions of democracy which may be called, in a sense, material or external; but there are also other conditions required which we may call, in comparison, internal or mental. Before government by discussion can exist at all, there must be the preliminary basis of a common national tradition and a common social structure; but when it has once come into existence upon this basis, it still needs for its working a mental habit of agreement upon a number of axioms which have to be generally accepted, and not only accepted but also obeyed, if it is to work successfully. The acceptance of these axioms is an *inherent* condition of any system of government by discussion. It is not something which is external or preliminary. It is something which must be present *in* discussion, from first to last, if it is to be a genuine play of ideas, and not a war of forces.

The first of the axioms which have to be accepted we may call by the name of Agreement to Differ. This agreement to differ means something more than is meant in ordinary speech, when a man says to his neighbour, ' We must agree to differ', intending only to suggest that personal friendship must not be broken by the continuance of a difference of opinion. It includes, indeed, this elementary virtue (a virtue difficult to attain, since we are all of us prone to take the rejection of our opinions as a rejection of ourselves ; and yet a virtue which may also become a vice, if we surrender the depth and tenacity of our convictions to the claims of social convenience) ; but it also includes a further element. It means that the members of a community agree—by a tacit agreement, made under the stress of its impact—to cluster round some great single issue, *pro et contra*. There is at once unity or agreement, in concentrating upon that issue, and difference or disagreement, in regard to the attitude to be adopted and the policy to be pursued towards that issue. A centripetal force and a centrifugal force are both at work. It is the centripetal force which we are apt to neglect when we think of government by discussion. We see the differences of attitude : we forget the unity of the issue. But the concentration of the general attention of all the community upon one agreed issue is a fact which is prior to the differences of attitude. It is also the cardinal fact of government by discussion. Political discussion is impossible, or at any rate it is sorely vexed and troubled, when there is a multiplicity of different issues which afford no common ground for debate. Its proper working requires some single *fundamentum divisionis*.

In our own history we have always had such a ' fundament of division ', though it has differed at different times. In 1688, and for long years afterwards, the issue was that of the succession to the throne and the position of the monarchy : by 1832 it had become the issue of the rate of change in the constitution, and more particularly, of the extension of the suffrage ; to-day it has become an issue of the nature of the social structure. Our history will also teach us a further lesson. An agreement to differ does not necessarily mean an agreement to form two, and only two, camps on the issue of division. There is no uniform system of two parties running through our history ; and there is nothing in the general logic of a system of government by discussion which demands that the parties to the discussion should be ranged in two camps. It is a far more important thing that there should be only one issue than that there should be only two different opinions in regard to that issue. It takes two to make an argument ; but three or four may also conduct an admirable discussion. On the other hand, as has already been noticed, there is one factor in an organized system of discussion—the factor of the cabinet—which inevitably tends to reduce any multiplicity of parties and of differences of opinion to a simple dualism between the Government side and the Opposition side. Discussion may be possible between three, or four, or even more parties. Considerations of government always tend to bring matters back to only two sides—the side of the Ins and the side of the Outs.

The second of the axioms on which democracy proceeds is that of the Majority Principle. The majority principle has two sides. It has an obvious or formal side, which is a matter of quantity and mathematics, or the number of voices saying ' Aye ' and ' No '. It has a less obvious, but more real and substantial side, which is a matter of quality, or of the content and character of the thing said. On its formal side, the majority principle implies an agreement or obligation of all to accept the decision of the greater number as the decision of all. *Quod majori parti placuit*, we may say, *ab omnibus approbatur*. Formally stated, in this way, the principle seems sufficiently clear ; but it instantly raises difficulties—difficulties which have been debated for many centuries. Why should the will of some, however numerous they may be, be identified with the will of all ? How can the will of a plurality be accepted as being, *ipso facto*, a univeral will ? When we begin to reflect upon these difficulties, we begin to ask ourselves whether the will of a majority must not have some attribute other than that of being, and in addition to that of being, the will of the greater number, before it can be accepted as the will of the whole community. If that is the case, what is the nature of this attribute ? There were some who argued, as early as the Middle Ages, that the will of a majority could only prevail, and receive general acceptance, if it were the will of the *major et sanior pars*. The effect of thus adding the words *et sanior* was to require quality as well as quantity. It was to proceed from the formal and external factor of the number of persons saying ' Aye ' or ' No ' to the substantial and internal factor of the character and value of the thing said. If we pursue this line of thought, we shall require two things, and not one only, before we give our consent to the validity of the majority principle. We shall require the extrinsic fact of number : we shall also require the intrinsic fact of value. But in that case, and if we thus import dualism into the majority principle, we soon begin to find that we have only escaped from one set of difficulties in order to fall into another.

We are confronted, in the first place, by the difficulty of the standard of value. By what criterion are we to measure the value of any particular will of a majority ? ' Sanity ' is a vague criterion. The criterion of ' generality ' which Rousseau sought to apply, when he argued in favour of a ' general will ' which was general in virtue of having the quality and the value of being directed to the general interest, is a more definite criterion. But even if we have some definite criterion of value, there are further difficulties which still await us (as Rousseau's own struggles are sufficient to show) when once we have imported dualism into the majority principle. Who is the final judge, superior to the decision of the majority, who will apply the criterion of value to its will ? If, when the judge is found and the criterion applied, the will of the majority is discovered to possess less value, and the will of the minority greater, must the will of the minority prevail ? To ask these two questions is to realize at once that the importation of the idea of quality, over and above the idea of quantity, and *as something separate from the idea of quantity*, may involve the destruction of the majority principle, and, *pro tanto*, the nega- tion of democracy. To enthrone a super-judge who may in turn enthrone a minority is to abandon democratic institutions.

Yet we cannot abandon the idea of value ; we cannot enthrone the majority just because it is a majority and superior in quantity. We have to find some way of linking value and quantity together as things inseparably connected, and not as separable factors which may quarrel and collide. There is one way of seeking to link quantity and value which we need only mention in order to dismiss. It is a way which we have already had reason to explore. According to this way of thinking, quantity is linked with value, and inherently possesses value, because it is linked with force, and because it possesses force. The will of the majority has the right to prevail because, if recourse were had to the *ultima ratio* of force, it could show that it had the might which would enable it to prevail. It is sufficient to observe that quantity is not always force, and that, even if it were, force is never value. We must find some other way of linking quantity with value. In order to find it we must go back to that process of discussion which, according to our argument, is the basis and the essence of all democracy.

Discussion implies a spirit, and can only act in a spirit, of mutual giving and taking. By the process of discussion one side learns from the other. Each has its attention drawn to some aspect of a problem, and to some facet of truth, which it had not taken into its reckoning ; and each is thus drawn to each in a process of giving and receiving. Discussion is not only like war : it is also like love. It is not only a battle of ideas ; it is also a marriage of minds. If a majority engages in discussion with a minority, and if that discussion is conducted in a spirit of giving and taking, the result will be that the ideas of the majority are widened to include some of the ideas of the minority which have established their truth in the give and take of debate.[1] When this happens, the will of the majority will not be the abstract or isolated will of a mere majority, considered in itself and as standing by itself in opposition to the similar will of a mere minority. Some fusion will have taken place : some accommodation will have been attained. The majority-will, when discussion is finished and the final vote is taken, will have assumed a new quality. It will not, indeed, have become the agreed and active will of all. But it may have accommodated itself so much to other wills, and absorbed so much of the elements of truth which they contain, that it has become a will which is tolerated by all and resented by none. It has assumed a certain quality, and attained a certain value. It is in this sense that discussion produces, if not unanimity, at any rate something so near it that we may speak of common consent. It is in this way that the will of a majority can become something of the nature of the will of all.

We can now see that there is a third axiom or principle on which democracy proceeds. This is the Principle of Compromise. The will of a majority does not prevail when it is merely the formal will of a mathematical majority. It prevails

[1] Conversely the ideas of the minority will also be widened to include some of the ideas of the majority ; and this widening may be conceivably (if also adventitiously) enhanced by the prestige of numbers and the natural liking of men for being ' in the swim '.

when it has been attained in a spirit, and when it has thus attained a content or substance, which does justice to the whole of the community and satisfies its general and universal character. The *spirit* which does justice to the whole of the community is a spirit which induces the majority to make concessions to the views of the minority, at the same time that it asks the minority to make the greater concession of accepting, or at any rate tolerating, the trend of its own view. The *substance* or content of any majority-will which does justice to the whole community is a substance or content which incorporates elements drawn from the whole. Granted such a spirit, resulting in such a substance—granted, in other words, the principle of compromise—we can believe that the majority is able to add quality to quantity not as something separable which has to be separately judged, but as something which is integrally connected with the fact and the action of quantity. If the spirit of discussion—which is a spirit of giving as well as of taking, and of learning as well as of teaching—is present from beginning to end, there is genuine reason for thinking that the opinion of the majority, intrinsically and inherently, will possess quality and value. Quality will not be a separable attribute, which may be or may not be present, and the presence or absence of which has to be determined by some judge who stands outside and above the process of discussion. It will be inherently and essentially connected with quantity.

In the first place the opinion of the majority, considered in its original form and before it has entered into conflict with the opinion of a minority or the opinions of minorities, will itself be based on an internal discussion and an internal compromise between the different views of the different elements of the majority. It will already have in its favour the fact that it rests on a broader basis, and is a larger synthesis, than the other opinion or opinions. In the second place, when discussion is engaged between the formed opinion of the majority and the formed opinion of the minority, the breadth of the opinion which has already been attained by the majority will be broadened further by the inclusion of new elements, or the modification of old elements, in proportion to the strength of the case which is urged by the other side and the skill of the advocacy with which it is urged. The ultimate result will be an opinion which is broadly based not only on the number of its immediate adherents, but also on the number of the facets of thought and the points of view to which it attempts to do justice. If the opinion of a majority has genuinely made this attempt, and has been genuinely inspired by some idea of doing justice, it may fairly be said to possess an inherent value and an intrinsic quality, derived from the very process of its formation. It is true that this value or quality of majority opinion simply consists in its reflecting, and comprehending, as far as it possibly can, the general trend of public opinion at large : it is true that, even if general public opinion is thus reflected and comprehended, the general public well-being is not necessarily secured, because public opinion, however general, *may* be mistaken in regard to the true nature of the public interest. But it is also true that the only practical criterion of public well-being is the general trend of public opinion about it. We may fairly assume that a process which has collected and distilled public opinion will have gone as far as is humanly possible toward the attainment of the public weal.

§ 10. THE CONVENTIONS OR VIRTUES REQUIRED IN A SYSTEM OF GOVERNMENT BY DISCUSSION

There are thus three axioms which have to be accepted and obeyed if government by discussion is to work successfully— the axiom of Agreement to Differ : the axiom of the Rule of the Majority : the axiom of Compromise. The central axiom is that of majority-rule ; and it is natural to concentrate attention upon that axiom. But it is only one of three ; and it is lame and halt without the other two. In order that the majority may rule, two other things must also happen, and two other conditions must also be present. In the first place, there must be a previous agreement of *all* to concentrate upon some central issue or set of issues, and to take sides upon it. There is thus an implied unanimity which is prior to majority decision and the condition of its possibility. In the second place there must also be (subsequent to this previous agreement of all, but still prior to majority decision) a previous compromise between the different sides which have been formed on the central issue—a compromise in which *all* the factors give and take, and which contains some sort of reconciliation between *all* the conflicting views. Without such a compromise a majority decision may be only a formal act, a one-sided expression of will which cannot be translated into effect because it is opposed by other and similarly one-sided expressions. If such a compromise has been attempted and attained, the will of the majority will be more than formal : it will be an operative and effective will, because the minority is ready to tolerate, or even support, a decision in which it has had its say and can recognize some of its handiwork.

If majority-rule is combined with agreement to differ and compromise, there will be no tyranny of the majority. The majority will not only agree to differ from the minority—tolerating, and even encouraging, the existence of opposition because opposition is necessary to the health of its own existence. It will also make concessions to the views of the minority. It will be passive as well as active, consenting to receive suggestions and to acquiesce in demands, even while it seeks to carry through its policy and to realize its programme. The majority is not always active ; and the minority is far from being always passive. It has been said that ' minorities must always suffer '. It is true that they must suffer ; but if they *always* suffered, and their fate was nothing but suffering, there would be little reason for their existence or prospect of their continuance. They act as well as suffer ; and in the same way, if to a less extent, majorities suffer as well as act. The intransigence which vindicates all action for the majority, and assigns nothing but suffering to minorities, is fatal to the essence of democracy, because it is fatal to discussion. It is an intransigence based upon the conviction that truth is a monopoly, and that a single side alone possesses ' the truth, the whole truth, and nothing but the truth '. When that conviction is entertained, there is no point in discussion and no reason for democracy. As soon as any political party begins to believe that it is the sole possessor of an exclusive truth, democracy is already dying or dead ; and it is only a formal registration of its death if such a party proceeds to act in the logic of its belief, and to suppress other parties on the ground that they believe in falsehood, ' and there is no truth in them '. There cannot be any discussion, or any system of government by discussion, except upon the assumption that truth dwells in more than one habitation, and that its elements have to be collected, and not only collected but reconciled, before it can be enthroned.

In any country we shall generally find a number of particular constitutional 'conventions' or 'understandings' which are distinct from the formal 'law of the constitution', but are yet inextricably connected with it, and indispensable for its operation. These particular conventions constitute in each country a body of political ethics or system of political morality : they are concerned with the spirit and temper of mind—we may almost say, the moral disposition—which along with the law, and in addition to the law, should control the course of political action. In much the same sense, but with a wider range and a deeper penetration, there are also indispensable conventions of the general system of government by discussion—conventions common to all countries and necessary to all constitutions in which that system is applied. They are conventions which go down far to the roots of human thought, and are concerned with the exercise of fundamental virtues. They involve toleration of differences of opinion : they involve the candour which is open to conviction by the weight of argument ; they involve moderation in the hour of strength, and reasonableness even in the throes of defeat. *Nil leges sine moribus*. The constitutional law and the formal institutions of democracy profit little in the absence of the conventions which are also an integral part of its being. From one point of view we may regard these conventions as intellectual rules or axioms ; and from this point of view we shall speak of the axiom of agreement to differ, the axiom of majority-rule, the axiom of compromise. From another point of view we may regard them as moral rules or habits consonant with these axioms ; and from this point of view we shall speak of the virtue of tolerance, the virtue of candour, the virtue of moderation. From whatever point of view we regard them, the implied conventions of any system of government by discussion are no less important than its overt institutions. It is possible, and it is vitally necessary, to regulate by constitutional law the structure of the different organs of such a system. It is possible, and it is vitally necessary, to regulate in the same way the formal action of each organ, and the formal relations of the different organs with one another. Men naturally concentrate their attention on these matters of regulation and the problems which they involve—problems such as proportional representation, the right of dissolution, the right of referendum, and whatever else can be made a matter of formal legal right. But when constitutional law has done its utmost, it leaves a sphere which needs control, and yet cannot be controlled by legal rule. Discussion, by its very nature and in its own essence, transcends the scope of legal control. What it cannot transcend is the rules of its own inner logic and its own inward ethics—or rather it can only transcend them at the cost of annihilating itself. Discussion which refuses any control becomes civil war ; and civil war is the end of discussion. What we have now to learn—in these days of great national parties, counting their millions of adherents, and tending, by their very weight, to carry discussion to the uttermost consequence—is how to practise that observance of self-imposed rules of political controversy which was a comparatively easy lesson for the old, small, and more or less aristocratic parties (playing politics as a game, and ready to follow rules of the game), but is a far more difficult lesson in a time of issues far more vital, debated in a far greater arena, under the blazing light of a new publicity.

III

THE INTERNAL DIFFICULTIES OF DEMOCRACY

§ 1. THE GREAT ELECTORATE AND ITS MENTAL TENDENCIES

ONE of the great difficulties of democratic government may be expressed in the one word 'size'. In the eighteenth century, when the idea of democracy was still associated with the city-states of ancient Greece and medieval Italy, or with the cantons of Switzerland, the democratic constitution was supposed, as Paley wrote in 1785, to 'suit only with the affairs of a small State; the mechanism is too complicated, and the motions too slow, for the operations of a great Empire'.[1] Paley, like Rousseau before him, and like the authors of the *Federalist* afterwards, was inclined to think that a system of federalism, associating the liberty of small commonwealths with the security of a great State, might enable the democratic system to be practised on a large scale. In much the same sense, though they begin at the opposite end (seeking to decompose a great state into small commonwealths, rather than to unite small commonwealths into a great State), the advocates of devolution to-day seek to invoke the federal idea in support of democracy. Their feeling is still the same : democracy and the great State are not good yoke-fellows.

The actual process of history confronts us to-day with great States which have committed themselves as they stand, without any federal qualification, to the principle and the practice of democratic government on the fullest scale. We have states with populations of 40 millions and more governing themselves on a basis of universal suffrage which involves electorates amounting to two-thirds, or even three-quarters, of the total population. Nor does the presence of federal institutions, where such institutions have been adopted, really alter the situation. Federal affairs from the first are the most important affairs : they increasingly tend, in the history of most federations, to become vastly the most important affairs ; and federal affairs depend on the vote of a federal electorate which may be greater than the electorate of even the greatest unitary State. Wherever democracy is practised, except in the smaller States of the world, we are faced with the fact of the great electorate, which counts its members in tens of millions.

[1] *Principles of Moral and Political Philosophy*, Book VI, ch. VI, *ad finem*.

Numbers are terrifying things. Our terror of an electorate so numerous will be augmented if we regard it as the hub and the pivot of the whole democratic system—the fountain and origin of the will of the State : the maker and master of all the organs of democracy. Fears will diminish, and they may even become hopes instead of fears, if we regard the electorate, on the lines of our previous argument, as itself only one of the organs of democracy, or one of the stages in the democratic process, similar to the other stages or organs, and co-operating in its measure, and according to its function, with the rest. Even so, and though we may thus conceive it as simply one of the parts of the system, aided and even guided by the other parts, the electorate still remains a great and essential part of a rational system of discussion ; and we may ask ourselves whether an organ apparently so unwieldy as the modern electorate, and acting on the level of intelligence which may presumably be expected from such a mass, can properly participate in a system so delicate and subtle. It is perhaps impossible to give a dispassionate and scientific answer to such a question. If the electorate votes in accordance with our own predilections, we call it wise : if it does otherwise, we use other language. But if we seek to lift ourselves above our predilections, and to see the electorate ' steadily and whole ', we may say that, tested by the historical experience of its action, it can give a great and simple answer on great and simple issues, and that, tried by the way in which it discharges its own particular function of election, it can judge effectively the general quality of the men who seek its suffrage.

We may add two other reflections. In the first place, the use and the value of the electorate are not to be judged merely by its knowledge. Whether the electorate be wise or foolish, and whether it has knowledge or is ignorant, it is still a matter of vital importance to learn what it feels. Popular feeling, in itself, is an integral factor and an essential element in the whole process of government by discussion (as it is, indeed, in any process of government) ; and in the absence of any ascertained knowledge of that feeling, such as the general vote and only the general vote can give, the whole process labours in the dark. An inspired autocrat may govern by intuition and delation, in the light of his own guess and the information of his secret agents about the state of public feeling ; a rational system of government by discussion must start from some rational and scientific method of discovering, in a tolerably clear and therefore in a quantitative expression, the actual state of such feeling. Not that the weight and volume of such feeling, in itself and by itself, will necessarily determine each issue. Other factors must also enter and play their part—the deliberations and policies of parties, parliamentary debate and vote, cabinet responsibility ; in a word, the various agencies which collectively constitute the general leadership of the community. Public feeling is not a fixed and unalterable datum ; it is malleable, and it can be modified by the various forces of leadership. But it still remains true that one of the essential factors in the formation of any decision by the process of discussion is the state and attitude of ascertained public feeling. In the light of that ascertained fact parties and parliaments and cabinets can decide more wisely how far they can go, and what risks they may properly take, in the way of leadership.

But there is also a second reflection, which affords a deeper justification of the great electorates of our times. We can not only defend them on the ground that they are vents and expressions of public feeling, in some sort of quantitative form, and that the broader the vent, the broader and clearer will be the resultant expression. We can also defend the great electorate on the ground that it is the vehicle of a collective experience of life, and a collective faculty of judgment, which belong to the domain of knowledge and reason, and which make it—even in that domain, and not merely as an expression of feeling—a congenial and integral part of a rational system of government. The growth of the electorate has coincided, in time, with the growth of popular education—adult as well as juvenile.[1] It has also coincided with the growth of trade unions and other organizations among the mass of the people, in which they have learned to handle affairs and to acquire that practical training which matters at least as much as formal education. It has coincided, again, with a great development of scientific knowledge, and with a diffusion of the scientific habit of mind among wider and wider circles.

[1] Movements of popular education—the Sunday school movement, and the movement for the ' voluntary ' day school—preceded the Reform Bill of 1832. The expansion of the suffrage in 1867 and 1884-5 was accompanied by the foundation of State schools and the introduction of universal compulsory education.

It has coincided, finally, with an era of scientific inventions which have contributed signally, if not intentionally, to the technique of discussion, and which now make it possible for an electorate of 30 millions to be linked together as closely as an electorate of a million was linked a hundred years ago. Every advance in the means of physical, and still more of mental, communication enables an increasingly greater circle to be formed for common deliberation and common action. We do not yet know the ultimate effects of the invention of broadcasting. Already it enables an audience of millions to listen together to reasoned argument. Already, by presenting that audience with reasoned arguments on *both* sides, it is familiarizing millions with the idea that there is something to be said on either side, and that truth is a thing which belongs exclusively to neither. This is an idea essential to discussion, and therefore essential to democracy ; and we may thus comfort ourselves by reflecting that if electorates have broadened far beyond the dreams of the Whigs of 1832, the mental resources at their disposal have broadened even further.

But we should be over-hasty if we believed in the perfection of man because he had at his service new instruments of perfection. While new instruments develop, old instruments, though they are still necessary, and even increasingly necessary, may decline. The Press is an example. It can be a singularly valuable instrument of discussion, collecting and clarifying public opinion, providing an open forum of debate, and serving as an institution of democracy. In our own country, from the Reform Bill of 1832 down to the end of the nineteenth century, it performed these functions admirably. It is not clear that it is performing them equally well to-day, either in England or elsewhere. The spread of popular education has been accompanied by the rise of popular papers supposed to be addressed to a new reading public, but hardly worthy of the public to which they are addressed. The Press has been largely removed from the realm of politics to that of business : business methods, involving the mass-production of commodities which are immediately and superficially attractive, have been applied to the newspaper ; business interests have tended to determine the purpose and the policy of its conduct. The change in the character of the Press, or rather of part of the Press (it does not affect the whole, and there are still papers which continue, and have even improved, the old tradition), may be regarded as a symptom of a larger and more general trend in human life.

For a century and more there has been, in most countries, a great increase of population, unparalleled in human history. This has provided a great body of potential consumers, who can be induced, by appropriate means, to accept a mass of wares, both material and intellectual. The appropriate means takes the form of applied psychology, which seeks, by the methods of suggestion and advertisement, to utilize the human instinct of imitation. All who have wares to vend, whether in the field of economics or in that of politics, have been tempted to become practitioners of such applied psychology. It may be that great masses of men are more prone to act by elementary instincts : it is certain that the art of appealing to those instincts, and of forcing a market for commodities and policies by the use of suggestion and the stimulation of reflex action, has been encouraged by the existence of such masses. We are thus driven to the conclusion that if the growth of great electorates has been accompanied by new intellectual developments, it has also been accompanied by new developments of another style, which we may call, in a rough and ready term, by the name ' psychological ' ; and these later developments have in many respects run counter to the first.

Whether the balance is in favour of the growth of intellectual or of that of ' psychological ' developments—whether, on the whole, mankind in the mass acts more by reason than it used to do, or more by instinct—is a question which is easily raised, but admits of no certain answer. One country differs from another : some are more mature and critical, and some are more prone to follow the call of the blood and obey the cry of the mystagogue. Even the same country may vary from time to time ; and even at one and the same time it may appear rational to one spectator, and merely emotional to another. The one thing that may safely be said is that it is folly to see nothing but intellect and the growth of reason, and an equal folly to see nothing but instinct and the growth of its exploitation. Man is a mixed being. Human nature in politics, like human nature in marriage and indeed in any other institution, is a mixed thing. Both reason and instinct are needed ; and they may agree and serve one another, if they may also pull different ways. Instinct and reflex action are economies of time ; and if they are linked to the service of reason, they may serve to leave reason more free for its own essential work. The danger arises when they become substitutes for reason instead of auxiliaries.

§ 2. ELECTORAL POWERS AND METHODS : PROPORTIONAL REPRE-SENTATION

The growth of the electorate in size has not only been accompanied by new mental developments, some favourable and some more dubious. It has also been accompanied by new claims on its behalf. The greater its increase in size, the greater, it may be argued, is the power which it is able to exercise and the claim which it may justly advance. . . . It may equally be argued, on the other side, that the greater the electorate, the greater is the difficulty of its operation and the less the demand which we are entitled to make upon it. The small electorate may be able not only to elect, but also to undertake other functions : the great electorate, at any rate while it is still new and feeling its way, will be wise if it confines itself to doing the one essential thing to the best of its ability. . . . The former of these arguments is the more obvious, though not necessarily the truer ; and in our own days the introduction of universal suffrage has in many countries been accompanied, or followed, by the introduction of institutions such as the initiative and referendum, and of ideas such as the mandate and recall. In the wave of democratic feeling which followed the end of the war of 1914-18—partly due to the democratic propaganda of the victors, and partly to reaction among the vanquished against their old and authoritarian governments—these accompaniments or sequels were common in the new constitutions which were then created in Central and Eastern Europe. Of an earlier date, though attaining a wider diffusion after the war, was another institution, designed, or at any rate calculated, to enhance the claims and the powers of the electorate. This was the institution of Proportional Representation.

Proportional representation differs from institutions such as the referendum and the initiative. It does not involve any right of the electorate over and above the essential right of election. It is simply a more elaborate and more strictly logical method of exercising that right. It is a method designed to secure not only that electors shall vote in some way for candidates, in some sort of constituency, but also that they shall vote in the particular sort of constituency (the multiple-member constituency) which will give the most positive weight to their vote,[1] and shall vote and have their votes counted in the particular way (the way of the long list of candidates, of the numbered statement of preferences, and of the transfer of votes in counting from preference to preference) which will secure the most exact representation of each shade of their opinion.

The purpose of proportional representation, from this point of view, is to clarify, and by clarifying to magnify, the voice of the electorate. The electorate will no longer speak, as it were, in a thick and husky voice : it will speak in clear and distinct accents, which can be nicely calculated and exactly recorded. Just for that reason, its verdict will carry a greater weight and exercise a more decisive influence : the *vox populi*, being a *vox clara, magna erit et praevalebit*. On the grounds of pure logic and pure mathematics, the argument seems impeccable. But if we look at the electorate not in the abstract, but as a part or organ of a general system of government by discussion—connected with parties on the one hand, and with parliament and cabinet on the other—we begin to see flaws in the logic and to entertain doubts about the mathematics. The electorate, as a whole, is treated too much in isolation from parliament and cabinet (though not, as we shall see later, from party) : it is reduced too much, in each of its constituencies, to a sum of quantitative fractions.

In the first place, the general aim of the method of proportional representation is directed primarily to excellence in the formal recording of the voice of the electorate, and not to excellence in the substantial activity of the electorate as a creative organ intended for the production of an effective parliament, and indirectly of an effective cabinet, themselves

---

[1] In a single-member constituency, with a single and non-transferable vote for one of the candidates, a majority of the electors (in the case of a three-cornered contest) may obviously vote without any positive result ; and their votes will be simply negative.   In a multiple-member constituency the votes of a large majority will necessarily be positive : that is to say, they will actually serve to determine the result.

intended in turn to play their substantial parts in the subsequent course of discussion. The emphasis which is laid by the method on the process of recording the voice of the electorate, considered in itself and considered by itself, tends to connect it, after all, with the institutions of the referendum and the initiative. Proportional representation may be concerned with the voice of the electorate only in the moment of election ; but the weight which it assigns to that voice at that moment leads easily to claims for a similar weight at later moments. And while the electorate may thus be exalted, parliament and the cabinet may be simultaneously depressed—the former by being made too tesselated and balanced for effective debate, and the latter by becoming too composite, and too much of a coalition, for any effective decision.

In the second place, the institution of the multiple-member constituency, which is a necessary means to the general aim of proportional representation, tends to isolate the electorate from the member (or rather members) of parliament whom it has chosen, and thus to prevent that contact and interplay of the different organs which is part of the system of government by discussion. The single-member constituency may expose a member more to the pressure of his constituents (though the danger of such pressure will be eliminated if the system of parliamentary procedure, and the method of appointments to the public service, render it impossible for a member to move for grants or press for posts on behalf of his constituency) ; but at any rate it ensures an easy contact and interplay.

In the third place, the attempt to secure an exact representation of shades of electoral opinion, by methods which may range from the transferable vote for particular candidates to compulsory voting for a party list, has the effect of confusing —rather than of clarifying—the voice of the electorate on large plain issues. Instead of giving a great and simple answer of ' Yes ' or ' No ' to a great and simple question, the electorate may return a series of qualified answers, coupled with a number of answers to entirely different questions which may have been raised under cover of proportional representation by ' single-question ' groups. In this way, and because it thus leads to the returning of a confused answer, proportional representation may again, and from a different point of view, become connected with the institution of the referendum.

The referendum may be its necessary complement, or corrective, for the purpose of giving the plain answer to a plain question which it has failed to secure.

Proportional representation tempts to digressions. But it cannot be neglected in any discussion of the internal difficulties of democracy. Those who criticize its principle and its methods regard it as an institution which increases and accentuates these difficulties. Those who advocate its adoption regard it as a rational and sober system which will encourage the temper of reason and ease the play of discussion, and thus diminish or even remove the difficulties of democracy. They plead that, by other methods of voting, party majorities of the electorate are artificially maximized in parliament, and minorities are artificially minimized ; that parliament thus fails to represent the electorate, and to keep in touch or act in harmony with it ; above all, that the artificially maximized majority is led to disdain compromise with an artificially minimized minority, and the necessary basis and condition of proper majority-rule accordingly disappears. This is a serious plea ; and it goes to the roots of democratic theory. It fairly demands a reconsideration of the merits and demerits of proportional representation from a point of view different from that which we have hitherto adopted. We have considered proportional representation in connection mainly with the electorate—the great electorate of modern times. But it must also be considered in connection with party, and in the light of its effect upon party and the relations of party to the electorate. . . . What, after all, is proportional representation? What is the factor or term to which representation should be 'proportional' ? The answer, in a word, is party. Proportional representation means representation for each party in proportion to the number of electors who have cast their votes for the party. We are thus led to the consideration of party. What are the difficulties with which its modern development presents us, and how far will proportional representation remove or increase these difficulties ?

§ 3. PARTY : THE GENERAL CAUSES OF ITS INTENSIFICATION

The Green Ribbon Club, which was the nucleus of the Whig party, existed as long ago as 1675. But parties, before the days of the great electorate, were little more than clubs, with an informal organization and scanty and casual resources. They were loose bodies of common opinion—sometimes, on an even more rudimentary level of development, they were simply bodies of common sentiment for a 'side' and its colour—rather than organized associations with their own officers, their own finances, and their own specific purposes of programme-making and election-managing. In France to-day (except for the highly organized parties of the Left), the political parties in the constituencies, as distinct from the political groups in parliament, are still of this loose nature. In most other countries the last sixty or seventy years— beginning with the Reform Bill of 1867 in England, the end of the Civil War in North America, and the introduction of manhood suffrage in Germany under the constitution of 1871— have witnessed a great extension and consolidation of party. The beginning of the great electorate instantly affected the character of political parties. The electorate needed organiza- tion ; and parties began to organize themselves for the organi- zation of the electorate. In England the very year of the Second Reform Bill saw the beginnings of this movement both on the Liberal and on the Conservative side. In October 1867 the Birmingham Liberal Association, the most active of all the local party organizations, was reconstituted on a more repre- sentative basis, with regular subscriptions, regular officers, and a regularly elected committee ; and ten years later, in 1877, the Birmingham model became the parent of a National Liberal Federation, covering the country at large and con- structed on similar lines. In November 1867, the Conservative party had already formed a National Union of local Conser- vative Associations ; and by 1883, under the inspiration of Lord Randolph Churchill, the National Union was beginning to bid for the same position on the Conservative side which the National Federation, led by Joseph Chamberlain, had been seeking since 1877 to vindicate for itself on the Liberal side.

The initial claim of the National Liberal Federation, which was popularly called the Caucus,[1] was remarkable. The Federation was not only to formulate policy, and to present to the electorate candidates who were pledged to that policy.

---

[1] The term ' caucus ', which began to come into use in 1878, was a misuse of an American word, which signified a private meeting of party-managers. The English caucus was not private, and it was not a meeting of party-managers : it was a public organization, representative in character.

'It was expected to be', as Mr. Chamberlain expressed it,
'a Liberal parliament outside the imperial legislature ; not,
indeed, doing the work of that body, but arranging what
work it should do, or rather what work the Liberal members
should bring before it, and what attitude they should assume.
By this process the initiative on all the greater issues, so far
as the Liberal party was concerned, would be largely transferred from the Treasury Bench to the Federation.'[1]   The
process of government by discussion was not only to be
afforced by a new organization of party : it was also to be
radically altered ; and a schooled parliament and a managed
cabinet (whenever the cabinet was Liberal) were to play a
new and humbler role in its conduct.   These claims of the
National Liberal Federation, which were paralleled,[2] if not
equalled, in the temporary ebullition of the Conservative
National Union during the years 1883 and 1884, were soon
abandoned on both sides.   Parliament and Cabinet were too
deeply rooted in the English system of government to be
schooled and managed by a caucus.   But the new organization
of party survived on both sides ; and when a third side was
added to English politics, with the appearance of the Labour
Party, history repeated itself in its claims.   Labour parties,
particularly when they are inspired by definite socialist conviction, are necessarily militant parties.   They may not espouse
the full doctrine of the class war ; but they inevitably feel that
they are fighting a battle against privilege and all its powers,
and they inevitably tend toward the rigour of a military
discipline.   The solidarity of the party, the full loyalty of all
its members, the control of the party over its representatives
in parliament, the control of those representatives over the
cabinet, and even the control, in turn, of the cabinet over
its prime minister—these are, at any rate initially, the tendencies of a Labour party.

   They are tendencies, however, which are by no means
peculiar to Labour parties.   If they are accentuated, at the

[1] A. L. Lowell, *Government of England*, I, p. 504.

[2] 'The old methods of party organization . . . were utterly obsolete, and
would not secure the confidence of the masses of the people who were enfranchised
by Mr. Disraeli's Reform Bill.   The organization of the party would have to
become an imitation . . . of the Birmingham Caucus.   The Caucus . . . is
undeniably the only form of political organization which can collect, guide, and
control for common objects, large masses of electors.'   Lord Randolph Churchill's
letter to Lord Salisbury (April 1884), quoted in Lowell, *op. cit.*, I, pp. 549-550.

moment, in Labour parties—partly owing to the militancy of
their attitude, which sharpens the rigour of party discipline ;
partly owing to the recency and the rapidity of their growth,
which makes them recapitulate, in a quick succession and in
an acute form, the ' distempers ' through which older parties
passed at an earlier date and with less vehemence—these
tendencies emerge from the very nature of *all* ardent parties,
as naturally as the sparks fly upward.　Labour and Socialist
parties are generally the most ardent and the most highly
organized of parties :　their members rate the merit and the
duty of party loyalty very high :　they have shown these
characteristics and this spirit, with a large measure of uniformity, in different countries, and even in different conti-
nents[1] ; and they have thus drawn on themselves an attention
which is natural and explicable, but which cannot in fairness
be confined to them only.　In England it is likely, if history
repeats itself still further, that just as the National Liberal
Federation and the National Conservative Union adjusted
themselves to the position and the tradition of parliament and
cabinet, so the Labour party, which has already moved a long
way in that direction, will do the like.　If this happens, all our
parties will follow a uniform trend, accommodating themselves to the other factors in the system of government by
discussion, and not seeking to emphasize their independence
(still less to proclaim their sovereignty) in regard to cabinet
and parliament.　But a different—and indeed, in many respects,
an opposite—trend has shown itself in the politics of many of
the States of the Continent.　Here the tradition of parliament
and cabinet has been comparatively recent, and it has shown
itself unable to cope on equal terms with the growth of party,
which, if also recent, has been fostered with particular vigour
and determination, and has been directed toward the organization of the electorate in disciplined party armies.　Under
these conditions all parties alike—the parties of the Right no
less than those of the Left—have been led to emphasize their
independence, and even their priority, in the general system
of democratic institutions.　Instead of all parties tending to
assimilate themselves to one another in a common respect for

---

[1] Lord Bryce, in his *Modern Democracies*, II, pp. 227-233, gives a vivid description of the Australian Labour party—its system of pledged members ; its method
of parliamentary caucus meetings to decide in advance the votes of the Labour
members ; its general moulding ' into a sort of Spartan or Prussian army '.

the rights and claims of other democratic institutions, they have tended to assimilate themselves to one another in a common insistence upon their own claims and rights. Not only cabinet and parliament, but also the electorate, have been brought into subordination to the primary zest of party.

It is perhaps the exaltation of party, and of the disciplines and loyalties of party, which has been the greatest of the internal difficulties of democracy, at any rate in the field of pure politics, during the present century. Whatever proportional representation may be capable of becoming under conditions less passionately partisan, it has not served to mitigate the passions of conflicting parties with which it has, by the fate of its history, been doomed to co-operate. On the contrary it may even be said to have served to exacerbate such passions. Proportional representation has helped, indeed, to prevent swollen majorities and attenuated minorities : but it has not helped to produce a spirit of compromise between majority and minority, or even to produce the definite majority and the definite minority which are the necessary bases of such compromise. Subdued to the material in which it has had to work, and adapted to the ends and ambitions of conflicting groups, it has been used to give each group its uttermost ounce of political representation, and to divorce party still further from party by making each concentrate its attention on securing for itself the greatest possible yield from the electorate. Under these conditions the electorate, instead of gaining new power, loses its dignity and its function. It becomes a passive field, divided into proprietary party plots which are intensively cultivated to yield the maximum of return. There is no room for a body of independent electors, sitting loose to strict party ties, and free to record general movements of opinion by moving their votes from time to time. The electorate tends to be fixed in allegiances ; and the play of political opinion tends to be fixed in rigid bodies of party belief. A method intended to give the electorate greater freedom may thus give it less ; and a system intended to increase the possibility of compromise may be used to foster the spirit of intransigence.

It would be folly to attribute to a method of voting any large share in producing the difficulties which confront the working of democracy. Political technique has its importance ; but the men who conduct politics, and the spirit in which they conduct them, have a vastly greater importance. The emergence of party leaders who set their whole faith in party, and the power of such leaders to attract and retain the absolute allegiance of followings which imitate and accept their faith, are things which matter more than the technical methods by which parties dominate the electorate, or even than the schemes by which parties organize themselves. Party satisfies deep human instincts for the stimulus of personal leadership and the warmth of personal contact. It meets emotional needs. Men in the mass have a natural desire for some system of ' sides ' to which they can pledge their loyalty. The desire is accentuated by the growth of great populations ; but it is also frustrated and baulked by the growth of impersonal institutions (alike in the field of politics and in that of economics) which accompanies the growth of great populations. The development of party ' sides ' and party loyalties releases and satisfies baulked desires. The rush of emotion into parties, both among leaders and followers, is one of the great causes of their modern prominence. It is because they satisfy emotions that they can readily be regarded, and treated, as ends in themselves. They then cease to be parts and organs of a rational system of discussion. They become emotional absolutes.

§ 4.   PARTY : ALTERATION OF ITS CONCEPTION AND PRACTICE

A number of causes have conspired to bring party into the foreground, and to give it priority over the other organs of democracy, particularly in those countries in which the whole system of democracy was new, and where there were no established traditions of parliament and cabinet to balance and counteract the growing vogue of party organization and party feeling. The numerical increase of the electorate has provided new scope and new material for the manipulation of party. The emergence of deep economic issues has produced ardent and disciplined Labour parties ; and their ardour and discipline have infected the other parties by a natural and inevitable contagion. The method and technique of proportional representation has been an effect, rather than a cause, of the growing importance of party ; but it is an effect which also becomes a cause when the method is pushed to its farthest limit and the elector is allowed to vote only for the party lists prepared by the different party organizations.   To these numerical, economic, and technical factors we have also to add the psychological, which is closely connected with the numerical and the economic. Great populations, often cantoned in urban centres, and divorced by their economic conditions from older outlets of personal emotion, have found a new vent and channel in the following of party leaders and the enthusiasm of party loyalty.

Under the influence of these causes the conception and the practice of party have been radically altered. In its nature and its origin a party was a voluntary club : not an organ of the State but an organ of society, which served the State by mediating between the play of social thought and the activity of political machinery. It formulated trends of social thought in definite programmes : it brought these programmes, and the persons who stood as candidates on their behalf, to the attention of the electorate ; and when it had done that work, it left the rest to the candidates who had been elected, trusting them so to act, in their capacity of members of parliament and ministers of the executive (in other words, as organs of the State), that the ideals of the party programmes would be carried into political effect. The new developments have altered this system. They turn the voluntary club into an organ of State, and they tend to make it the dominant organ. When the electoral laws specifically recognize party as a legal body, which may prepare legal lists of candidates for which the elector is legally bound to record his vote, they definitely recognize party as an organ of the State.[1] But short of being thus legally recognized as an organ of the State, a party may act *de facto* in that capacity, and may even seek to act as the dominant organ. If a party conference in the country at large seeks to determine by its vote the policy which is to be adopted in parliament by the members who belong to that party, and if these members accept the result of that vote, the party becomes an organ, or super-organ, of the State. If a party

---

[1] In Czechoslovakia a deputy who had been elected on a party list, and then excluded from membership by the party which prepared the list, might be deprived of his seat by the electoral court established under the Constitution (article 19) to determine the validity of elections. Mirkine-Guetzevitch, *Les Constitutions de l'Europe Nouvelle*, p. 27.

meeting of members of parliament, held before a division which is to be taken in parliament, seeks to determine by its vote the votes to be given by each member in the division, the result is similar—though the fact that the body dictating to members of parliament is itself composed of members makes a difference in the position.[1]

The tendency of parties to claim authority as organs of State is general. Even in France, where the political parties in the country at large are generally loose, and the political parties in the Chamber are often separate formations, made in the Chamber itself and relating only to the Chamber, the national party conferences of some of the parties have tended to assume new powers in regard to the Chamber and the Cabinet. But the claims and the activities of party can go beyond the function of an organ of the State. A party may claim to be not only an organ of State, but a State. It may go even farther, and claim to be *the* State. This is the final consummation of the zeal of party, and it is a consummation which has already been attained in some of the great States of Europe.

Parties, we should all admit, are necessary means of democracy. But the means may become the end. This is what happens when electorate, parliaments, and cabinets are all, in their different ways, subordinated to the exigencies and brought under the control of party. In the same way and by the same process that the means becomes the end, the part may become a whole, and assume what is nowadays called a 'total' or 'totalitarian' character. There are two stages in the development by which the part or party becomes the whole. In the first stage each party turns itself into a whole State (with the whole apparatus of a State), but continues to exist side by side with other parties in a State which is thus composed of a number of States. Not content with being an 'emotional absolute', party becomes an active and organized absolute. Each party professes a *Weltanschauung*, a general set of social and political ideas which covers and colours the whole

---

[1] The question may be raised whether there is any difference between the control of a member by the party whip and control by the vote of a party meeting. The answer may be given that the vote of the party meeting in parliament generally implies the ultimate authority of the vote of a party conference outside parliament, while the control of the party whip only implies the leadership of the cabinet (or the anti-cabinet, as the case may be) within the walls of parliament.

of life, and in that sense is total, but is yet, and at the same time, exclusive and peculiar to itself. Each party seeks to provide its members with a whole apparatus of life, for sport, for education, for material benefit, for every social purpose : each aims at ' autarky ', and encourages its members to look to itself, and only to itself, for every social utility. Each party, in the last resort, turns its adherents into an army, with uniforms and military formations. It has already assumed the generality of a State : it is natural that it should also assume the coercive power and the armed force of a State. In this first stage of development, and at this point of the first stage, each party is already a State : there are as many States as there are parties ; and the conflict of rival party States is the inevitable result.

That conflict involves the second stage of the development. One of the rival party-States triumphs. Unity returns ; the State is re-integrated ; but it is re-integrated on the basis, and under the control, of the victorious party-State. Party, which had already become a State, now becomes *the* State. A single party, proscribing and eliminating all others, climbs the throne and clutches the crown. The democratic State suffers a complete *bouleversement* ; and the cause of that *bouleversement* is the encroachment of party. Not content to be a mediator between social thought and political action, party has made three successive and increasing encroachments. First, it has made itself an organ of State, entrenched within the State either by legal right or by the *de facto* power exercised by party conferences in the country or party meetings in the legislature. Secondly, it has made itself a State within the State, an *imperium in imperio*, with a totalitarian claim on its members and a totalitarian apparatus of action. Finally, some one victorious party, disdaining to be an *imperium in imperio* by the side of other and rival *imperia*, has ejected the other *imperia* and become the one and only *imperium*. In this consummation party ceases to be a part of the State ; and the State becomes a part, or an expression, of the life of party.

The titanic insurrection of parties is a mark of our times ; but it is not peculiar to our times. The radical Greens and the conservative Blues who fought in the Hippodrome of Constantinople, fourteen hundred years ago, almost overturned the Byzantine autocracy, and came near to driving Justinian from his throne during the Nika revolt of 532.[1] The *parte Guelfa*, led by its *capitano*, dominated the politics of Florence, and monopolized political office, during a large part of the fourteenth century.   Even farther back in history, in the city states of classical Greece and in ancient Rome, we may remember the hot party feuds of democrats and oligarchs, of *populares* and *optimates*. There is nothing very new under the sun ; but if we are repeating the past, we are at any rate repeating it with a greater and more systematic logic and perhaps with a less fury of hot vendettas and bloody proscription (though such things are far from being entirely absent) than marked, let us say, the party triumph of Sulla, and his temporary institution of a one-party State at Rome, some two thousand years ago.

§ 5. PARTY : ITS RELATION TO THE GROWTH OF PROFESSIONALISM
IN POLITICS

Those who believe in the economic interpretation of history will ascribe these recurrent exacerbations of party to the recurrent eruption of economic motives and economic animosities. It would be a folly to deny the influence of such motives and feelings ; and we must turn, in the issue, to examine their operation and their effect. But parties are primarily political phenomena ; and the primary causes of their behaviour and development are political causes. Some of the political causes which have accentuated party—the numerical increase of the electorate, and the tendency of parties, in a period of growing organization, to organize more elaborately their activities and their methods—have already been mentioned. Mention has also been made of the half political, half psychological (or, as a modern Italian might simply call it, the ' demographic ') factor of great urbanized populations, which find in party and party loyalty a substitute for the old loyalties of the countryside and the soil. But there are other and simpler political

---

[1] History repeats itself in curious ways. The Blue faction in Constantinople sought to distinguish themselves by wearing a peculiar uniform. " Thus they discarded the use of the razor, and wore full Persian beards, allowed their back hair to grow long in imitation of the Huns, and donned richly embroidered tunics furnished with sleeves which bellied out in an extraordinary fashion from the wrist up to the shoulder." Some of them carried weapons regularly, ostensibly to chastise the Greens, but often for the real purpose of robbery and murder. See W. G. Holmes, *The Age of Justinian and Theodora*, II, p. 454.

factors which have also to be taken into account in explaining the modern intensity of party.

As late as the nineteenth century, the sphere of party politics was still largely a sphere of the amateur. Politics was a great game, played by those who had sufficient leisure and were willing to devote their leisure to its excitements and its intricacies. But even games, when they are played on a great enough scale and offer a sufficient prospect of remuneration, run readily into professionalism ; and the great game of politics ran the more readily in that direction because it was always more than a game. Too much hung upon it for it to be left entirely to the amateur : it was too much a matter of general weal and woe to be ever merely a sport. Even in the aristocratic days of the eighteenth century Burke is already a professional politician ; and he did not stand alone. When the days of aristocracy had passed away, and first the middle class, and then the working classes, were drawn into the fray, professionalism necessarily assumed a wider scope. Large party organizations required paid and permanent managers, who devoted themselves with zest to extending the scope and pressing the claims of the organizations which they served. Acquiring officers and offices, and acquiring, along with them, the funds necessary for their support, parties became organized undertakings, analogous to the great industrial and commercial undertakings among which they moved. The movement did not stop there. Not only did the secretaries and managers of parties become professionals. The candidates who fought constituencies on behalf of parties, and who, if they were successful, embraced a parliamentary career as representatives of their party and advocates of its policy, followed the same trend. The professional party manager was accompanied by the professional party politician, who devoted his whole time to the struggle of party politics and was remunerated for his devotion. At first the remuneration was private, in the sense that it came only from party funds : eventually it became also public, and by the beginning of the twentieth century the payment of members of parliament from State funds was a part of the general policy of parliamentary government.

This professionalism of party politics was an inevitable movement. On the one hand it was the necessary result of the increased business and the prolonged sessions of legislative bodies, which made demands on the time of their members that could only be generally met on the basis of full-time paid professional work. On the other hand it was the necessary concomitant of the democratic process of enfranchisement ; for it was impossible to secure a true representation of the enfranchised masses by members who were drawn from their own ranks, and were in touch with their real feelings, unless those members were secured a livelihood which enabled them to devote themselves fully to their duties of representation. But the new profession of the party politician, at any rate in its initial stages and until it has settled down on the lees, none the less constitutes one of the difficulties of contemporary democracy. It does so in two ways. In the first place, the zeal of the professional representative of party, whose life is devoted to its interests, and whose aim is the triumph of its policies, is a cause—though it is not the only cause—of that accentuation of party which imperils the balance and adjustment of democratic institutions. From one point of view professionalism in politics is not different in kind from professionalism in medicine, or engineering, or journalism ; and from this point of view it is not to be blamed—or, for that matter, praised—any more than these other forms of professionalism. Like them, it is in its nature a rendering of skilled service, which is based on training and experience, in return for remuneration. But from another point of view, there is a great difference. The doctor or engineer or journalist may press the interests and the claims of his profession ; but at the most he is only seeking to increase the prestige and the remuneration which he and the other members of his profession enjoy, in comparison with those enjoyed by the members of other professions or occupations. The professional party politician—less self-interested, but more dangerous—does not seek to increase the standing or the reward of his profession, as such, in comparison with those of other professions : he seeks to magnify the claims and the authority of his party, with which he has identified himself, against the claims and the authority of other parties, and even, in the last resort, against the claims and the authority of anything else in the State. The professionalization of party politics not only strengthens the spirit of rivalry between the different parties : it also tends to produce an idolization of party at the expense of the general State.

There is another way in which the system of professional party politics, in its early stages and before it has acquired the moderation which comes from length of experience, may adversely affect the State. Every profession needs some code of professional ethics—some body of rules of honour by which the members voluntarily abide, in the interest of their own good name, and for the sake of the general standing of their profession in the eyes of the community. The code of ethics of the medical profession is as old as the oath of Hippocrates, and it thus goes back as far as the fifth century B.C. The essence of all such codes of professional ethics is that skilled service shall be faithfully rendered, with no ulterior object and without any breach of trust. The danger of a system of professional party politics, while it is still a new system, is the absence of this spirit of honourable obligation. The practitioners of the system are close to the mainsprings of the State. They are justified in using that position in the interests of the programme and the policy of their party ; but they will be tempted to use it in the interests of their party organization and their party adherents. It is difficult—though it is no less imperative than it is difficult—to draw a clear line of division between promotion of the policy of a party and promotion of the interests of its supporters. But if this line is not drawn, skilled service sinks into interested manipulation ; ulterior objects are allowed to enter, and breaches of professional trust are committed. This is the cause of the cry of political corruption which has been raised, in many countries, against party politics, and against the whole system of democracy of which party politics is an essential part. It is also a cause of the cry of inefficiency which has also been raised. Instead of rendering skilled service, the party politician has seemed to be guilty of the disservice of interested management of patronage and spoils ; and devoting himself to such management, he has been accused of the crime of neglecting the cardinal interests of the State. Purity has revolted against corruption : patriotism has revolted against inefficiency added to corruption ; and in the name both of purity and of patriotism, party politics and democracy at large have been brought to the bar of judgment. Too often the judgment has been pronounced by one of the parties in the case. Some party group, claiming a monopoly of purity and patriotism, has been the judge of other groups, and has pronounced a sentence of excommunication upon them. But there has been some real fire behind all the volume of smoke ; and there has been enough of corruption, and enough of consequent inefficiency, in many systems of professional party politics, to establish a case against them. Not that such defects are peculiar to these systems. Corruption and inefficiency are possible in any government ; they are even possible under the dictatorships which profess to save the State from them. But professional party governments, working under democratic conditions, necessarily live in the blaze of publicity, and wash their linen on the house-tops. Their scandals leap to the eye ; and there is no veil of censorship to shroud them from general view.

§ 6.   LEGISLATIVE ABSOLUTISM AND THE REACTION AGAINST IT

The great electorate and the highly organized party with its system of professional politics are two of the internal political difficulties of democracy. A third, which is closely connected with both, but more particularly with the modern development of party, is the tendency of legislative bodies to encroach on the necessary powers and authority of the executive. The development of parliamentary democracy on the Continent, owing to a number of reasons, has been parliamentary (in a narrow sense) rather than democratic. It has been a development of one part of the system of democracy rather than a general development of all the parts. The example of France has been followed rather than that of England ; and the logic of formal reason, conjoined with a different set of historical memories, and more particularly with the memory of a Napoleonic executive absolutism and its perils, has installed a sovereign Chamber as the residence and essence of the principle of democratic self-government.

In England the various factors of democracy—the electorate, party, parliament, cabinet—are all as old (at any rate in the germ) as the seventeenth century, and they have all pursued a continuous evolution together since 1688. They have settled down together in a working system under which each has found its place and function ; and while they have changed, both in themselves and in their relations to one another, none of them has altered its essential nature or the essential nature of its relations to the other factors. In particular the continued survival of the Crown, with a continuous prestige even if with altered prerogatives, has preserved the dignity and the authority of the executive. The members of the cabinet advise the Crown and determine its action by their advice : they do so because they command the confidence and represent the authority of parliament ; but they are none the less ministers of the Crown, and they derive a real dignity from the formal fact that they are in its service. It would be a paradox to argue that a balanced system of democracy postulates the existence of a monarchy. But it is none the less true that the survival of monarchy in England is integrally connected with the balance of our democratic system. The fact that the cabinet advises the Crown in the use of its prerogative powers, including the power of dissolution, is vital to its position, and vitally affects its relation to parliament and the electorate.

In France the course of development has been different, and a different logic has been applied to the results of a different development. Before 1789 there was no parliament, no electorate, no system of parties ; there was only a traditional but discredited system of monarchical absolutism. The system collapsed in 1789 ; and France passed *per saltum* to the other extreme. A legislature, professing to be the expression and the incarnation of the 'national sovereignty' of the people of France, dethroned the King and assumed the Crown. For some years the executive became as dust in the balance : the legislature, with an untrained electorate, and with equally untrained and violent parties, held the field. But an executive expelled by a pitchfork tends to recur ; and in France it recurred in the new and imperial form of a popular dictatorship, which used the machinery of the plebiscite to marry its autocracy to the idea, or rather the form, of democracy. The revolutionary period between 1789 and 1815 thus left France with two different and opposed legacies—the legacy of legislative omnipotence, and the legacy of the Napoleonic dictatorship. There was a nominal Restoration ; but it was never more than nominal. The Revolution was always triumphant in idea ; and the real issue which vexed France was not that of Restoration or Revolution, but that of one interpretation of the Revolution or another. After 1870 the interpretation which made the legislative body sovereign and omnipotent eventually triumphed. There was still, indeed, through the length and breadth of France, the tradition of a strong local executive operative in the shape of the prefects of the departments, as there had always been since the time of the Napoleonic reconstruction. There was also, in the capital, a strong central body of administrative officials, as there had always been since the days of Louis XIV. But the master of both was the Assembly, which controlled them through cabinets of its own creation dependent for their existence upon its precarious favour. It was now no longer a Napoleon, but a legislative assembly, which controlled the destinies of France ; and that assembly was resolved to be master of cabinets, master of prefects, master of administrative officials, and general master of France. It stood constantly on the alert against the whole executive side of government. It professed the doctrine of separation of powers ; but it interpreted that doctrine to limit the executive—and not itself.

The example of France has affected deeply the development of continental democracy ; but similar causes have also tended to produce a similar result even independently of the example of France. The place of the executive in the system of democracy has been generally depressed, because memories of an old and indigenous régime of executive absolutism have generally inspired a fear of its ambitions. On the one hand, the legislative has felt that it was itself the true heir and successor of the old plenary executive, and it has magnified its inheritance ; on the other hand, it has watched with a jealous surveillance the operation of the new and diminished form of the executive, in order to prevent its reversion to the old type. But it has also felt, and it has also emphasized, its own independent titles to power and authority. Elected by the people, and sustained by the tributary currents of electoral opinion, a plenary legislative can claim to be the general reservoir and the central clearing-house of the whole electorate. The hive of parties, and the focus on which all the many lines of party formation converge, it can also claim to be the general bank in which all the capital of social thought is invested. The logic which seeks to find a personal *primum mobile* of the forces and factors of democracy, and is not content to think of each factor as playing its appointed part in a general and impersonal scheme of discussion, can easily find satisfaction in the enthronement of the legislature.

The enthroned legislature sits permanently for the whole of its appointed term, without any fear of dissolution. There is nothing to send it back to an electorate which may have ceased to sustain it, and which it may have ceased to reflect. The parties in such a legislature are free, for the whole period of its tenure, to weave and unweave the webs of cabinet in a succession of combinations. The committees appointed by such a legislature become permanent commissions, sharing authority with the cabinet in the sphere of their operation ; they turn the opposition into a plurality of oppositions, which not only can criticize, but may actively thwart, the responsible government. Even the individual members of such a legislature may become so many sovereigns. They may move grants of supply for purposes which they seek to promote : they may exert pressure on ministers in the exercise of patronage or the general course of administrative action : they may make the individual legislator, as well as the corporate legislature, a master of the executive.

Even in point of logic the enthroned legislature is vulnerable. If it can be argued that the legislature is a *primum mobile*, it can also be argued that the electorate, or the party, is a *prius mobile*. Behind legislatures stand the electorates from which they proceed : behind both legislatures and electorates stand the parties which seek to be the ultimate main-springs of both. If we seek a ' first cause ', we may find the legislature dethroned in favour of some other force which claims to be even more ultimate ; or, short of that, we may find other forces seeking to associate themselves with the legislature in the position of ' joint first cause.' The latter is what actually happened under some of the new democratic constitutions which arose after 1918. There was a supreme legislature—sometimes unicameral—with its permanent committees and its general claim to dominate executive government : there was a supreme electorate, armed with powers of referendum and initiative : there were would-be supreme parties, with their party lists and their schemes of ' integral ' proportional representation for enforcing the lists upon the electorate. The supremacy of the legislature was thus combined with rival supremacies which it evoked into sympathetic but rival action ; and whatever it might have achieved if it had enjoyed a free field, it was actually doomed to work with allies who were also rivals and adversaries.

If it is vulnerable in logic, the enthroned legislature is still more vulnerable in its personnel and its actual composition. A legislature is not an abstraction or an impersonal force : it is an actual body of men, which will command as much power and authority as its members command respect and deference. Every government is grounded in opinion. If the government is conducted by a large legislature, which is not secluded in awful state, but acts on the public stage in the ordinary light of day, it must be grounded in opinion even more deeply than other forms if it is to command an equal authority. But the hold of legislatures on general opinion has not increased with their claims. It has rather decreased. Even if the quality and status of their members had remained constant, their prestige would none the less have diminished under the conditions of modern life. Publicity has a fierce glare : it breeds familiarity ; and familiarity, even if it does not breed contempt, is not the parent of deference. This is not all. The legislatures of the nineteenth century, newly risen to life, and encircled by the halo of a successful vindication of liberty, were a glory, a myth, a political cult. The legislatures of the twentieth century have been soiled by use and staled by custom : they are not a new song, and they are less grateful to the ear. We might thus have expected, in any event, some decline in the prestige of legislative bodies ; but the decline has been hastened by a growing suspicion, just or unjust, that the quality and status of the members of these bodies is not what it was. They are felt to be no longer amateurs, but the professional players of the commercialized game of party politics. They are paid ; and while we pay lip-service to the saying that the labourer is worthy of his hire, we also feel that he is somehow less worthy because he receives it. They serve, more obviously than ever before, the needs of their party and their side : they seem to be the sectaries of party rather than the free representatives of the whole commonwealth ; and while we admit the need of party, and are ready to applaud the party of our choice, we are not equally ready to admit the need, or to applaud the role, of the professional partisan. An attitude of distrust has taken the place of the older attitude of deference. Lord Bryce, writing some twenty years ago, ended his study of modern democracies with the words, ' Democracy will never perish till after Hope has expired '. But his own hopes had grown somewhat dim ; and he confesses, on a page which is headed ' Decline of Legislatures ', that ' the reputation and moral authority of elected legislatures . . . have been declining in almost every country.'[1]

Lord Bryce's book was published in 1921. It was followed, in the very next year, by the beginning of a movement which has since spread far and wide. It is a movement of what may be called ' executive reaction ', and the Fascist march on Rome was its first great manifestation. It is a movement broader and deeper, as we shall see in the issue, than mere executive reaction ; but that reaction is one of its cardinal and primary elements. The executive which had been eliminated, or at any rate subjugated, by the legislature has returned into the field, and turned on its subjugator. The extreme of an enthroned legislature has been met and answered by the other extreme of an executive dictatorship. True, the executive dictator can claim that he has party behind him, no less than the legislature had. The only difference—but it is large—is that he has a single party at his back, while the legislature had a plethora of parties. True, again, the executive dictator can claim that he has the electorate with him, and that he is its reservoir and general bank, as much as (or more than) the legislature was. He can accordingly plead that democracy is not dead, but has only suffered a change, and a change for the better, into a system of representation by one great popular leader. But if party and the electorate still subsist, and if (we may also add) there still survives some form of legislature, for the sake of etiquette and in order to preserve the ceremonials of legislation, the primary and cardinal element in the new system is the enthroned executive. It is the executive which has now its permanent tenure of office ; and just as the old legislature could not be dissolved by the executive, so the new executive cannot be dismissed by the legislature. It is the executive which is now master of the legislature, just as the old legislature had been the master of the executive. But the new executive, in its reaction, goes even further in the way

[1] Bryce, *Modern Democracies*, II, p. 632.

of executive control than the legislature had gone in the way of legislative control. It vests itself with legislative power by some form of *Lex regia*, ceremonially passed in the legislature, which gives the force of law to its proclamations. It becomes, in form as well as in substance, an organ of legislation as well as an executive organ.

§ 7. DEMOCRACY IN AN ERA OF ECONOMIC AND SCIENTIFIC CHANGE

To the catalogue of the difficulties of democracy there is another still to be added. This is a difficulty which is due, not to the organs of democracy and the defects into which they may fall, but to the nature of the functions which they have to discharge and the speed with which they have to discharge them under the conditions of modern life. The functions of government have become largely economic : the speed at which they have to be discharged has become bewildering. The difficulty is not peculiar to democracy : it is common to all forms of government. But it presses with particular weight upon democracy. Democracy is the government of all : economic problems affect all, but they also affect different sections differently ; and how can all arrive at any agreed solution, or indeed at any solution, when they are vexed by deep differences of outlook and interest ? Democracy, again, is not in its nature congenial to rapid decision : based on a process of discussion, it has a great need *godere il beneficio del tempo* ; and time is now flying too rapidly to dispense its benefits.

Democracy in its nature has always carried economic implications. In the days of struggle, when men were agitating for a democratic suffrage and parliamentary institutions, they were also agitating for something which lay behind and beyond their more immediate objects. They did not merely desire the vote : they desired a key to unlock a new world in which the sinister interests of privilege would be corrected, and equal justice, directed to a more equal distribution of happiness, would be established. In the days of achievement, when a general suffrage and a representative parliament had become accomplished facts, the economic consequences of democracy became still clearer. New social classes had been enfranchised : their interests and their desires found public expression ; and political reorganization was seen to involve, by a natural and inevitable logic, an increasing measure of social reconstruction. To stop short at political change is to stop in the middle of a river. Few will be content with such a position ; and most hands will be outstretched *ripae ulterioris amore*.

The economic consequences of democracy become still more obvious when we consider the new capitalistic epoch of mechanical change and industrial revolution in which it has struggled to birth and in which it is still engaged. In a period of static methods of production and traditional standards of distribution there may be but little incentive to questioning. In a period in which methods of production are rapidly changing and the standards of distribution are constantly changing with them—changing too, as it seems, erratically, and in flat violation of all established tradition—there will be an abundance of questions. It was among such questions that modern democracy was born : we may almost say that it was *from* these questions that it was born. In that sense capitalism—in its modern form, and so far as it has been the parent, or at any rate the brother, of change—has not been hostile to democracy : it has rather been the incentive and stimulus to democratic thought and democratic aspiration. It has produced a vast material which invited and demanded universal discussion ; it has led, above everything else, to the institution of systems of government by discussion. Capitalism did not invent democracy in order to govern under its shadow. But it has helped, none the less, to produce it—*malgré lui*.

But if the questions provided by capitalism have helped to produce democracy, it does not follow that democracy is able to provide the answers to those questions. Apart from the fundamental difficulty, to which we must presently return, that those who have to give the answers are themselves divided by deep divisions of outlook and interest, there is another and minor difficulty, which is none the less becoming increasingly grave and serious. The ultimate result of long years of scientific discovery and mechanical invention, from the steam-engine to wireless telegraphy and the aeroplane, has been an obvious acceleration of the pace of human life. The production and the distribution of wealth have been revolutionized ; but that is not the whole of the revolution. Our minds too work with different tools ; and a different apparatus of life affects the whole process of deliberation and decision. Rapidity of communication, both physical and mental, has become the mark of our times. Rapidity of communication not only involves a new rapidity of deliberation and decision ; it also involves a new and increasing centralization of decision. The great business settles its affairs in the head office ; scattered ambassadors, of old almost plenipotentiaries, have become the dependents of the Foreign Office. The commissioner of an Indian district has to look to the provincial governor, the governor to the Viceroy, the Viceroy to the Secretary of State in Whitehall. In itself this process of the centralization of decision does not seem necessarily adverse to the power and prestige of legislative bodies. They are central organs ; and they can, as such, vindicate a right to the privilege of central decision. But the rules of procedure of legislative bodies are intended to secure the benefit of time for a protracted discussion of policies and measures ; and though such bodies are capable of acting with sudden rapidity in an emergency, they cannot in their nature act with a regular rapidity. Meanwhile the pace of the mutations of foreign affairs increases ; the wheel of economic vicissitudes, in the relations between country and country, revolves more rapidly, and throws up sudden problems of currency, quotas, and tariffs ; even internally there may be sudden emergencies in the working of a scheme of unemployment relief, or in the relations between employers and workers in a ' key ' industry, or on some political issue of freedom of speech or meeting. All this enures to the benefit of the central executive. Whether or no an instant decision is really necessary, it is expected by the temper of our minds ; and we naturally look to those who can give it most instantly. We are taught—not only by the Press, which has its own reasons for loving the word, but also by all the rush which we see around us—to think in terms of ' crisis ' ; and the word ' crisis ' (which in its original Greek form means simply decision) evokes the idea and the expectation of instant solution. The whole spiritual process of democracy thus seems to be challenged by the new pace of matter in our modern world. We have set matter, in all its forms, to move more quickly ; and we are inevitably influenced, in the motion of our own minds, by the increasing motion of matter which we have ourselves produced. Physics react upon politics : the new physical environment with which we have surrounded the whole of our life affects our political systems and the whole order of our societies.

There is an old and simple proverb which says, ' The more haste, the less speed '. It does not follow from our greater rapidity that we are attaining better solutions, or even that we are attaining any solution. Perhaps all great decisions on cardinal issues are slowly and surely matured. But for our own day, and in this generation, we have to reckon with a mood of impatience, which belongs to a period of rapid mechanical change and may pass away when we settle down into our new environment. This impatience is one of the causes of that ' crisis of democracy ' which, in its turn, is one of the many ' crises ' among which we live. It leads us to look for sudden salvations and sudden saviours. It throws out of gear, for the time being, the steady process of democratic discussion. With all the means of rapid publicity and instantaneous com- munication—the talking film, the broadcast voice, the rapid dash by aeroplane—a new system of electric and instan- taneous executive leadership now finds its opportunity. Nor is it only the technology of physics, and the new marvels of physical invention, which provide the opportunity. It is also what may be called the technology of psychology. The pure and experimental study of psychology, like the pure and experimental study of physics, is a pure addition to the total sum of human knowledge. But there is a form of technical or applied psychology—the psychology not of the laboratory and the student, but of the market-place and the man of affairs— which has also to be taken into account. It provides a tech- nique which can substitute an induced mass-emotion, by the use of appropriate stimuli, for the rational process of general discussion. When we are taking stock of the influence which applied science, in all its various forms, is exerting upon the conduct and temper of politics, we must not forget the influence of applied psychology.

It is a facile and a foolish generalization which makes modern science, in any of its applications, the natural foe of a democratic government. The student of natural science is not responsible for the application of the results which he attains ; and it would be a treason to the cause of science if any scientist allowed himself to be stopped, by a prophetic fear of possible results, from treading the path of discovery and invention to its ultimate end. The evils of scientific invention will be gradually interred : the ultimate good will live permanently. Initially, and on a short run, it is those who can make a quick profit who hasten to adopt the results of scientific invention ; in the long run the general community turns them to the benefit of its own general and permanent purposes. If democracy has the root of life in it (and on all our argument it has), it will not be bent by a whole multitude of new inventions : it will bend them to itself. All the new speed of communication, all the new methods of influencing opinion, everything which physics and psychology can give, can be taken up into the process of democracy and used to improve its working. If, in the beginning, the pace flusters, and if, in the early stages, the electorate and parliament are left behind, and the executive (voluntarily and through ambition, or involuntarily and in its own despite) runs ahead and in solitude, these are the incidents of the beginning and of the early stages. Even in the early stages a scientific invention such as broadcasting, if it is caught betimes and made serviceable to the general intention and character of the State, can prove itself a new asset and an added power to the working of democratic institutions. It can provide a forum of discussion, as wide as the nation and open to the ears of the whole nation, in which issues can be debated gravely by representatives of different views and policies : it can serve, as we have already had reason to note, to make the great electorate of our times no less capable of reasoned and sustained argument than the far smaller electorates of the nineteenth century. Applied psychology itself, whatever the level of its present achievements may be, can render, and may yet render, large services to the cause of reasonable human self-government. Men have to understand themselves as individuals in all their range, in their dim instincts as well as in their conscious purposes, before they can govern themselves as individuals. What is true of the individual is also true, in this respect, of the whole community. The more the community understands the instincts to which it is prone, and the emotions by which it is liable to be swayed, the more it becomes their master and the master of the whole of its life. There is room, and to spare, for an applied science of social psychology which will seek to give this understanding, and, by giving it, to lay a healing hand on our perturbations. Social psychology may well develop into a form of social therapeutics which can ease the whole process of social life.[1]

§ 8.   DEMOCRACY IN RELATION TO MODERN METHODS OF PRODUCTION AND DISTRIBUTION

The material and mechanical changes in the equipment and the pace of life, and their influences on the behaviour of nations and the conduct of national government, form only one aspect of the general revolution of environment which affects all the activity of modern society. There is another and more fundamental aspect, which has already been mentioned, and to which we must now return. The general revolution of environment not only involves physical changes in the equipment and pace of life : it also involves economic changes in the production and distribution of wealth. It is not only a revolution in the world of physics : it is also a revolution in the world of economics. Behind all systems of politics, including the system of democracy, there stands the system of economics. That system, in its present form, presents every system of politics with the profoundest and the most persistent problems which it has to face. But it presents them to democracy in the acutest and most serious form.

There is the problem, in the first place, of the organization of the economic system for its primary purpose of production. That organization, in almost all States, is capitalistic. The owner of capital resources, or the agent who acts on behalf

---

[1] This was the aim of Graham Wallas. In a letter to the writer, written on the eve of the last War (22 July 1914), he defined it as follows : ' The social psychologist is bound to deal essentially and primarily with types of behaviour. His purpose, as I conceive it, is entirely practical. He is aiming . . . at a sort of social therapeutics. For that purpose he wants to find out how a normal man will behave in the presence of a given stimulus, and how far, by changing the stimulus, you can change his behaviour.'
There are two further sentences in the letter of July 1914 which are worth quoting. We are apt to distinguish between the processes of emotion and instinct, and those of reason and reflection. Graham Wallas drew the writer's attention to the ' false dichotomy of all processes leading to action as consisting either of unreflecting obedience to instinctive impulse, or of a series of fully conscious logical conclusions '. ' I believe ', he continued, ' that the normal alternative for the ordinary man in actual life is between the following of instinct and [the following of] reflection ; but that reflection in ordinary life consists of processes largely sub-conscious, making small use of language, and directed by no logical system.' In a word, we are less rational than we think in what we call our reasoning, and perhaps just for that reason more rational than we think in what we call our instinctive impulses. A basis is thus laid for the work of the social psychologist in seeking to rationalize impulse.

of the owner or a number of associated owners, controls and determines, in virtue of such ownership, the process of production and the action of the workers who are engaged in the process. In its unqualified form, capitalistic organization is a form of autocracy or absolutism. In practice it is never unqualified. On the one hand the legislation of States, whatever the form of their government, generally imposes conditions (beginning with what are called factory laws, but not ending with such laws) on the process of production. On the other hand combinations of workers apply the force of numbers and the menace of a concerted withdrawal of labour to impose further conditions of their own. But the qualified autocracy or absolutism of capitalistic organization still falls short of economic democracy. We may call it, by a contradiction of terms, a limited absolutism, which naturally seeks to escape its limits, and on which (so long as it exists) combinations of workers will as naturally seek to impose new limits.

When we turn from production to the distribution of the product, we are confronted by the same general situation. The owners of capital resources, or the agents for the owners, control and determine, in virtue of such ownership, the process by which the results of industry are distributed in profits and wages. The control is qualified in the same way as the control of the process of production is qualified ; though it is seldom qualified (at any rate in so far as the action of the State is concerned) to the same extent. On the one hand the State may correct the distribution of the results of production by instituting a minimum wage for workers, or by limiting profits, or by imposing taxes which largely fall on owners of capital and go to provide social services for the benefit of workers. On the other hand combinations of workers may seek to use their bargaining power to affect the process of distribution in their own favour. By both of these methods, a limited absolutism is again made to take the place of unqualified autocracy.

Democratic States, like other forms of State, have used their authority to limit capitalism by law, and they have left scope to Trade Unions (though never an absolutely free scope) to impose further limits by the method of collective bargaining with employers. We need not here pause to enquire whether they have imposed *more* limits, or have left Trade Unions *more* scope to impose further limits, than other forms of States have done. We have to face larger questions. There is, first of all, a question of logic. Can democracy, in its nature, co-exist with any form of economic absolutism, however limited ? Does it not naturally and logically involve a parallel system of economic democracy, under which the control of production and distribution, in every industry and in every factory, is vested not in a limited autocracy, but in a free partnership of all the agents concerned, who will all determine by common rules, based on a common agreement and attained by a process of common discussion, both the processes of production and the methods of distribution ? Such a partnership would not necessarily involve the substitution of a system of social ownership of capital resources for the existing system of private ownership. In other words, it would not necessarily entail the institution of socialism. On the contrary, it would be compatible with the private ownership of capital resources, if only that ownership were diffused, or agreement could be attained that it should be progressively diffused, among all the agents engaged in production. But if the ideal of economic democracy, thus expressed in the form of free partnership, would not necessarily involve the institution of socialism, it would necessarily entail the ending of capitalism in its present form, as a system which vests the control of production and distribution in a body of owners distinct from, and superior to, the other agents concerned in the economic process. We are thus brought to a second question. This is a question of fact and practice. Can any democratic community, as a matter of fact and in actual practice, reasonably hope to achieve, by the democratic process of discussion and compromise, a solution of the economic problem which involves the ending of capitalism in its present form ? Is it not too hopelessly divided into two camps, one standing stiffly for the present form of capitalism, and the other standing no less stiffly for the institution of a new system of socialism ? We seem to be plunged into a dilemma. On the one hand, democracy ought to secure some economic order of society which is congenial with its own nature and is attained by its own process. On the other hand, its process seems inadequate to attain the solution which is congenial with its nature. The process of debate and compromise seems incapable of attaining that solution, or indeed any solution at all, when there is no common ground on which to debate, and no middle term on which we can compromise.

It is the second of these questions—the question of fact and practice—which is the cardinal question. If the members of a democratic community can agree to think together about a solution of economic problems which agrees with the logic and character of their community, they will find one. We cannot predict the exact solution which they will find, and we cannot lay down in advance the precise conditions to which it must conform. If we seek to do so, we shall be contradicting the spirit of democracy : we shall be saying what men must think, and not leaving them free to think. If we believe in democracy we must believe in the ' heuristic ' of democracy, and we must not seek to prescribe for it exactly what it shall find. The question before us is not therefore the question of the precise nature of the solution which has to be found : it is the question of the capacity for finding *any* solution, when the issue in question is the issue of economics. Can the members of a democratic community agree to think together on that issue, or must they think separately, in two distinct and divided camps ? Is it possible, on that issue, and in that respect, to believe in the democratic process and the heuristic of democracy, or are we condemned to disbelief and despair ? The answer we give to that question will transcend the immediate economic issue, and will determine our general attitude to the general capacity of democracy. If it cannot solve the greatest of issues, it will stand condemned, whatever the triumphs which it can celebrate, or the hopes which it may nourish, in other fields.

§ 9. THE IDEA OF CAPITALISTIC DEMOCRACY

Disraeli, over ninety years ago, published a novel, entitled *Sybil, or the Two Nations*. A few years afterwards, in 1848, Marx and Engels issued the Communist Manifesto, in which the two nations were baptized as the proletariat and the bourgeoisie. Names have power. When once we have taken a notion and given it a sounding name, we readily transplant it from the notional world into the actual, and we vest it with life and motion. The two nations, the proletariat and the bourgeoisie, capital and labour—these names and labels have been turned into living and personal forces, engaged in a struggle which overshadows and dominates everything else.

The dualism is simple—too simple to do justice to the multiplicity of actual life, which is not all plain black and white ; but its very simplicity is cogent. Under the influence of this dualism it is easy to see everywhere ' two and two, one against another '. Politics, like the rest of life, can be schematized on this system. There will then be, on the one hand, an organized wealth-owning class, anxious to preserve and increase its wealth, and striving to use the machinery of politics for this object : there will equally be, on the other, an organized non-wealthy class, anxious (under the same impulse of economic necessity) to redistribute wealth, and striving to use the machinery of politics for the achievement of that object. On this basis the process of democracy is subjected to two contrary stresses ; and the result of the process will necessarily depend on their relative strength. It will not be common deliberation which will decide economic issues. It will be different and conflicting stresses. When one of the stresses is greater, we shall have what is called capitalistic democracy. When the other is greater, the victory will lie with what is termed social democracy. But there will never be pure and simple democracy. That can never exist after the two antagonists have once entered the scene—or until they both leave it.

If we pursue this line of interpretation, we are confronted by the fact that ' capitalistic democracy ' is now generally in the ascendant. This seems, at first sight, a paradox. Universal suffrage is now the rule : under universal suffrage the non-wealthy class is the great majority of the electorate ; and the stress of that class should therefore be far the greater. But there is an explanation of this paradox which may easily, and not unjustly, be pressed. The electorate is not the whole of the system of democratic machinery. It is only one part of the system ; and it is influenced by other parts. We must therefore study the whole of the system of democracy in order to understand the actual play of the stresses to which it is subject. If we do so, it is contended, we shall readily see why the stress (or ' pull ') of capitalism is the stronger.

The argument may be stated in some such terms as these. Democracy is a process of discussion. Discussion requires publicity—full and fair publicity—for every point of view. That requirement is not satisfied so long as the power of wealth controls the means of publicity. The wealth-owning

class can at present acquire a predominant weight in the
process of discussion, not in the strength of what it has to say,
and not by the inherent value of the case which it seeks to
put, but in the strength of its purse and by the adventitious
power of its monetary resources. In this way the process of
discussion is perverted. It is not controlled by the weight of
argument : it is directed by the power of wealth. That power
is able to influence every organ of democracy. In the first
place it can influence party. The subventions of the wealthy
to party funds help to determine the policies of parties and the
programmes which they put before the electorate. The first
beginnings and the original springs of deliberation are already
choked. In the second place, wealth can influence the Press
and the whole of the machinery by which opinions are published. It can provide an easy course for the dissemination
of its own particular set of opinions : it can multiply the papers
and publications by which they are expressed : it can create
the illusion that they are universally held ; and it may
succeed in imposing the illusion upon the electorate. Influencing party and the Press, wealth can already influence, indirectly, the electorate and parliament ; but it also influences
them immediately. The rich can woo and win constituencies :
they have the leisure for parliaments, or if they leave parliamentary duties to others they have the means for securing
assiduous advocates of their views in the Chamber and its
lobbies. In a word, ' money talks ' ; and government by talk
is really government by money. Lenin had a solid basis for
his opinion when he wrote that ' the democratic republic is
the best possible form for capitalism, and therefore, once capital
has gained control . . . of this very best form, it establishes its
power so securely, so firmly, that no change of persons, or
institutions, or parties, in the bourgeois republic can shake it '.[1]

---

[1] *The State and Revolution*, I, § 3. Towards the end of § 4 Lenin also writes :
' We are in favour of a democratic republic as the best form of the State for the
proletariat under capitalism.' There is no real inconsistency between the two
statements. The democratic State offers a free field for both sides—with a great
deal of favour, initially, for the side of capital ; but that favour is gradually
corrected by the growth of the organization of labour, and this is the reason why
the democratic State is (or rather becomes) ' the best form of the State for the
proletariat under capitalism.' The correction, however, can never result, in
Lenin's view, in the establishment of balance or compromise. It can only result
in a final Armageddon, which shatters the democratic State. The receptacle
which has contained, and even sustained, both sides is finally exploded by their
last conflict.

Crudely stated, in such a form, the theory of ' capitalistic democracy ' is hardly convincing. It is true enough that, on any argument, the dice are loaded in favour of the wealthy advocate of opinion. It is seldom that opinions carry weight in pure proportion to their intrinsic merit. A little experience of life is sufficient to teach us that the opinions of those who command prestige—whether the prestige be derived from official position, or from birth, or from wealth—have an influence which is out of proportion with their inherent value. Those who have held office, and then relinquished or lost it, are sufficiently aware of this simple truth. The pure struggle of opinions, on their own merits, is hardly ever achieved in any community. But it is one thing to admit that wealth, like office or birth, adds an inevitable (and yet, in a sense, an artificial) weight to the opinions of its possessor : it is another thing to contend that wealth can purchase and pervert general opinion. We pay too great a compliment to the power of wealth when we think that it can purchase the victory not merely of its own opinions, but of its own interested opinions, for the price of mere money. The victory of any cause has to be bought at a higher price ; and that price is the reason and justice inherent in the cause. It is a low view of human nature, as well as too great a compliment to the power of wealth, to imagine that any other price will ever be generally accepted. Men sell many things for money ; but one thing which they do not readily sell is their convictions. There is a curious blend of lofty idealism and bitter cynicism in those who hate the idea, but magnify the power, of capitalism. They believe with passion in a new and ideal dispensation which transcends capitalism, and they must therefore also logically believe in the higher capacities of human nature which are necessary for its achievement ; but they believe equally, and with no less passion, in the corrupting power of the present order of capitalism, and in the liability of human nature to succumb to the power of corruption. It is often the tendency of the idealist to divorce his ideal from the ground of reality—to magnify the ideal beyond the reach of realization, and to vilify the real beyond the power of recognition. This mixture of idealism and pessimism—this divorce between reality and the ideal—naturally issues in an advocacy of the method of revolution. When the ideal is absolutely divorced from the real, it is only the use of force which can bring them together again.

If we explore the ground of actual reality, we shall hardly find that it warrants the theory of ' capitalistic democracy.' Any democratic government must indeed be influenced by the stress of capitalism ; and that stress may even be traced, by those who limit the field of their vision but use strong glasses within that field, in the courts of law as well as in parties and the Press. But democratic governments are also influenced by the stress of organized labour ; and the capitalist himself is prone to think that the democracy under which he lives, and in which he is taxed and otherwise regulated, is the opposite of capitalistic. If we are to interpret politics in terms of class, we must admit that the non-wealthy class is at least as well organized as the wealth-owning class : indeed, to all appearances, it is better organized, and it is certainly far more united by a spirit of solidarity. Organized labour can raise its own funds to sustain a party devoted to its interests. The policies and programme of that party are presented steadily to the electorate : they are present in the very beginnings, and at the spring-head, of national deliberation. Labour, again, has its Press and its publications ; and just because it is news, even if for no other reason, it also commands the attention, and receives the notice, of the general Press. Oral report and the spoken word are also at its service in the cities in which men congregate ; and even though it may be held to be weaker in the Press, it must be accounted stronger on the platform than any of the other parties. Labour, too, no less than wealth, can woo and win constituencies : it can hold them permanently in the great centres of industry ; it can provide advocates of its cause in parliament who are no less assiduous, and no less effective, than the advocates of other causes. In the face of the electorate, and in the field of party, the Press, and parliament, labour thus stands on a general equality with its opponents. In some other respects it has even the advantage. Labour has an economic organization, parallel to and connected with its political organization, which generally, and on the whole, adds to its strength, though it may sometimes prove an embarrassment. In England the two organizations are connected with a peculiar intimacy. The Trade Union movement has never been with us, as the

Confédération Générale du Travail has been in France, a movement separate from the political organization of the Labour
party : it has not even, as was the case in Germany down to
1933, contented itself with acting as an independent economic
ally of the workers' political party. The English Trade Unions,
since the beginning of the present century, have been regular
members of the Labour party, affiliated to it for political
purposes even while they also continue to act independently,
for economic purposes, in their own field. But in any case,
and in all countries, whether the economic organization of
labour is dovetailed into or separate from its political organization, it is generally an integral part and a powerful factor in a
solid and sympathetic organization of labour. When we speak
in terms of two nations or classes, we must not forget that
if one of them can rely on the subtle and pervasive effects of
wealth, the other can rely on the massive weight not only of its
political party, but also of its organized and cohesive economic
associations.

§ 10. THE IDEA OF THE TWO RIVAL DEMOCRACIES

So far as the argument has gone, it may be said to prove,
or at any rate to suggest, that on the ground of actual reality it
is impossible to speak in the over-simplified terms of ' capitalistic democracy ', in which the capitalistic class is supposed to
exclude the workers from any effective share in the exercise
of power by the subtlety and the ramifications of its influence.
At the very least we must set by the side of ' capitalistic
democracy ' another and rival ' labour democracy ', with its
own equipment and its own native source of strength. Are
we then to believe in two democracies, and not one ; and are
we to hold that the two are irretrievably divided ? Is that
the lesson which we must learn if we place ourselves on the
ground of actual reality ? In that case we shall have escaped
from the over-simplicity of capitalistic democracy only to fall
into the utter dualism of two opposed democracies which
somehow co-exist but cannot co-operate. We shall have one
democracy based on the primary principle of private property
in capital resources, with all its corollaries ; we shall have
another based on the primary principle of public ownership of
those resources ; and since the difference is held to be a
difference of primary principle—since it is conceived as turning

on the essential first idea which creates and constitutes the whole nature of society—we shall not have a single society in which the two can act, and react, upon one another.

The dualistic picture of life with which we are thus presented is, however, an arbitrary picture, which depends on an arbitrary assumption of the principle of interpretation, and an equally arbitrary selection of the features and facts to be brought into the light and thrown into vivid relief. It is a large assumption of principle when the whole nature of society is made to depend upon its system of ownership. Private property and public ownership are important factors in social life ; and a society based on the one will differ in many respects from a society based on the other. But there are also other important factors besides the system of ownership—none of them, indeed, independent of it (any more than it is independent of them), and this for the simple reason that all the factors are interconnected, and necessarily interact, in the common unity of any society. The general scheme of law, which is something larger than the law of property : the faith and the organization of churches : the tradition and the content of general culture—these are all factors in social life ; and it is possible to believe that a society which preserves the continuity of these factors may remain fundamentally the same, without undergoing any great change of character, even if it alters radically its system of ownership and its economic basis.[1] We have also to remember, in this connection, that there are few of the older States of the world which are based exclusively on private property. There is no clear distinction between private property States and public ownership States. The economic basis of the political community, in a country such as Great Britain, covers a range which stretches from public ownership and management, through an area of undertakings operating with private capital but subject to public control or even to public management, until it reaches the area of private property and private management. The economic factor, so far as ownership and management is

---

[1] Russia is an example to the contrary. Here the alteration of the system of ownership has been accompanied by a general alteration of the scheme of law, of religious life, and of general culture. But it is none the less possible that in older and more settled societies great economic changes might be effected without any general revolution in the whole character of social life. Russia is not a typical example—though it is conceivable that deliberate imitation of Russia *might* make the Russian example typical.

concerned, is accordingly mixed. The two supposed opposites live side by side ; systems which are neither live side by side with both ; and all amicably play their different parts in the one society. There would be no great change if the balance were gradually tilted towards the side of complete public ownership and public management—provided only that the tilting was due to a process of steady and continuous adjustment, and not to a sudden cataclysm.

When we turn from things and the ownership of things to persons and the status of persons, we are again confronted by the fact of mixture. The dualistic picture of two separate and opposed classes, ' two and two, one against another ', is an arbitrary picture. The class scheme is an abstraction, drawn from the actual world by the process of selecting some and neglecting other features which it presents, and then imposed upon it as its true form or ' idea '. It is, in a sense, an artistic or imaginative creation, comparable to the creations of the poet and the painter ; but it is not clear that such an imaginative creation can be made the basis of scientific analysis of the present or scientific prediction of the future. If the features and facts which are neglected for the purpose of such creation are both numerous and essential, we may indeed be stirred and moved by the result, as we are moved by a work of art ; but such emotion will not be a safe guide to a reasonable and tenable theory of the whole evidence.

The class scheme, with its simple dualism, may be said to omit two sorts of facts which are both essential. Even if we admit the existence of two opposed classes, we have also to admit the existence of other social groups, which are not based on the principle of class, but may none the less cherish their own convictions and formulate their own policies on the issues of economics. Society is not only the home of classes : it is also the home of churches, and of voluntary associations intended for the promotion of social purposes and programmes. The Roman Catholic Church, in every country, gathers its adherents together around its own doctrine of social economics, as that doctrine has been expressed in the encyclicals of 1891 and 1931[1] ; and in every country bodies of opinion, formed irrespective of class, and existing for the pure advocacy of

---

[1] *Rerum Novarum*, issued by Leo XIII, 15 May 1891 : *Quadragesimo Anno*, issued by Pius XI, 15 May 1931.

some economic plan or some more general social programme, are a part of the general play of social forces. Classes are mixed with other elements : however large they may seem to bulk, they do not occupy the whole field. Political parties, in particular, are forms of voluntary association which exist by the side of class formations, and can only be identified with them by a violent interpretation of their structure and composition. It would hardly be a paradox to maintain that there is nowhere a party which contains all the members of a single class, and contains nothing but the members of that class.

Not only are other social elements mixed with the element of class : that element is itself a mixed and multitudinous thing. Modern life does not present us with any simple cleavage of distinct and separate classes. In the Middle Ages it was possible to distinguish three classes, or forms of status, or ' estates '—the baronage, the clergy, and the commons, or, as they were termed in the Latin of the day, the *bellatores*, the *oratores*, and the *laboratores*. In nineteenth century Germany, in which the tradition of the Estates and the *Ständestaat* still survived, it was an easy leap for the theorists of socialism to modify the medieval distinction, and to postulate a plain opposition between the capitalistic class, which had succeeded to the baronage, and a proletarian class which was the depressed heir of the medieval commons. But this modified medievalism did not sit easily on the new industrial age which it professed to describe. The industrial age, with its rapid changes and its new mobility, obliterates the old and simple distinctions of a fixed and static society ; but far from putting in their place an even simpler system of distinctions, it substitutes a much more complicated, and a much less stable, system. It is true that it consolidates, and thus differentiates, the class of the community which lives by the wages it earns as the price of its manual labour. In that sense the growth of industry may be said to constitute, or at any rate to define and accentuate, a separate proletarian class. But it is far from true that it consolidates, or in any way constitutes, any other single separate class. The more it develops, the more it produces a mixture or complication of social elements. One of these elements may indeed be called capitalistic. But even this element is divided into a financial section, which manipulates capital and credit, and an industrial section which applies a capital that is mainly borrowed to the actual work of production ; and the interests of the two sections may disagree with one another.   Nor is this all.   By the side of this capitalistic element there are also other elements, which may count even more in the general play of society.   There are, for example, the professions, which steadily increase not only in numbers, but also in the efficiency of their organization : there are again the technical and managerial staffs in industry (perhaps only a new form or variety of profession), which belong neither to the capitalistic nor to the proletarian side. There is thus no organized single class to confront the class of wage-earning manual workers : there is only a number of different elements ; and some of these may feel that their interests, far from separating them from the class of the workers, unite them in harmony with it on many, if not on all, issues.   Nor must we exaggerate the homogeneity of the class of manual workers.   The interest of one of its sections may conflict with those of others ; and many of its members may, by the process of saving and investment, acquire possession of capital and begin to identify their interests with those of other elements of the community.   When we consider these facts, we are bound to reject the idea of a necessary dualism of classes.   We may even reject the very idea of classes, for the simple reason that we cannot discover any community which is really arranged in a number of distinct and distinguishable classes.   ' The belief in the existence of social classes ', it has been said, ' or even of one social class, the interests of the members of which are identical, or nearly so, and opposed to the interests of the rest of the community, is the result of studying social theory of doubtful value and of neglecting social facts '.[1]

§ 11. SOCIAL DIVISIONS AND THE POLITICAL BRIDGE

The study of social facts does not warrant us in believing that there is any unbridgeable gulf (deep as one of the cañons in the New World) between the different social elements contained in the modern State.   At the most it might conceivably lead us to conclude, first, that the great body of manual workers has attained a new consolidation (partly

---

[1] A. M. Carr-Saunders and D. Caradog Jones, *The Social Structure of England and Wales*, p. 72.

through the increasing mechanization of industry, which assimilates the activities of all manual workers in a common process of repetition work, and partly through the parallel development of Trade Unions, once organized on the basis of different ' crafts ', into great and comprehensive ' industrial ' unions which tend to a close alliance) ; and, secondly, that the other social elements, varied though they may be, are none the less steeped in a common spirit of private property, and dyed in a common colour of private enterprise, which are alien to—or at any rate remote from—the spirit and colour of the world of manual labour. But even if we go to the length of that conclusion—which is, after all, an extreme conclusion, exaggerating the unity of either of the two sides, and exaggerating equally the difference between them—we are not compelled to believe in the doctrine of the unbridgeable gulf, and still less to hold that the State is lodged on one side of the gulf and acts in the interest of that side. The facts testify to the contrary. For at least a century the State, even under a so-called ' capitalistic ' system (which is really a ' mixed ' system of private property and public ownership, steadily altering its proportions and its character), has imposed conditions upon the system, which have secured new rights for manual workers, imposed new liabilities on their employers, and restricted the whole of the wealthier section of the community. It has bestridden the gulf, so far as there was a gulf ; and, as Solon claimed for himself, it has striven to hold ' a strong shield over either side '. The record of social legislation cannot be simply dismissed under the facile appellation of ' palliatives ' or ' ransoms ' or ' sops ', as if it were something thrown out, in desperation, to a pack of pursuing wolves. It has been advocated by those who believed, without any *arrière pensée*, in the general and impartial cause of social justice ; it has been won, in no small measure, by the honest effort and the concerted strength of the workers themselves, standing for their own rights. Men are driven to curious shifts of interpretation when they seek to make the record of fact fit into the scheme of their own abstractions. The doctrine of ransom or palliatives is one of the most curious of such shifts.[1]

---

[1] The doctrine of ransom or palliative is sometimes extended, by some modern writers, to a further conclusion. It is argued that palliatives, for what they are worth, can only be provided by capitalism in a period of prosperity ; and it is

If the State in general does not live on one side of a gulf, but can pass to and fro—bridging, adjusting, and reconciling differences, after its nature and according to its function—there seems to be no fundamental reason for despairing of the democratic form of State. No doubt such a form of State has its own special difficulties. It does not compress social forces and social elements, as the autocratic State is able to do—or rather, can *attempt* to do : it lets them play, and it sets them free to engage in the battle of agitation and debate. It is true that if the forces thus liberated are essentially hostile and fundamentally opposed, their play will be something more than play, and their battle will be more than a battle of agitation and debate. If they are so hostile and so opposed, they will be unable to argue together, because there are no common terms in which they can argue : they will be unable to compromise, because neither is willing to make a concession to the other, or to receive a concession from it. But there is no evidence to prove that the forces which are liberated under the system of democracy necessarily must, or actually do, believe in this stiff and intransigent spirit of buckram logic. It is only intellectual abstractions, ' hatched in the schools ' of neo-scholasticism, which are thus unyielding. In the world of flesh and blood there is always a spirit of accommodation which makes men stretch out tentative hands to find ways and means of living together in some measure of comfort. Good sense has its quiet victories, which, if less renowned, are more substantial than the victories of the remorseless logic of doctrine. The dialectic of practical life is not the dialectic which seeks to refute : it is the dialectic which seeks to persuade.

This temper of accommodation, good sense, and persuasion, is a temper which needs to be cultivated. But we may also say, with no little truth, that it also needs to be left alone. Left to itself, it will produce peace and the fruits of peace. If it be troubled, by constant ingeminations of the doctrine of

urged that, since capitalism is now in difficulties, and its period of prosperity has passed, there are no more palliatives to be expected. The record of social legislation is finished, and its last word has been written. . . . This seems to be ' too quick despairing '. The world's great age may begin anew. Moreover, the argument seems to prove too much. If capitalism is in so desperate a pass that it can no longer pay the smallest of ransoms, it has passed beyond our praise or blame, and we must simply write its epitaph. There is no need of denunciation : still less of a revolution. The old and inefficient king, who can no longer provide even a bribe, is dead. It only remains to proclaim his successor . . . if he can be found.

social war, it may disappear. It is not the social facts of our time which are dangerous : it is rather the social doctrines. It is perfectly possible for democracy to work, and to work well, on the basis of existing social facts and existing social temper. It is possible for a party of the Right and a party of the Left to exist and act in the same society—both acting on democratic principles ; each seeking to win a majority ; and each willing, if it wins what it seeks, to come to some agreement with the minority, and to make some compromise with it which it will consent to accept. But the possibility may be killed. The spirit of democracy—and with it the system, which can only exist when it is informed by the spirit—may be extinguished. A dualistic abstraction, urged as a gospel, and urged until it creates the reality of dualism, may become the great and compelling factor in human life ; and if that happens the presuppositions of democracy will have vanished. There will be no single society : there will be no common terms of debate ; there will be differences of opinion far too acute for any agreement to differ, and divisions of policy far too deep to be bridged by any compromise.

As we stand to-day, there is no war of classes. It is difficult even to say that there are any organized classes. But there is a war of ideas ; and ideas, when they grip the mind and drink the blood of conviction, become stern realities. The idea of democracy (which is not only an idea, but also an organized system of institutions) is fighting to-day on a double front. It is opposed on one front, as we have already seen, by the idea of dualism. Those who hold that idea deny both the unity of democratic society and the reality of democratic government. They deny the unity, because they see, through the veil of the single society, the deep division of classes : they deny the reality, because they see, behind the façade of popular institutions, the fact of class domination. But the idea of democracy is also opposed, on another front, by another and different idea which we have still to study—the idea of unitarianism, or (as it is nowadays called) ' totalitarianism '. Those who hold that idea agree with the dualists in denying the unity of democratic society ; and they agree again in denying not, indeed, the reality, but at any rate the value and the efficacy of democratic government. The dualist holds that democracy shipwrecks on the fact of class : the totalitarian believes that, in its traditional form, it is vitiated by the fact of party. In his view a democratic society is only a congeries of warring parties, each devoted to its own views ; and on his philosophy the true unity of any society demands an agreement, not to discuss and reconcile differences of opinion, but to eliminate all differences by the common acceptance of a single body of opinion sustained by a single party. The value of democratic government, at any rate in its present forms, thus disappears. It is dismissed as a legalized system of schism, fundamentally inimical to unity ; and a system of single leadership, based on a single body of opinion, is proclaimed in its place as the true representation of social unity and the true form of authentic democracy. Dualism itself, opposed as it seems by its very nature to this absolute unitarianism, may tend in its ultimate consequences towards the same result. For if dualism is reduced to unity by the victory of one of the warring classes, one body of opinion triumphs, one system of single leadership may be instituted, and the whole apparatus of the unitarian State may thus be established.

The ultimate issue with which we are thus confronted is an issue which transcends the difference between classes, or that between parties, or indeed any difference which is merely a difference of parts or sections of the community. It is an issue between two different spirits, two different tempers of mind—the spirit and temper of accommodation, and the spirit and temper of intransigence. The real war of our times is not a class war : it is a war between two mental worlds. From this point of view we may argue that the fundamental difficulties of democracy are not internal, but external. Democracy belongs to a mental world inspired and controlled by the temper of accommodation—a world that is patient and tolerant of differences, accepting them as the necessary ingredients of unity, and trusting them to achieve it by the method of voluntary adjustment. Belonging to this mental world, democracy is confronted by figures, and forces, and factors, which belong to another. First, there is the figure of the guiding and compelling Hero. Next, there is the force and the exultation of group-sentiment. Lastly, there is the factor of new economic stresses and strains, different from any hitherto studied, which demand, or seem to demand, new and non-democratic methods of easing. All these belong, in their different ways, to the world of intransigence. The difficulties which they oppose to the successful conduct of democracy are external difficulties ; and it is under that head that they must be studied. If democracy is under eclipse in many countries, the fundamental reason is the interposition of another world of ideas, which darkens its sphere and blocks its light.

PART II

DEMOCRACY AND ITS EXTERNAL DIFFICULTIES

IV

THE ERUPTION OF THE PERSONAL : THE ROMANTIC FACTOR[1]

§ 1. THE VOGUE OF THE EMERGENT LEADER

ONE of the marks of our times is a new eruption of the personal. Systems and institutions of politics are clouded over. The impersonal principles on which these systems and institutions depend are still more deeply obscured. Men turn for their inspiration to the living flow of personality. Some leader who has burst from hidden and elemental depths commands a passion of personal loyalty. Leadership has always been a great factor in the history of human communities. The deification of the ruler was the cement of the Hellenistic monarchies and of the Roman Empire which inherited their tradition. It may seem a strange atavism that we should now be apparently recurring, in the twentieth century, to a similar practice. But there are exigencies of contemporary life which explain the new vogue of leadership, and there is a tide of contemporary thought which leads on to the current doctrine of the emergent leader.

Among the exigencies of contemporary life there are two to which some reference has already been made. On the one hand, the growth of great populations—particularly in urban centres, where they are divorced from the old outlets of personal emotion—has pushed men in the mass towards new and stirring loyalties, which appear to promise the emancipation of a dormant faculty. A party leader is the immediate beneficiary of this trend ; but if the growing volume of his party, and the rising surge of its emotion, lead him to victory, he becomes the leader not only of a party, but also of a whole people. On the other hand, the recent growth of enthroned legislatures, sovereign over the executive, and seeking to attenuate personal leadership into a shadow, has provoked a reaction of the

---

[1] This chapter was originally published in *Philosophy*, the Journal of the British Institute of Philosophy, in October 1936.

executive, and a return of personal leadership, which have carried a number of European countries to the opposite extreme. The leaders of to-day are not only new outlets for old popular passions of personal attachment and loyalty. They are also new incarnations of an old political tradition on the Continent—a tradition of executive power and executive responsibility—which had been overlaid, and almost stifled, by an extreme form of parliamentarianism.

But the leader is something more than a satisfaction of the personal emotions of a great electorate and a restoration (exaggerated, as all restorations immediately are) of executive power and responsibility. If he were only that, he would be a phenomenon in the world of democratic ideas and practice, produced by causes inherent in that world. He would not represent the incursion of another world. We shall not do justice to his claims, or his significance, unless we realize that he represents such an incursion. He has sprung from roots, and he is grounded in causes, which go beyond the immediate occasions of his emergence. If we are to understand those causes, we must turn to the tides of contemporary thought which run against democracy and in favour of a new idea and practice of the art of political life.

§ 2.   PHILOSOPHIC CURRENTS SETTING TOWARDS PERSONAL LEADERSHIP

There is one tide of contemporary thought which begins with Nietzsche. Nietzsche was not a logical thinker. He was a master of trenchant aphorisms which could cut both ways and might often contradict one another. But he had a general hatred of the slave-morality which was based on the calculus of general advantage, and he had a genuine passion for the master-morality which was founded on the rock of power. Under the head of slave-morality he sets the principle of democracy, as he also sets socialism and Christianity : they all stand for the advantage of the weak, and they all contravene the great hierarchy of nature by which the strong rule the weak. Under the head of master-morality he sets the will to power, which makes a man deploy all the force and resources of his nature and impose himself on the universe. This may seem mere subscription to the doctrine of tyranny ; and it is easy to interpret Nietzsche's conception of the superman in that sense. But if it is easy, it is also erroneous. The superman of whom Nietzsche dreamed was really a new super-species, to be achieved in some future age by the intervening travail and self-discipline of strong and chosen spirits, who mastered themselves in order that their descendants might enter into their labours and master the universe. The ' will to power ' of which he wrote was not a will to power over other men ; it was a will to power over the self, which would ultimately lead to power over the universe in which the self is set. Nietzsche was not an apostle of the national totalitarian State inspired and controlled by the genius of a dominant personality. He denounced the State as the ' coldest of monsters and most frigid of liars ' : he looked to the emergence of a free *élite* which, transcending the idea of ' bovine nationalism ', would guide a united Europe first to the dignity of ' higher man ' and then to the majesty of ' supermen '. But the effect of a philosophy is often different from the intentions of its creator ; and in any case the philosophy of Nietzsche, even if it was not a proclamation of the dictator, was a denunciation of democracy. He saw democracy as a static system, which was content, and indeed designed, to keep men as they were, with uniform rights and liberties which, just because they were uniform, were merely pitched on the level of average humanity. He wanted to see, in place of the democratic form of State, and indeed of all forms of the State, a dynamic surge, beginning immediately with the strong, but ultimately drawing all men in its wake, from the level of the average to the height of the maximum. His desire, in its full consequences, ran contrary to all political organization ; but it was particularly contrary to democracy because democracy was the current form. And the interpretation of his theory was even more contrary to democracy than was his theory itself. His superman, who belonged to the future, and was a species rather than an individual, was translated into the present, and turned into an individual. Foreign to the State and the nation, and transcending them both, he was fitted into them, and made their mainspring. The interpretation of Nietzsche, if not Nietzsche himself, is a parent of the dictator.

The theory of Nietzsche may be termed a spiritualized form of Darwinism. It is a theory of evolution translated from the sphere of biology to a higher and more spiritual sphere. There is a second current of contemporary thought which shows a similar character. It is a current which begins with Bergson, and may be seen flowing, in different and altered forms, in the writings of Sorel and Pareto. ' All morality ', Bergson has said, ' is in essence biological '.[1] In other words it is ultimately a product of the life-force which moves the whole world of creation. In man, and in his moral world, the life-force works in two different ways. On the one hand it arms man with instinct, and creates a primary morality of social pressure which is ' a system of orders dictated by impersonal social requirements '. On the other hand it arms man with intelligence, and creates a secondary morality of individual aspiration, vested with personal emotion and answering ' a series of appeals made to the conscience of each of us by persons who represent the best there is in humanity '.[2] This secondary morality of aspiration is the result of a ' sudden leap '. Individuals emerge ' who each represent, as the appearance of a new species would have represented, an effect of creative evolution '[3]; or, to express the same point in other words, ' life . . . imparts a new impetus to exceptional individuals who have immersed themselves anew in it, so that they can help society further along its way '.[4] The emergent individual —strong in the new impetus imparted to him by life—who creates a new morality, or rather adds new truths to the existing morality of aspiration, has something of a Nietzschean flavour. He is, however, in Bergson's view, compatible with democracy. It is he and his associates who discover the ideas of democracy : who vest them with emotion : who make them magnets for the minds of millions. When they forecast and seek to realize the ideas of liberty, equality, and fraternity, they add a new democratic content to morality ; and that content becomes a part of its permanent substance, because it involves a higher and finer form of the social cohesion at which life is always aiming. On this view, therefore, the emergent individual is not the master of society. He is rather the servant, who ' can help society further along its way '. He is not the enemy of democracy. He is its agent.

---

[1] *Two Sources of Morality and Religion* (English translation), p. 82.
[2] *Ibid.*, p. 68.
[3] *Ibid.*, p. 79.
[4] *Ibid.*, p. 82.

But if the *principles* of democracy, or the ideas associated with democracy, are thus connected with the emergence of ' exceptional individuals ', and indeed proceed from that emergence, it is not equally clear that the *process* of democracy is compatible with the role which such individuals are appointed to play. Democracy involves a reliance on time and tentative effort : the philosophy of Bergson is a philosophy of the ' sudden leap '. Democracy, again, is a matter of discussion and the collaboration of many minds. The philosophy of Bergson assumes that ' masses of men have been carried along by one or several individuals ' : it even allows that ' nature . . . must have intended the ruthless leader if she provided for leaders at all '.[1] The process of the life-force, as it works in our human field and produces our human morality, is not a democratic process, even if it issues in the creation of democratic principles. It proceeds by sudden leaps or emergences, and the motive force of these leaps is the exceptional individual, who incarnates the appetite of life for some new and original form of individuation, some new variation of species.

The theory of Bergson thus seems to be coloured by an aristocratic tinge. Sometimes, it is true, the emergent leaders are prophets who freely arise from the depths ; but it is also true that they are sometimes members of the upper class, or of the intellectual *élite*, who from a sentiment of justice (or, it may be, personal ambition) espouse the cause and express the views of the rest of society. Georges Sorel, while he was animated by the fundamental ideas of Bergson, preferred to find the leaders who would ' help society further along its way ' among the working classes. The middle and upper classes lived on the fruits of the past, and for the defence of those fruits : it was only the workers who could produce a new *élite*, and only that new *élite* which could carry men with it in a new leap into the unseen future. The new leaders emerging from their immersion in the life of the working class would incarnate its ideas and its demands ; they would vest them with the glow of their own deep personal emotion, and they would communicate that emotion to their followers by preaching the ' myth ' of the general strike ; nor would they shrink from the actual use of a clean and surgical violence, realizing that just

[1] *Ibid.*, pp. 241 and 266.

as force was naturally used to defend the custom of the past, so it might also, and no less naturally, be used to secure the conquests of the future. There are additions to Bergson's theory, or transmutations of Bergson's theory, in this philosophy. The life of which Bergson speaks in general terms is transmuted into the particular form of the life of the working classes. The general idea of the emergence of exceptional individuals is turned into the particular conception of the appearance of a workers' *élite*. The notion of the sudden leap is charged with the added notion of violence. In a word, Georges Sorel has added elements drawn from Marx to a system of thought which belongs to Bergson. But the additions and transmutations have not abolished the fundamental core. There is still the personalism of the emergent leader, or group of leaders, creating a new morality of aspiration. There is still the emotionalism which, in Bergson's theory, attaches to this morality of aspiration. There is still the leap, under the *élan* of emotion, and under the guidance of the person, into the unseen future.

The doctrine of Pareto, a friend of Sorel, and one of the teachers of Mussolini, is a continuation and a development of the same strain of thought. It is a doctrine of the *élite*, and of the part which is played by force in that circulation of *élites* which characterizes the life of a society. In the course of history some governing *élite* establishes a social leadership by personal qualities and personal prestige. It seeks to retain its position even when it has lost its title. But the presence of a new *élite*, rising from the depths of society, and carrying a new and energetic belief supported by a ' myth ', impinges upon its position. The social law of the circulation of *élites* demands the establishment of the new *élite* : the conservative instincts of social pressure resist. The demand and the resistance create a state of tension ; and the ending of this state may involve the use of force, by the leader or leaders of the new *élite*, on behalf of the new belief. The personal coming and going of *élites*, and the role of force in determining the sequence of their succession—these are the themes of a doctrine which has played its part in the making of the doctrine of Fascism.

There is thus, in the writings of Bergson, Sorel, and Pareto, a tide of thought which runs in the direction of personalism.

This personalism, if it may be so called, is associated with three other factors—the factor of emotion, which is its natural concomitant ; the factor of the sudden leap, which for Bergson is the leap of life itself, through the individual in whom its new impetus is incarnate, towards a fresh variety, but which may be interpreted, or extended, into the simple explosion of pure and immediate personal force ; and, finally, the factor of the ' myth '—a factor which recurs, in various forms, in all these writers, but which is always connected with the other factors of emotion and the sudden leap.[1] Led by the man ; stirred by the contagion of his emotion ; prepared for the leap and its contingencies of violence ; nerved by the myth— with these auspices, and under this aegis, men can shed the past and move into the future. This may be called a Latin tide of thought, which beginning in France has flowed into Italy and there attained its height and its consummation. Italy has again and again, in the course of its long history, produced great and arresting personalities which have deeply affected its life, and even affected the destinies of Europe. Caius Gracchus, Sulla, and Julius Caesar ; the Viscontis and Sforzas ; Eccelino da Romano and Cesare Borgia ; Hildebrand and Savonarola ; Mazzini and Garibaldi—there is a long list, and the name of Bonaparte may be added to the list. English history is largely a history of the impersonal—of the expansion of precedents : the development of institutions : the slow solidification of a body of law proceeding from the steady activity of the general legal profession, and free from the personal impetus of a would-be maker of codes. Italian history has always shown a more personal character ; and this old

[1] In Bergson the myth belongs to the field of religion. The intellect of man, representing to itself the facts of death and chance, and being dismayed by these intellectual representations, evolves intellectual counter-representations, by means of ' a myth-making function ' with which it is furnished, in order to arm itself against its own discoveries and to nerve itself for continued activity. This is the origin of the various forms of religious myth. But the myth-making function, though it works with exceptional force in the realm of religion, continues its myth-making work in other realms and in different forms (*op. cit.*, p. 168). Sorel can thus assume the operation of this function in the form of the myth of the general strike, by which the leaders of the working class insure and nerve themselves and their followers against the difficulties of the future. Pareto similarly invents a theory of myths, or ' enthusiastic derivations ' (drawn from social facts, but transcending those facts, and based on sentiment rather than reason, so that they assume the form of religions), by which men insure themselves against the mere calculations of inductive reason and nerve themselves for the leap in the dark. The connection of the idea of the myth with that of the leap is subtly explained by Bergson (*op. cit.*, 167–8) : it is more obvious in the theories of Sorel and Pareto.

and historic character still marks the life of contemporary Italy. In a country which has suffered from a long past of disunion, personal figures become the necessary symbols of national unity : in a country largely peopled by an agricultural population, hitherto depressed and uneducated, the leader can find a following which is ready to be led ; in a country responsive to personal magnetism, both in the life of art and the life of politics, personality will carry prestige. It is no wonder that the Latin tide of thought which moves towards personalism has found a ready entry into Italian affairs. It is the less wonderful when we reflect that currents of German thought—not only the thought of Nietzsche, but also the general ideas and philosophy of German Romanticism, with all its zest for the factor of personality—have also found their way through the Alps. There is a German as well as a Latin ingredient in the general creed of personalism.

Before we examine that ingredient, we may turn to one of the documents of Italian Fascism which summarizes, in succinct phrases, the core of the Latin version of personalism. This is the preamble to the *Statuto* (or, in other words, the constitution) of the Fascist party, as it was originally drafted by the Grand Council of the party in 1926, and afterwards approved by royal decree in 1929. The crucial words of the preamble are those which turn on the position of the leader. ' The people recognize the Leader by the marks of his will, his force, and his achievement.[1] The people must receive light and leading from above, where there is the full vision of the attributes to be given and the tasks to be assigned, of function and of desert, and where the only standard is that of the general interest '. But the essential factor of leadership carries corollaries and adjuncts. There is first the corollary of emotion or faith. ' Fascism is above all a faith, which has had its confessors, and under the impulse of which new Italians to-day are vigorous as combatants '. There is next the corollary of struggle, of *élan*, of the sudden leap. ' Fascism has always considered itself as being in a state of war. . . . Removed from dogmatic formulas and rigid plans, it feels that life consists in the possibility of continuous renewal '. The pragmatism of a ' will to believe ' in

---

[1] The Tibetans recognize their Grand Lama by external marks. The Western leader is known by the inward marks of his will and force, and by the fruits of achievement in which they issue.

the faith—a will which proves the truth of the faith by simply acting upon it—is also another corollary and adjunct of the creed. The leader ; the emotion or faith he inspires ; the struggle he leads ; the will to believe generated in the struggle, and the action which follows upon it—all these are thus in the foreground. Beyond, in the distant background, stand the law to be ultimately made and the ends to be finally realized. ' In the ardour of struggle action always preceded law. Fascism is living to-day in terms of the future ; it regards the generations to come as the forces destined to realize all the ends designed by our wills '. This is the opposite of the temper of Wordsworth's Happy Warrior,

> Who, through the heat of conflict, keeps the law
> In calmness made, and sees what he foresaw.

It is not mere opportunism ; but it is at any rate a homage to contingency and chance. But that homage is always involved in the creed of personalism. The personality of the leader is in the domain of contingency.

The creed of personalism, in this stage of its evolution, not only affects the idea of democracy ; it also affects the idea of law. It challenges democracy as a mere impersonal system of many voices—supposed to be blended and attuned, by the method of discussion, in a common harmony of public thought, but really discordant and jangled—and it seeks to substitute for it the personal note of the dominant voice, followed and echoed by the rest. Challenging the impersonality of democracy, it is led to challenge equally the impersonality of law. Here too it asks that the impersonal shall put on personality. It makes personal action precede and determine law ; it turns the general rule into an act of personal will.

The challenge which is thus offered both to the general process of discussion and to the system of general rules of law (two things which are closely connected, and are therefore challenged together) has a long ancestry. It goes beyond contemporary philosophy. It is as old as German Romanticism. Perhaps we may even say that it is as old as the German woods : ce beau système a été trouvé dans les bois. We are thus brought back to that German ingredient in the creed of personalism which has already been mentioned, and which must now enter the stage as protagonist of the drama.

§ 3. THE IDEAS OF GERMAN ROMANTICISM[1]

Romanticism is a word so general and so comprehensive that we may include under it, according to our predilections, everything which we like—or everything which we dislike. It is primarily a term in the language of art and literature ; but it is also a term in the language of morals and politics. If we confine it to the latter of these applications, we shall still find it a Protean term. Originally and etymologically, it seems to signify a return to the Middle Ages and the tradition of their vernacular literature or ' romances '. It thus acquires a note of what may be called ' antiquarian idealism '. The restoration of the past becomes the goal of the future : *antiquam exquirite matrem* is made the motto of life. But a return to the past will not stop at a proximate and particular epoch : it will run back beyond the Middle (or intervening) Ages to the first and immediate beginnings. From the days of Herder and Schelling, in the last quarter of the eighteenth century, the German Romantics who carried their theory into the moral and political sphere began to speak of the Folk. They went back, like the school of natural rights, to original and primary nature. But unlike the school of natural rights, they did not posit a state of nature with free individuals who had to make social contracts before they could form a society : they discovered the given and existing society of the Folk, or tribe, or stem, already united by the personal bond of a common loyalty. In the early, and also, indeed, in the later Romanticism of Germany, down to the twentieth century, this spiritual bond of common loyalty was still held to be the ultimate bond. The biological idea of the unity of a common blood (or ' race ') could only emerge into the foreground with the further development of natural science ; and though the Folk was already regarded by the Romantic thinkers as a tribe or stem, possessing a physical quality of consanguinity, and thus sharing the nature of the family, it was envisaged primarily as a spiritual being, which owed its unity to the *spirit* of a common loyalty.

---

[1] Since this section, and indeed this chapter, were written and originally published, the writer has read with attention and profit the work of a young scholar—R. d'O. Butler's *The Roots of National Socialism, 1783–1933*. The reader is referred to it for a detailed treatment of the theme here briefly handled.

In the Romantic view the Folk is thus a spiritual being
(*Volksgeist*), which acknowledges, as such, a common loyalty.
To whom, or to what, is the loyalty due ? The philosopher
gives one answer : the ordinary man, in his simplicity and his
personalism, gives another ; and it is the answer of the
ordinary man which eventually wins the day—even in the
theory of the philosopher. The answer of the Romantic
philosopher, in its first intention, ascribes the loyalty owed by
the Folk to the spirit of the Universe (*Weltgeist*). God is a
pervading spirit, who manifests Himself in many ways : each
Folk is a manifestation of Him, or as Ranke said, a ' thought
of God ' : the members of each Folk acknowledge Him, in the
manifestation of His nature given to them in their area of
space and their epoch of time, as the common centre and
magnet of their common loyalty. This is a creed of personalism
which ends in the super-personal. It makes the Folk—and
the State in which the Folk issues—into a personal group,
united by personal bonds of common loyalty ; but it carries
this Folk ' back into the life of the universal substance ', and
attaches it to the immanent spirit of a pantheistic universe.
There was a simpler form of personalism which appealed to
the ordinary man, and which could be discovered by the
historian in the cultural records of the early German Folk.
This was the figure of the human leader—the *princeps* with his
particular body of retainers or followers, gathered around his
person in an elementary loyalty ; or the *dux* or *führer* of a whole
people, chosen and followed by it for his personal quality.
Tacitus had written of such figures ; they could still be
discovered in old popular legends and tales. Nor did they
belong only to the past. The leader, with his dynamic personality, was a perennial factor of human life. He was the
core and centre of the community : he was the magnet which
drew its members together in a common attraction towards
his dynamism. The world and its Folks, dissolved by the
philosophers into a fluid play of the spirit, were thus solidified
again in terms of concrete personality. The Romantic philosophers themselves were ready to make their peace with this
process of solidification. The super-personal spiritual force
could be depicted as caught in, and reflected by, the leader ;
and it has thus been said of German Romanticism that ' it
placed leadership in the hands of great men, from whom the

spirit of the whole essentially radiated and by whom it was organised '.[1]

This solidification of Romanticism into a doctrine of personal (and, in the last resort, autocratic) leadership may be traced both in the political philosophy and the legal theory of nineteenth-century Germany. In political philosophy the spiritual Folk becomes the living fountain of an organized and canalized State ; and the leader who incarnates the spirit of the Folk (and thereby the spirit of the Universe, in the particular manifestation which it has assumed in his particular Folk) becomes the directing and organizing force of such a State. Hegel can thus regard the universal spirit (the *Weltgeist*) as necessarily concrete and solidified in individual personality—concrete generally in all the persons who form a Folk, but particularly concrete in the highest and most representative personality. A modern German writer, whose work appeared in the beginning of 1933, has expressed the significance of Hegel's theory in the following terms[2] :

> The highest universality is also the highest individuality. It is in the most perfect union of the universal and the individual that the essence of an historically important personality consists. It follows that the statesman who wills the universal—that is to say, the State—is not only the organ or instrument of the State : *he is the State* ; he is, in the instant of his activity, so thoroughly identified with it, that it is active and conscious of itself in him and in his being. On the other hand, since the State is also, at the same time, indubitably something more than any of its temporary representatives, it is true that even the active statesman is never, in himself alone, the State : he needs the complement, the other factor, that is to say the community of the Folk which acknowledges him and recognizes itself in him.

These are words which cover and illuminate much of the development of Germany in the nineteenth century—and afterwards. They cover and illuminate the legal theory which found in the person of the monarch *der Träger der Staatgewalt*— the bearer of the authority of the State. They cover the career of Bismarck—the minister provided by the *Zeitgeist* for the monarch. They cover the coming and the triumph of Herr

---

[1] Ernst Troeltsch, in a lecture of the year 1922, translated in an appendix to the author's translation of Gierke's *Natural Law and the Theory of Society*, vol. i, p. 213.

[2] K. Larenz, ' Die rechts- und staatsphilosophie des deutschen Idealismus und ihre gegenwarts Bedeutung ' (in *Staatsphilosophie*, a part of *Abt. IV des Handbuchs der Philosophie*), p. 168.

Hitler—the leader whom, when the monarch was gone, the Volksgeist found for itself, and in whom it ' recognized itself'.

There is a sense in which Romanticism is the negation of personality. It is the negation of moral personality, as such personality was conceived by Kant—the personality which belongs to all men equally, in virtue of the simple fact of their being men : the personality which, true to the nature of its own being, respects its fellows everywhere, and therefore respects the claims of others and its own responsibility for meeting those claims. The rock of moral personality—which is the foundation of the moral law, as that in turn is the foundation of the law of the State and the whole system of the State[1]—is submerged by the waters of Romantic theory. Super-personal forces or spirits emerge in its place : with them, and energized by them, there appear the giant forms of groups, communities, or Folks, driven towards constant development by the working of their immanent spirit ; and though we are told that the group exists for the individual, whom it lifts into a larger liberty, we are also told that the individual exists for the group, to which he owes the gift of his life and the debt of his loyalty.

In another sense, however, it may be said that Romanticism is the assertion, and indeed the exaggeration, of personality. It creates new dimensions of personality. It seeks to enrich the world with higher (or larger) group-persons : it insists on the unique and personal individuality of each Folk. Again, it adds a new extension to personality. It emphasizes the idea of *development* : it projects each particular Folk on its own personal voyage of constant becoming and perennial discovery. Law is thus personalized into a matter of fluid personal growth ; and we may see the result in the doctrines of that historical school of law which was one of the expressions of Romanticism. ' For the historical school of law, the Volksgeist is not only the origin and the . . . creator of law, . . . it is also the canon of judgment : only that law is " true " and " living ", which keeps its connection intact with its particular Volksgeist, and has " grown " historically in the " organic " development and expansion of this Volksgeist'.[2]   But the

---

[1] ' A true theory of politics must begin by doing homage to moral obligation ' (Kant, *Perpetual Peace*, Appendix 1).

[2] K. Larenz, *op. cit.*, p. 145.

personal note in Romanticism not only leads to new dimensions and a new extension of personality ; nor is it content with the personalization of law in terms of these new dimensions and this new extension. In the last resort it returns to plain human personality ; but it returns on the basis of a fundamental inequality of persons. The leader who is at one with the super-personal force of spirit, and who can thus ' will the universal ', becomes the residuary legatee of the whole philosophy. He may be the greater and finer leader if he has the sense upon him of his oneness with the Spirit, and of the Universal behind his will ; but he is *primus inter impares*, and any sense of responsibility which he feels is not so much to his fellows or equals, as to the higher being and the transcendent cause which he represents in his person. He may cover his position with the form of popular election, and clothe his acts with the form of popular approbation ; but this formal homage is not a duty, and he is really an incarnation of the super-personal rather than a representative of true and actual human persons.

§ 4. THE PRINCIPLE OF LEADERSHIP IN GERMAN THOUGHT AND HISTORY

The principle of personal leadership which dominates contemporary Germany is not a new and sudden eruption. It has assumed, indeed, a new form by entering into an alliance with the democratic factor of party, and by creating a personal party-following to serve the leader as the immediate source of acknowledgement and recognition. But there is an old substance behind the new form ; and even the new form itself, if we see it under the guise of the old institution of the retinue or *Gefolgschaft,* has an antiquity of its own, and is an ancient corollary of leadership. The substance of the *Führer-prinzip* is as old as German Romanticism ; and in so far as Romanticism goes back to primitive Germany, it is as old as primitive Germany. In Western Europe men have slowly built an impersonal State, acting through impersonal institutions and by impersonal rules of law, but acting always to protect the claims and to guarantee the rights of each human personality. The democratic form of State is the last stage of this building. Across the Rhine the personal has endured ; and it has sublimated itself in a philosophy of personal leadership which makes the leader, himself inspired, the inspiration of his people's life.

There is something here which is different from the antithesis of democracy and dictatorship. That antithesis does not cover the facts, or express their significance. The leader is something more—and also something less—than the dictator. He is the vehicle of something more than his own individual force and his own individual will. Just for that reason, he puts less trust in himself and his own resources. The leader is not, like the dictator, an absolute antithesis of democracy : he may be said to be rather an alternative form, at once like it and different from it—like it, in seeking to serve as the channel of a people's thought and aspirations ; unlike it, in seeking to resume that thought and those aspirations in the single channel of his own personality. From this point of view it may be urged that a truer form of antithesis would be that between democracy of discussion, with a whole people painfully seeking the truth through the organs and institutions of discussion, and democracy of intuition, with a people content to see the truth through the eyes of a ' chosen leader ' who possesses the higher vision. But to state the antithesis in these terms is to be guilty of giving the name of democracy to something which is not democracy at all. The antithesis between democracy and dictatorship may not cover the facts ; but the antithesis between ' democracy of discussion ' and ' democracy of intuition ' only serves to conceal them. There is a fundamental division between the doctrine of democracy, as we know it in Western Europe, and the German doctrine of leadership. The one is an impersonal system which, just because it is impersonal, gives the opportunity to every person of expressing his thought and will, and results in the guidance of national life by the combined thoughts and wills of all persons. The other is the personal explosion of a single individuality, which, though it may allege its ' representative ' character, and though it may actually receive a general allegiance in the moment of its explosion, is fatal to the general expression of persons and inimical to democracy. The impersonal liberates *persons*. The personal liberates *a* person. That is why it may be said, in a paradox, that the impersonal is based on the fundamental rock of personality. That is why it may also be said, in another paradox, that the personal, not being founded on this rock, has to base itself on the misty and impersonal clouds of an assumed Folk-person and its *Volksgeist*.

The general theory of German Romanticism, as we have already had reason to note, has not been active in Germany only. It is one of the forces at work in contemporary Italy. The stream of Fascist ideas has not only been fed by currents of thought which flow from Bergson and Sorel and Pareto. It has also been augmented by a Romantic current flowing from Germany. Italian thinkers have accepted, and added to the common stock, the doctrine of the higher personality of the People, expressed and realized in the person of its leader. The Italian *Carta del Lavoro*, one of the great documents of Fascism, starts from the assertion that ' the Italian nation, by its power and its duration, is an organism with a being, and with ends and means of action, superior to those of the individuals, whether separate or grouped, of whom it is composed '. Assume the ' superior organism ', and you naturally assume, as its inevitable corollary, the superior person who represents its being and gives ' light and leading from above '. In the varied and kaleidoscopic theory of Fascism, drawn together and welded into a *dottrina* during the last fifteen years, we may thus trace a German as well as a Latin strain— a German strain independent of the peculiar doctrine of Nietzsche, and derived from the permanent trend and general character of the Romantic theory of Germany.

But the principle of personal leadership has a longer historical pedigree, and a larger and more mature philosophical ancestry, in Germany than elsewhere. The leader and his following belong to the primitive records of the early German tribes ; and the doctrine of heroic personality is steadily and deeply imbedded in the history of German thought from the end of the eighteenth century to the present day—all the more because that thought has again and again recurred to the inspiration of pure Teutonic antiquity. Nor is the principle of personal leadership merely a fact of the primitive past, or a factor in the modern thought which finds inspiration in that past. It is a principle which is also illustrated in the general course of German history. If the medieval history of England is largely a history of the making of the common law and the evolution of parliament, the medieval history of Germany is mainly a history of the achievements and the failures of kings and emperors. The German Reformation is something more than the personality of Luther, but the explosion of his fiery spirit is a great part of its history. Prussia was made by its electors and kings ; and when Prussia began to pass into Germany, in the latter half of the nineteenth century, it passed into Germany through the spirit and personality of Bismarck. The leader and the following—*Führer und Gefolgschaft*—have played a part in German development for which there is no parallel in our insular history. The great men we have produced seem cut on a smaller scale. . . . Perhaps that is only an illusion ; and perhaps the real fact is that they have had to work in co-operation, or in conflict, with other men who felt themselves to be of an equal temper. . . . At any rate the only votary of Heroes and Hero-worship in the history of English thought was a romantic Scotsman who had steeped himself in German philosophy.

For all its antiquity, the principle of leadership has suffered a change in our times. It has come under the influence of levelling tendencies to which it seems by its nature opposed, but with which it has made its peace. In the past it was only the religious leader who emerged from the depths : the political leader was generally drawn from the heights. To-day the political leaders of the countries which have accepted the principle of leadership are drawn from the depths. They have emerged without advantage of birth or wealth, and espousing or founding a party they have used the popular arts of journalism and propaganda to prove their magnetism and to establish their title. The origin from which they start and the methods by which they arrive can both be acclaimed as in some sense democratic. If they then act, or profess to act, in the days of their power, as representatives of the depths and spokesmen of the people, the acclamation may be redoubled, and their followers may claim that a new and higher form of democracy has been achieved. That claim, for the reasons already stated, is a claim which cannot be sustained. The principle of leadership is not the same thing as the principle of democracy. On the contrary, if the principle of democracy consists in the free expression and the free reconciliation of different views, it is the opposite of that principle. But the matter does not end there. Leadership may be different from democracy, and the opposite of democracy ; but it may still have qualities and merits which make it an alternative to democracy. It may satisfy human emotions of loyalty which democracy leaves starved. It may provide springs of continuous and concentrated action in which democracy is deficient.

There was never, indeed, a democracy which was destitute of leaders. The defect which may be charged against it is not the absence of leadership, but the multiplicity of leaders and the refusal of the led to give to any one leader a continuous enough allegiance. The new principle of leadership may claim the merit of providing a single leader, and of providing that leader with the continuous allegiance which enables him to pursue a continuous and long-range policy. But if it may claim that merit, it also suffers from serious disabilities— disabilities which affect the choice of the leader : disabilities which affect his action : disabilities which affect the eventual succession to his office. Under the system of democracy a reserve of potential leaders is steadily accumulated : their powers are tried and tested in the open and public process of debate ; and the eventual choice of the final leader is determined by the known and regular methods of a constitutional system. The new system of leadership abrogates any system of choice ; it depends on the spontaneous emergence of a dominant personality ; it works in the dark. The continuity of the leader in his office, which is another of the essential features of the new leadership, may affect his action for evil as well as for good, and prove a disability as well as a merit. He has indeed the opportunity of long-range policies ; but he also incurs the danger of petrifaction. True leadership demands a fresh and vital impulse ; and the period for which any one man can give such an impulse must necessarily be measured by a brief span of years. Democracy is wise in changing its leaders, because it secures a continuity of fresh impulse ; it may even be said, from that point of view, to do the truest homage to the nature of true leadership. It is thus ready—sometimes only too ready—to solve the problem of succession. The personal leader who has won his office by a right of emergence can offer no certain solution to that problem. By the very nature of his solitary position, he cannot accumulate a reserve of genuine political leaders from whom his successor may eventually emerge. They would be too dangerous to his power. He tends, voluntarily or involuntarily, to starve the supply of the future, and to leave the succession, at the best to mediocrity, and at the worst to chance. In its end, as in its beginning and its intervening course, the Romantic principle of leadership defeats itself, and fails to secure its own ultimate aim.

V

THE ERUPTION OF THE GROUP

§ 1. THE WORSHIP OF THE GROUP AND ITS CAUSES

THE eruption of the personal is not the only eruption of our times. There is also another, which seems to be its opposite, but which is really its complement—the eruption of the group and of the worship of the group. The solitary personal leader who claims to hold a representative position must find some body or being which he can profess to represent. That body or being will not be an electorate of individual voters. If it were, he would be committed to ideas of his own election ; of the giving and withholding of free assent to his action ; of the possibility of dismissal. Indeed he would be committed to even more. An active electorate is by its nature divided into a majority and a minority part, and the leader who bases himself upon it will necessarily find by his side an anti-leader with a similar basis who opposes his claims and his policy. The single leader who stands alone in the claim of a representative position must find some body or being other than the electorate to serve as his basis. He will therefore evoke some unity—something undivided and indivisible— which he can claim to express and to represent. He may call it nation : he may call it race : he may even call it by the name of class, if the class be sufficiently large, and if it can be regarded as destined to embrace all others in a final unity. Whatever it be—race, nation, or class—the unity represented must be something super-personal. It must be something other than, and something which can be held to stand above, a definite body of individual persons who can express their own views and formulate their own wishes. The person who claims to represent this super-personal entity has a far freer scope for his own personality. He can claim to be the one organ of its views, or rather of its necessities. Directing allegiance to it, and claiming allegiance only on its behalf, he consolidates his own position in the act of seeming to abnegate direct allegiance to himself.

It would be absurd to believe that the leader invents the myth of the group. It would be hardly less absurd to believe that, finding it ready to his hand, he exploits it consciously in his own interest. He may be the pure and convinced prophet of what he believes to be absolute and ultimate reality. But it is true, none the less, that the mysticism of the group is a welcome ally to the personalism of the leader. It consecrates him, and it consecrates his party—no party in the ordinary sense of a section of the electorate, but a body of chosen believers in the unity, the reality, and the transcendency of the group. It may seem a paradox to connect the personality of the leader (and the personal allegiance of his party or following) with the cause of the super-personal group. If it be a paradox, it is, as we have seen, a paradox as old as the history of German Romantic thought. The leader who expresses the spirit of a group which is a person above the persons of its own members is not a figure of to-day, or even of yesterday. He is a figure of hoar antiquity.

When we consider the current idea of the unity, the reality, and the transcendency of the group, we may be struck by another paradox—a paradox which, on reflection, becomes an obvious truism. It is the countries of an imperfect actual unity which cultivate most ardently the idea of a perfect and transcendental unity. Where unity is in the very air, and is taken for granted without reflection, differences are tolerated, parties emerge, and individual variety of taste and opinion is accepted and even expected. Countries of an old and established unity, with a traditional form of State and a generally accepted scheme of law and order, can easily afford to follow the philosophy of ' identity in difference '. They will regard variety as a proof of vitality ; they may even regard it as the normal and natural pattern of life, to which the State must adjust its structure and its activity. Countries vexed by a long process of historical disintegration, from which they have only recently emerged, and of which they fear the recurrence, will follow a different line of thought. For them identity will be something which cannot be found in difference, and cannot even be reconciled with difference. It will be something which transcends all difference and has to wage a constant war with difference. Local varieties become local particularisms which are a treason against the spirit of the whole ; parties become factions which rend the unity of the nation ; classes and their social aspirations become schisms in the body politic ; churches and their claims on the allegiance of their members become secessions from the cause of national unanimity ;

and the idea of individual development becomes the idea of desertion.

It seemed, a generation ago, as if national unification had been definitely achieved in all the great countries of Europe. It seemed as if it only remained for historians to write the history of the achievement, and for statesmen (now provided with the necessary basis of unity) to pursue the democratic method of discussion of differences and compromise between them which the achievement had rendered possible. To-day we are beginning to realize that unification was not completed when it seemed to be. The past is not liquidated so easily ; and the first and formal achievement of unity is only the beginning of actual unification. There is a sense in which we may say that Italian Fascism and German National Socialism are simply new phases of the still incomplete and still continuing process of Italian and German unification. Three causes have combined to provoke a new and vigorous reassertion of the cause of unity. In the first place, the old provincialisms and local particularisms, forgotten in the enthusiastic moment of the first and formal unification, but still surviving undiminished, have come to be felt as alien and irritating substances which must be eliminated from the body of the State. This, in itself, is a mere matter of the liquidation of an internal past ; and by itself it would not provoke a passionate worship of unity. But, in the second place, the newly unified countries have found themselves confronted by general European movements, political and social—the movement of democracy and the movement of Socialism—which might be interpreted as invasions and disruptions of their unity. Democracy brought the conflict of parties : socialism preached the conflict of classes ; and both of them could be regarded as the allies of local particularisms which could now be used as a cover for the interests of a political party or of a social creed.[1] Those who believed in the cause of unity could plead that unless it conquered parties and creeds, thus allied with local divisions, and unless it absorbed them into a single national party professing a single creed, it would itself be conquered and lost. In the third place, and perhaps more powerful and more

[1] Herr Hitler, in a speech to his party at Nuremberg (1 September 1933) referred to ' the party egoists who made a cold and calculated identification of their perverse party interests with provincial traditions of particularism (*einzelstaatlichen Ländertraditionen*), and thus sought to bring the unity of the Reich into danger.'

explosive than any other cause, there was the external corollary
and sequel of national unification. Even if it *were* actually
united at home, a newly united country would inevitably feel
that it had not achieved its unification, or consolidated its
unity before the world, until it had found a place in the sun
proportionate to its new strength. ' When we were disunited,
we did not count ; now that we are united, we must count
for all the worth of our unity '. This is instinctive feeling. It
issues in a collective mood of sensitive pride, disturbing the old
equilibrium of States (and with it all the old States which are
content to sleep in an equilibrium), but rallying the members
of each new State in a new devotion to a new and higher
power of unity. It is in this sense, and from this point of view,
that we say that the history of national unification is a process
which was not, after all, completed in the nineteenth century,
but is still active—and indeed more volcanically active than
ever—in the twentieth. Our hopes were vain when we dreamed
of the consummation of a national unity which would henceforth be content to follow the tranquil methods of national
self-government. We did not know the strength of the national
ferment, or how it would continue to work—without as well
as within.

But there is another way in which men may press the idea
of unity as something transcending, and therefore determining,
the individual. They may not only start from the idea of the
nation, and exalt the claims of national loyalty ; they may
also start from the idea of the class, and proclaim the duty of
class solidarity. The two ways may seem, at first sight, to lead
in opposite directions. The nationalist is ready enough to
claim that his cause is the cause of unity ; but he is equally
ready to insist that the cause of class is the cause of disunity.
His claim and insistence are just if we admit the assumption
he makes—the assumption that his idea of unity is the only
true idea, or at any rate the higher idea to which all others
must be adjusted. But it is obvious that the idea of class is also
a major idea of unity for those who believe only, or believe
pre-eminently, in the unity of class ; and if the idea of the
unity of class be made a transcendent and determining unity,
there will be no intrinsic difference between the high nationalist's conception of the claims of unity and that of the high
socialist. There may of course be extrinsic differences. There

may be differences in the number of persons who are united, or supposed to be united, in the group. The nation may include more persons, and may, in that merely quantitative sense, be said to be a greater unity. On the other hand a class which claims and attempts to be international may seek to surpass the nation even in point of quantity. Again there may be differences in the number of interests which one form of group includes in comparison with another. Here the nation, *prima facie*, is the more comprehensive group ; and including a wider range of interests—more especially all the great interests which go by the name of national culture—it may claim a pre-eminence of quality. On the other hand a class may also vindicate for itself the possession of a culture which is peculiar to itself and gives it a peculiar quality. It may regard itself as equal to the nation in the number of interests which it comprehends, and superior, by virtue of its community of economic status and feeling, in the solidarity with which it supports those interests. The extrinsic differences between nation and class are not, after all, so great that only one of the two can claim to be the vehicle of unity. Both can make that claim ; and both may press the claim to the ultimate conclusion in which unity becomes the dominating and determining principle of human life and action.

It is thus not only the unspent tide of national unification, but also a new and rising tide of class consciousness and class solidarity, which has led to the contemporary eruption of the group and the worship of the group. The liberal or democratic State, which simply assumes the existence of a national society, and directs itself by the policy of discussion between its members, is challenged on two fronts. There are those, on the one hand, who feel that the existence of national society cannot be simply assumed, and that its continuance is incompatible with the free play of discussion. To them national unity is an end which is still to be attained, and can only be attained by devotion and sacrifice : to them the leader, who inspires the devotion and claims the sacrifice, is the only form of government consistent with the end. On the other hand there are those who see no value in any form of national society, whether it be assumed as a tacit condition or exalted as an ultimate end ; who substitute class for nation, and demand for the class the same devotion, and the same system of leadership, which the nationalist demands for the nation. In the triangular contest which is thus engaged it is not always clear which antagonist is opposed to which. From one point of view it may be said that the democrat is so far at one with the high nationalist that he accepts the nation as the normal unit of political organization, and on that ground is opposed to the theory of the high socialist. From this point of view, communism becomes the enemy of enemies, which must be opposed by all forms of State which are based on the idea of national society. From another point of view the Fascist form of State, which has arisen on the ruins of the democratic form and continues to denounce its disunity, may find more affinities with the unitary system of communist government than with any other ; and democracy may thus appear as the common enemy of the planned authoritarian State in both of its forms. From still a third point of view the democratic and the communist State may find that they have common principles, or at any rate a common antagonist. Both of them, if in different ways, pay homage to the principle of human equality ; both of them, if for different reasons, oppose the fervent nationalism which claims total allegiance for the national State at the expense of all other groups.

§ 2. THE TOTALITARIAN GROUP IN ITS RELATION TO INDIVIDUALS AND TO SOCIETIES OF INDIVIDUALS

In this confusion of alliances and oppositions it is necessary to find and follow some guiding thread. The thread which has emerged from the previous argument is simple. It depends entirely on the idea of the relation of the individual to his community—whatever the community may be. It does not greatly matter (at any rate in comparison) whether the community is held to be primarily a nation, or primarily a class. Most of us would prefer to start from the nation, for the simple reason (if no other) that the nation is a great and given fact of history. But we should admit that the nation is coloured in some degree by a class or system of classes, just as we should also contend, in the same way but in the opposite sense, that a class which claims to be the whole of the community (as in Russia) at once colours itself with national characteristics and tends to become a nation. (The development of Russia, during the last quarter of a century, is the development of a would-be international proletariat into an actual national community.) The ultimate issue, therefore, is not the issue of nation versus class, though that issue has its own deep importance ; it is an issue between what is nowadays called the totalitarian community, which transcends and determines its members, and the simple community of co-operation, which has no existence apart from its members and whose purposes and activities are determined by its members. In a word we have to decide whether we start from the conception of individual moral personality, with its moral claims on others and its moral responsibilities to others, or from that of the transcendent personality of the community (however it is held to be constituted), with its total claims on individual allegiance and its responsibility only to itself.

Totalitarianism, with its insistence on the rounded O of the whole society, has a deep appeal to some of the finer instincts of men. It summons the devoted spirit to service and sacrifice. It strikes the same strings of human nature which have always been struck by religion : indeed it may almost be called a form of religion—or of anti-religion. It is something which goes deeper than the mere assertion of unity against its enemies ; and it is more than a negative protest against that ' atomism ' of individuals, and that ' particularism ' of parties, which it charges against the cause of contemporary democracy. It has its own positive quality. It makes an historic appeal, beyond the present, to an idealized past—here to the ancient Roman unity, when all were for the State ; there to the old German tradition of the mystic unity of the Folk. It offers, through the resuscitation of that past, to provide a way of future salvation for those who are weary of the burden of individual responsibility. Vexed by fluctuations—of currency and income, of parties and ministries, of individual and of communal life—men are summoned to an assured stability. They are bidden home from their wanderings—back into the life of the universal substance ; back into the historic tradition of their people ; back into the comfort of community. There is something in totalitarianism which has a positive attraction both to the strong and to the weak—to the strong, because it commands a devotion of service and sacrifice ; to the weak, because it promises the comfort and security of guidance. But paternalism, authoritarianism, absolutism—by whatever name it may be called—has always had that attraction. Charles I could rally to his cause both the vigorous Strafford and the unreflecting Royalist. It would be wrong to say that the only new thing about totalitarianism is its name. But it may perhaps be said, without error, that it only seeks to corroborate an old cause by giving it the support of a new idea. The cause of authority (and with it, of security) is strengthened when it is made to appear as the cause not of a person, or of a government, but of the whole. Each giving himself to the whole gives himself to no person. He gives himself to something which at once includes him and stands above him—his folk, his nation, his class. Immersed in its totality, he finds in its existence the reason for his own. He is content to be merged because he finds himself not only sustained, but also explained, by the body in which he is merged.

The old authoritarian governments, while they relied on the human passion for security, sought also to find their basis in the religious motive. They pleaded some form of divine right, vested by God in his vicar and vicegerent ; and some of the greatest of their servants (among them Bismarck himself) were rallied to their service by this plea. The new totalitarianism has also its religious aspect and its connection with the religious motive ; but the connection is different, and it raises different and graver questions. The authoritarian monarch who claimed a sanctity for his authority was not claiming that his authority was a religion, but only that it was a part of religion. Totalitarianism, in its strict logic, is not a part of religion, but a religion. Professing to be a whole, and to embrace the whole man, it leaves no room in its theory (though it may in its practice, which for reasons of convenience may fall short of its theory) for the area of religious life. It does not seek to find a place or a foothold for itself within that area ; it seeks to penetrate and absorb it. A logical totalitarianism has no room for religion and churches. It may accommodate itself to them, but only on the condition that they accommodate themselves to it, by becoming parts of the whole and serving its purposes. It is true that in this respect totalitarianism is not absolutely unique. Any new political doctrine which claims and receives a passionate adhesion attracts to itself the religious motive and tends to become a religion. The creed of Liberty, Equality, and Fraternity, which swept through France in the days of the Revolution, was a creed which gravely affected religion and the Churches. The Republic 'one and indivisible' implied, if it did not enunciate, the doctrine of totality; and the Civil Constitution of the clergy, which brought the organization of the Church into harmony with revolutionary principles, was an attempt to accommodate religious institutions to the spirit of an ardent and all-embracing republicanism. Monarchism, too, no less than republicanism, has sought to be all-embracing; and the reform of the Church by Henry VIII, if it followed a different direction, was in the same spirit as the French reforms of 1790. But though the totalitarianism of our own day has its analogies in the past, it has also its differences from the past. Just because it is definitely and avowedly totalitarian, it leave less room for religion and the Churches. In one of its forms it eliminates them; in another, it assimilates them; in a third form, it consents to recognize them by a concordat, but still continues to claim a total allegiance for itself.

The relation of totalitarianism to religion and the Churches raises an even larger issue—the issue of the relation between society and the State. In our current English conception we draw a distinction between them. We regard a national society as a general body of different cohesions, or associations, existing for a number of different purposes—legal, religious, economic, charitable, educational, cultural. We regard the State as one, but only one, of the different cohesions or associations in and through which the national society acts. In our view the State is an association, which differs indeed from other associations in including all the members of the national society, as no other association does, and again in using a final power of legal coercion, as no other association can, but which is none the less an association like other associations, and like other associations has a particular and specific purpose—that of declaring and enforcing a scheme of legal order obligatory on its members in the sphere of external conduct. No doubt the purpose is particularly important; no doubt its achievement is the necessary basis and background of the achievement of other social purposes; no doubt the associations which are concerned with those other purposes will be affected, and even controlled, on all questions of legal order arising in the sphere of external conduct, by the rules of the legal association. But the purpose of a scheme of legal order is none the less particular and specific : it is not total and absolute. It does not include or abolish other social purposes ; and the association which is its agent does not include or abolish the other associations which are the agents of other purposes. On this view, therefore, the State can never be totalitarian. It is, indeed, the whole society, so far as its membership goes : in other words it includes all the members of the national society on which it is based. But it is not totalitarian, so far as its purposes go : it is not the agent of all the purposes of the society : it has its own specific legal purpose, which will carry it, indeed, into the fields of other associations which seek to achieve other purposes, but will carry it into those fields only in so far as legal questions are raised which relate to matters of external conduct and are capable of solution by the methods of legal coercion.

It follows upon our argument that the worship of the group, in its modern form, involves two different, and yet connected, consequences. In the first place, the group is made to transcend, to explain, and to determine the existence of individuals. It becomes something above them and apart from them, for which they must live and to which they are means. In the second place, one form or aspect of the group—the form or aspect of legal regulation and coercive control—is made to absorb and abolish the rest. The State is identified with society ; the coercive power of the legal association, extended beyond its legal purpose, is made to include all other purposes, and to serve as the general agent of every purpose. The idea of the transcendence of the group is thus accompanied by the idea of its pure and indifferentiated unity. The two ideas are naturally and logically connected. If the individual ceases to retain his own existence as a being who possesses an intrinsic value in himself, the voluntary associations in which he has sought to find expression and fulfilment will suffer a corresponding change. They too will cease to possess an inherent value and an independent title to existence. They will either be abolished (as Trade Unions, for example, have been abolished in Germany) on the ground that they are inimical to the cause of unity, or they will be absorbed and transformed (on the corporative plan adopted in Italy) into ' organs of State ' which are charged by the State with the duty of achieving one of its purposes under its auspices. It is not merely political parties, or the democratic institutions with which they are connected, that perish or suffer a transformation in the totalitarian States. It is very much more. It is the whole idea and system of society, in the sense of the word in which it signifies something more than the State—something broader and richer than the State—something of which the State is indeed a very necessary form or aspect, but of which there are other forms, and other aspects, with a necessity of their own. If we believe that there are Churches as well as States—and not only so, but also that there are other forms of society, and other associations, as well as Churches, which also serve in their way the expression and the fulfilment of the human spirit—we cannot but realize the gravity of the issue with which we are faced.

The idea of the transcendent and unitarian group—the idea which is expressed in the word ' totalitarianism '—is thus far more than a challenge to the idea of the democratic State. It is a challenge to a whole scheme of ideas in regard to the relation of society and the State. It affects society as well as the State ; it affects any form of State (the authoritarian or non-democratic as well as the democratic) which conceives its function as specific, limits itself to the purpose of a legal association, and recognizes the existence and the purposes of other associations. There is, of course, point and sense in the antithesis which is currently made between the totalitarian State and democracy. The States which confront the totalitarian State are actually, for the most part, democratic. The apologists of the totalitarian State attack them on the ground of their democratic form of government ; and the form of government adopted in the totalitarian State, while it is alleged to be ' pure ' and ' true ' democracy, is ostentatiously the opposite of actual democratic forms. It is natural enough, with such evidence before us, to speak of the antithesis of democracy and totalitarianism as if the issue were a simple issue between two forms or methods of government. But though it is natural, it is erroneous, or at any rate misleading. It is not the form of its government which makes the totalitarian State what it is. A State with an authoritarian form of government need not be totalitarian. What makes a totalitarian State is not the particular form of its government (though that will be generally, and even necessarily, authoritarian) : it is the conception on which it acts of the whole purpose and function of the State. We know a totalitarian State much more by what it does than by the form of government which it employs. A totalitarian State is one which, whatever its form of government and its method of political action, acts on the principles (1) that the whole (however conceived, in terms of race, or of nationality, or of class) is a transcendent being or ' organism ' which determines the life of its members, (2) that the whole is ' integrally realized ', or entirely comprehended, in the one association called the State, and (3) that the State has therefore a complete and solitary control of human life and activity.

Before we turn to discuss the different terms in which the whole may be conceived, we may pause to consider a little further the relation of the idea of totalitarianism to the idea of democracy. Our view of the relation will depend upon our interpretation of the idea of democracy. If democracy is interpreted as the government of will—the will of the people, which means in effect the will of a majority of the people—it seems possible to believe, at any rate theoretically, in the combination of totalitarianism with democracy. A State organized on the basis of universal suffrage *might* claim to be the only association, and *might* seek to exercise total control over the lives of all its members. But it would be difficult for such a State to appeal to any transcendent being which warranted its activity and inspired its will. It would be too obviously itself to allege any impulse of its activity beyond itself ; it could invoke no mysticism ; and it would thus lack the crucial and essential ingredient of totalitarianism. The appeal to the will of the people, however devoutly it may be proclaimed by apostles of the sovereignty of that will, must always be, in the last resort, an appeal to the actual will of an actual people ; and there is no transcendence in such a will. Even if we identify democracy with the will of number, we cannot, after all, reconcile it with totalitarianism. The will of number has not enough divinity for the purposes of totalitarianism.

It is even less possible to reconcile democracy with totalitarianism if it be identified not with the will of number, but with the process of discussion. A State which acts on that process makes the fundamental assumption that individuals, and groups of individuals, determine the lines of its action by the agreement or compromise which they finally attain after freely expressing, and freely debating, the different views from which they start about the lines to be followed. On this assumption there is no superior and separate whole, with its own inherent and dominant demands which have to be detected, and translated into effect, by an intuitive intelligence which emerges to act as their organ and commands and receives a general assent in that capacity. On this assumption, again, there is no given and pre-existent will of the people, which has to be elicited and registered by the method of voting and the election of representatives. There is a simple community of individuals, already organized in a number of groups or associations, who have to think out together, in common and open discussion, the rules of their common life. This common effort and process is the *primum mobile* of political action. By it the individuals, and the groups of individuals, who participate in its activity, determine their mutual relations, their common purposes, and the modes of the execution of those purposes. They determine the whole which is immanent in them and ' actuated ' by them : they are not determined by it as something transcending them and ' actuating ' their wills. The view of democracy which finds its essence in the power of discussion begins with free individuals and free groups of individuals, and trusts them, by the pooling of their thoughts, to construct a whole in which they can live together at peace and in liberty. The whole is their construction : it is a legal association, with common rules of law, which they have made for themselves ; and though it could not exist unless there were a pre-existent society in which free individuals, and free groups of individuals, were already accustomed to act, it is something distinct from that society—something which has supervened upon it, by deliberate creation directed to a definite and limited purpose, and which is operated, for that purpose, by the deliberate will of its constituent members.[1]

---

[1] This may seem pure individualism. But if the line of argument here suggested were pursued to its conclusion, we should discover that it implies two corollaries which transcend individualism. (a) The individuals who determine the whole do not determine it as separate individuals, or isolated groups, from calculations of individual interest or of the interests of particular groups : they determine it as co-operating individuals and groups, engaged in a common effort of thought with a view to attaining and realizing a common conception of a common good. It is this co-operation of all, and not the separate action of

§ 3. THE DIFFERENT IDEAS OF THE TOTALITARIAN GROUP : RACE,
NATION, AND CLASS

The terms in which the dominant whole is conceived by the advocates of totalitarianism are various. They all proceed from the fertile thought of Germany, incessantly vexed by the problem of unity, and constantly impelled to fly from an actual world of local particularism and social cleavage to an ideal world in which the One comes by its own. When the unity of society is a simple fact which is taken for granted, there is little need to speculate about its nature, or to emphasize its claims. When its very existence seems in question, it provokes enquiry and invites assertion. German philosophy, traversing the hills of divided thought, has thus been naturally led to detect some great figure, looming in the mist, which might satisfy an urgent need. In the early history of Romanticism the figure was that of the Folk—the spirit of the Folk, with open arms ready to enfold and sustain. The romantic idea of the Folk was primarily the idea of a common spiritual substance, ' a community of values ', a common culture in which (however they might be divided otherwise) the ' folk-mates ' who shared it were fundamentally united. But this common spiritual substance was also regarded as something more than substance, or rather as necessarily involving something beyond itself which alone would explain its existence. If there was a spiritual substance, there must be a creative spiritual being—a unit, like itself—which brought it into existence and continued to be its ' bearer '. The argument was not impeccable : a common spiritual substance may be the creation of co-operative individual minds, and may be carried

each, which is the determining factor. (b) Before the common effort of thought can begin, it must necessarily be assumed that there is a common good to be discovered. Men cannot co-operate in a common effort of discussion unless they already entertain the idea that a common good exists, and that it can and must be discovered by common effort. In that sense the idea of a common good of the whole is prior to discussion, and is the cause of all discussion ; and in that sense (but only in that sense) men may be said to be determined by the whole.

On the other hand two notes must be added to these two corollaries. (i) The whole which determines individuals and groups to co-operate is simply and solely the *idea* of a common good of the whole community—an idea resident and immanent in the minds of its individual members, and resident nowhere else. (ii) This idea, which forms or constitutes the whole, only determines individuals, as an idea, in so far as they freely accept it and determine themselves by it—just as all ideas only determine us, as ideas, in so far as we make them our own and act by our own faith in them. If we are determined by some other man's idea of the whole, we are not determined by the idea itself : we are determined by *him*—by the prestige *he* carries or the force *he* commands.

and contained in the common thought of individuals. If, however, the argument be accepted, the Folk becomes a spirit and a being ; and we have thus a world of different Folk-spirits or Folk-beings, each creating and each sustaining a spiritual substance or culture of its own. It is no ignoble conception ; but it is somewhat tenuous. These spirits, who move in the sphere of culture, must drink blood before they can speak to us audibly. They must assume some physical shape. It is here that variety of interpretation begins.

One variety of interpretation, current in modern Germany, may be called by the name of ' Folk into Race '. On this interpretation the Folk, instead of being primarily conceived in terms of the spiritual culture which it creates and carries, is primarily and essentially conceived in terms of blood and physical attributes. In a sense this means a materialization of the conception of Folk-society and the nature of the Folk-being. They become a matter of physical rather than of spiritual substance. In another sense, since the factor of race is closely connected with that of culture, and since it can be contended that peculiarity of race is the primordial source of each peculiar culture, the theory of ' Folk into Race ' continues the tradition of a common spiritual substance, but gives it a ground or basis in physical idiosyncrasy. It can be argued that the Folk-being, without this physical substratum, is vague and unexplained. The *Volksgeist* is supposed to live, and to produce its fruits of culture ; but it has no attachment to the solid earth from which life ultimately springs. Race and blood provide the attachment. A Folk which is a simple system of culture, or simply produces a system of culture, has no very obvious or definite membership. Strangers may profess to share in the system, and may claim to be members : in any case culture, in itself and without a precise attachment, is a cosmopolitan sort of term, which may rally adherents indiscriminately. Blood is a known and definite sign ; and a community which begins by being a community of blood, and then issues in its own and peculiar system of culture, is a known and definite community.

The idea of Race has thus a double advantage. It provides something prior to the Folk, which explains its peculiarity and its power of producing a peculiar culture ; and again it provides a sign or note by which the true members of the

Folk may be known and recognized. The vogue of the idea of Race in modern Germany is partly to be explained by the double advantage which it thus offers : it is also to be explained by historical facts and developments. Biological science, with its emphasis on the physical inheritance of natural characteristics, is a contributory cause ; but it is a cause which is not peculiar to Germany, and which, by itself, will not explain the cult of the idea of race in Germany.[1] Anthropology, with its categories of races—Nordic, Alpine, Mediterranean, and as many others as each exponent of classification may find a reason for detecting—is a more proximate cause ; but the study of anthropology is, again, not peculiar to Germany, and indeed the theory which assigns a peculiar virtue to the Nordic race is a theory which originated in France. The real causes which have produced a racial philosophy in Germany are practical rather than theoretical. It is the practical effort to find some final core of unity which has harnessed science to its needs. The formula of ' Folk into Race ' is the answer to an urgent question of actual German life ; ' What is our unity, and what is the sign by which we can know that we are one ? ' To the ardent nationalist, living in the days of the Weimar constitution, unity was not to be found in the fact of a common government and a common constitution. Government was a matter of multiple and conflicting parties ; and each territory or *Land* had its own constitution as well as the *Reich*. Nor, again, was unity to be found in the common culture, the community of values, proclaimed by Möller van den Bruck. In a critical and self-conscious age the very idea of a common culture became a matter of doubt and uncertainty[2] ; and in any case culture was a term too vague, and too comprehensive, to satisfy those who hungered for a definite and intimate unity. The unity of a common blood, proclaimed by a *Volkspartei* which identified Folk with Race, seemed a unity rooted in nature itself— a unity which could not be lost, like political unity ; a unity which could not be shared, like cultural unity. It seemed an ultimate, on which all other forms of unity would follow, and without which no other form of unity could permanently

---

[1] But I remember vividly a lecture on Race, with the recurrent theme of the *Erbmasse*, delivered by a scientific professor in one of the German universities, in the Spring of 1934, to a crowded audience of colleagues and university students.

[2] See P. Viénot, *Incertitudes allemandes*, especially pp. 19 sqq.

exist. The historic memory of the old German ' stems ' and ' tribes ', knit (or alleged to be knit) by the bond of blood, might be alleged in its favour. Anti-Semitic feeling, always latent, and always provocative of the idea of a profound and inescapable difference of blood and breed, might be elicited in its support. Whatever science might say (and German science might give a favourable testimony if the gospel of race were pragmatically established), the exigencies of life seemed to demand a saving idea ; and race, backed by historic memories and contemporary feeling, became that idea.

The transformation of Folk into Race is from one point of view the raising of the Folk to a higher power. The Folk remains a creative spirit which produces the spiritual substance of a common culture ; but it also becomes a body, breed, or blood. In this body the spirit finds its necessary residence ; and through this body it will maintain its spiritual purity, by the mere process of heredity, if only the body itself maintains its physical purity. The racial theory thus makes a double assumption. It assumes that a folk has its ultimate unity in race, and is essentially a race : it also assumes that the racial factor is the cause of the culture of the folk. Both of these assumptions may be challenged.

Even if a folk *is* a race, it does not follow that the culture which it develops in the course of its history is determined purely by the factor of race. No culture develops in isolation. Every culture is an amalgam of ingredients, borrowed (or rather, diffused) as well as native—ingredients drawn from the long historical development of the Mediterranean world, in its Semitic, Greek, and Roman areas, as well as from the more recent development of Northern Europe. The racial genius of a Folk, even if we admit its existence, is only a colouring matter which gives a peculiar tincture to the common cultural inheritance of civilized humanity.

But there is no valid reason for admitting the existence of a racial genius in a Folk. The assumption that a folk is a race is a pure assumption, which is not warranted by any evidence. A folk or a nation is not a race, whatever else it may be, and whatever a race may be. Every nation of which we know is an amalgam of different racial ingredients, which the long process of historical migration has deposited on the national soil. The unity of a Folk is never the unity of a single race.

To assert that it is, is to be oblivious of the simple fact of human movement and migration, and to create an abstraction based on oblivion. . . . We do not therefore, raise the Folk to a higher power when we transform it into a Race. We only give it a body which is even more imaginary than the creative spirit which it is imagined to possess. The elusive ideal of unity has eluded us once more.

Another variety of interpretation of the transcendent group, current in modern Italy, may be termed by the name of ' Folk into Nation '. This is a very simple transformation ; indeed it may be said to be merely a verbal translation, which turns the German *Volk* into the Italian *Nazione*. Such a saying, however, would be an exaggeration. It is certainly true that the current Italian conception of the nation is deeply coloured by German ideas and German philosophy. But words have a magic of their own ; and there is an Italian magic, or quality, about the word *Nazione*. The Italian Nation is different from the German Folk. It is not primarily a system of culture : still less is it a unity of race. ' Race—that is a sentiment, not a reality ', Signor Mussolini is reported to have said ; ' 95 per cent is sentiment '.[1] The essence of the nation, in modern Italian thought, is ' spirit ', issuing in the form of will: ' a will for existence and for power ; self-consciousness ; personality '.[2] A nation, therefore, is not race ; it is not territory : it is not number : it is a personality with the supreme attribute of will, which expresses itself in willing its own continued existence and its own increase of power. ' For us the nation is above all spirit. . . . A nation is great when it translates into reality the force of its spirit '.[3] A consequence follows upon this emphasis of will as the supreme attribute of the personality of the nation. It is a consequence of primary and fatal importance. In order that it may will, the nation must have a will-centre. That will-centre is the State. The nation, on this view, cannot exist without the concurrent existence of the State ; we may even say, if we follow this view, that it cannot exist without the previous existence of the State. ' The Nation does not exist to generate the State. The Nation is

[1] B. Mussolini, *Scritti e Discorsi*, VIII, p. 95, note 19. But this saying belongs to an epoch earlier than that of the new racial idea later adopted in Italy in the course of 1938.

[2] *Ibid.*, p. 72, § 9, *ad finem*.

[3] *Ibid.*, p. 96.

created by the State, which gives to the people, conscious of its own moral unity, a will, and thereby an effective existence.'[1] The Nation is indeed a personality ; but it is a personality which could not exist, because it would not possess its essential attribute of will, unless it were brought into existence, and unless it were continually sustained, by the inspiration of the State.

Two conceptions are thus implied in the formula of ' Folk into Nation '. The first is the conception of the Nation as a self-conscious spirit which exists in the form of explosive will, and seeks to translate its force of will into action. Here the Romantic Folk-mind has become less of a mind, and more of a will ; less a creator of culture, and more a doer of deeds. *Spirito*, after all, is different from *Geist*. But the Nation is still, like the Folk of German Romantic philosophy, a transcendent being, with an existence of its own distinct from that of its members. It is a personality : it is a personality of a higher order (*personalità superiore*) : it has a being, and it has ends and means of action, superior to those of the individuals of whom it is composed. The second conception implied in the formula is that of the relation of this personality to the State. The personality cannot exist apart from the State, and except on the presupposition of the State. Its being consists in the exercise of will ; and without the State it is without a will, and therefore without any real existence. The Nation without the State is a brute aggregate, and not a spirit. There must at the least be a State *in fieri*—a political will already in action among the *élite*, and already inspiring an active sense of unity among the masses—before there can be the beginnings of a nation.

A national personality active in the area of will, and directing the activity of its will to the assertion of its force—a personality so connected with the State that it is fanned into being by it, and receives its will and its effective existence from it—this is the essence of the Italian version of the transcendent group. The nation is simply an Ego, with its own inevitable egoism ; but the egoism is held to be ' sacred ' because it is collective— or more exactly because, in seeking its own satisfaction, the national Ego seeks the satisfaction of all. This is a facile philosophy ; but it depends on two assumptions. The first

[1] B. Mussolini, *Scritti e Discorsi*, VIII, p. 72. But see p. 340, note 2.

is that there can be no real conflict between the will of the national Ego and those of the individual members of the nation. The second is that the national Ego is moving in a bare universe in which it does not come into contact with other and similar beings, impinging on its egoism and necessarily limiting its will. Neither of these assumptions can be readily granted. It is true that the first assumption may not only be made in theory, but also asserted by force. Agreement between the will of the nation, ' given ' to it by the State, in some particular form or constitution which the State has happened to assume, and the will of its individual members, may be secured by the way of fact. But a forcible identification is not the same as identity ; and the egoism of the nation will not be sacred, even to its own members, if it simply imposes its purposes on their wills. In the sphere of external relations the sanctity of the virile affirmation of national will is still less obvious. Such an affirmation is indeed a fact. It may even be, in a given conjuncture, a fact which imposes itself. But the mere affirmation of national will can never be more than a fact, or acquire the dignity of a ' sacred ' right, unless it adjusts itself to other wills, and until it enters a system of wills based on a common recognition of limits and a common respect for those limits.

Even if we admit the existence of a national personality, expressing itself in the area of will, we are thus left with a double problem—the problem of the adjustment of national personality to the personality of the individual members of the nation, and the problem of its adjustment to the personality of other nations. These problems are not solved—on the contrary, they are simply shelved—if we make the national person a lonely absolute which is entirely free to enforce, both within and without, its will for existence and power. We have simply added one supposition to another. We have first supposed a national personality ; and we have then supposed a solitude in which it is free to operate. We may well be led to doubt, when we reflect on the unwarranted character of the second of these suppositions, whether the first supposition is any more warranted than the second, and whether we can really admit the existence of a national personality. Our doubts will be increased when we reflect that the national personality, as it is conceived in Italian theory, is not an original or self-existing personality. It is created by the State, and it derives its essential character of will from the State. The Nation as a personality (and not only a personality, but a ' higher personality ') is thus a derivative fact. It has no inherent being and no original will. In its present form, it is the creation of the present form of the Italian State. Its being is what the Fascist party and its leader think it to be ; its will is the will which is given to it by them. It is a shadow rather than a substance—a State-created shadow, in the name of which the creating State can subsequently profess to act. In the last resort, therefore, the formula of ' Folk into Nation ' presents us, like the formula of ' Folk into Race ', with an imagination. But the metaphysical nation of Italian Fascist theory, with its higher being and its higher ends, is not only an imagination : it is a self-confessed imagination. The racial folk of German National Socialist theory, conceived as the creator and carrier of a peculiar Folk-culture and a corresponding and protecting Folk-State, may be criticized as imaginary, but it cannot be fairly criticized as a work of self-confessed imagination. If in either case a political party has erected an idol, or imaginary recipient of worship, the Fascist idol of the metaphysical nation, created by the State and posterior to the State, is even more fictitious than the National Socialist idol of the racial Folk.

The third interpretation of the transcendent group, prevalent in the scheme of Communism, may be called by the name of ' Folk into Class '. Here, indeed, we must begin by admitting that, at the first blush, Communism would seem to be the very antithesis of the whole Romantic tradition of the transcendent group. It does not, on its own showing, deal in mysticism : it is severely materialistic. The Communist does not start from any belief in the *Volksgeist*, or in the spirit of the nation : he starts from matter, the modes of acquiring material subsistence, and the system of classes which springs from those modes. On this basis he is led to deny the unity of the Folk or nation—so long as it is still distracted by the war of conflicting classes. The nation, in his view, is the product of a false idealism, intended to disguise and gloss the reality of class ; and the true ideal—true because it is based on the essential material factor—is the international solidarity of the whole international proletariat. The whole of the Romantic theory, subjected to this corrosive, appears to be dissolved ; and the solid residuum is the unromantic but poignant reality of economic class.

But Communism, after all, is only a form of Romanticism. It may be inverted Romanticism ; but it is Romanticism none the less.[1] When it develops into action, as it has done in Russia, it displays this character more and more clearly in the successive stages of its development. In the first place, whatever its theory of internationalism may be, and however much it may seek to conduct international propaganda, it necessarily operates, under the conditions of modern life, in the area of a national State. In the second place, and within that area, it sets itself to create the unity which it fails to find, but is all the more resolved to make. The proletarian class (or more exactly a section of that class—the urban and industrial section) is assumed to be the core of unity : the capitalistic class is suppressed : the semi-proletarian classes, engaged on the land or in the professions, are incorporated into the core ; and a single and homogeneous workers' society is substituted for the system of conflicting classes. Finally, this society assumes the romantic quality of a creative being which creates a new culture in its own image and inspires the whole life of every worker. The proletarian class, turned into a workers' society, inherits the mantle of the Folk.

Primarily, because it is primarily economic in its own basis and intention, it creates an economic ideal of rationalized mechanization—a new mode of acquiring material subsistence, congruous with its own unity and necessary to its own unity, by which each member of the society is made a contributory cog. It creates a romance of tractors and power-stations ; it imposes it on the imagination, by the method of propaganda, as the aim of the hive is imposed by instinct on the motions of the bee. Next, and because machinery is not enough, the creative being of ' Folk into Class ' produces its own proletarian art and literature, and its own total scheme of proletarian culture. Here the wheel has come full circle. The

---

[1] Marx (in the preface to the 1873 edition of *Das Kapital*), referring more particularly to the dialectic of Hegel, spoke of himself as having inverted the teaching of his master. ' With him it is standing on its head. It must be turned right side up again, if you would discover the rational kernel within the mystical shell.' But Hegel inverted is still Hegel ; and inverted Romanticism is still Romanticism.

Folk, decomposed into classes, and then reconstituted on the basis of one (and one only) of these classes, has attained a new scheme of composition ; and while, on this new scheme, it is engaged in doing new things, it is also doing the old. True, on the communist philosophy of material determination, it is doing them not as spirit, or at any rate as free spirit, but as a materially determined being which simply does what it must. But it is active none the less ; and it is active as a being which transcends and controls individuals.

§ 4. THE COMMON FEATURES OF THE DIFFERENT IDEAS OF THE TOTALITARIAN GROUP

It is difficult to compare the three idols, or to say which imposes the heaviest burden of worship. Class proscribes other classes ; race proscribes other races ; the metaphysical nation, though it seems to rally all to its service, proscribes none the less all those of its members who are not ' true ' to the national spirit, and it also proscribes other nations. Each form of exclusive absolute makes its own particular exclusions ; and when we make comparisons, we are apt to measure each absolute in terms of our own particular sympathies with the particular elements which it excludes—falling ourselves, to that extent, under the sway of our own class feeling, or our own racial sense, or our own national pride, and thus succumbing ourselves to our own form of counter-idol. Comparisons are idle, and even dangerous ; we shall profit more and lose less if, instead of seeking to establish a hierarchy of these absolutes, we note their common features and the similarity of their results.

Each absolute weds itself to a State, which it makes equally absolute with itself. It finds a person who becomes its incarnation ; he in his turn finds a party, on the basis of the absolute which he incarnates ; he and his party then capture the State, and use its machinery to stamp their absolute on the community. First the absolute (the class, the race, the national organism) ; then the person of the leader ; then the party ; then the absolute party-State, dominated by the person—this is the logic of the development. Sometimes the logic may seem ideal rather than actual. It may be argued that, in Italy for example, the future leader had emerged, had founded his party, and had even captured the State, before he discovered the absolute which he and his party were destined to serve. It is certainly true that there is a large element of contingency in human affairs, and it is no less true that a dynamic personality is often an incalculable factor. But it is equally true that the Italian creed of nationalism was prior to the leader ; and whatever the vicissitudes of his opinions may have been, there is as good a reason for saying that the creed chose him as there is for saying that he chose the creed. In Russia, at any rate, the sequence of history squares with the logic of development ; and the same may be said of Germany. The leader is seldom, after all, the creator of the cause which he leads—though he may deify himself afterwards, or be deified afterwards by his followers, into the position of its creator. He is the user rather than the inventor. He uses the cause invented by thinkers as the basis of his own inventions (the party and the party-State) and the ground of his own position.[1]

The end of the absolute, when it has achieved its development, is political absolutism. But it is also something more. It is totalitarianism. Totalitarianism goes beyond absolutism. The absolute ruler is simply a ruler unlimited by any political constitution standing above him, or by any political organs of government (legislative or judicial) standing by his side. He has a giant's strength ; but it is a strength which belongs to the political sphere, and he does not in his nature invade the field of society. Exigency may sometimes compel him to do so ; but exigency will generally persuade him to purchase political power at the price of tolerating the general play of such social institutions as do not directly affect the exercise of his power. A totalitarian government follows a different policy. The absolute on which it is based must be carried into every domain of life—the social no less than the political : religion, education, economics, the methods of sport and the uses of leisure, as well as politics proper. Any form of group for any activity is a potential rival ; it is a possible magnet of loyalty, which, however insignificant it may seem in comparison with the great loadstone, may none the less succeed in deflecting the quivering point of allegiance. From early life, and in every activity of life, the individual must be taught to

---

[1] Lenin is unique among the leaders of the twentieth century (and perhaps in history) in being an inventor as well as a user. But even Lenin may be called the developer of an invention,r ather than an inventor. He was the re-interpreter of Marx.

point true : he will be enlisted early in the Octobrists or the Balilla or the Hitler Youth : his games, his holidays, the very life of his family, will be drawn into the field of the party, the party-State, the leader, the ultimate absolute. Zeal is more powerful, and more consuming, than power. The zeal of race, or class, or national spirit, can eat men up in its fire as no Leviathan, at his most ' dragonish ', ever can.

Totalitarianism professes to be modern : to be a matter of scientific engineering : to be a system of deliberate planning. But it is an old idea that men should be engineered, and that their life should be made to move according to plan. There is a sense in which we may say that the totalitarian States are living in the sixteenth century.

The Tudor period of our English history had its totalitarian features. One society, one State, one Church, one system of economics controlled by the King in Parliament—these were the ideals of that period. There were dissidents, there were rebellions, there were repressions ; but a ground of unity was achieved sufficient to allow the subsequent growth, from the Great Rebellion onwards, of the spirit which tolerates difference and is ready to consider compromise. There are no exact parallels in history ; but similar causes at any rate tend to produce similar results. Whenever a group of men is shaken by a nervous tremor, it will tend to draw closely together for comfort and reassurance. There were tremors and alarms in the England of the sixteenth century : there are tremors and alarms in Germany, Italy, and Russia to-day. Solidarity seems dearly precious in such times ; its name is exalted, and it carries the day. Men are always apt, in each troubled moment, to see the eternal in the moment, and to find eternal verities in the occasions of the hour. Our own sophisticated age, troubled by old problems, has invented more imposing and high-sounding verities than ever occurred to the age of the Tudors To explain and to expedite an instinctive closing up of the ranks, it has called into existence transcendent beings on which men can suppose themselves to be closing ; it has constructed, in order to organize the movement, hurrying parties, urgent leaders, and a general system of tension. Faced by such tendencies, which are relative to particular occasions and the sentiments which they evoke, we may find comfort in seeking the perspective of history and remembering the relativity of our own human reactions. It is true that the closing up of the ranks in any one country, or set of countries, will tend to induce, by the force of contagious excitement, a similar movement in others. It is also true that a general tendency will appear, from its very generality, to be permanent as well as general. But if we seek the perspective of history, we shall see that such things have come—and gone—before now ; and if we remember the relativity of human reactions, we shall see that they are answers to a particular stimulus, which may not always last, and which, if it is active in some countries, need not be active in all. Totalitarianism has happened before ; and it may happen again. It is happening here ; and it may also happen there. But it will not necessarily endure ; nor will it necessarily spread.

Meanwhile it is good to arm ourselves against contagious excitement, and to ask ourselves, before we too begin to close up, whether there are any occasions in our life which demand it ; whether there is any ' being ' on which we can close ; and whether the open order in which we are moving is not true to the best tactics of social life. For nearly three hundred years—ever since the New Model Army debated the ultimate foundations of politics—we have been trying to develop the open order of a society of free individuals freely determining their common purposes, and the methods of their execution, in the forum of discussion. We have assumed that this society was constituted and actuated by its members ; we have assumed that they could freely debate a number of alternative purposes, or alternative schemes of social life, as well as alternative methods of realizing a single particular purpose or scheme ; we have assumed that they could group themselves freely, in political parties and otherwise, for the advocacy both of alternative purposes and of alternative methods. A wide area of choice, among ends as well as among means ; free discussion of the alternatives ; free association for the purpose of formulating choices and advocating their adoption—these have been the tactics (sometimes clumsily followed, and sometimes sadly impeded by the prejudice of confessions and the bias of classes) which have controlled our general life. We shall hardly surrender them readily to the eruption of the group, and the worship of the group, which is connected with the eruption of the personal.

VI

ECONOMIC MOVEMENTS AND POLITICAL MOTION

§ I. ECONOMIC DEVELOPMENT AND THE THREE QUESTIONS IT RAISES

THERE is still a third eruption by which we are now confronted. This is the eruption of the economic factor, which seems to claim and dominate the whole of our modern life. Can the system of democracy face it, and absorb it into its working ; or must the system yield to the demands of an economic development which is the final and ultimate imperative ?

The course of the previous argument has already led us into economic questions. In dealing with the internal difficulties of democracy, we had to face the problem whether the development of class differences and class-consciousness had not destroyed that basis of social homogeneity which must necessarily be present if men are to discuss their differences in common terms and to reconcile them, after discussion, by some commonly accepted compromise. In dealing with the external difficulties of democracy, we have had to face the problem raised by the idealization of economic class, translated into an absolute which claims a total allegiance. But the idea of class, whether it presents itself as an internal or as an external difficulty, is not the only economic difficulty. There is something further and, as it seems, vaster. There is the whole economic machine—mass-production, mass-consumption, the maladjustment of the one to the other ; the consequent cycles of unemployment ; the whole paradox of a vastly increased control over nature and a rapidly growing loss of control over human life. Democracy may seem an excellent method of the control of human life so long as the issues of control are tolerably simple, and so long as the need of control is not too terribly urgent. Complicate the issues ; intensify the urgency —and will the democracy work ? Must not control become direction ; and does not direction involve the reign of the expert ? Not democracy, but technocracy—or, if democracy, a democracy so qualified by respect for the expert that it circumscribes the area of discussion within narrow limits— this may be the new politics imposed by the new growth of economics.

What are the changes in the structure of economics which confront the old structure of politics with new interrogations and new demands—interrogations so searching, and demands so imperative, that the old structure may have to be modified, or even superseded, in order to meet their stress ? There are different answers which may be given to that question. One of the answers commonly given turns on the growth and accentuation of economic classes, produced by the growth of large-scale industry, and made acutely conscious of their opposing interests by the greater propinquity and the closer contact which comes with industrial agglomeration. If we pursue the logic of this answer, we shall find that it tends to a larger argument about the influence of class divisions than any we have yet been led to consider. That argument goes beyond the view that the fact and the idea of class constitute difficulties for democracy, both internal and external. It advances to the conclusion that they suggest, and even demand, the supersession of democracy.

The old society, with its many local centres, each divided from the rest, and each tending to develop its own local solidarity, is gone. The new society is in one sense more united, in virtue of a common and national scheme of economic activity : in another and deeper sense it is more divided, because the difference between the parts played in that scheme by the various factors concerned (on the one side ownership, management, and technical skill ; on the other side, manual labour) stands out in bolder relief on a scale of national magnitude, and is more readily apprehended and more acutely felt when it stands out on that scale. A national economy thus involves new forms of national division ; and it is not clear that the old political machinery, devised for the old society, will suit the needs of the new, or can meet its stresses and strains. The old parliamentarianism—based on the representation of localities, modified and qualified by the activity of national political parties—seems to labour heavily in a time in which localities hardly count, and in which parties are ceasing to be mainly bodies of political opinion and are tending to become expressions of conflicting economic interests. Some general plan for the new society, more congruous with its nature, and more capable of solving its problems and reconciling its divisions, seems demanded by the law of change.

The growth and accentuation of economic classes is not the only change which demands, or rather is alleged to demand, a new conception of politics and new political methods. Those who fix their attention on that fact, and that fact alone, are drawn either into Communism or into Fascism—into Communism, if they believe that the triumph of one particular proletarian class, and the compulsory assimilation of other classes to it, is the one way of introducing a plan of social unity into the conflict of classes ; into Fascism, if they believe that the triumph of a superior national authority (which in practice, however, may be merely the middle or lower middle class) is the only way to social cohesion and social order. But there are thinkers, neither Communist nor Fascist, who see other economic changes besides the growth of organized and opposing classes, and who feel that these changes demand a method of government at once swifter and more scientific than the method of parliamentary democracy. Economic development has not only presented a problem of the conflict of classes to the political system : it has also forced upon it a chaos of problems—problems which involve all classes indiscriminately, and affect employer and employed in common ; problems which seem to transcend the method of debate (only applicable in its nature to plain data and simple alternatives), and to demand scientific methods of investigation and solution. Debate will not solve the vexed problem of currency, or provide a stable medium of general international exchange. Discussion will not achieve an adjustment between the effective demand of millions of consumers and the mechanical output of millions of producers. Parliament cannot cope with cycles of trade which revolve in their courses over its head, beyond its comprehension and outside its control. A new method of politics, calculated on the model of the laboratory rather than on that of the hustings, seems to be required by a new age not only of complex data, which need accurate quantitative measurement, but also of complicated alternatives, which involve scientific estimates of their probable consequences and a deliberate plan of choice based on those estimates.

We may logically distinguish, as separate in origin and separable in the conclusions to which they lead, the argument against democracy which springs from the idea of ' class ' and the argument against it which springs from the idea of 'planning' or scientific direction. The one argument, springing from a *social* origin, leads to a form of State which is either totally classless or, if it still retains classes, has a no-class or super-class government : the other, which has its origin in *technical* considerations, leads to a form of State which possesses a government capable of discovering and realizing a planned system of economics. In practice, however, the two arguments blend and coalesce ; and the idea of planning is closely connected with the altering, or even eliminating, of the system of classes. To think of altering the system of classes is already to plan, and since classes are rooted in economics, the plan must be ultimately carried down to their economic roots. Similarly to plan a system of economics is already to affect and to alter the existing relations of classes, and to introduce, in a greater or less degree, a different system of classes.

This interconnection is obvious in both of the rival systems which are now disputing the field. The Communist argues that the capitalist class, with its worship of free competition, is inevitably averse from any general plan. He argues that parliamentary democracy is similarly, and no less inevitably, averse—partly because it is managed by the capitalist, and consequently shares his aversion ; partly because it has always been, and still is, connected with a ' liberal ' doctrine of non-intervention in the field of economics. He therefore concludes that the overthrow of capitalism and of parliamentary democracy by a revolutionary proletariat, resolved on the institution of a new and classless State, is the indispensable condition of any planned system of economics. (Perhaps this is but wisdom after the event. The system of planning under Soviet Communism is rather an unforeseen aftermath of revolution than a matter of previous and calculated design. But the fact remains that, even if it was not intended, it was none the less involved ; and the Communist may fairly plead that by a revolutionary reconstruction of the system of class he makes a system of planning possible and even inevitable.) The Fascist arrives at a similar result by a different route. He argues, not that the capitalist class defeats the possibility of a plan, but that the general idea of class, and of the rights of classes, is the general enemy of all planning. So long as classes are free to fight, and to form class-parties for the purposes of war, as they are in the democratic State, there can only be a perpetuation of chaos. The higher idea of the nation must be substituted for that of class ; the régime of parliamentary democracy, wedded to the conflict of class-parties and to the doctrine of non-intervention in its issues, must yield to the régime of a standing national government based on the idea of the nation ; and a planned economy, reconciling the interests of classes and directed to the long-time interests of the whole of society, will then be the fruit of the new régime. The leader of the standing national government, in the strength of the idea on which he is based and in the added strength of the activity of his office, will be the *nuovo principe* of our times, who, planning the unitary national economy which the times demand, and which cannot otherwise be attained, will bring order out of chaos in Machiavelli's style.

The general ground on which the capacity of parliamentary democracy is challenged by both of these systems may be called the ground of relativism. Democracy is held to be an outworn mode, suited to the social structure, the social needs, and the social habits of a bygone age, but not relevant to our own. Its constituencies, its parties, its parliaments, its parliamentary executive—all these belonged to a vanished world of local groups and London clubs, of oratorical combats at Westminster and amateur conclaves in Pall Mall. Its general method of discussion assumed a placid society and an economic system which worked by its own momentum.[1] Many things have changed to-day. In the first place, there is the new schism of the body politic, and the new and deep gulf between political parties—parties which are now of the nature of social camps rather than of rival clubs. If the State should be one—and not many—in order that it may plan and realize a single scheme of life, the democratic State is contrary to that elementary necessity. In the second place, there is a new need of deliberate intervention, to regulate the working of an economic system which can no longer be left to its own momentum, because, on the present gigantic scale of the system, the results of its own momentum are intolerable to all concerned—

---

[1] When one looks back over a century, to the profound agitations of the Reform movement, the Chartist movement, and the Anti-Corn Law League, one wonders what our forefathers would have said to such a description of their times. Each age is convinced of its own crisis, and unconsciously glosses over the crises of the past. Yet perhaps it is better to say ' O passi graviora ' to our forefathers than ' O patientes gravissima ' to ourselves. The ' changing world ', of which we are nowadays so prone to talk, has always been changing.

showing a general maladjustment (here depressed areas, and there prosperous centres of new industries : here sheltered occupations, and there occupations exposed to the full blast of competition) which affects both employed and employer and offends any notion of justice. If the action of the State, confronted by such results, ought to be positive and not negative, the democratic State is once more contrary to an elementary necessity. It is wedded, by its whole history, to a general doctrine of non-intervention : it belongs, by its general logic, to a system of unregulated multiple initiatives, jostling one another in the debate of the council-chamber as they also jostle one another in the competition of the market. In the third place, there is a new and quicker pace of events, a new and accelerated tempo of action, which cannot stay for the old and slow processes of discussion. A revolution has taken place in our methods of communication, physical and mental ; we can travel and speak on the wings of the wind ; emergencies arise in a moment, and demand an immediate answer. If, in such a new world of time, the action of the State must correspond to its movement, the democratic State once more is contrary to an elementary necessity. It produces a succession of short-time governments, each slow in getting under way, and all denied the chance of acquiring that automatic rapidity of reaction to stimulus which comes from habit and practice. It produces a parliament which luxuriates in debate and indulges itself in obstruction : it produces a general temper of mind which worries about the rules of action rather than about action itself, and is more interested in process and procedure than it is in actual performance.

Before we consider the alternatives or amendments to the system of parliamentary democracy which are proposed on these and similar grounds, it is worth our while to examine the validity of the grounds. Three questions confront us. Is the democratic State really rent and paralysed by schism ? Is it by its nature, even if it were not rent and paralysed, pledged to non-intervention ? Is it, in any case, too slow for the pace of events and the hurry of contingencies ?

§ 2. THE FIRST QUESTION : DEMOCRACY AND THE ECONOMIC SCHISM

Each party tends to think itself the antithesis of other parties ; and each therefore tends to express itself in terms of schism. Parties forget that they are complements, and even colleagues, in the general running of the democratic State ; and each is prone to regard itself as the only true 'friend of the people' and its only faithful trustee. The new labour or socialist parties which have arisen in Europe during the last half century have a specially vivid sense of their difference from other parties, partly because they feel the strong zest of new creations, and partly because they feel themselves peculiarly and intimately connected with the people. Whatever is not with them is against them, and whatever is against them is against the truth. Their sense of difference breeds a corresponding counter-sense in other parties ; and this accentuation of party difference, as we have already had reason to note,[1] is a grave internal difficulty to-day in systems of parliamentary democracy. Is it more than an internal difficulty, peculiar to our age, which may be gradually overcome in another age ? Does it mean the permanent appearance of something really external—something foreign to the very nature and the essential method of democracy—which, as it grows in strength, must mean the abrogation of democratic institutions ?

On the strict Marxian view it is clear that not only must the democratic form of State be abrogated, but the State itself, in any and every form, must totally disappear. The State, in its nature, is the organ of the domination of an economic class ; and it is therefore, by its nature, opposed to the pure and unsullied unity which is only to be found in a classless society. In logic a labouring class which founds a labour party, and seeks to put that party, through the machinery of election, in control of a majority in Parliament and thus in control of the government, is condoning the iniquity of the State. Logic demands revolution against the State, the elimination of classes by a revolutionary party (acting, it is true, as a State, but only as a temporary State), and the institution of a classless society in lieu of the State. In practice, however, the way of reform has generally been followed instead of the way of revolution. 'Reformist' parties, based on the labouring class, and professing a general adherence to Marxianism, have accepted the assumptions of the democratic State, and have acted as parts of the system.

[1] *Supra*, pp. 84-90.

But there is a difficulty in being simultaneously a Marxian and a democrat. The more you are of the one, the less you are of the other. If you are more of a democrat, you recognize that your party is a political party, like other political parties, pledged to the same system of electoral vicissitudes, alternations of power and opposition, changes of national will and policy, and the general tacking to and fro which is involved by vicissitudes, alterations, and changes. You learn the virtues of accommodation and practise the art of compromise. If you are more of a Marxian, you retain and emphasize the idea of class—which is essentially different from that of party—even in the very act of joining and serving a party. (A class is a body of persons determined by the common fact of economic status and occupation : a party is a body of persons determined by a common choice of political convictions, and including all who share such convictions, whatever their status or occupation.) Retaining the idea of class, you retain the idea of the conflict of classes : you feel the dividing gulf : you become intransigent in policy : you move uneasily and reluctantly in the area of vicissitudes, accommodation, and compromise. You do not believe in the internal logic of the democratic process : you believe in the transcendental logic of a revealed doctrine, above the reach of compromise and the chance of modification.

It is hard to live in the half-way house between Marxianism and democracy. They are two incompatible things ; and the man who attempts to believe in them both simultaneously—not in parts of either, but in the whole of both—will find himself irretrievably divided, and will be a cause of social division. Democracy has no doctrine (not even, as we shall see, a doctrine of non-intervention) : it is its essence that it is hospitable to all doctrines, and is only pledged to the process of free discussion of doctrines—a process which implies not only free choice between them, but also freedom to make some reconciliation or compromise among them, or to give each its trial in turn. (If it be said that belief in that process is itself a doctrine, the answer is that just as the doctrine of religious tolerance is different from any particular religious doctrine, so the doctrine of political tolerance—which is only another name for democracy—is also different from any particular political doctrine.) Marxianism has not only a doctrine—that, in itself, far from being incompatible with democracy, would be a service to it, because it would add to the riches of its choice—it has also an exclusive doctrine, which, in the sphere that it covers, is essentially intolerant. Since that sphere is the whole of economics, and since economics, on the Marxian principle, determines the whole of life (including religion as well as politics), the intolerance is large and comprehensive. True, it will be an actual intolerance only if the strict logic of the creed be followed : true, again, intolerance will be practised only on the ground (but when has intolerance ever taken any other ground ?) that toleration of other creeds is treason to the one true creed. None the less, there will always be intolerance in the logic of Marxianism ; and that intolerance is necessarily foreign, and even fatal, to the tolerant process of democracy.[1]

There is nothing to be said in theory against—on the contrary, there is everything to be said both in theory and in practice for—a political party which directs itself *primarily* to the benefit of the labouring class, and seeks to rally to its support all those who believe that that welfare should be the *primary* aim of their endeavour. There is equally nothing to be said against the *gradual* transference of undertakings from private to public management, if such a transference produces a greater measure of general welfare—judged not only in terms of the material dividends of the undertakings transferred, but also in terms of the mental and moral energy which they enlist or elicit from the whole community. But there is much which may be said against that trend of opinion, professing to be democratic, which bases its policy *wholly and solely* on class, and directs its programme to *immediate and total* socialization. Not that a community in which the whole of production is socialized, and the antithesis between an employing and an employed class has vanished (only to be replaced by some other form of differentiation inevitable in human society), may not be the outcome of future social development. That is not the issue in question. The real issue is that of the process by which the outcome is to be attained. It is on that issue—and that issue only—that the policy of a wholly class party, and the programme of immediate

---

[1] It is often said that Marxianism, in its strict or Communist form, is a religion. It is more than that. It is a religion of a special form—the convinced form which cannot tolerate or associate with others. The analogy of the medieval Church is sometimes cited. The answer to that analogy is that the medieval Church belongs to the Middle Ages, and not to modern life.

and total socialization, may raise grave doubts in a democratic community, and for that matter in any community.

The frank policy of absolute Marxianism, which rejects entirely the democratic process, and is committed to the rigour of a class war and the arbitrament of revolution, is an open enemy. The frank policy of a political Labour party of the reformist type, which fully accepts the democratic process, and is committed to its consequences, is an open friend. What is neither an open enemy nor an open friend is the ambiguous policy of the half-way house, which at once accepts and rejects both Marxianism and democracy. True and untrue to Marxianism, the policy of the half-way house is almost wholly untrue and subtly and peculiarly dangerous to the cause of democracy. Divided against itself, it also tends to divide democracy against itself. Professing to move within the system of democratic ideas, but using methods and advocating policies which are foreign to the system, it tends to pervert its working and to threaten its survival.

The reason for the development of the policy of the half-way house, which is neither absolute Marxianism, nor reformist Marxianism, but a curious *tertium quid*, is partly theoretical. It is an attempt of the theorist to combine the doctrine of Marxianism, to which he has given an intellectual and emotional adherence, with a belief in the democratic process which is part of the inherited furniture of his mind, but which (just for that reason) has not been submitted to the same intellectual investigation or vested with the same emotional quality. But there is also another and practical reason. The experience of practical politics, in States which profess to be democratic, has convinced the ardent Socialist that there must be something wrong in the current idea and practice of democracy. Universal suffrage has been established. His party is the party of the People. Why has it not triumphed, as it should have done? How can it be made to triumph, as it ought to do?

The simple answer to the question why socialist parties have not triumphed under the democratic system would seem to be that they have not yet succeeded in achieving a clear and absolute majority in parliament, or in providing a sufficient number of adequate and commanding leaders capable of forming a government and of carrying into effect, with the aid of such a majority, the far-reaching policies of social transformation which they advocate. These are not defects of democracy : they are defects of the socialist parties themselves, in failing to meet the necessary requirements of democracy. But it is easy for us all to charge our defects not on ourselves but on our stars—not on our own want of power, but on the system which, we cannot but feel, frustrates our power. In this mood the argument begins to be advanced that there are great and hidden forces militating against the triumph of any socialist party. There is a conspiracy of wealth which perverts the electoral process, and prevents the electorate from returning the verdict which it would otherwise return ; there is a similar but even greater conspiracy which, even if the verdict of the electorate were favourable, would paralyse the victor by the force of social obstruction and the use of economic power. In a word, the exercise of political mastery is stopped by an economic mystery which both prevents its attainment and would frustrate its operation even if it were attained.

It is possible to understand such feelings, and not only to understand them, but even to sympathize with them. All radical parties, whether socialistic or no, must inevitably feel that they stand outside a charmed circle which possesses not only political power but also a subtle social authority—a circle in which all things are managed, and every member of which is connected with every other. ' How can we win, when the dice are loaded against us ? ' A radical party which is also socialistic will have another and deeper feeling. It is not concerned with the simple issues of the old Radicals. It is pledged to large and complicated schemes of social transformation. It knows that, if it were returned to power, it would find it difficult to realize these schemes even in the absence of opposition. It feels that, in actual fact, there would be an abundance of opposition ; that all the resources of parliamentary obstruction would be employed, and that these resources would be backed by the force of social agitation and social obstruction. Once more the question arises, in an even graver form : ' How can we win, when the dice are loaded against us ? '

§ 3. THE MARXIST-DEMOCRAT'S ANSWER TO THE FIRST QUESTION

These feelings suggest a policy of drawing away from the tactics and process of democracy, and of gravitating towards the tactics and the logic of strict Marxianism—but without overt

desertion of the cause of democracy, and without overt acceptance of the cause of strict Marxianism. In the first place there
is to be a class war—which yet is not a class war. In the
second place, and as its outcome, there is to be a revolution—
which yet is not a revolution.

The class war which yet is not a class war may be expressed
under the name of the unbridgeable gulf. In a democratic
system there is of course a difference of parties, but there
cannot be a gulf between them—for the simple reason that
they succeed one another in office, and must necessarily pursue
some generally continuous policy in the general conduct of
affairs. It is impossible that the history of a State should be a
series of discontinuous episodes. The Marxist-democrat[1] is
generally willing to accept this contention : indeed, as we shall
see, he is anxious to press it himself and to urge the need of
continuity for the period which will ensue after the triumph
of his own cause. But he argues that there is *one* point of time—
the hour when the transference takes place from capitalism to
socialism—at which there must necessarily be discontinuity.
This is a grave *petitio principii* ; for it is obviously possible that
such a transference *can* be made over a period of time, and it
is further clear that, if it is to be made by the democratic process, it *must* be made over a period of time, during which it has
been fully debated between parties and successively worked
out in a generally continuous series of majority-minority
compromises.[2] But having made this *petitio principii*, the
Marxist-democrat proceeds to argue that this future point of
time, at which there will necessarily be discontinuity, must
control the present feeling and action of all who believe in
socialism. Seeing the gulf ahead, they must proceed at once
to divide themselves by a gulf from their opponents. The
coming revolution (which yet is not a revolution) casts its
shadow before ; and that shadow is the class war, which yet
is not a class war, but only an unbridgeable gulf.

[1] I have used this term to designate the policy called above by the name of
the half-way house—the policy advocated by writers such as Professor Laski.

[2] The history of parliamentary reform suggests an analogy. There was nearly
a century between the Representation of the People Act of 1832 and the Representation of the People Act of 1918. Cold comfort, perhaps, for those of us who
desire socialism in our time. But the world also gives cold comfort to those of us
who desire peace in our time. The wills of men (and of nations) change slowly.
Perhaps for that reason they change the more surely. What would the result have
been if the Act of 1918 had been passed in 1832 ?

On this basis, and with this forward-looking view to the great and abrupt ' fault ' of a future discontinuity, the strategy of the present is constructed. Two camps are arranged. The assumption is made, on strictly military lines, that ' the other ' camp presents a solid front of capitalist defence which is resolved on no surrender. The other camp may, as a matter of fact, be rent by divisions of interest and conflicts of opinion : it may be so far from presenting a solid front that it is not even a camp ; indeed, if the régime of capitalism is a régime of competition, the capitalist army will be an army which is mainly engaged in its own civil war. But it is natural to magnify the solidarity of the enemy ; and from the assumption of his unity it is an easy step to the inculcation of a counter-unity. The solidarity of the labouring class is accordingly affirmed : it is conceived as a group which deserves and demands the supreme loyalty—as a nascent state which it is ' treason ' not to support, and a present army or ' front ' which it is ' desertion ' ever to leave. Treason and desertion are indeed current words in the exaggerated vocabulary of party polemics ; but they acquire a new and more poignant sense when they are linked to the conception of class. They accentuate the idea of division ; they suggest that it is ultimate and irretrievable ; they propose to the mind a picture of two States—the State which is, and the State which ought to be— struggling for mastery and engaged in war within the community. True the war is still only verbal ; it is a war which is yet not a war : it is formally a struggle of parties, conducted in terms of democracy and waged under the rules of democracy—a struggle for a parliamentary majority which will carry control of the government. But if we get behind form to substance, we shall notice a fundamental change. The temper of war has been substituted for the temper of discussion. Discussion always implies that agreement can be found. The Marxist-democrat is convinced that agreement *cannot* be found. Having arranged his camps, and exaggerated their difference—having assumed that the other camp is united, and having preached the necessity of unity to his own—he naturally reaches the conclusion (which he has already begun by assuming) that they can never agree on any compromise. He has thus kept the form of democracy, and rejected its essence. He has kept the form of party ; but he has altered the basis of its composition (making it consist in identity of class rather than community of opinion), and he has changed the spirit of its action. He has equally kept the form of discussion ; but he has made discussion impotent to perform its essential function.

A virtual class war, in which there can be no compromise, naturally entails a virtual revolution. The essence of a revolution is that it is an abrupt and absolute solution of some problem—abrupt, in the sense that it is discontinuous with the past ; absolute, in the sense that it is unqualified by any transaction or compromise. The Marxist-democrat is a revolutionary, just as he is a believer in the class war ; but he disguises the revolution, just as he disguises the class war. He suggests a revolution which is not a revolution because it is to be conducted by democratic forms. When the hour has finally struck, and his party has finally secured a clear victory at the polls, he proposes a double policy. In the first place the new government, in order to realize integrally the programme for which it stands, must be armed with plenary powers, on the plea of emergency, by an enabling act of the new parliament. The emergency will be there ; the other side (on which the onus is conveniently thrown) will stand armed with all the resources of parliamentary opposition and extra-parliamentary obstruction ; and the emergency must be met.[1] The effect of the plenary powers by which it is to be met is the abrogation, at any rate for the time being, of any power of effective opposition. The abrogation will be made by parliamentary process, and it will therefore be consistent with the form of parliamentary democracy. In essence, however, it will obviously be a mode of revolution. It is meant to secure an absolute solution, which is the essence of revolution. It is

[1] This may be called the argument of the bugbear. It is the quasi-military argument which naturally springs from the idea of quasi-war—the class war which yet is not a class war. You start from an hypothesis of what your opponent is likely to do, guessing his action from the action which you yourself would be likely to take if you were he. You proceed to the conclusion, based upon this hypothesis, that you must undertake corresponding counter-action in order to anticipate the action which you expect that he will take. The only non-military thing about this policy is that the counter-action is frankly announced in advance. This may be homage to democracy. On the strictly military ground it is bad strategy. But it is part of the contradiction of Marxist democracy that it can be neither strictly military nor strictly democratic. It is curious, by the way, to notice that the policy of an enabling act, and of the suspension of any power of effective opposition, suggested by English advocates of the half-way house, is a copy (conscious or unconscious) of the National Socialist policy of 1933.

meant to suspend opposition, which is essential to democracy.

There is a second policy which is also entailed, in addition to the policy of plenary powers and the enabling act. Let us assume that the absolute solution has been actually achieved by means of the powers conferred by that act. We are still left with a difficulty. How can the solution be maintained? The crucial moment of discontinuity has been reached, and even passed ; but the problem which now emerges is that of securing the continuity of the new régime. It may be threatened by a counter-revolution, either undisguised, or disguised in the same sort of democratic trappings which the revolution itself has just worn. Short of that, if we suppose the survival of democracy, and if we do not assume the disappearance or the suspension of its institutions, the new régime will be faced by the ordinary electoral vicissitudes. There will be a general election : the victorious side may suffer defeat at the polls, and the other side may return to power. Will that other side honour the legislation of its predecessor, which was not based on that principle of majority-minority agreement which leads one party to honour the previous acts of another? The Marxist-democrat assumes that it will so honour that legislation, or rather that it *must*. ' The continuance of parliamentary government would depend upon its [the Labour party's] possession of guarantees from the Conservative party that its work of transformation would not be disrupted by repeal in the event of its defeat at the polls.'[1] The doctrine of continuity thus returns, after the moment of discontinuity ; and the sanction which secures its return is that otherwise there is to be a discontinuance of parliamentary government. The essence of the Marxist-democratic argument is here revealed. ' Democracy, if democracy produces a particular result—but otherwise some system other than democracy '. It can only be said that democracy on terms is not democracy. The Marxist-democrat who accepts democracy only when it conforms to Marxianism does not accept democracy. If one victorious party is to be all-powerful, breaking abruptly with continuity and imposing its absolute solution, while other parties are to be bound by continuity and limited by conditions, there is no equality of parties. Once more, if from the opposite point of view, the dice are loaded.

[1] H. J. Laski, *Democracy in Crisis*, p. 81.

The reply may be made : ' All this is but words, and idle words. The facts are there, and they are the iron masters of life. There *is* an unbridgeable gulf between classes ; there *is* a dividing cañon between the régime of private property and the régime of common property. In the evolution of man, there *must* come a point of discontinuity, when he crosses from the law, the beliefs, and the whole system of society and the State, inherent in the institution of private property, to the law, the beliefs, and the whole system of society and the State, inherent in the institution of common property. And when the crossing has once been made, there equally *must* be, and there inevitably *will* be, a continuity of the new régime.' This is plain, frank, and total Marxianism, without any of the disguises and shifts of the half-way house : and it is a plain contradiction of democracy—something incompatible with it, and something frankly hostile to it. If this diagnosis is correct, there is no room for the democratic method or for any half-way policy of juggling with that method. The surgeon's knife is the only cure.

We can only challenge the diagnosis of the plain and total Marxist. We can only repeat that the conception of two warring classes is not a fact of life, but a dogma imposed upon the facts, and contradicted by the facts.[1] We can only repeat that the idea of the absolute antithesis between the State and society based on private property and the State and society based on common property is equally a dogma, which is equally contradicted by the facts.[2] In actual fact there is always a mixed system of property, partly private and partly common, and there are a number of possible adjustments between the proportions of the two sorts. In actual fact, again, there is always a mixed system of classes, with each social section shading into others, and with the members of each section (so far as sections can be distinguished) covering so large a range of different interests and opinions that no section forms a solid and separate block. These are precisely the conditions under which the method of democracy naturally emerges and can operate successfully. Just because there are a number of possible adjustments in a mixed system of property, it is also possible to debate, without any irremediable antagonism and without any desperate haste, what is the next

[1] *Supra*, pp. 117–120.   [2] *Supra*, pp. 114–115.

adjustment which it would be wise and opportune to make. There is room for progressive experiments, for occasional halts, and even for some temporary recoil, according to the movement of opinion and the lessons of experience. This is the natural stuff of the democratic method ; and this is the stuff by which we are actually confronted. Similarly, just because there are a number of different bodies of opinion in a mixed system of society—bodies of opinion which are not coincident with membership of a class, but each of which runs through the whole of society and attracts to itself a mixed membership—the agents or parties of debate, and the temper in which they can act, are naturally provided by such a society. General bodies of opinion, based on the common ground of a mixed society, can agree to differ : they will seek to discuss their differences : they will be impelled, by the common ground on which they are based, towards some compromise of their differences. In a word, just as a mixed system of property provides the material which is congenial to the democratic method, so a mixed system of society (the concomitant and the corollary of a mixed system of property) provides the active forces, and also the mental habits, which incline men's minds to that method.

It is folly to ' ingeminate the word, Peace, Peace,' when there is no peace. It is also a folly to ingeminate the word, ' War, War,' when there is no war. Of the two, the second is the greater. The pacifist in social affairs, who puts his trust in reason and in reasonable debate, may be accused of being blind to an actual conflict of social interests and social wants. He may even be accused of taking a side by the act of refusing to take a side, and of bolstering up capitalism by failing to recognize that the only argument which it will own is some version of the argument of force. But the militant in social affairs is also open to criticism, and to even more serious criticism. He too may be accused of being blind to the actual play of the society in which he lives, by failing to recognize that its true colour is something more complicated, and more neutral, than plain black and white. He too may be accused of tending to produce grave consequences—not indeed, the consequence of bolstering up capitalism, but the even graver consequence of pulling down democracy. If, within the democratic State and under cover of democracy, he seeks to enlist in his service the argument and the temper of force, emphasizing the idea of a war which yet stops short of the fact, he will tend to produce the fact by his emphasis on the idea. Proclaiming war when there is no war, and alleging that the war he proclaims is only an intensified form of democratic discussion, and indeed a truer form of discussion (because more sincere and more convinced), he may find that he has abrogated discussion and introduced a more terrible arbitrament. Whether or no there is a class war in the nature of things, the temper of war can be aroused by the use of language and by the feelings which such use breeds ; and when the temper of war appears, the process of democracy is already at an end.

The problem before the Marxist-democrat is to determine where he stands, and whether he is really a Marxist or really a democrat. If he is really a democrat, his Marxism will be relative to democracy. In other words, it will be one of the alternative doctrines submitted to the process of discussion ; it will triumph in so far as its case is made good in the course of that process ; and its triumph will take the form of an alteration of the mixed system of property by some new compromise peacefully attained between the minority and the triumphant majority. If he is really a Marxist, his adhesion to democracy will be relative to his Marxism. In other words, he will accept the process of democracy when, and in so far, as it is favourable to his doctrine ; he will seek to alter the process where, and in so far as, it is unfavourable ; he will be ready to abandon it entirely if he comes to believe that it is utterly unfavourable. His attitude will be one of opportunism ; and his opportunism will always be sliding into scepticism—scepticism about the rationality of a process which fails to recognize immediately and conclusively the rationality of his own doctrine, or that even deeper and final scepticism which affirms that, even if democracy be rational, reason itself is powerless to solve the passionate conflict of ultimate interests.

The Marxist-democrat who is primarily a Marxist, and only secondarily and relatively a democrat, is really an opponent of democracy, and an opponent all the more dangerous because he professes to speak its language and espouse its principles. He assumes a divided society which does not exist, and in which genuine democracy could not exist ; and he then proceeds to suggest the new terms, and the new form, under which a sort

of democracy might still be allowed to exist in this hypothetical society. We need not accept the terms he suggests or
adopt the form he is willing to allow. What we have to do is
simply to deny the assumptions on which they are based ; and
they perish with that denial. The divided community—the
unbridgeable gulf—the schism which rends and paralyses the
democratic State—all these, as the world now stands, are
dogmas about the facts, and not the facts themselves. It is
true enough that there are clashes of interests in any society.
They have always existed, and they will always exist : their
existence is the cause of the existence of political organization :
their voluntary reconciliation is the aim and end of the form
of political society which we call the democratic State. But
we cannot reduce the clash of interests to the simple formula
of two sides, since the interests are far too numerous and
variegated ; nor can we forget the existence, and the general
recognition, of a common interest with which we know that
they have to be reconciled. Life shows us a multiplicity of
interests, at once jarring and blending, here opposed and
there united ; and it shows us a common interest—a common
respect for one another's rights, and a common consciousness
of our duties towards one another—by which the jars and
oppositions can be freely reconciled.

§ 4. THE SECOND QUESTION : DEMOCRACY AND LAISSEZ-FAIRE

To speak in these terms is already to offer, in advance,
something of an answer to the second of the objections to the
democratic State—the objection that it is pledged, by the
nature of its being, to a policy of non-intervention in the
sphere of economics, and is therefore precluded inevitably, by
its own fundamental principle, from planning any scheme of
economic order and justice. No State can be pledged to non-
intervention in any sphere in which there are jars and oppositions ; and the democratic State, like all other forms of
State, is not only free, but also bound, to intervene in any such
sphere—though it is pledged, by its nature, to intervene only
after full and free discussion between conflicting opinions and
by action which represents the greatest common measure of
general agreement. Subject to these limits, which will affect
both the rapidity and the amount of its action, the democratic State can enter the economic sphere in the same way as

it enters others, and to the same extent as it enters others. If it looks at that sphere before it leaps, and if it only leaps with general assent, the same is true of its action in all other spheres.

But if this is true of democracy in its nature, there is a qualification to be made when we study democracy in its history. Historically, the growth of modern democracy, from the time of the French Revolution, has coincided with a period of economic development in which free initiative, and the competition of free initiatives, seemed to be demanded, and were certainly practised, in every progressive country. It was a period of rapid industrial and commercial development : it was a period of fresh invention and free enterprise : economics escaped the bonds of the old ' State House-Keeping ' (which is the meaning of political economy, in the strict and etymological sense of the term),[1] and became the individualist house-keeping of the system of *laissez-faire*. No doubt there was some internal conjunction between the new spirit of democratic liberty and the new system of *laissez-faire* : no doubt the free political man hailed the free economic man as his peer and coadjutor. But the conjunction was, in the main, an accidental and external conjunction imposed by historic contingencies. The union of democracy with the so-called ' liberalism ' of *laissez-faire* (which was never liberalism in any generous or even true sense of the word) was a coincidence in time rather than a congruity in spirit. When the times changed, democracy—remaining itself, and remaining the same in its process and its spirit—changed its action with the times. As soon as the jars and oppositions of the new economic system became manifest, the democratic State moved towards intervention. In England we may even trace, from the time of the Reform Bill of 1832, a conjunction between a new growth of the formal institutions of parliamentary democracy and a new growth of State intervention in the sphere of economics. So far was democracy from being wedded to the ' liberalism ' and individualism of *laissez-faire* that its further development coincided with the beginnings of effective factory legislation and the general regulation of industry. Nor was

---

[1] The very adjective ' political ' in the term ' Political Economy ' obviously implies the conception of an active State, which brings the political conception of the general welfare of the whole to bear on the acquisition and use of wealth. The whole of Aristotle's *Politics*, wherever it touches economics, is informed by this conception.

this a mere coincidence. When general public opinion, concerned by its nature with the general common interest, finds greater freedom of political expression, it will inevitably seek to satisfy the demands of that interest.[1]

This is an argument which may be challenged. It may be urged that the connection between democracy and a policy of intervention is no less accidental, or even more accidental, than the connection between democracy and a policy of *laissez-faire*. Why should the connection be made a matter of coincidence in the one case, and of something more in the other ? If there is any presumption either way, is there not a presumption in favour of a real and permanent connection—which may sometimes be interrupted, but is always tending to recur—between the cause of democracy and the cause of non-intervention ? Even if the democratic State wishes to intervene, the admission has already been made that it is so much conditioned by its process that it may tend to intervene slowly, and will be unlikely to intervene largely. But will it actually wish to intervene at all, if it is true to its character and its principle ? It is vowed to the cause of liberty ; and liberty, if it has any definite meaning, must surely signify freedom from intervention, for each individual and group, so far as it can be vindicated and so far as it can be enjoyed.

This is an old and vexed problem, with which we have already been confronted. As it confronts us again, with particular reference to the economic sphere, it seems to present an insoluble dilemma. On the one hand the democratic State must be free to intervene—otherwise *it* is not free ; on the other hand individuals and groups must be free from intervention—otherwise *they* are not free. Either side tugs and gets what it can ; neither side is free ; both are left with fragments. The State cannot plan a system of economic order, though it gets some fragments of economic control : individuals and groups cannot fend for themselves, though they are free to

[1] Professor Dicey, in his *Law and Opinion in England*, c. vii., traces the transition from the ' individualism ' of 1832 to the ' collectivism ' (or intervention) of 1870–1900. He ascribes the transition not to the advance of democracy, but to a number of other factors, some of which (e.g. the introduction of household suffrage in 1867) would seem, however, to belong to the advance of democracy. In any case the gist of his book, which goes to show the growth of collectivism after 1832, and its dominance after 1870, attests the fact that democracy is compatible not only with acts of intervention, but also with a general policy of intervention.

wage war, and to call it freedom, in the area which escapes control. There is thus, on this showing, a radical dualism at the heart of the democratic State—not merely a dualism between the conflicting interests or classes which it contains within itself, but a dualism between the whole of itself and each and all of its members. It can gain only by their loss : they can gain only by its loss ; and in either case the self-defeating cause of liberty is bound to suffer.

The dilemma seems formidable ; but it is less formidable than it seems. It is true enough that the democratic State is pledged to the cause of liberty. Indeed it is doubly pledged. It is pledged to liberty in the *process* of its intervention, which must take the form of free discussion, directed to the free conclusion of a voluntary agreement between the parties to that discussion. It is pledged to liberty in the *end* or aim of its intervention, which is to secure, by a common agreement expressed in law, the general framework of rules which best conduces to the general personal liberty of all its members. But the fact that it is thus doubly pledged to the cause of liberty is very far from meaning that it is pledged to non-intervention. The opposite is the case. In the first place, the process of the democratic State enables policies of intervention to be propounded and pressed, by the advocates of this and that cause (prohibition or protection, Sabbatarianism or the censorship of the theatre), in greater volume than in any other form of State. They will not all triumph ; but it is always possible that some such policy, even though it transcends the limits of what can actually be done by law (as prohibition, for example, does), may win a victory. One of the problems of the democratic State is to adjust its process to its aim, and to ensure that the free movement of general opinion is not inimical to the free action of human beings. In the second place, the end or aim of the democratic State demands a constant and complicated intervention, above all in the sphere of economics. The liberty of all, shared equally by all, is so far from being a natural condition that it may be described, without any paradox, as the most artificial of all conditions. It is so far from existing without intervention that it can only be created and maintained by means of intervention. To introduce the spirit and method of liberty into the system of economics—not for employers only, but also for workers ;

not for employers and workers only, but also for others who are also concerned—involves an interference with the natural order which is perhaps greater than any other object could involve. It is comparatively simple to intervene in the system of economics with a view to securing the maximum production of national wealth, or the maximum insurance of national power or national independence. It is a more complicated matter to intervene in the system with the object of securing the maximum energy of individual freedom for all alike, without any respect for persons.

Democracy was once allied, or seemed to be allied, with the cause of *laissez-faire*, because the range of persons as yet covered by its view was small. It had not gone down into the depths : its view was confined to a limited class of employers, independent producers, and traders, which seemed capable of managing for itself ; and the members of this class were given a virtual monopoly of personal freedom—necessarily prejudicial, but not yet recognized as prejudicial, to the personal freedom of the members of other classes—because they were regarded as possessing a virtual monopoly of personal capacity. The suffrage was a limited suffrage : economic independence was the independence of a limited class ; and both limitations were connected with, and derived from, a limited view of the range of personal capacity. No intervention seemed necessary to secure the freedom of a small and limited class, whose members seemed competent, and certainly desired, to act for themselves : on the contrary, the absence of intervention could be held to be the one thing necessary. It may seem curious, and even self-contradictory, that respect for the rights of personality should stop so soon, so short, and at so limited a circle of persons ; but it is a lesson hard to learn that every man—and every woman—is a full person, and that personal freedom, if it belongs to any, belongs by the same title to all. As soon as the democratic State began to learn this lesson, and to recognize that personal freedom was not the monopoly of a section, but the universal right of all, it moved inevitably towards intervention. If the worker was to be a free agent in his work, there had to be intervention with the employer in the contract of employment ; and the measure of that intervention would extend and grow with the extension and growth of the worker's idea of freedom. The freedom of all the members of a community is an arduous reconciliation of many freedoms ; and the greater the reconciliation to be achieved, the greater will be the intervention which it demands. By the same title by which it had abdicated, when it concerned itself with a limited circle, the democratic State assumed full sovereignty when it began to deal with the whole circle of all its members.

Intervention with the ' natural ' economic order, and the planning of an artificial (and higher) system of economic order, are thus compatible with democracy, and indeed are dictated to it by the essence of its end or aim, when once that aim is seen and applied in the full width of its range. On the other hand the intervention of the democratic State will always be a limited intervention—limited both by the process through which it is achieved and by the purpose to which it is directed. The limitations imposed by the process of demo-cracy will best be discussed under the head of the argument of time, for the main indictment against democracy, so far as its process is concerned, is an indictment of the pace of its motion. The limitations imposed by the purpose are more fundamental, and demand an immediate discussion.

The democratic State will intervene only—or rather it will intervene primarily and ordinarily (for other purposes will enter in time of emergency or war)—for the purpose of ensuring the maximum of general liberty. It is true that, as has just been argued, this purpose permits—and not only permits, but also invites—a constant and complicated intervention. To remove all hindrances to liberty at all the points of friction, and to reconcile all the jars of conflicting liberties, involves action no less permanent and no less various—it may even be said *more* permanent and *more* various—than any other object can possibly involve. But from another point of view the intervention of the democratic State will never be positive and whole-hearted. The foot will always be on the brake, and the presumption will always be against intervention, even in the act of intervention. The end is always individual self-help and individual self-determination ; the action of the State, however constant and complicated it may be, is always a means to that end. The State intervenes to prevent an intervention more dangerous than its own.

A large assumption is implicitly involved in such a policy— the assumption that men in the mass, in the name and as the organ of whose opinion the State is acting, are genuinely and ultimately devoted to the right of individual liberty—a right which has, for its other and reverse side, the duty of individual responsibility. It is a high assumption ; but is it justified ? Are men in the mass genuinely and ultimately devoted to a cause so arduous ? If they are, they will colour with their devotion the democratic State which serves the cause, and they will see in its action and intervention a positive quality of service to a positive and exacting cause. But if they are not thus devoted, the question may well be asked whether the whole action of the democratic State is not a shadow—a service on behalf of a cause which is not felt *as a cause* by those to whom the service is rendered. If this be so, the intervention of the democratic State is not only limited : it is sterile. It has not given men what they want, or the thing on which their hearts are set. Proceeding ever so delicately, and with an infinite circumspection, the democratic State has done everything to liberate a capacity and to satisfy a passion which do not exist ; and therefore it has done nothing.

This is an ultimate issue. If we are frank with ourselves, we must confess that there must be a capacity and a passion for the enjoyment of liberty—there must be a sense of personality in each, and of respect for personality in all, generally spread through the whole community—before the democratic State can be truly effective. It thus demands a high degree of general conformity of moral outlook : a general consensus, both about the moral claims to the conditions of free development which each can reasonably make on others, and about the answering moral responsibility to satisfy those claims which each can reasonably be expected to show to others. A sense of rounded and definite personality, backed by a common feeling about the nature of the claims and the answering responsibilities which spring from that sense, is a large thing to demand. Perhaps it can be fairly demanded only in a community which has achieved a sufficient standard of material existence, and a sufficient degree of national homogeneity, to devote itself to an ideal of liberty which has to be worked out in each by the common effort of all. If the problems of material existence are still absorbing, if a sufficient standard of material existence has not been achieved, if the primary effort is merely an effort to live, the ideal of living a common life of freedom—in other words, of attaining a *particular quality of life*—will seem an idle dream. If, again, the problems of national homogeneity are still insistent, and there is no common feeling of fellowship —if some sections of the community are regarded by others, whether on the ground of their inferior education, or on the ground of their inferior stock, or any other ground, as essentially alien and heterogeneous—the ideal of the common life of freedom will equally seem illusory : the mere and bare necessity of attaining the common life itself, apart from any consideration of its quality, will absorb men's attention and effort. A sufficient level of material existence, and a sufficient degree of national homogeneity, are things which men must possess before they can enter into the full inheritance of democratic self-government.

Bearing these things in mind, we can see how, at the end of the account, democracy can still be indicted for negativism and non-intervention. Not that it actually fails to intervene : on the contrary, it intervenes constantly, and in a large variety of ways, to achieve its aim of liberty. But that very aim also limits its intervention. It specifies intervention in a particular form and direction—the form and direction of recognizing claims of persons upon other persons, and making them rights by such recognition ; the form and direction of recognizing the responsibilities of persons to other persons, and making them duties by such recognition. Tied to a scheme of personal rights and personal duties, which in turn is tied to an ideal of the freedom of every personality, the democratic State has no absolute or positive power of intervention ; and whenever such absolute or positive power is claimed and annexed by the State, the democratic system of government must necessarily disappear. It may survive in the form of plebiscite ; it cannot survive in substance. Plenary intervention—whether it is based on the exigencies of material existence, and directed to an economic reconstruction of society without respect for persons, or whether it is based on the demands (or alleged demands) of national unity, and directed to the formation of a common front at all costs and by any sacrifice—requires other instruments, and another temper, than the instruments and temper of democracy.

We may thus confess that there is a sense in which democracy, both in its methods and in its aim, but particularly in its aim, is relative. Its aim of respecting persons (even in the act of intervention on behalf of their liberty, and never more than in that act) is relative to a state of society in which the idea of personality has a statuesque precision, and each person stands out firm and clear in his own existence, but in which, just for that reason, there is a common recognition, equally firm and clear, that all are persons alike, united, and not divided, by that essential fact, and united by it in a common respect for one another and a common effort to express that respect in a common scheme of personal rights. We may express this relativity either by admitting that there may be times and societies for which democracy is not fitted, or by contending that there are times and societies which are not fitted for democracy. It would be a folly to expect that a mode of common life which is the expression of a particular temper, and the outcome of a particular development, should be appropriate to another temper and a different stage of development. On the other hand it would be an error to carry relativity to the length of admitting that democracy, and the democratic ideal of intervention, are on the same level as other modes of common life and the activities in which they issue. Democracy, though it may be like other forms in being relative to a particular temper and a particular development, may also be unlike them in being relative to a better temper and a higher development. Here we enter into the realm of values and of the judgments based on our estimate of values. If we believe in the intrinsic and ultimate value of individual personality, we shall also believe that—so far as we can see into the mist of time—the democratic State has the future on its side. On the basis of that belief, it corresponds to the 'idea' of the State. It is not merely a form, among other forms : it is the norm. If therefore it intervenes in the scheme of our common life not with a stretched-out arm, but with a restrained and cautious hand, that is not its defect or its own peculiar limit. It is a limit inherent in the idea of the State itself, if the idea of the State be accommodated, as it needs must be, to the ultimate value of individual personality on which it ultimately depends.[1]

[1] In the theory of Communism itself the idea of the free society of free men is pushed to the length of ultimate anarchism—the anarchism of a self-acting society which exists independently of any regulating State. But this free society is also pushed into the future : it is not for our generation, and we must go

§ 5. THE THIRD QUESTION : DEMOCRACY AND THE URGENCY OF
ECONOMIC PROBLEMS : THE AUTHORITARIAN ANSWER

A third objection which may be made to democracy when
it enters the sphere of economics (though it is not an objection
peculiar to its action in that sphere) is that it moves too slowly
for the pace of events and the hurry of contingencies. This is
the argument of time ; and it turns on the process of democracy. Considered in its essence, and according to its own logic,
the democratic process already involves a double delay of
action—the delay involved during the period in which different
policies are formulated and submitted to the electorate ; and
the delay involved during the period in which the eventual
compromise between majority and minority is slowly con-
cluded by a long and arduous trial of parliamentary strength.
Considered as it actually works, under the practical difficulties
which are added to its essence—multiple parties, embarrassed
and short-time governments, the luxuriance of opposition in
parliament and outside—the democratic State seems condemned, at the best to slow motion, except for fitful spasms
of activity due to some driving personality or some sudden
eruption of a popular demand, and at the worst to total
inaction. When there is motion, it is not steady : and in times
of the gravest issues, motion may simply stop. Embarrassed by
opposition, the government is forced too often to struggle for
mere existence, ' et propter vitam vivendi perdere causas '.

Meanwhile the pace of events and the urgency of issues have
been quickened for our generation—partly by revolutions in
physical transport and mental communication ; partly by the
rapidity of general economic development and the swift
accumulation of new economic problems ; partly by a closer
interconnection of States, which has multiplied the issues
impinging on each and increased the need of general

through a purgatory in order that our descendants may enter into paradise. The
democrat is an idealist not of the future, but of the present. He is also the practical
idealist, who believes that, so long as human nature remains the same, there will
necessarily be jars and oppositions, and therefore a regulating State. He therefore
seeks to make the regulating State, here and now (because it will always be
with us, and there is no virtue in waiting for a future in which it will have withered
away), compatible with human liberty. After all, if liberty be the ultimate good,
and man by his nature is free, we are guilty of treason to the cause of liberty, and
we are using the men of our generation merely as tools to an end beyond themselves, if we sacrifice the liberty which they might actually enjoy to some supposed
greater liberty which their descendants may possibly enjoy. To undergo material
privation for the sake of the future is one thing. To undergo *spiritual* privation is
another.

expedition ; partly by the growth of a general temper, consequent on all these changes but accentuating their effects, which
demands quick solutions and immediate answers. More than
ever, as we reflect upon these facts, it may seem as if the
democratic process were antiquated. In the mere pace of its
action, as well as in the nature of its institutions, the democratic State may be accused of being an out-worn mode, relative
to a by-gone age.[1] It is government by ' the word ', suited to
a slow and deliberate age which loved, and could afford to love,
the mere process of deliberation. When government by ' the
deed ' and the ' hammer-stroke ' is necessary, it ceases to count.

The argument of ' time ', and ' pressure ', and ' urgency ',
is nothing new to our age. It is one of the ' idols ' or illusions
to which men's minds are prone, and by which they seek to
escape from the anxious and racking process of deliberation.
Magnifying the particularity of the occasion, and the peculiarity of its urgency, we precipitate issues and resort to short
cuts. Urgency is often real ; but there is also a fallacy of
urgency—a self-contradictory belief that urgency is a chronic
and permanent condition—which readily besets the mind, and
issues in the idea of a standing emergency. The idea of the
standing emergency is a recurrent idea in politics. It is the
standing temptation both of governments and of ardent
reformers. It encourages governments to substitute the method
of dictation for the process of deliberation. In emergency
action must come first, and deliberation, if it comes at all,
must follow on the heels of action. Similarly it encourages
the ardent reformer to substitute the method of revolution
for the process of persuasion. Once more, if from the opposite
point of view, immediate action must be the answer to the
immediate pressure of emergency.

The argument of time and the plea of urgency were used
by the early Stuarts to justify the rapid use of the royal prerogative, for the restraint and direction of trade, in preference
to the slow methods of parliamentary deliberation.[2] The

---

[1] See above, p. 169, p. 172.

[2] Whitelocke states and then answers the plea in the debate on impositions
(1610). If a duty is levied by another country on English traders, so he states the
plea, ' the counterpose is, to set on the like here upon the subjects of that prince ;
which policy, if it be not speedily executed but stayed until a parliament, may
in the meantime prove vain and idle, and much damage may be sustained that
cannot afterwards be remedied.' But he instantly follows this statement of the
plea by its answer. ' This strain of policy maketh nothing *to the point of right*.'

same argument and the same plea are used in the theory of contemporary Fascism. Upon a short view it is obvious that time is saved by the suspension of debate and the supersession —or, short of that, the drastic modification—of parliamentary methods. Even on a long view it must be conceded that there are some issues—grave and urgent at the moment, but belonging only to the moment—which may be permanently solved, and had therefore better be solved, by rapid action taken at the moment of their emergence. But if we take a long view in regard to those issues which are at once insistent and permanent—the issue of unemployment, for example, or the still broader issue of the general organization of national industry and the general conduct of national trade—it is far from clear that time can be saved, and it may even be argued that time will be lost, by the supersession of the process of electoral and parliamentary debate. The real issues which vex political life have this double quality of insistence and permanence. Because they are insistent, they seem to demand immediate solution. Because they are permanent, any solution —or rather, any immediate solution—will only bring them up again in a new form. If attention is paid only to the quality of insistence, and if the apparent need of immediate solution is alone regarded, the first steps are easy enough. Some particular and positive policy of solution is enthroned, either by acclamation or by a *coup d'état*. The party behind the policy takes command : it eliminates other parties, because they are mere negatives to its own positivism and obstructive brakes on its own rapidity : it destroys opposition, abolishes debate (except within its own ranks, and within the limits of its own formulas), and proceeds by pure unilateral action. So far, motion is simple ; but then there comes a check. The very vacuum which has been created proves to be an obstruction. New forms of the insistent problems arise, not only because those problems are always permanent as well as insistent, but also because any attempted solution will always—merely of itself, and purely by the alteration of conditions which it has itself produced—produce some new sort of problem. Confronted by these difficulties, the solitary party finds itself alone in the vacuum it has created. There are no sign-posts and danger signals. There are no other parties which can collaborate with it by indicating—as they could when the party was climbing to power and formulating its original policy—what other views can be taken of the difficulties and what other policies can be proposed for their solution. The solitary party, and in the last resort its solitary leader, thrown back on native and elementary resources, can only attempt experiments by the crude method of trial and error. There is no rapidity in that method. The path of error has to be retraced as slowly as may be, in order that the error may not be too obvious. The path of trial itself has to be trodden slowly, and in doubt, because it may prove to be the path of error. Even if trials are rapid, and even if errors are rapidly repaired, the total progress may be slow. The history of contemporary dictatorships shows more suddenness than speed.

The bright initial speed of non-democratic methods has its attraction. But speed is not everything, even in an age so bemused by speed, and so enamoured of speed, as our own. There may be a price to be paid for speed which men will not readily offer. Fox once said that he would not barter English trade for Irish liberty : ' that is not the price I would pay, nor is this the thing that I would purchase.' Fascism proposes a barter of civic liberty for executive speed. We may confess that executive speed may well be a thing worth purchasing, especially in great issues of the common life, when grievances and anxieties press heavily ; but even so the price must be reasonable, and the thing must be genuine. There is the less need to pay the heavy price which Fascism demands, since the commodity which it offers seems itself to be dubious. If Fascism starts with a bright speed, it does not continue at the same pace. Its initial speed is due to the very democratic method against which it protests : it can act quickly because its leaders start with a knowledge, which only democratic institutions can give, of the currents of opinion and the trends of feeling in which, and on which, they have to act. The further it recedes from its beginnings, the more it loses this initial advantage, which was always extraneous and borrowed, and the more it is condemned to slow navigation along an uncharted course. Not only do the issues prove to be permanent which at first seemed merely insistent, and therefore capable of some immediate and final solution. There is something more than that.

The issues of the common life do not exist in themselves, or

merely as ' things '—things which can be done, and then put
away. They exist in persons : they are rooted and grounded
in opinions and feelings. Indeed it may even be said that the
real issues *are* opinions and feelings. The ' reorganization of
industry ' is really the reorganization of human beings, the
re-direction of their opinions and feelings. The action of
government is fundamentally psychological. It is not a
mechanical construction, or reconstruction, of objects : it is a
psychological adjustment of the opinions and sentiments of
human ' subjects ', or, more exactly, it is a constant readjustment, an unending reconciliation. These opinions and sentiments—particularly the sentiments—are not merely passive.
They cannot be altogether, or even in any large measure,
created, inspired, and directed at will. However greatly the
art of propaganda may be developed, there will always be a
large area of unbidden and uninspired sentiments, which are
the natural and spontaneous reactions of individual men and
women to the pressure or stimulus of the ordinary needs and
desires of their lives. This area of unbidden and uninspired
sentiments, and of opinions connected with these sentiments,
is a vital datum of government, and the vital problem of
government. It presents the real issues ; and no government
can deal promptly with those real issues, or indeed deal with
them at all in any way likely to be successful, unless it is aware,
by knowledge and not by guess, of the area in which it is
moving. A government is in the dark about the issues with
which it is concerned, unless it knows at first hand the opinions
and the sentiments which constitute the core of those issues,
and unless it constantly renews its knowledge to meet the
constant renewal of these opinions and sentiments. This is a
fundamental justification of the democratic process. It is also
a fundamental reason for believing that, merely on the ground
of time and speed, the democratic process will in the long run,
and on a long view, prove its efficiency.

§ 6. THE REVOLUTIONARY'S ANSWER TO THE THIRD QUESTION

The argument of time and the plea of emergency may be
pressed not only by governments, but also by the opponents of
governments. ' Time ' and ' emergency ' can support the
cause of revolution as well as the cause of high prerogative.
It may even be said that they suit the cause of revolution

best, and that the Fascist, after all, is simply a crowned revolutionary, perpetuating the temper and the logic of revolution. Certainly the idea of the desperate hurry, and the strong sense of emergency, are strongly entrenched in the mind of the Marxist-democrat. The word ' immediate ' is common in his vocabulary. His use of the word, and his insistence on the idea, are connected with his theory of ' the point of discontinuity '. Believing, as we have already noticed, that a system of private property and a system of common property are opponents, which cannot co-exist, he also believes that there cannot be any process of evolution from the one to the other —any period of gradual transition during which the one is increasingly mixed with elements of the other. He is thus led, as we have also noticed, to assume the necessity of some abrupt and sudden transformation, which—whenever it comes, and however slow it may be in coming—must itself, in the moment of its coming, be discontinuous. But it is an easy leap from the notion of discontinuity to the notion of immediacy. If change, whenever it comes, must be discontinuous, why should it not come quickly and be made immediately ? The greater the benefit of the change, the less should it be delayed. Since the surgeon is needed, and the methods of the physician are not available, the surgeon had better be summoned at once.

Such an argument, in its pure form, is based on assumptions so obviously untrue to the actual facts that it does not require an answer. Private property and common property *can* co-exist : and it is therefore possible to conceive a period of gradual transition from a system mainly based on the one to a system mainly, or even exclusively, based on the other. The transference to a system of general social ownership need not, in its nature, be achieved *per saltum* : it is not, in its nature, unique, or totally different from other forms of social change and modification. It is a form of social change which, like other and similar forms, is compatible with the ordinary methods and process of democracy : it is a change in degree and not in kind, which permits discussion about the next degree of social ownership to be introduced and the successive stages by which successive degrees can best be attained.

There is, however, another line of argument which presents more serious difficulties. Admitting that the transformation of property, in its own nature and in the abstract, is an ordinary form of social change, the social reformer may still feel and contend that in its concomitants, and in the feelings which it excites, this particular form of change is peculiar and peculiarly arduous. If opinions and sentiments are the real core of political issues, here is an issue with a hard and bitter core. At each stage, the opinions and sentiments gathered on the side of private property stand tenaciously and obstinately on the defensive, and delay any change till the last possible moment : at each stage, the opinions and sentiments gathered on the side of social ownership, whatever their strength, find themselves thwarted and baulked. Democracy may not be capitalistic, in the sense that it is managed and manipulated by the owners of capital ; but it seems, none the less, to play into the hands of capitalism, in the sense that its slow process of debate, and the methods of lingering obstruction which it provides, give a definite advantage to the defensive, and paralyse the strategy of advance.

Every reformer, whatever the issue of reform and wherever it may be debated (in a club, in a society, or on a local council, no less than in a general election or in parliament) must necessarily feel a sense of baulked and thwarted ardour. It is the penalty of his cause ; and it is a penalty generally exacted. Men rally readily to the *status quo* ; and when pecuniary motives are added to that instinctive conservatism which sanctifies vested interests even for those who have no private interest in their defence, the way to change is doubly blocked. It is always easier to object than it is to suggest ; and the rules of procedure, from the standing orders of a club to those standing orders of the State which we call ' the Constitution ', are readily invoked in favour of objection. The social reformer who seeks to alter the system of property undergoes a common fate ; and his cause only differs from others in the peculiar degree to which pecuniary interest nerves opposition to his policy. Most reforms affect some body of pecuniary interest ; most reforms tend to be obstructed, delayed, or even thwarted, by those who feel their interests affected. We are thus confronted by a general problem, which is not peculiar to policies of socialization, though it may be peculiarly acute in regard to such policies. Do the institutions and the methods of democracy tend to favour those who oppose reform at the cost of

those who propose it ? Do they give an advantage to the
general cause of vested interests, and, behind that, to the still
more dubious cause of mere pecuniary interest ? If this is
really the case, the argument of time assumes a serious character. Reform will be delayed until feelings become acute :
even if it is achieved, it will bring no satisfaction, because it
comes too late to give a glow of pride or a sense of accom-
plishment ; and each late-won gain will only be a signal for
a fresh and equally protracted struggle. The result will be a
steady tension of frayed tempers ; and the end of that tension
will be explosion and revolution.

It is obvious that democracy offers a greater scope for
opposition than other forms of government. Indeed we may
almost say that its essential and cardinal feature is the presence
of opposition—in the electorate ; in parliament ; and even in
the anti-cabinet which confronts and challenges the cabinet.
But it would be a folly to interpret the fact of opposition as
something entirely negative or only concerned with obstruction
and delay. In the first place an organized opposition, free to
express its views, is the safety valve of the State. Even on the
theory of communism, if the communist theory of ' the dialec-
tical process ' be extended to the process of current politics
(as it seldom or never is), an opposition represents the
' antithesis ' which is the necessary corollary of every ' thesis '.
In the second place, the opposition cannot be identified with
the cause of vested interests. In the vicissitudes of democracy,
which now enthrones the progressive and now the conservative
cause, the opposition varies, and if it is sometimes an opposition to reform it is sometimes an opposition to stagnation and
reaction. Opposition serves both causes ; its strength enures
no less to the benefit of change than to the benefit of vested
interests. Finally, an opposition is never entirely critical, or
utterly negative. The function which it discharges in the
process of democracy is fundamentally positive. It contributes
to the making of that majority-minority agreement which is
the end and aim of the process. True, every opposition begins
with the challenge of a ' No ', and by contradicting the policy
of the government in power—as that policy stands, in its
original enunciation. But no opposition ends where it began.
If it did, it would leave the policy of government unaffected
and unchanged, and would fail to achieve its own object. It

seeks to amend and alter the policy, and in so far as it follows that aim it helps to construct and affirm what it began by seeking to destroy and deny. No doubt this is all a difficult and delicate operation ; and opposition is always tempted to stop in its first and easy beginnings, and to shirk its ultimate goal. The more it yields to temptation, the more it postpones the pace of action. The more it fulfils its ultimate constructive duty, the more it hastens the pace of considered and effective action, weighted with the volume of general consent, and moving with the momentum which only that volume can give.

Democracy may liberate opposition ; but in the same act, and by the same token, it equally liberates action. It may liberate the criticism of minorities (whether the minority of the moment be on the Left or the Right) ; but it never trammels up the action of the majority. Whatever the strength of an opposition, and whatever the classes from which it is drawn, a convinced and definite majority will carry that major part of its policy to which it is entitled by the fact of being such a majority —*so long as the democratic process continues*, and unless the minority, either discontented with that minor part of its policy to which it is also entitled, or defrauded of that minor part by the intransigency of the majority, refuses its collaboration and presses its opposition to the ultimate consequence of force. A convinced and ardent majority which is really a majority ; which, conscious of being a majority, is free from terror of the other side ; which, free from terror of it, is willing to persuade it, by making concessions to the terrors which *it* may naturally feel from the fact of being the weaker—such a majority, even if it be a reforming majority, and even if it be arrayed against the cause of vested interests, has no need to quarrel with the democratic process. The quarrel with that process, where such a quarrel exists or is fomented into existence, is not the quarrel of an actual and substantive majority : it is the quarrel of an expectant or potential majority—of a majority not yet there, but hoping to be there, believing that it ought to be there, and angry because for some reason it is not actually there. If the expectant or potential majority is kept long in a state of expectation by the uncertainty of the electorate (and by its own consequent failure to make itself actual, and not merely potential), the tension may be prolonged, and the quarrel of the expectant majority with the democratic process may grow. It is true that the fault lies in itself rather than in the process with which it quarrels. The expectant majority has not become what it hoped to be and continues to think that it ought to be. It has not converted to its views a sufficient volume of the electorate. But it is always easy, as we have already had reason to notice, to ' find the fault . . . not in ourselves, but in our stars '.

We are thus brought to a final danger which may arise from an embittered sense of time and urgency. It is not the danger which arises from the slow and protracted rear-guard action of vested interests, with their inveterate tenacity and their infinite variety of *ruses de guerre*. It is the danger which arises from the halted or flagging advance of the reforming interest, retarded by the uncertainty of the electorate. In such a position two different lines of opinion may declare themselves. There will be those who say that every issue must ripen for a solution before it can be solved ; that it is impossible to move generally towards a clear-cut solution when the electorate has given no clear-cut verdict and the general opinion is still divided ; that it is best to trust to time and tentative effort for an outcome. But there will also be those who feel that a long protracted issue is something which is intrinsically and inherently wrong. It makes life stale and dull : it prevents, not only in its own sphere, but also in others, any generous undertaking and any constructive effort. From this feeling it is an easy leap to a policy of audacity. To wait upon the people is to wait until the Greek Calends. Instead of waiting for them to decide, why not decide for them ? There is the magic of the thing once done ; and men will often accept, and even join in working, a scheme which they would not have chosen if they had been free to choose. When time stands still, we must give it an impulse to set it in motion. When the people halts, or faces both ways, we must give an inclination to the poised and quivering balance.[1]

It is not a mere impatience, bred of the feverish hustle of an age of rapid motion, which leads many men to feel so strongly to-day the force of the argument of time. It is rather the sense of a hanging and postponed issue, which stifles action and must be settled. Nor is the solution suggested

---

[1] This was the gist of the policy once advocated by the Socialist League, with its plan of emergency action, suddenly and dramatically passed without any pausing for compromise.

purely a suggestion of force. It is a solution which comes from the dramatic (or melodramatic) factor : solution not by big battalions, but by resolute and decisive strokes of policy ; solution which, in a sense, belongs to the area of discussion (we may even say of persuasion), but which brings into that area the emotional cogency and the sentimental quality of arguments which are also acts. The democratic process of discussion is not altogether intellectual. Sudden and dramatic interventions may sway its course and determine its outcome, not because they are based on physical force or appeal to emotions of physical fear, but because they seem to proceed from decisive certainty of thought, and because they appeal for acceptance to something higher than fear, if also to something lower than reasoned and genuine conviction. Without being drilled into action by fear (which is the way of tyranny or dictation), and without being persuaded into it freely by the balance of argument (which is the way of democracy and discussion), we may be led into it by something which is neither, but shares the nature of both. There is a borderland which lies between compulsion and consent. It is in this borderland, peculiarly dangerous because it is peculiarly hazy and vague, that the spirits of impatience dwell. Hot for certainties, and eager for final solutions of delayed and hanging questions in the light of their burning certainties, they are ready to risk the bold stroke before the hour of general acceptance has struck, believing that the bold stroke will of itself precipitate the hour of striking.

Just because there is this borderland, and because this borderland is even more dangerous than the frankly hostile territory which lies on its further side, the democratic cause must be kept distinct and separate. Those who, instead of waiting for the people to decide, elect to decide for them, are not subscribers to the principle of government by consent, even if they gamble on eventual consent. Those who obtrude the rapid dramatic stroke into the process of discussion may believe that they are adding an argument ; but an argument which is really an act admits of no answer but a counter-act, and when politics become a matter of acts and counter-acts discussion has ceased and faction begun. Dramatized imitation of civil war may easily produce something more than ' dramatic ' or emotional effects. It may produce what it imitates.

PART III
AMENDMENTS TO DEMOCRACY
VII
THE REFORM OF PARLIAMENTARY DEMOCRACY : PROCEDURE

§ 1. THE RULE OF THE GAME AND THE RULES OF PARLIAMENTARY PROCEDURE

WE have examined, in the second part of these reflections, the external difficulties which confront the parliamentary system of democracy. We have studied the eruption of personalism and the new doctrine of leadership. We have studied the eruption of the group and of the worship of the group, expressed in the new national egoism of Italy and the new racialism of Germany. We have studied the eruption of economics and its lava of economic problems ; and in the course of that study we have been led to investigate a number of grounds, belonging to the sphere of social economics, on which objection may be taken to the process of democracy. One was the ground that the democratic State was so paralysed by economic schism that it was unable to conceive or to achieve a single scheme of common life. Another was the ground that, even if it were not so paralysed, it was barred by its own nature, and by its own principle of liberty, from any real intervention in the problems of economic society. Another was the ground that, even if it were inherently free to intervene, its complicated machinery made its intervention too slow for the pace of economic development.

The next step in the argument would logically seem to be an examination of the alternatives to democracy—the alternatives which, in different forms and with different combinations of elements, espouse the cause of personalism ; adopt the cult of the group (be it nation or race or class) ; transcend the economic schism, launch boldly into a policy of economic intervention, and offer a bright new speed of action with a general plan of attack on the whole of the economic front. If we took this step, we should proceed at once to study the recent recession of democracy in Europe, the growth of a new single-party system of government which seems and claims to provide an alternative to democracy, and the various forms which that system of government has assumed in different countries. But before we proceed to take this step, there is a prior line of investigation which deserves to be pursued.

We have already had reason to speak, in passing, of the idea of ' technocracy ' or scientific government : the idea, as it may be called, of ' good engineering ' : the idea of planned design and expert execution. It is an idea which has some resemblance to the systems of planning (the Five-Year Plan of the Russian State Planning Commission, or the Four-Year Plan of German National Socialism) which have been followed in States of the single-party type. In those States, however, it is associated with other factors—with personal leadership ; with the cult of the group ; with a drastic recasting of the economic order and the social life of the whole community. But in itself it is a cool and calm idea, moving in the domain of science, which deserves to be investigated by itself. Its concern is with quieter problems of the proper procedure of government, and of the place to be assigned to planning and expert skill in the solution of the economic and other issues which vex governments and communities. This is a rational concern, divorced from any passion for leaders or groups or mysticisms, which must command the attention, and even the sympathy, of all who believe in the rational system of government by discussion. It deserves the most serious study. In particular, it invites us to face the question whether technocracy may not be the friend and ally, rather than the foe, of democracy. Before we connect technocracy with the alternatives to democracy, we shall do well to consider whether it is not compatible with democracy—not perhaps with democracy as it stands, in its present form and on its present basis of procedure, but with a reformed democracy. We shall thus be led to consider the theme of amendments to democracy, and we shall pause to consider that theme before we turn to investigate the alternatives to democracy by which we are now confronted.

Every form of government tends to harden not only into fixed institutions, but also into fixed and formal methods of procedure which are regularly followed both in each institution and in the relations between the different institutions. The absolutism of the French monarchy under Louis XIV and Louis XV was a highly formal absolutism, with prescribed instances and methods for each act. The autocracy of the Tsars was of the same pattern. It is only in new and revolutionary governments that procedure is fluid ; and even a revolutionary government, when it ceases to be new, solidifies steadily into its own fixed rules of procedure. There is nothing which is peculiar in the procedural rules of a representative parliament. Every public meeting, every local council, and every voluntary association has its standing orders, which (since such bodies are analogous to parliaments) are similar to the standing orders and procedural rules of parliaments. With the passage of time the procedural rules of all these bodies harden, and they also multiply. New problems and difficulties arise in the conduct of business : new rules are made to solve the problems and avoid the difficulties : a whole code is evolved. A class of experts arises, who are skilled in the rules of the code and insist on the observance of the rules as a proper safeguard for the proper conduct of business ; another class arises, equally or even more skilled, who insist no less on the observance of rules, but do so with a view to preventing business (at any rate business to which they object) from being done at all. All of us who attend meetings (from college meetings to the meetings of lodges of Trade Unions or Oddfellows) are familiar with both classes ; and if we ourselves are anxious, as we say, ' to get something done ', we become impatient with both. We thus find ourselves apt to draw a distinction between two sorts of rules—the rules which are antiquated or merely ' formal ', and the rules which are living, or ' real ' ; the rules which may be neglected or evaded, and the rules which must be observed and enforced. There is this truth in our distinction, that a code of rules, as it grows and grows, will tend to contain some elements which had their reason in past states of mind and past conditions of business, but have much less reason to-day. There is this ground for our impatience, that interest in the thing to be done and the action to be undertaken may often be diverted from the thing and the action to the form in which the thing is to be done and the procedure by which the action is to be undertaken. When this happens, the ground of reality is deserted for the ground of formality. The rules really exist for the sake of the game. But they tend to become the game itself, and to assume the character of ends in themselves.

The analogy of the game is apposite. Every human activity tends to clothe itself in rules, which are intended to ease and improve its running. The activity of hitting or kicking a ball first specifies itself into the various forms of hitting or kicking ; and a code of procedure is then gradually built for each of the forms, intended to ease the particular form, or game, by giving the participants (and also the spectators) a certain and established expectation that some things never will happen, or should never be allowed to happen, because their happening would clog and impede the game. The game assumes shape, and achieves a pattern, in virtue of this expectation ; and the more it achieves a pattern, the more it becomes a work of art. In just the same way as the activities of sport are reduced to shape, and enabled to achieve a pattern, by the gradual building of rules of procedure, so, and by the same means, the activities of earnest are also reduced to shape and enabled to achieve a pattern. Rules of procedure are built for judges (mainly by the judges themselves) which are essential to the practice of a judicial art[1] : rules of procedure are built for legislators (generally by the legislators themselves) which are essential to the practice of a legislative art. The point about the rules of judicial procedure which are followed in courts of law is that they determine, not the content or substance of judgment, but the form or method of judgment.[2] They determine *how* the judge shall proceed in collecting and formulating a judgment, but not *what* his judgment shall be. Similarly the point about the rules of parliamentary procedure which are

[1] In the United States the rules of judicial procedure are mainly made by legislative bodies. In England, under the Judicature Act of 1873, they are made by a rules committee which consists of the Lord Chancellor, seven other judges, and four practising lawyers. All new rules, or revisions of rules, made by this committee must be laid before, and may be disallowed by, Parliament. Parliament, however, has hitherto disallowed none.

[2] This was a distinction which grew upon Bentham's mind in the course of his thinking, and which he ultimately formulated, in 1802, as the distinction between ' adjective ' and ' substantive ' law. Already, in 1791, in the *Essay on Political Tactics*, intended for the French National Assembly, he had begun to interest himself in the rules of parliamentary procedure, as a form or species of what he was later to call ' adjective ' law which ran parallel to the rules of judicial procedure. ' The object is to avoid the inconveniences . . . which must result from a large assembly of men being called to deliberate in common. The art of the legislator is limited to the prevention of everything which might prevent the development of their liberty and their intelligence ' (quoted in E. Halévy, *The Growth of Philosophic Radicalism*, Eng. Trans. p. 166). Bentham here shows his sense of the importance of rules of the game, intended to secure greater ease in its playing. He even remarks, of the English rules of parliamentary procedure, ' In this bye-corner an observing eye may trace the original seed-plot of English liberty ' (*Ibid*).

P

followed in representative bodies is that they determine how such bodies shall act, but not what acts they shall do. They are, in Bentham's phrase, ' adjective' and not ' substantive' rules.

The ' adjective' rules of parliamentary procedure are none the less of the greatest importance. If parliamentary democracy be, as we have argued, a *process* of discussion, or a *method* of collecting views and taking decisions on the views so collected, the rules of procedure which regulate the process and the method of the central and representative organs of the democratic system will be closely connected with its essence. We may even call them a part of the constitution, and we may find it difficult to draw any distinction between the rules of parliamentary procedure and the rules, or law, of the constitution. This was a difficulty which Bentham found. It is true that he defines constitutional law as one of the branches (along with civil and criminal law) of ' substantive' law; but it is also true that, when he comes to define its scope, he finds that it is a law composed of general rules of procedure in regard to the making and application of ' substantive' law, and is therefore itself of the nature of ' adjective' law. If this be so, the general rules of procedure which make up constitutional law, and the particular rules of procedure which form the standing orders of the legislature, may both be regarded as ' adjective' law; and the latter may even be counted as simply a species or variety of the former.

In any case the rules of procedure of parliamentary bodies have a vital significance in the operation of democracy. Whether or no we regard them as a part of the constitution and a form of constitutional law, they affect the whole process of democratic discussion in its most crucial stage—the stage of parliamentary debate and decision. And they affect it not by trammelling it, but by easing its operation. They make it possible for discussion to achieve a pattern, and to become a work of art. They do so, as Bentham justly said, by avoiding and barring ' the inconveniences' which may beset common deliberation, and by preventing everything which might prevent the common ' development of the liberty and the intelligence' of all the participants. This, again, is also the character of the rules of games. They too have an immediately negative aim, which is calculated to produce an ultimately positive result. They too have the object of avoiding inconveniences and preventing everything which might prevent free and intelligent action.

It is only just to emphasize the general aim of the rules of parliamentary procedure. It is to ease deliberation in common : to raise it to an art : to ensure the hearing of every opinion and side in a just and due proportion. But it is equally just to notice the defects to which rules of parliamentary procedure are liable, both as they actually work in the legislature and in their own proper field of deliberation, and again as they affect the executive organs of government (and thereby the general business of the community) in that ultimate field of decision and action which lies beyond, but is already implied in, the field of deliberation.

Within the legislature itself, as in any form of meeting or place of deliberation, it is always possible that a true dialectic, which aims at producing some synthesis between thesis and antithesis, may turn into a mere eristic, which stands sharply on mere thesis or mere antithesis, but particularly on the latter. In other words, opposition, losing its constructive character, may sink into mere obstruction. Actually this happens to a far less extent than most of us are inclined to think. We are most of us partisans enough to interpret genuine and constructive opposition, when it is opposition to our own views, as mere obstruction. A study of parliamentary debates after the event (say, at a year's interval) will generally convince the reader who belongs to the other side that there *was* something, after all, in the case made by the opposition—though it may also convince the reader who belongs to the same side as the opposition that there was not as much in the case as he passionately believed at the time. When pure obstruction is practised, without any constructive purpose, it is not the fault of rules of procedure, though it may be covered by those rules. The point of the rules is to ease constructive criticism : if they also, and incidentally, ease other forms of criticism, the price may be well worth paying. Nor can it be said that parliaments labour under antiquated or obsolete rules which lend themselves to abuse. Of the hundred or so standing orders of our own House of Commons, relative to public business, there are only five which have not been passed, in their present form, since the accession of Queen Victoria ; and some of the most important have been made in the last fifty years.

So far as deliberation is concerned, there is little to be said in criticism of our rules of procedure. The proceedings themselves, as distinct from the rules, may be criticized, but the defects which they show are defects due to human temper. Party spirit, a too exclusive sense of the side and its interests, a disposition to stickle entirely for party position, a general eristic on behalf of an exclusive thesis—these are defects beyond the reach of rules of procedure. They are not defects peculiar to democracies ; the one-party authoritarian States show them even more ; and party uses its giant's strength most like a giant when it stands solitary.

§ 2.   THE RULES OF PARLIAMENTARY PROCEDURE IN THEIR
BEARING ON EXECUTIVE ACTION

But it is parliamentary procedure as it affects action, rather than as it affects deliberation, which is the peculiar object of criticism. Parliaments are not themselves active or executive bodies ; but they control action and execution. They control it doubly. In the first place they make the general rules or laws which determine the general lines and fix the channels of action : in the second place they control the executive or active organ itself, both in its work of enforcing the laws and in its exercise of discretionary authority (the conduct, for instance, of foreign relations). Now in regard to both sorts of control it is possible that the rules of parliamentary procedure may hinder action. Primarily intended to ease deliberation, they are not made with a view to action ; but just for that reason they may in practice affect it adversely. In the matter of public bills, for example, which propose new general rules, it is part of the system of procedure that they must be considered and agreed by both houses, and that the one may propose amendments to bills which have passed the other. In each house, too, there is a complicated system of stages or readings, with provisions for amendment and scope for continuous opposition. Again there are rules which divide money bills from other bills in point of procedure ; and while the effect of these rules is partly to strengthen the hands of the executive ministers in respect of such bills,[1] another effect is

---

[1] All money bills go to a committee of the whole House, which, acting on the ground of party, is swayed and determined by the party leaders who form the executive ministry. Other bills, as a rule, go to standing committees, in which party is not so strong and compromise is more likely.

to impede the promotion of large measures of social reconstruction which involve financial consequences, and thus to
erect a barrier against policies of constructive reform.

Yet the development of parliamentary procedure in Great
Britain, especially in the last fifty years, has greatly eased the
way of action ; and when we reflect that parliament is always
the master of its own procedure, we are bound to admit that
there is no necessary limit to the process of easing—except the
one limit, always inherent in the idea of democracy, that the
other side *must* be heard, and not only heard but also considered, and that time *must* be given for it to be heard and
considered. Time cannot be escaped or eluded—time not
merely in the sense of a flat dimension of so many hours and
days, but time in the sense of the psychological duration
needed (by the nature of our minds) for different ideas to lay
hold, to sink in, to produce mental concessions, to achieve
combination. The whole process of democracy involves this
notion of psychological duration ; and its worst enemy is an
unreflecting emphasis on the mere bare sequence of time, and
an unreflecting passion for shortening the length of the
sequence. Subject to that one—but fundamental—limit, the
demands of action have their claim ; and their claim has been
recognized in the normal development of modern democracy.
The cabinet, which is an integral part of parliament, and indeed
the most powerful part of parliament, is always alive to the
demands of action, and always ready to press their claim on the
attention of parliament. When the agents of action are
enthroned in the midst of parliament, action will not be
neglected. With us parliamentary democracy has developed
rapidly, in the last half century, into what almost might be
called cabinet democracy. The central core of parliament
has almost become the parliament itself. Strong in its power
and its prestige, it has adjusted parliamentary procedure to
its needs. Government business has priority on most days of
the parliamentary session[1] ; and government business includes
practically all legislation that matters. Public bills, other than
money bills, have been expedited, since 1907, by a system
under which they are mostly sent for detailed consideration to
one of five standing committees, composed partly on party
lines, but partly on grounds of personal competence ; and these

[1] Standing Order 4, 1927.

committees, while they secure less partisan treatment of measures, and thus allow more room for the method of compromise, are also more informed and more expeditious.[1] These are not the only methods by which the procedure of parliament has been adjusted to the demands of action and expedition. The procedure for the closure of debate has been tightened by new methods, and especially by the method which enables the Speaker to select amendments for discussion.[2] Above all, the method of what may be called administrative exercise of legislative powers, or supplementary legislation, has been introduced, and practised on an increasing scale, in regard to both public and private bills.

The method of supplementary legislation is simple. It is a method by which, under the authority of parliament, specifically given in a law, orders having the force and character of law may be made either by the executive at large (acting in and through the Privy Council) or by an executive department, provided that they are made within the terms and for the purposes specified in the law. It is an old device ; and it is as widespread as it is old. The *constitutiones principum* made by the Roman Emperors were orders issued in virtue of an authorizing *Lex Regia* duly passed by the *populus Romanus*. The proclamations of Henry VIII, under the Proclamations Act of 1539 (the so-called *Lex Regia*), were orders 'set forth . . . by authority of this Act', which were to be 'obeyed observed and kept as though they were made by Act of Parliament'.[3] The legislation of Italy since 1922, and of Germany since 1933, contains (as we shall see later) examples of similar Enabling Acts devolving limited or general powers of law-making upon the executive authority. The method, as these instances suffice

---

[1] The standing committees were instituted as long ago as 1882, though their general use dates only from 1907. They can sit while the House itself is sitting ; and they thus increase the working power (and we may even say the time) of the House. These committees are not specialized : bills are distributed among them, at his discretion, by the Speaker ; and thus they do not (like the specialized committees of parliament in France) develop a policy and an *esprit de corps* which may lead to the difficulty, and the delay, involved in struggles between them and the cabinet. On the other hand Scottish bills are referred to a special Scottish standing committee ; and bills relating exclusively to Wales are referred to a committee comprising all members for Welsh constituencies. The standing committees are, to this extent, territorially specialized ; and in them the idea of regional devolution already finds a measure of recognition.

[2] Standing Order 27 A, 1919. This incorporated in the standing orders of the House the method of the 'Kangaroo' closure.

[3] See K. Pickthorn, *Early Tudor Government—Henry Eighth*, pp. 414-18.

to show, can transcend the scope of democratic institutions, and may be used in a way inimical to such institutions. Delegation may be either a surrender of the essential core, or a jettison of unessential detail in order to preserve and strengthen the core. With us delegation of legislative power to the executive has been, since 1689, of the latter sort. It has been done not by a general act, but by a particular act in each case : it has been limited by the terms, and to the purposes, specified in the case.[1] It is a method which began to be applied on a larger scale after 1832, with the new flood of legislation which began with the passage of the Reform Bill : it is a method which has been applied on an even larger scale since 1906, with the new development of social legislation which ensued on that crucial year. It is a method obviously dangerous to the cause of parliamentary democracy, unless parliament watchfully surveys, and is aided by the courts in surveying, the use which the executive makes of the powers delegated to it ; but it is also a method which is obviously necessary to that cause. It enables the general and summary rules of legislation to be passed both with fuller discussion and with greater rapidity : it enables the details to be settled both rapidly, as the occasion arises, and also gradually, as different occasions successively arise. The isolation of the general rules for one mode of consideration and making, the separate building of the detailed rules by another mode which is both prompt and experimental (since the building may be spread over a period of years)—these are great advantages.

On the other hand it is only in theory that it is easy to separate the general and the detailed. In practice a matter of apparent detail may raise large general issues ; and it is to be observed that, by the method of supplementary legislation, a matter which raises such issues appears to be removed from the area of discussion (and thereby from the operation of the

[1] All supplementary legislation, or, as it may more properly be called, delegated legislation, depends on a parliamentary Statute by which such delegation is made. (Orders in Council made in virtue of Royal Prerogative—as distinct from ' Statutory ' Orders in Council made in virtue of a parliamentary Statute—are of course an exception ; but such Orders ' resemble delegated legislation in name but not in substance '. Report of Committee on Ministers' Powers, Cmd 4060, p. 24.) The extent of the legislative power delegated by Statutes may vary from case to case : in exceptional cases it may include the power to legislate on matters of principle, and even the power to amend Acts of Parliament ; but in ordinary and normal practice neither of these powers is conferred (*ibid.*, pp. 30 ff).

democratic process), and to be settled at a stroke in an office. But that is a theoretical possibility rather than an actual fact. If the office, as our British offices generally are, is in constant contact and consultation with all the organizations concerned with the interests which it handles (whether they be local authorities or voluntary societies), there will be some amount of discussion before it proceeds to supplementary legislation. The essential thing for the cause of democracy is that the method of discussion, consultation, and 'give and take', should find admission somewhere, and not necessarily that it should be applied in Parliament and in Parliament only. That does not eliminate the necessity of the standing and continual presence and action of Parliament. Parliament is the mainspring of discussion ; and without its presence, and its incessant insistence on the method, there would be no safeguard, and no likelihood, of the use of the method elsewhere than in Parliament. We can dispense with Parliament occasionally because it is so ubiquitous (and on condition that it remains so ubiquitous) that we can trust bodies other than Parliament to do the sort of thing which it would do if it were acting itself.

We may therefore accept the method of delegated legislation as part of the general method of parliamentary democracy. Having accepted it, we can face the argument of time, pressure, and urgency with some measure of confidence.[1] If time has a quicker pace to-day, the same is also true of the procedure of parliamentary democracy, which has been greatly expedited. The rules of procedure are indeed complicated ; but the very complication is partly due to a new zeal for expedition, which has produced a crop of new rules, if it is also due in part to an ancient (and very wise) zeal for

[1] Another, and an important method, by which time has been saved in the British system for the despatch of public bills, or general legislation, is the method by which private bills (affecting local or particular interests) never come before the full Parliament, but are referred to, and despatched by, committees of Parliament acting under a separate and quasi-judicial mode of procedure. To save time for Parliament still further (even in the handling of private bills themselves) a system of supplementary legislation by the executive, under which provisional orders can be made by executive departments in lieu of private bills, is largely used. There is thus supplementary legislation by the executive both in the sphere of public and in that of private bills. Provisional orders issued by executive departments in lieu of private bills stand in need of parliamentary confirmation ; but this is given annually, and almost automatically, by a series of 'provisional orders confirmation Acts' for the different executive departments concerned.

mature and many-sided deliberation. However complicated the rules, and however ardently they may be cherished, they can all be suspended in a trice if occasion urgently demands, and if the urgency of the demand is genuinely and generally felt. It is not unknown that a British Act of Parliament should be passed through all its stages, in both Houses, within a single day. But normally the pace of action will be slower : indeed, far slower. It is not that a democratic form of government is unable to achieve speed, if it wishes. It is rather that it will not wish to achieve speed, if it remains true to its own nature. It will always be inherently a respecter of time—the time which consists in the psychological duration necessary for the completion of a psychological process. It can only telescope time if time telescopes itself—in other words, if the time of psychological duration becomes (as it may become in moments of generally apprehended emergency) a pin-point and not a line.

§ 3. THE FLEXIBILITY OF THE RULES OF PARLIAMENTARY PROCEDURE

Time cannot always, or often, be telescoped, but it can always be saved. The benefit of parliamentary time and deliberation can be confined to the issues which demand them, and other issues can be shunted on to other and new lines of traffic. This is what parliamentary democracy has already been engaged in doing ; and it may do even more in the future than it has hitherto done. Some new lines of traffic have already been constructed and used—notably, as has just been mentioned, the line of deliberating on legislative measures in committee, and the line of supplementary legislation by the executive. But it is easy to imagine the engineering of other new lines for the easier and speedier passage of legislative traffic. One would be the line of unicameralism. It is not clear, however, that the abolition of the Second Chamber would save the time of the First : on the contrary, if the First Chamber were the one and only Chamber, with no reserve and no qualification, the internal struggles by which it would tend to be vexed might be more desperate and more prolonged. In any case the passing of the Parliament Act in 1911 was a revolution in general parliamentary procedure which has already made for expedition, particularly in money

bills, and which, by its consequential and long-time effects
on the temper and attitude of the two Chambers, may ease
their relations even more. Another line which is possible is
that of territorial devolution, by which the central Parliament
might remit local legislation to new local legislatures, in Scot-
land, Wales, and England. Here, again, however, it is not
clear that time would be saved, or that, in a country so interconnected and intertwined as Great Britain, it would be
possible to find separable local issues of sufficient importance
to engage the attention of local legislatures.[1] Finally, it is
possible that the whole system of money bills, which with us
goes back to a time when money was carefully doled out by
the whole House to an executive still under suspicion, should
be overhauled. Under that system such bills are considered
by a committee styled the committee of the whole House,
which is simply the House itself sitting under the name and
style of a committee. The effect of the system is that the
House, instead of controlling the executive, is itself controlled
by it : for the executive ministers, who are also the party
leaders, inevitably dominate the party majority which dominates the House when it sits as a whole. Another, and consequential, effect is that money bills are separated, not only in
form, but also in the spirit in which they are handled, from
the ordinary public bills which are now generally remitted
to standing committees of mixed composition and less partisan
flavour. This separation becomes the more serious, when we
reflect that money bills may involve matter of general public
policy, just as, conversely, ordinary public bills may involve
issues of financial consequence. The result of the separation
may be, as has already been suggested, to impede measures of
social reconstruction which involve financial effects. But if it
is possible to see the defects of the present system, it is not so
easy to see the remedies. The whole House naturally clings
to its *de jure* exercise of financial powers. The cabinet naturally
clings to a system which secures its *de facto* authority, and would
no less naturally oppose a system of financial standing committees (analogous to the standing committees for public bills)
which might menace or rival its authority. The knot

---

[1] The machinery of the central parliament already provides, in the system of
standing committees, a method by which local representatives consider proposed
legislation which has a local reference (*supra*, p. 214, n. 1).

continues to exist ; and while there are proposals for cutting it,[1] no successful proposal for untying it has yet been made.

In some of these observations the argument has travelled outside the realm of procedure, in the ordinary and proper sense of the word. The relations of the two Chambers, for example, are not strictly a matter of procedure (although they are partly that)[2] ; and it would be more than a matter of procedure if local legislatures were established to share or divide the work of legislation with the central Parliament. But rules of procedure, as we have already had reason to notice, run up into rules of the constitution ; and there is no great difference in importance between the development and extension of legislation delegated to the executive (which seems to be purely a matter of procedure) and the development and extension of legislation devolved upon local parliaments. The issue of the whole matter is that there is no fixed or unalterable method for the conduct of the process of democracy. By procedural change or by constitutional amendment it is constantly growing, or at any rate altering. It can meet the demands of time by changing with the times. It is always, as we have said, the master of its own procedure, though it is always, as we have also said, subject to the conditions of its own process. Being subject to the conditions of its own process, it can never eliminate opposition : it can never eliminate the necessity of discussion between the government side and the opposition

---

[1] The regular Labour party, in facing the problem of parliamentary procedure, has been content with (*a*) a ' committee on time ', to make a time-table for each Government Bill, (*b*) an increase of the number of standing committees (coupled with a reduction of their size), and (*c*) an increase of supplementary legislation. In connection with the work of the ' committee on time ', it is suggested that there might be some abbreviation of financial procedure, but without any altera- tion of its general nature. Some of the more advanced Labour thinkers and politicians have gone further. *Inter alia* (one of the most drastic *alia* being the passing of emergency legislation, in a single day, when a Labour Government first takes office with a majority, for the purpose of authorizing it to take initial economic measures to clear the way for its eventual policy), they propose an annual (or biennial) Planning and Finance Bill, which would generally run together, in procedure and passage, money bills and all related public bills in a short and brusque shrift of procedure. (See e.g. Sir Stafford Cripps, in the *Political Quarterly*, vol. IV, no. 4.) This is to cut the knot ; but it is also to install a dictatorial government, which, if in intention only initial and temporary, might come to illustrate the saying that nothing is more permanent than the temporary. The Government of the day would control finance : it would therefore control the related public bills which were connected with finance ; and it would there- fore control practically everything.

[2] The method of conference between ' managers ' from the two Houses, and that of the exchange of messages between one House and the other, in case of difference, are both matters of procedure which affect and regulate their relations.

side : it can never telescope the time required for that effective discussion which produces some modification of attitude on either side : it can never dismiss the practice of compromise, which is the object of discussion and the reason for the existence of discussion : it can never abandon that general national continuity of policy which is vitally connected with the practice of compromise, and which demands that each party, while it is in office, should neither totally repudiate its predecessor nor so act that it will be totally repudiated by its successor.[1] On the other hand, being the master of its own procedure as well as the servant of its own process, a system of parliamentary democracy is always free to alter the methods of its action within the limits of these governing conditions. Its methods are not its essence ; the rules of its procedure are merely the tools with which it works ; and though we may condemn a particular form of parliamentary democracy if it uses bad tools, or uses good tools badly, we do not necessarily condemn the whole system by condemning the particular form upon a particular ground.

There is no inherent reason why a parliamentary democracy should not be capable of constructing for itself good tools of procedure and using them well. Certainly the development of our own system, in recent years, attests that capacity. One example is particularly apposite. It might be contended, *a priori*, that the parliamentary method of procedure would be incapable of working a system of protection. Interests would obtrude themselves into the discussion of its details : corruption would be engendered : time would be lost in interminable debate ; parliament would be hampered in its work as well as degraded in its temper. In fact, the remission of the actual regulation of imports to an Import Duties Advisory Committee has shown that the contention is ungrounded. The parliamentary system has been accommodated to rapidity of action, by this method of procedure, at the same time that it has also been freed from the intrusion of interests. There is a system of ' indirect rule ' which has been introduced recently into some of the British Colonies. It is one of the greatest of

---

[1] It may thus be said that democracy involves compromise not only in each present moment, between the present thesis and the present antithesis, but also between the present and the immediate past, and again between the present and the immediate future. This is the reason why compromise is connected with continuity.

our political inventions : it reconciles the need of central guidance and central direction with the need of local autonomy. In another sense of the term, we may say that our parliament at home has also embarked on a great experiment of indirect rule. The Import Duties Advisory Committee is only one example. There are many other matters (from broadcasting to agricultural marketing) which are now being ' indirectly ruled ' by Parliament. If Parliament is stooping to conquer, it is still conquering—conquering both the difficulties of time (with its incessant demands ' do this, do that, and do quickly whatever you do ') and the difficulties, which time also brings, of the multiplication and congestion of business.

VIII

THE REFORM OF PARLIAMENTARY DEMOCRACY : PLANNING

§ 1. THE METHOD OF SCIENTIFIC INVESTIGATION IN THE POLITICAL SPHERE

THE multiplication and congestion of business is a problem common to all forms of government. It is partly the result of a period of rapid economic transformation (with the old industrial revolution in a new period of eruption, and with an agricultural revolution added to it) ; partly the product of a growing sense of social justice, involving new measures of social reform ; partly the effect of a growing tendency (itself the effect of new and more intimate communications) to bring more and more for adjustment to the central bar of the State. The body politic has new afferent nerves ; the new messages and demands they bring require new central answers. We may thus speak of a concentration of tasks as well as of a congestion of business. This concentration of tasks demands something more than rapidity of action or changes of procedure designed to secure such rapidity. It is not enough to give an immediate answer to each of the multitudinous questions. It is also necessary to give co-ordinated answers which hang together and fit into one another. The piecemeal solution of problems may be so far from being a solution that it creates a whole crop of new problems, more numerous and more vexing than those which seemed to be solved. In this way the idea of planning emerges. And the idea of planning leads to the idea of scientific government, acting on the basis of a scientific survey, and proceeding by a scientific scheme which emerges from the survey.

Soviet Russia, the devotee of science, is also the apostle of the General Plan. The United States, the home of engineering and of scientific management, has produced missionaries of technocracy. In both cases the idea of scientific government seems to be associated with that of mechanism. It is a matter of ' rationalizing ' the whole machinery of production ; indeed it may even be a matter of ' rationalizing ' the whole system of economics ; but it stops short at the stage and in the sphere of economics. The idea of scientific government, properly understood, must necessarily go further than that. It is true that the State, in some of its ranges, may be like a business, and on the level of a business : it is true that, so far as it is, and so far as business ought to be rationalized (a matter which admits of discussion, and of a certain latitude of opinion), the State ought to be made an example of rationalized business method. But the State is more than a business. It is concerned with large issues of human life (peace and war, religion and education, marriage and family life, the promotion of human health and the diffusion of human happiness) which transcend the world of business, though they are none of them entirely separable from that world. When we argue for the scientific government of the State, we are arguing, therefore, for scientific regulation of more than economic issues, even if we have those issues particularly in our mind. We are arguing for the scientific conduct of the general life of the community, so far as that life falls within the scope of State action and State adjustment.

A plea for general scientific government was advanced by General Smuts, in an address on democracy delivered at Cambridge in 1929. As a lawyer, he had been impressed by the achievements of the science of law (the ' first science '), as applied to human affairs by the expert judge. As a statesman concerned with international affairs, he had watched and admired the achievements of impartial commissions of experts, dealing with thorny problems which had baffled the passions and intuitions of empirical politicians. On these analogies he proposed the inoculation of democracy by science. ' Universal suffrage has to be tempered with universal science.' Without such inoculation and tempering, he argued, democracy was exposed to two great dangers. On the one hand the Press and other forms of publicity might produce popular and party passions which stampeded statesmen and made governments impotent : on the other hand the rules of procedure and debate in legislatures might equally reduce to impotence any sense which a people might have of what was right, and any desire to act in that sense. From the blast of publicity, and from the toils and tangles of procedure in legislatures, a refuge might be found in ' the cool, serious, gentle spirit of science '. Expert scientific commissions, dealing with the issues which needed to be removed from the party and partisan arena, might be interpolated between the public and popular leaders. Their recommendations might serve as a guide both for public opinion and for the government ; and in this way science, essential to the working of the State both as a method of acquiring knowledge and as a body of results and truths, might yet become the governing factor in our human organization.

Such a scheme does not involve the substitution of scientific government for democracy. It involves only what may be called a mixed government—partly composed of a scientific procedure and personnel, and partly of what may be called (at any rate in comparison) the non-scientific and empirical process of democracy. Accepting, for the moment, the distinction which is suggested, and admitting, for the moment, the implication that democracy is in its nature something non-scientific, we may pause to remark that this form of mixed government—half science, and half democracy—has long been at work in our country. It was the scientific surveys made by the English system of parliamentary democracy, and faithfully recorded in its Blue Books for the guidance of public opinion and the government, which formed the main bases of Marx's *Das Kapital*.[1] The same method of scientific survey, ending in cool and calm recommendations, has been steadily pursued in the 75 years since *Das Kapital* was published. Royal commissions, ordinary commissions, and departmental committees, on the executive side ; on the legislative side, statutory commissions appointed under Act of Parliament, select committees appointed by either House of Parliament, and joint select committees appointed by both Houses—in various forms, and with various powers, expert scientific commissions always abound.[2] Indeed the general criticism is that they over-

[1] Compare Marx's own words, in the preface to the first edition of 1867. ' We should be appalled at the state of things at home (i.e. in Germany), if, as in England, our governments and parliaments appointed periodically commissions of inquiry into economic conditions ; if these commissions were armed with the same plenary powers to get at the truth [scientific method] ; if it was possible to find for this purpose men as competent, as free from partisanship and respect of persons [scientific personnel], as are the English factory-inspectors, her medical reporters on public health, her commissioners of inquiry into the exploitation of women and children, into housing and food.' It is curious to reflect that what is nowadays called, by modern Marxists, ' capitalist democracy ' received this great compliment from Marx himself.

[2] The method adopted in preparing the Government of India Act of 1935 may fairly be described as scientific. (*a*) It began in 1927 with the appointment of a statutory commission in virtue of a section in the Government of India Act of 1919. That commission, after visiting India, reported in 1929. (*b*) The second stage was an Indian Round Table Conference (composed of representatives convened from India by the government to join with representatives of British political parties, drawn from both Houses of Parliament, in discussing the

abound : that to appoint a commission and invite a report is a way of salving conscience and shelving action ; that libraries are stacked with the records of good intentions which remain at the stage of intentions, and still more with the voluminous records of data on which these intentions are based. The criticism is too simple to be just. Not every scientific investigation bears immediate fruit, and there are many which bear no fruit at all ; but that is no reason for condemning the general method of such investigation. The record of investigation stands ; if it is compelling enough to demand action, there will be action : if it is not, there is still the record, and that may be used by a Marx (with large results) even if it is not used by the statesman.

Nor need the method of investigation be confined only to particular problems as they arise, or pursued only by *ad hoc* commissions. There is also a virtue in standing commissions of inquiry and report ; and such standing commissions have also been incorporated in the general machinery of parliamentary government. These standing commissions (or, as they are styled, consultative committees or councils) may be attached to particular departments, to conduct investigations and to make recommendations in the general field which each covers. An example is the consultative committee of the Board of Education, established by Statute in 1899, which, among other reports on issues remitted to it by the President of the Board, prepared (after two years of preliminary investigation) a report on the Education of the Adolescent which has largely affected the course of elementary education during the last

report of the statutory commission and the general problems involved), which sat in London and held three main sessions from the end of 1930 to 1932. The result of the Conference was a White Paper, issued by the Government in 1933, containing its eventual proposals for Indian Constitutional Reform. (*c*) After the statutory commission and the Round Table Conference, the third stage was a joint committee of both Houses, to consider the future government of India and in particular the White Paper, which the committee proceeded to do, in consultation with delegates from India, from the spring of 1933 to the end of 1934. The Report of the Joint Committee, at the end of 1934, issued (after long and anxious debates) in the final Government of India Act of 1935. Three successive Governments were in power between 1927 and 1935—a Conservative Government, a Labour Government, and a National Government. The changes of government did not disturb, in any essential respect, the working of the scientific method by which the final Act was prepared. That the Act should since have partially failed was in no sense due to defects of proper procedure (unless it be held that it was such a defect that a constitution for India should not have been prepared in India, by an Indian National Assembly) : it was due to deep-seated causes in India.

dozen years.[1] Besides such consultative committees attached to specific ministries, there are also similar bodies attached to the government at large. The Committee of Imperial Defence (if it be not a committee *of* the cabinet rather than a committee attached *to* the cabinet), and the Economic Advisory Council, are both of this nature, different as they otherwise are in powers and in general standing.

But the question still remains whether the institution of expert scientific commissions (temporary or permanent ; purely and wholly composed of scientific experts, or also including, in addition to such experts, laymen versed and immersed in current politics) can properly be described as a ' tempering ' or qualification of democracy. If it can properly be so described, we may justly speak of our government as a ' mixed government ', partly scientific, and partly something other than scientific. But in speaking of a mixed government, we are also speaking in terms of antithesis or dualism. We are implying that the process of democracy, by itself, and until there is added some qualification or tempering of its nature, is different from the scientific process, and opposed to (or at any rate alien from) that process. This is an implication which demands examination. Is there really any antithesis between the method of science and the method of democracy ? Is the method of democracy, in its nature, non-scientific ?

§ 2. THE PROCESS OF DEMOCRACY REGARDED AS, IN ITSELF, AN EXAMPLE OF SCIENTIFIC METHOD

There is an obvious, and a profound, sense in which the process of democracy is itself scientific, and indeed may justly be called the most scientific process possible, in view of the nature of the material which has to be handled and the character of the problem which has to be solved ; nor is the process any the less scientific because it is conducted by ordinary men and women, acting not in a laboratory or in a temper of quiet abstraction, but in the hurly-burly of their contacts and among the frictions which contacts produce.

The material to be handled is man : the problem to be solved is the government of man. It is the never-ending

[1] The Advisory Council of scientific experts, attached to the department of Scientific and Industrial Research, brings the spirit of science, in the strictest sense of the word, into collaboration with a department of government itself established to promote scientific work and to produce scientific results.

problem—always being solved, and never finally solved—of making, repairing, and maintaining an adjustment of human relations which satisfies (or is generally calculated to satisfy) the moral claims of right made upon one another by human individuals and by groups of such individuals. Now such an adjustment, which satisfies claims of right, can only be attained if there is present, in addition to claims of right and in answer to claims of right, a corresponding and responsive body of acknowledgements of duty. If we have a sense of right and make claims of right for ourselves, we have also a sense of duty and make acknowledgements of duty to others ; and without this sense and these acknowledgements no claims of right (our own included) would ever be more than claims. It is acknowledgements of duty which turn claims of right into actual rights, actively recognized and therefore really enjoyed. We may therefore say that the government of man, or the adjustment of human relations within a political society, is ultimately based upon, and cannot exist without, the moral foundation of an acknowledgement of duty to others. This is the same as to say that it is based upon, and cannot exist without, a sense of moral obligation—the sense that I have, and must admit, and must fulfil, certain duties to my neighbour. It is true that the sense of our rights, and our claims of right, spring first to our mind. It is true again that, for this reason, political philosophy has often based itself on claims of right, and has often been couched in terms of ‘ natural rights ’ or ‘ the rights of man ’. But it also is true that reflection must always carry us back to the sense of duty and the acknowledgment of obligation. Rights without duties are like men without shadows : they only exist in fairy tales. Any claim of right is ultimately an appeal to the sense of duty and the acknowledgment of obligation. ‘ I must give ’ is something which must underlie ‘ I ought to have ’. That is why Kant proclaimed that true politics must first do homage to morals, and why political philosophy must always turn from the theory of Tom Paine to the theory of Kant.

The problem handled by government is therefore that of making an adjustment of human relations which satisfies moral claims of right because, and to the extent that, it is supported by moral acknowledgments of duty. What is the scientific method of attaining this adjustment ?

There is one method which is not in itself scientific, though it may be the beginning and the first stage of a scientifc method. This is the method of simple quantitative measurement. In itself, and in isolation, it is the method of a thin or mathematical democracy, which is something different from a rounded or scientific democracy. If we pursue only this method, we are guilty of a double abstraction. In the first place we confine our attention to abstract claims of right, forgetting the necessary foundation of acknowledgments of duty. In the second place we confine ourselves to measuring abstractly the number of persons who advance one claim of right, or one set of claims of right (grouped, for example, in the programme of a party), over against the number of those who advance another and opposing claim or set of claims. On the basis of this mathematical datum we proceed to make an adjustment, which may obviously range (if we still confine ourselves to mathematical considerations) over the whole indeterminate area which lies between the alternative of conceding the whole of its claim to the majority and the alternative of conceding a part of their claims to both sides in proportion to their numbers. This procedure has one merit. It supplies one definite datum : it registers exactly the number of claimants of right. On the other it has some obvious defects. In the first place, though the datum, so far as it goes, is certain, the adjustment is uncertain. There is nothing scientific in an adjustment which is left with so large a latitude of undetermined discretion. In the second place, the datum supplied, although it is definite, is far from adequate. We want to know the quantity of claimants of rights, but we also want to know something more. We want to know the quality, or the value, of the claim which they make. In order to know that, we want to know how far, and with what degree of intensity, the claim appeals to, and is backed by, an acknowledgment of duty. For unless there is that acknowledgment of duty, the claim is only an abstract claim to which there is no foundation.

We are thus driven to demand a method of adjustment which starts from an adequate knowledge of the whole of the relevant data, and then proceeds, by an adequate assessment of the significance of the different data, to action based on that knowledge. The only scientific method of government—the only scientific way of adjusting human relations—will be a method which can satisfy that double demand. Democracy—provided that it is something more than the thin and mathematical democracy of mere measurement of majorities and minorities ; provided that it attains the dimensions of a rounded or scientific democracy, engaged in the rational process of discussion, and constructing by means of discussion a reasonable adjustment or compromise—can meet and satisfy the demand. In the first place, it collects, in a full and unparalleled way, a complete survey not only of claims of right, but also of acknowledgments of duty.   It sets the community itself to speak and to produce its own register and record of the data. No survey made from outside can produce the record : no external observation can register the data : the claims of right and the acknowledgements of duty, being things of the mind, must come forth and speak for themselves, through every organ by which they can find their speech and utterance. If they do this, then, in the very act of its being done, democracy already begins to achieve a second result. The process of collecting the data of the problem proves itself to be also a beginning of solution. The differences do not merely register themselves as what they separately are : they do not merely state themselves independently and in isolation : they begin, in the act and moment of statement, to enter into relations with one another—relations of attack and defence, of action and re-action—by which they are modified and adjusted even while they are being formulated and expressed. An adjustment is thus already immanent in the very statement of the problem. It is also ' immanent ' in another sense. Adjustment does not proceed from any authority outside the parties themselves, or follow any process except the process in which they are themselves engaged. It is no act of external imposition, which might be this, or that, or that : it has no quality of arbitrary selection : it comes, as a scientific solution should always come, from the very data of the problem.

So far as democracy proceeds by way of genuine discussion ; so far as it succeeds in bringing one claim of right into argument with another, and in eliciting acknowledgements of duty to meet and face claims of right ; so far, again, as it succeeds in inducing men to make for themselves compromises between different claims, and to achieve for themselves a union and correspondence between rights claimed and duties acknowledged ; so far it does these things, it is already true, in itself and as it stands, to the ideal of scientific government. If it then adds to its general method the particular machinery of expert scientific commissions, it is not tempering or qualifying its methods by that addition. Still retaining its own complete and final responsibility—still setting different claims to speak for themselves and present their own cases, and still seeking to promote a voluntary adjustment between the different cases presented—it has simply erected a special court to give a preliminary hearing to the cases, and it has simply empowered that court to make recommendations for the guidance of the community in achieving a voluntary adjustment between the cases. The method of the expert scientific commission is ancillary to, and in accordance with, the general method of parliamentary democracy—a method, in its nature and intention, no less scientific, but working on a grander scale, and with an unbroken continuity, in the ultimate court of final and absolute decision. It is true, and it must be frankly admitted, that the actual conduct of parliamentary democracy often falls very short of the ideals of its method. Passions obtrude on the scientific art of discussion : bungles and botches take the place of genuine solutions. There is nothing peculiar in the imperfections of actual democracy : wherever there is an ideal, there is also a falling short ; and the higher the ideal, the greater the falling short. It is only the pragmatic and authoritarian governments, which govern by the method of *ipse dixit*, that need never fall short of the standard of their own method. But such governments, which act by the external imposition of an external and authoritative adjustment, have no claim to the title of scientific. They do not (because they cannot, so long as discussion is silent) proceed on the basis of a complete survey of the data. The essential data are human feelings, convictions, longings ; and those data (except in so far as *some* of them find expression through the authoritarian party which surrounds, and even impels, the authoritarian government) remain unknown, in the dark. Proceeding in the absence of real data, and providing solutions which, instead of issuing from the real data, are imposed and stamped upon them, the authoritarian government is opposed by its nature not only to the process of democracy, but also to the method of science. If mere mathematical democracy is bad science, dictatorship is not science at all.

§ 3. THE AUTHORITY OF NATURAL SCIENCE AND THE PLACE OF THE SCIENTIFIC EXPERT

We may thus, in a broad and general sense, vindicate a scientific character for the general method of parliamentary democracy. We may even say that, if the stuff of government is human beings, human minds, and the claims of right and acknowledgments of duty which spring from human minds, the democratic system is a ' planned ' system, or an adjustment of human relations according to a general plan. But when we apply the ideas of ' science ' and of ' planning ' to government, we are apt to apply them in a special, a restricted, and (it may even be said) a physical sense. We leave out of account the subtle web of mental relations which is spun between mind and mind, and the need of some process of psychological adjustment which will give the web an intelligible pattern and a rational plan. We turn from human minds to human bodies and their physical-economic necessities. We begin to ask for a science which will produce a fit race of fine bodies, eugenically bred : we begin to ask for a system of scientific planning which will produce and distribute material necessities with the maximum of efficiency and the minimum of waste.

The physical and the material have always their fascination. They are obvious ; and in their sphere there is always something which can be done, or at any rate arranged. Not that they are ever purely physical or merely material. Body and mind are interlocked ; and the economic necessities of life are largely the substance of the claims of right and acknowledgments of duty which are made by human minds. But we readily isolate things physical and material ; and applying the ideas of science and planning merely to these isolations we fall, consciously or unconsciously, into a non-democratic frame of mind which is also, in the ultimate analysis, non-scientific. We begin to remit the solution of our difficulties from ourselves to something other than ourselves which possesses a wisdom, and therefore an authority, about things physical and material, which *we* do not possess. Authority for the production of a fit race thus becomes vested—if we follow the logic of our premises—in those who possess a full knowledge of biological

and anthropological matters ; authority for the production of
a planned system of economics similarly becomes vested—
again if we follow the logic of our premises—in those who
possess a full knowledge (in practice, or in theory, or both in
practice and theory) of economic matters.   Actually the
demands of logic will seldom, if ever, be followed.   The
authority which logically belongs to the expert will suffer a
curious .but explicable transference.   It will glide from the
possessor of the higher knowledge to the government which is
closeted with him, and which has shown its possession of a
still higher knowledge by knowing that he should be invoked.
The authority of science will be used to perfect the science of
authority.[1]

We are thus led to the old question (already discussed in the
lectures of Aristotle) of the true place of the expert in the
State. We should all agree that within his sphere he has not
only the right, but also the duty to speak. We should also all
agree that when he speaks, he should speak with his own
intrinsic and independent authority—the pure authority of
scientific knowledge, resident in the knowledge itself, and
proceeding only from that knowledge. Disagreement begins
when we turn to consider the *exact* extent of the expert's sphere,
and the *precise* nature of his authority. Let us assume, however, as a simple but important axiom, that the sphere of the
expert is limited to the field and subject in which he possesses
peculiar knowledge. Let us also assume, as another simple
but important axiom, that the nature of his authority is
confined to giving authoritative information (that is to say,
information which is particularly likely to be true and particularly demands our attention) in regard to the present
state of knowledge in his field or subject. If we proceed on the
basis of these axioms, we arrive at conclusions which may

[1] We use the word ' authority ' in two senses. In the one sense we use it to
describe the weight and cogency, in his field, of a person possessing scientific
knowledge in that field. In the other sense we use it to describe the cogency, in
the political field, of a person or body of persons competent to issue compulsory
orders in that field. It is natural to confuse, but it is necessary to distinguish, the
two different kinds of authority or cogency. If the two are confused, both science
and government are adversely affected. Science which is held to possess some
sort of political authority is twisted into a tool of politics. Appearing to issue
compulsory orders, it is made in reality subservient to the policies of those who
actually issue such orders. Again a government which is held to possess some
sort of scientific authority converts itself into absolutism. Being deemed to possess,
in some measure, the intrinsic and inherent authority of science, it acts as if its
political authority were totally intrinsic and inherent.

indeed be challenged, but which none the less follow logically
on this basis and are true if these axioms are true.

The first is that information (however authoritative) in
regard to any particular field (however important) must
necessarily be compared with, and adjusted to, information in
regard to other fields.   There is no issue in politics which falls
within one scientific field and one only.   It is only in the
procedure of science that particular fields are abstracted and
isolated for inquiry.   In the actual life of the State every issue
is a general issue ; issues of public health, for example, raise
economic and moral considerations ; issues of economics, such
as that of the proper place of agriculture in a national system
of production, raise considerations of national health, national
defence, and international policy as well as of pure economics.
Some synthesis of information is necessary, by some general
body, even if we assume that all that is needed is to correlate
the different bodies of information drawn from the different
fields concerned.   But that is an assumption which we are not
entitled to make.

There is a second conclusion, based on the axioms already
stated, which warns us to the contrary.   The information
furnished by the expert in regard to his field, or by a number
of different experts in regard to their different fields, is information which touches only the actual body of knowledge in
the field or fields concerned.   That knowledge, by its nature,
is confined, on the whole and in the main, to quantitative and
measurable data.   It is based on a general statistical basis.
It deals with measurable things ; or if it deals with persons, it
deals with them only as uniform integers which can be summed
and divided and multiplied.   It proceeds by vital statistics,
anthropological measurements, economic tables and calculations ; and it elicits from these data the uniform rules, or
uniform tendencies, which—whether or no they ought to be—
are actually at work.   Now it is not the defect (it is rather the
quality) of scientific knowledge that it has this basis, and that
it proceeds in this way on its basis.   It is vastly important to
measure the measurable and to discover the general rules or
tendencies of the behaviour of things or persons on the basis
of such measurement.   Whether it be Malthus or Mendel, he
who does work of this kind furnishes information which may
bear profoundly on social life, and which must be taken

strictly into account by all who are concerned in its regulation
The cool certainty of such information, within its field and in
regard to the data with which it is concerned, has of itself a
healing power. But it still remains at the level of information
in regard to measurable data. It cannot solve, and it is not
intended to solve, the problems of action. It may indeed set
limits to action, and in that sense and to that extent it may
determine action ; but even here the will of man may prove
strong enough to limit the limits and to set the boundaries
back.[1] The solution of the problems of action, in the sphere
of social and political life, depends on more than the measurement of measurable data and the results which such measurement can give. It depends on a process, which at its best can
also be scientific, and can also achieve a cool certainty—the
process by which different claims of right and acknowledgments
of duty, which cannot be measured in terms of quantity and
yet must be made sufficiently commensurable to be adjusted
to one another, are set to give information about themselves
and, in the process of giving it, to reconcile themselves to one
another in the certainty of a uniform and accepted law.

§ 4. THE BUSINESS EXPERT AND THE APPLICATION OF THE ANALOGY
OF THE BUSINESS WORLD TO THE WORLD OF POLITICS

The expert, in the sense of the scientific expert, can thus give
information in regard to the measurable data with which he
deals and the rules or tendencies of such data. His information
may even take the form of advice ; but it is advice about the
limits of action, or the measurable factors which enter into
the problem of action, and not about the actual action itself.
These are the limits of the expert, so far as the expert acts in
the name and by the authority of science. But there is another
sense in which the word ' expert ' may also be used ; and it is
with that sense that the cult of the expert, the idea of ' technocracy ', and the vogue of management or planning, are all
connected. Expert suggests experience : and when men speak
of expert knowledge, it is often experience, and not scientific
knowledge, which they have really in mind. They are thinking
of something which is superficially like scientific knowledge,
but fundamentally different—the empirical skill of the prac-

---

[1] The limits set by Malthus, for example, have proved to be movable limits—
real limits, indeed, but none the less movable.

tical engineer, the practical financier, the practical manager
of a factory or a commercial enterprise. Such men possess a
special knowledge, which may readily be identified with
scientific knowledge, all the more as it is concerned with
measurable factors ; but their knowledge really consists not
in a science, but in a skill—a skill of instinctive calculation (the
product of habit mixed with insight), and a consequent skill
of instinctive manipulation of the factors with which they
deal. Within its field this skill can easily move and easily
deploy the factors it handles, human as well as material, in
such a way as to produce the maximum of result with the
minimum of effort. The spectacle of such skill, so engaged,
suggests tempting prospects in the field of politics. Here, in
this skill, there seems to be a reserve of wisdom which may
be used to give advice about the running of the political
' machine ' and the ' business ' of politics, or even to conduct
its actual running. There may even seem to be something
more. If a great business can be run in this way—calculated,
manipulated, planned, and managed—why should not the
State itself be similarly run ? There may not only be a reserve
of wisdom in this world of practical business skill. There may
also be, what is even greater, an analogy or example which
should be copied by the State.

It is hardly necessary to examine the idea of a reserve of
power or wisdom. There is the less need to do so, because the
reserve is already constantly able, and seldom if ever unready,
to offer advice and aid in the business of politics. It can speak
in parliament and through the press : it can issue its own
manifestos, and send its own deputations to ministers. In the
same way the organizations of workers, with their skilled
leaders, also versed (if from the other side) in the factors of
commerce and industry, have also a similar power. The idea
which needs examination is not the idea that the expert skill
of the business world can supply a reserve of wisdom to the
world of politics ; that reserve is already in action. It is the
idea that the business world can supply an analogy or example
which the political world should copy.

One form of this idea has been expressed in the phrase that
politics and law are matters of ' scientific engineering '. It
was a common thing in the eighteenth century to regard the
State as a form of machine, in which, just as in other machines,

there must be pulleys and wheels, weights and counterweights, to produce compensation and balance. The notion is at once endorsed and criticized by Tom Paine (a would-be engineer and designer of bridges as well as a political theorist) in a passage of his *Common Sense*.[1] In a new form of the eighteenth century notion which is current to-day, the State is regarded less as an engine, and more as an engineering business, which should, as such, be managed by engineers.[2] The new form carries larger and more sweeping consequences than the old. An engineering business is something different from a machine. It is indeed concerned with wheels and weights ; but its essential concern is with the planning of human activities. When men spoke of the State as a machine, they were thinking simply of its instruments of government (the Crown, the two Houses, the judicature), and of the adjustment of these instruments in relation to one another. When we speak of the State as an engineering business, we are thinking of the whole community and all its members, and we are assuming that all their activities must be adjusted and planned in order to produce the maximum of result with the minimum of effort. We are turning the general community into a producing concern intended to furnish some visible and material result ; and we are asking that, as such a concern, it should be managed by the methods which are shown by the general experience of managing engineers to be most likely to furnish the greatest amount of such a result.

The organized community, acting as a State, is certainly intended, or rather intends, to produce a result. We may call that result by the name of general satisfaction : we may call it by the name of general, or greatest, happiness. But the true satisfaction or happiness which is the aim of the community, and the result which it intends to produce, consists in a consciousness that all claims have had a satisfactory chance to

[1] Paine accepts the idea of the machine, but argues against the theory of compensation and balance, on the ground that *one* of the weights must control the going of the machine. 'As the greater weight will always carry up the less, and as all the wheels of the machine are put in motion by one, it only remains to know which power in the constitution has the most weight ; for that will govern.'

[2] Compare Roscoe Pound's *Introduction to the Philosophy of Law*, p. 235. 'We may believe that the law of property is a wise bit of social engineering in the world as we know it, and that we satisfy more human wants, secure more interests, with a sacrifice of less thereby, than by anything [else] we are likely to devise.' Compare also p. 99, where the history of law is defined as that of 'a continually more efficacious social engineering'

express themselves, have been given a satisfactory hearing over against other claims, and have received a satisfactory adjustment to other claims. The production of such a consciousness requires something more than, and something entirely different frcm, the practical skill which guides the production of visible and material results. We may indeed imagine an absolute authority possessing the skill and the wisdom to give a fair hearing to every claim made by its subjects, and to make a fair adjustment between all their claims. Even so, the skill and the wisdom of such an authority would be something totally different from the practical skill of calculating and manipulating the factors of material production. It would be the wisdom of an acute sensitiveness to conflicting human aspirations, and the skill of a delicate power of balancing their claims. Short of such an authority, possessed of such skill and wisdom (for which we have only the warrant of our own imagination), we are left with the democratic alternative. The production of the state of consciousness which is satisfaction or happiness must be achieved by an immanent process. It is only an adjustment made by our minds that can be fairly expected to produce in our minds the intended result of satisfaction.

The conception of the planned State, managed by experts in the art of material production, is not only alien to the general aim of the modern State ; it is also alien to the mental assumptions and preconceptions on which the life of the modern State has nowadays come to proceed. It is one of those assumptions that, within the State and so far as the State is concerned, one man counts equally with another. The old inequalities of grade and status, issuing in inequalities of legal position, have gone. To-day, in authoritarian States as well as in democratic—or, as the advocates of authoritarian States would urge, in authoritarian States even more than in democratic—there is a subscription to the principle that all men are on the same footing before the State, and on the same level in the eyes of the State. If the analogy of the business enterprise and its planning be adopted for the State, this assumption or principle falls to the ground. The planning of the business enterprise segregates and distinguishes the planner from the planned. It involves inherent and radical inequalities of position. These inequalities may conceivably be necessary and defensible in *their sphere* : they may, that is to say, be necessary means, in the sphere of business, to the production of the maximum of material results with the minimum of effort ; but that does not mean that they are either necessary or defensible in a different sphere.[1]

Much the same may be said with regard to another of the assumptions or preconceptions on which the life of the modern State proceeds. This is the assumption that, though they must be treated as equals—or rather, *because* they must be treated as equals—men must be recognized as different, with different claims which require different satisfactions. Those who are different are not treated equally if they are treated as though they were simply identical. The State, on its principle of equality, necessarily adjusts its action to the differences and the different requirements of its members—even though, compelled to deal with men in the mass or the gross, it can only deal with mass or gross differences. The method of the business enterprise is of another pattern. It may indeed use, and even (for instance by differential payments) encourage, individual differences of productive capacity, in order to achieve its results. But so far as it recognizes differences, it adjusts them to itself rather than itself to them ; and its general postulate is that of the identity of the factors employed, which are all regarded in an identical capacity, and from a single point of view, as merely so many agents of production.[2]

The analogy between the business enterprise and the State may be pressed in either of two opposite directions. We may seek to assimilate the conduct of a State to the conduct of a business enterprise ; or we may seek to assimilate the conduct of a business enterprise to the conduct of a State. It is the first of these alternatives which has hitherto been discussed. It is

---

[1] If the State actually becomes a business enterprise (i.e., does not follow the analogy of such an enterprise, but *is* the thing itself), it will necessarily adopt business methods. This is what has happened in Soviet Russia ; and this is why Soviet Russia plans. Whether a State which has become a business enterprise is still a State, in the proper sense of that word, is another question.

[2] This is not to say that a business enterprise may not be conducted on different lines—as a co-operative enterprise in which there is a large measure of equality between employer and employed, or as a genuine community in which different human requirements are studied and satisfied by the management. So far as this is the case, the business enterprise becomes something in the nature of a State. How far a business enterprise can become a State, and yet remain a successful enterprise, is one of our modern problems. In any case there is more to be said for the business enterprise becoming a State than for the State becoming a business enterprise.

an alternative which naturally presents itself in the days of great industrial undertakings which impress the imagination ; it is an alternative which presents itself all the more readily at a time when the State itself, for one reason or another, has embarked on business enterprises and assumed (in part) the character of a business concern. But the second alternative may also be pressed. It may be argued that a business enterprise essentially involves the problem of relations of persons and the adjustment of those relations, and that it should therefore follow the analogy of the State, which is the great type and example of an undertaking devoted to the solution of that problem. If this argument be followed, we shall not seek to make the State a planned system, scientifically managed on the analogy of the business enterprise, but rather to make the business enterprise a democratic system, managed by the co-operation and consultation of its members on the analogy of the modern democratic State.[1] There is this to be said for the second alternative, that it leads to the interpreting of the less in terms of the greater, and not of the greater in terms of the less. It may also be pleaded, in favour of the conversion of the business enterprise into a co-operative society analogous to the State, that such a policy rests on more than analogy, and depends, in the last resort, on the intrinsic ground of the worker's claim of right to a satisfactory status in the economic system in which he is engaged—whatever may be the political system which stands beyond or behind it. The question may also be asked whether the business enterprise, after all, is so successful, and so free from friction, that it should be accepted as an example ; and whether, so far as it suffers from friction or failure, the reason of its defect is not the absence, or the imperfect development, of the methods of open discussion and voluntary agreement which have been so highly developed in the State.

§ 5. THE JUST DISTINCTION OF POLITICS AND ECONOMICS

In these ways, and on these lines, the argument from business to politics may be inverted into an argument from politics to

---

[1] This was the argument and the plan of the report of the Liberal Industrial Enquiry, issued under the title of Britain's Industrial Future (1928). ' If the status of the worker in industry is to be made satisfactory . . . he should be given . . . the sense that he is genuinely and fully consulted . . . and that he is a member of a really free society because it is one in which " the laws rule, and the people are a party to these rules " ' (p. 238).

economics. But while it is true that politics and economics are in some ways connected, and while it is true that considerations drawn from the one may be in some respects applied to the other, the fundamental fact is the fact of their distinction. It is not that they move in separate worlds, or that the one is entirely independent of the other—any more than Church and State move in separate worlds, or are entirely independent of one another. The same community lives, at the same time, an economic life, a religious life, a political life, and a life of the general culture of the faculties of body and mind. The lives are all interconnected ; and yet they are different lives. Politics and economics have always been interconnected, from the early days when an embryonic State began to form the germ of a law of property in order to regulate and adjust men's economic activity, and, on the other hand and conversely, dimly felt economic interests began to affect and modify the decisions of early doomsmen and the actions of early chiefs. But though they have always been interconnected, politics and economics remain distinct, both in the purposes of their activities and in the methods which their purposes entail. It is the very riches of man's nature and endowment which issue in these different modes ; and it is an impatient passion of simplification which would reduce them to uniformity. We do not ' lay waste our powers ' in ' getting and spending ' : we fulfil one part of them ; but that part is not the whole, and there are other powers, with their own appropriate modes, which must also be exercised and breathed. There is a just autonomy which the economic powers of man may claim within their sphere ; but that autonomy is not absolute, and it has to be adjusted to, and reconciled with, other autonomies which are no less just.

The just autonomy of the economic process consists in the planning and conduct of the production and distribution of commodities in such a way as to maximize their amount and minimize their cost. Whether the State itself is competent to undertake the process and to become a business enterprise as well as a State, or whether the State, by its nature, is estopped from being also a business enterprise, is a question which may be debated and answered in different ways ; but whatever the answer which we give to that question, and whether the State, or agencies other than the State, receive the benefit of our verdict, we have still to acknowledge the general principle of the just autonomy of the economic process. There *must*, in our days, be large-scale planning of production and distribution : there *must* be a previous calculation, and a deliberate manipulation, of the various factors concerned, both material and human. With the multiplication of the machinery of production and the machinery of communication and transport—with the multiplication of the population, and with the added multiplication of the *needs* of that population (which makes each unit of consumption greater than it was, and is therefore equivalent to a new and further increase of the population)—nothing else is possible. Whether, therefore, the State is itself a business enterprise, or whether enterprises exist separately and independently—whether there is socialism, or whether there is capitalism—there will be planning, calculation, manipulation and management. In the Union of Socialist Soviet Republics and in the United States of America the same system of mechanization and rationalization exists—so far as the economic process is concerned. In either case that process asserts its just autonomy. If it is to function for its own purpose, there is a method by which it *must* function. It must proceed by way of planning and management.

We are thus brought back to the old difficulty already stated[1]—a fundamental difficulty of our times—whether the changes which have taken place in the structure of economics do not involve a new method of action (planned, calculated, and managed) which is the one categorical imperative on which we must henceforth act. The answer which we are now in a position to give is simple. A new method of action is indeed an imperative ; but it is not the one categorical imperative which covers the whole of the common life. There is no escaping from the necessity of planning in the process of economics. There has been no escaping for many years past ; and to-day the necessity is an even larger and still more clear-cut necessity, because it is the obvious necessity of large-scale planning for a new and large-scale world. But the necessity exists *within* the economic process ; and the economic is not the only process. There is also the political process ; and the political process may have—indeed in the democratic

[1] See above, pp. 168–9.

form of State it actually has—another method. The method of the political process is not necessarily wrong because it differs from that of the economic process ; nor is the old method of free discussion and free adjustment in the one sphere invalidated by the growing vogue of a new method of planning and management in the other. On the contrary, the very fact of its difference from the method of the economic process may be the essential justification of the method of the political process. While the State may acknowledge the necessity for the planning of the economic process, and may even help the agents of the process to form and to execute plans, it may still claim that it is, in itself, and in the nature of its own process, the corrective of such planning. In the general balance of a community, different lives have to be lived together and simultaneously. Men are citizens, church-men, and civilized beings with a tradition of humane culture, as well as economic agents. One aspect has indeed to fit into another, and all have to wear some sort of common hue. But equally, or even more, one aspect is different from another ; each is the corrective of the others ; and it is just because there is this difference, and this mutual correction, that every aspect is the complement of the rest.

Unitarianism is a natural passion. It is an easy thing to cherish a faith in some whole, or totality, which engulfs the whole mind and the whole devotion. The whole may assume different forms. It may assume the form of a magic and magnetic leader inevitably followed by his retainers : it may take the form of a transcendental group : it may wear the more prosaic shape of a synthesis of politics and economics, in which economics is the Procrustes and politics lies on the bed. Perhaps it will tend to assume all these forms, and to take all these shapes, simultaneously ; and whenever it does, the idea of an economico-political synthesis, if less romantic than that of the leader, and less lofty than that of the group, will tend to carry the day. The integration of life for the greater satisfaction of material needs and wants will become the eventual plea ; and the management of life to that end will be the eventual issue. In Russia, Germany, and Italy, however different the origins of the cult of unitarianism, and however discrepant the syntheses in which the cult has issued, the ultimate event is equally a controlled and planned economy and a fusion of politics and economics—whether it bears the name of the General Plan, or that of corporativism, or that of autarky.

It is not dualism—still less is it ' pluralism '—to believe that different forms of human activity follow different modes of action, which interact, correct, and supplement one another. On such a view unity still remains, and indeed remains in its highest form, through the correction and completion which the different modes bring to one another ; but the differences also remain in the unity, and are essential to the unity. The political mode of action, when it is conducted on the democratic scheme, is the corrective and complement of the economic, when it is conducted on the scheme of mechanization and rationalization. It is a corrective equally needed whether the economic process is conducted on that scheme under capitalist, or under socialist, auspices. The essence of the political mode of action, in the democratic State, is that each man counts as a person, and not as an instrument ; that each, as a person or living spirit, advances claims of right, and makes acknowledgments of duty, in the spiritual field of personal relations ; and that an adjustment is attained in this field which is self-adjustment, and, as such, consistent with personal autonomy. We may doubt whether the essence of this mode can ever be transferred, wholly and integrally, into the economic mode. We may doubt, in other words, whether man as an economic agent can ever have the full dignity to which he may aspire as a political being and a citizen. But such doubts only make it the more imperative that we should cling to the essence of the political mode within its own field and for its own purposes, and should cling to it at its highest reach and its greatest power—the reach and the power which it attains in the democratic State. Here is the great corrective and complement. In one sphere of our lives we may be stationed on a moving belt ; we may be scientifically managed ; we may be units in a plan ; we may be the subjects of a technocracy. In another we remain ourselves : we cherish the idea and practice of self-adjustment : we follow, in the midst of all the revolving uniformities of the machine, a vital and vitalizing principle of free discussion and voluntary agreement.

From this point of view we may see in the democratic State

not a thing or structure which is to be adjusted to the march
of economic progress, but rather a spirit and a power which is
to be maintained in its own true nature and individuality.
The democratic State is not a Church, and democracy is not
a religion. Neither, again, is democracy ' a way of life ', or a
general body and scheme of culture. It is simply itself, and
simply a mode of human government ; and Churches and
cultures exist by its side in their own right and with their own
roots. But in so far as the democratic State is a spiritual
force, it takes its stand by the side of Churches and cultures,
and it makes its own contribution, within its own field, to the
development of the human spirit. It is one of the ways—no
more, but no less—in which the spirit of man exercises its
powers and realizes its capacities. It is a form of affirmation
of the spirit : one of the modes of *Der Geist der stets bejaht* :
one of its great and everlasting ' Yeas '. It is idle, therefore,
to argue that ' political democracy ' is meaningless and empty
so long as it remains without the complement of ' economic
democracy ', or to contend that economic inequality and
economic dictation make political equality and political
liberty nugatory. On the contrary, political democracy
already has meaning and content, and is already a complement to the economic process, simply by virtue of being itself.
The values of equality and liberty which it carries are not
neutralized by the presence of inequality or the absence of
liberty in the economic field. They are made all the more
precious ; and they are, at the very least, as likely to neutralize
their opposites, wheresoever they are found, as they are to be
neutralized by them. It would be a curious reading of English
history during the hundred years since 1832 which did not
recognize how much political liberty and equality had done
to neutralize and correct economic disabilities and disadvan-
tages. But it would equally be a facile optimism which did
not recognize how constantly political liberty and equality
have had to be defended against the incursion of economic
forces which tended to neutralize or curtail them.

§ 6. THE NECESSARY CONTRIBUTION OF THE POLITICAL ORDER TO
THE ECONOMIC SYSTEM

The general conclusion to which we are thus brought is
that the growth of the magnitude of the economic structure,

the development of mechanization and rationalization, the increase of planning and expert management—all these have in no way superannuated or antiquated the democratic State : they have rather made it the more necessary, and given it a new youth and vitality.   These developments do not demand a new system of government, more suited to their nature in the sense of being more similar to it ; they rather require a system—old or new—which is suited to their nature in virtue of being different from it.   This is not to say that the democratic system of government must differ from the system of economic management to the extent of being its opposite, or that democratic politics must be planless and inexpert because modern economics is a field of planning and experts.   If the political process must be a complement to the economic in the sense of being a corrective, it must also be a complement in another sense.   So far as economics falls short of its own aim—so far as its agents, acting in their own sphere and by their own lights, fail to plan and to manage their own system adequately—the democratic State, like all other forms of State, has to make its contribution and to add its supplement. The State has a general charge of the general interests of its members.   It has to adjust accordingly all claims and counter-claims, with a view to a general satisfaction and a general system of harmony.   Claims and counter-claims will arise in the sphere of economics no less than in other spheres : indeed they will be particularly prolific in that sphere.   In the first place there will be the claims and counter-claims of the employers and the employed.   The employer, seeking to plan production, is face to face with human agents as well as with inanimate material and instruments.   He is thus confronted by the problem of establishing a system of human relations between himself and those agents : but they, too, will necessarily have their say about the nature of the system. Bargaining between the parties concerned may go a long way to establish such a system ; but it will always leave a residuary sphere of unsolved questions which necessarily come to the ultimate authority for final adjustment.   However wisely expert employers, bargaining with expert representatives of the employed, may plan as much as they can of the system of economic production, the ultimate planning of the system of human relations which is involved in economic production will still

remain an ineluctable duty of the State. In the second place—
apart from the claims and counter-claims of employers and
employed, and in addition to them—there are the claims and
counter-claims between industry and industry ; between manufacture and agriculture ; between productive activity in
general and the distributive activity of commerce ; and,
finally, between both of these and that new power of ' finance '
which is affecting and tending to control both. All economic
planning, so long as it remains on the economic plane and
does not rise to the political, is a planning in compartments.
It is normally planning in a particular undertaking: at its
best it is the planning or rationalization of a whole industry :
it is never, so long as it remains economic, a *general* plan.
Even when the power of ' finance ', which tends to become
the most powerful of economic powers, plans and adjusts the
whole gamut of economic activity in some particular area,
beginning with the raw material in the field and ending at
the consumer's door, it is still confined to that particular
area ; and it raises new and acute problems of general adjustment by the particular adjustment which it attempts.

So far, then, from economics importing its own planned
system into politics, it is the business of politics to import a
planned system into economics. But the plan which politics
has to introduce is not an economic plan. It is a political
plan. In other words it is a plan for adjusting those claims
and counter-claims of right which affect the whole political
community (as a body existing for the conciliation of such
claims and counter-claims), and which therefore come before
the whole of that community for settlement. It is not a plan
for the management of production, distribution, and exchange.
These are separate human activities, with their own peculiar
technique, which proceed in their different orbit and follow
their different plan. It is simply a plan for adjusting claims and
counter-claims of *right* which arise in the course of the conduct
of these activities—the claim, for instance, of those who are
engaged in the activity of agriculture to some sort of equality
with those who are engaged in the activity of manufacture, or
the claim of those who are labourers, whether in agriculture
or manufacture, to a status and remuneration which afford
some tolerable standard of liberty and comfort, comparable, in
its measure, to that enjoyed by other grades.

The planning which the State is thus called upon to bring into the economic field is not different in kind from the rest of its planning. It may, indeed, be greater in degree : more claims may arise in this field, from more quarters, than in any other ; and their adjustment may be a heavier burden. But the essential business and activity of the State in economics is the same as it is elsewhere—to deal with claims of right (in connection with recognitions of duty, and on the basis of recognitions of duty), and to provide a mode for their adjustment, which, in the democratic State, will be a mode of self-adjustment. Now it is possible to urge, on more than one ground, that the democratic mode of self-adjustment of claims and duties cannot be applied to the economic field, or can only be partially applied. In the first place, the ground may be taken that the claims advanced in this field are so opposed, and so incompatible, that they cannot be self-adjusted by any process of discussion, but should rather be externally adjusted, either by a neutral and authoritarian power acting in the name of a State which transcends its members, or by a partisan power (capitalistic or proletarian) acting on behalf of some part of the community and imposing the adjustment which suits that part. If we admit this ground, we relegate the democratic State to chaos and planlessness. But there is no reason for believing that economic claims are peculiarly and utterly incompatible with one another. The history of England in the last century is the history of a gradual process of their self-adjustment ; and it is a history which is not unique.

In the second place the ground may be taken that even if economic claims are not in their nature incompatible, they are in their number, and in the rapidity with which they are constantly emerging, different from other claims. Other fields of human life, and the claims which arise in these fields, have more of a static quality. Confessions, for example, are not constantly changing ; confessional claims, however strongly they may be felt and however much they may be opposed, remain comparatively fixed ; time is given, and time permits the process of self-adjustment. In the economic field it is different ; there is a constant dynamism and a perpetual change. Revolutions in methods of production, beginning and gathering weight in far distant countries, may suddenly produce internal dislocations ; they may suddenly breed new needs and distresses, and suddenly create new personal situations and consequent new claims. Within a country itself, change is equally at work ; industry may migrate from one region to another ; new needs, new situations, new claims may arise from internal movements. If we wait till the situations are created and the claims are advanced, it may be urged that we are condemning ourselves to a policy of waiting until there is sickness before we attempt to ensure health. Better to refuse to wait upon events ; better to provide ourselves with means and machinery for thinking and planning ahead. The new situations will then be prevented from arising : the new distresses, needs, and claims may be avoided by a wise pre-science ; adjustments may be made in advance to anticipate the necessity of later and far more difficult adjustments.

There is weight in the argument ; but it is not necessarily fatal to the democratic cause. We have to ask ourselves whether it is not possible for the democratic State, as much as any other, to make what may be called economic ' pre-adjustments ' ; to deal with economic problems before they have become so acute as to provoke a bitter dissension ; to arrange in advance for the adjustment of what may be termed ' contingent claims '. May not economic planning, understood in this sense, be compatible with the general democratic system of self-adjustment ? Both enemies and friends of the system may be ready to offer a negative answer. The enemies may say that democracy, living a hand-to-mouth existence, can never find time to think of contingencies, or to accumulate a capital of planned and deliberate thought for meeting contingencies. The friends may say that democracy will be imperilled by pre-adjustments which anticipate and short-circuit the process of democratic discussion, and that to plan the future for the community is, in effect, to dictate the future to the community. There is substance in the objections both of enemies and friends. A democracy cannot make a complete and thorough-going plan for its future. It cannot sufficiently escape the pre-occupations of the present ; nor can it properly deny or abridge the liberties of the future. But it is possible to plan for the future without going to the length of the complete and thorough-going plan. There are limits to the length to which planning can go in the democratic State. But there is nothing in the nature of such a State to prevent some measure of planning.   And indeed some measure of planning is inherent in its nature.

§ 7.   THE CAPACITY OF DEMOCRACY TO MEET THE NEEDS OF ECONOMIC PLANNING

Every party programme is a plan of preadjustments. True, it is a plan which is already based on a compromise between the conflicting views within the party itself : true, it is also a plan which must be subjected to further compromise with the plans of other parties before it can be carried into effect. (That is a reason why party plans, or programmes which are ambitiously full and precise, and cast in a definite mould which leaves little room for subsequent accommodations, have seldom exercised any great influence, and are generally eschewed by those who have a practical sense of the conduct of politics.) But a party programme remains a *plan* ; and the democratic State, far from suffering from the absence of plans, is apt to suffer from their abundance. These plans, however, are all embryonic ; and the real question is less one of the embryonic plans that parties project than of the actual plan which a responsible government is prepared and able to execute.

It is easy to object to the responsible government of a democratic State that it cannot ' plan ahead ' ; that it has too short an assurance of life to project in advance any achievement which needs long breath ; that, even if it had sufficient assurance, it is too much distracted and diverted by opposition to pursue a straight course to the end. But such objections are only valid if the ' planning ahead ' involves some total and sweeping reconstruction, along one definite and undeviating line, and if a new and revolutionary State, and a new and altered society, is to be substituted for the old.[1] No ordinary democratic government can construct a totally new racial, or corporative, or communist, State. But where there is some continuity of political tradition, resident in the general mind of a homogeneous nation (not so discontented with its present but that it expects it, in the main, to survive intact in the future), and where, as a consequence, there is also some general continuity between the parties which succeed one

---

[1] It is the particular exigencies of revolutionary governments, where the revolution is not simply the substitution of one *form of State* for another, but the substitution of *one form of society* for another, that explain many of the modern attacks on democracy. The attacks are relevant only to the particular exigencies.

another in office, it *is* possible for an ordinary democratic government, during its tenure of office, to make and to execute plans for the future in which even its opponents can collaborate (if only by way of criticism), and which they too will continue to maintain (if not without modification) when their own day of office comes.

Democratic governments, like men in general, are apt to obey the sun, and to plan in terms of the year. There is an annual parliamentary session ; and each session becomes an end or cycle in itself. Again, like men in general, they are apt to make separate plans for what seem to be separate subjects ; and they thus proceed on a scheme of disconnected compartments (or separate ' bills ') within the cycle of the year. There is nothing sacred in the solar year, though it is a very obvious fact which is deeply impressed on the temper and the behaviour of all mankind ; and there is no necessary reason why a democratic government, if it sees fit, should not adopt a *magnus annus*, or a *lustrum*, of five years (all the more if the duration of parliament be quinquennial), for the purpose of planning ahead the necessary economic pre-adjustments. Similarly there is nothing sacred in the compartments which men create for the despatch of business piecemeal ; and if a general ' planning bill ' on economic issues (whether for five years or for some less period) commends itself to a democratic government, there is no necessary reason why such a government should not proceed by such a bill. Some changes of organization and method would be required ; but they would not be—or rather they need not be—changes which altered the essential nature of a democratic system. A cabinet which planned an economic scheme for a *magnus annus*, and planned it as a single and co-ordinated whole, would have to establish a planning committee of its members, and possibly to add new members to its own body, untrammelled by departmental duties, in order to strengthen such a committee.[1] It would also need the assistance of a consultative body of experts, partly drawn from the relevant departments of the civil service, but partly (and perhaps mainly) from the active world

---

[1] It is not clear, however, that such a committee would not become an inner cabinet, or a super-cabinet, analogous to the ' war cabinet ' of 1917–18. If there were such a development, the essential nature of the democratic system would be affected, because the full responsibility of the whole Cabinet to Parliament, and ultimately to the electorate, would be affected.

of industry and labour. But there is nothing in cabinet committees, or in consultative councils attached to the cabinet, which is essentially new or strange. The only novelties would be the longer duration, and the larger scope, of the work of a ' planning committee ' of cabinet, in comparison with its other committees, and the attachment of the economic consultative council not to a particular minister (as other such councils or committees are attached) but to a group of ministers.

A further development of democratic institutions has often been advocated, and sometimes adopted, in connection with the planning of economic legislation. This is an Economic Parliament, or National Economic Council, attached in some relation of co-ordination or subordination to *the general legislative body*, rather than to the cabinet or executive. The idea of such an economic parliament or council is of some age ; it has been canvassed or attempted in a number of countries ; and it has assumed a bewildering variety of forms. One of the earliest forms was the Prussian Economic Council (the forerunner of the provisional National Economic Council of the German Reich under the Weimar constitution) which was established by Bismarck over fifty years ago ; but this was a body advisory to a number of the Prussian Ministries rather than a body attached to the Prussian legislature. It is since the War of 1914–18 that the idea of an economic council or parliament has been mainly active. Sometimes, and in some countries, it has been suggested that the second chamber itself should be an economic chamber, attached to a political first chamber. More generally the idea has been mooted that by the side of the two political chambers there should be instituted an economic chamber ; but there has been a great and general uncertainty about the composition and about the powers of this chamber, and especially on the issue whether it should be attached as an advisory body to the executive or attached (and if so, in what relation of co-ordination or subordination) to the legislature.[1] A third scheme, the most drastic of all, has

[1] These problems particularly vexed the history of the provisional National Economic Council established in Germany under the Weimar constitution. In the event, it became a body advisory to the cabinet, with a less status and less powers than had been originally contemplated in the constitution. The Italian Council of Corporations, instituted in 1926, and modified in 1930 and again in 1934, stood for a time in co-ordination with the Chamber of Deputies (under the paramount authority of the leader of the Fascist Party, acting also as the head of the government of the State) ; but in 1939 the Chamber of Deputies was turned

also been suggested, by which the first chamber itself is to be turned into an economic chamber, representative of economic interests and claims, and deputies elected on the basis of syndicates or corporations are to take the place of deputies elected on the basis of geographical constituencies. This is a scheme which was discussed by some statesmen and thinkers in Great Britain over a hundred years ago, in the period before the Reform Bill of 1832, when Lord Liverpool toyed with the idea of representation of interests, and Sir William Mackintosh advocated the idea of ' varied representation ' in the *Edinburgh Review*. It is a scheme which has appealed, in our own times, to French Syndicalist thought, and which, after some years of discussion, has recently been carried into effect in Italy, by the turning of the Chamber of Deputies into a Chamber of Fasci and Corporations.[1]

The disappearance of the political first chamber, and the substitution of an economic chamber, is obviously the disappearance of democracy—or an aftermath and corollary of its disappearance. Whatever the nominal powers of a chamber constructed on an economic basis, and whether they are expressed as general or merely as economic powers, such a

---

into a Chamber of Fasci and Corporations, still standing apparently by the side of the Council of Corporations, but with 500 of its 650 members drawn from the members of that Council. The French National Economic Council, instituted by decree in 1925, and placed on a statutory basis in 1936, was a body of over 100 members representing different economic groups, attached to the Prime Minister for the study of economic questions ; and the Czechoslovak Advisory Council for Economic affairs (of 150 members) was similarly attached to the executive government and its departments. In our own country a proposal was discussed in an industrial conference convened by the Prime Minister, in 1919, for the institution of a National Industrial Council of 400 members, elected by the employers and workers (voting separately) in each industry, with the power of advising the government on industrial legislation. Nothing came of the proposal ; and the Economic Advisory Council actually established by the Prime Minister in 1930 is a sort of mixture of a Cabinet committee (including as it does the Prime Minister and four other Cabinet Ministers) with a consultative council of economic experts drawn from outside (employers, representatives of Trade Unions, and economists, to the number of a dozen). The French National Economic Council had a wider composition : it contained delegates (one or more) elected by 21 economic groups designated by the government. The same was true of the Czechoslovak Council, with its 60 members designated by employers, 60 by workers, and 30 appointed by the government to represent consumers, men of independent means, and economic science.

[1] In the Austrian Constitution of 1934 the legislature was also constituted on the basis of representation of economic (or social-economic) groups. This seems to be partly an inheritance of the old medieval idea of a parliament composed of Estates or *Stände* (hence the phrase *auf ständischer Grundlage* in the first words of the constitution) and partly an application of the Catholic notion of *ordines*, as expounded in the papal Encyclical Quadragesimo Anno of 1931 (hence the phrase *Christliche Staat*, also in the first words of the constitution). See below, p. 365.

chamber, representing different interests, can possess no inherent cohesion ; and any unity of action which it may attain will be an imposed unity. Constructed on an economic basis, it will in any case devote its attention mainly to economic issues ; and the rest of the life of the State will be largely subtracted from the effective cognizance of any representative body. More may be said in favour of schemes for the juxtaposition of an economic parliament with a political parliament ; but no such schemes have worked, or are likely to work, satisfactorily. In a democratic State an added economic parliament, elected by economic groups, and deriving its power and such prestige as it possessed from its representation of such groups, might be welcome neither to the political parliament, to which it might appear in the light of a possible rival, nor to the government, to which it might appear, if it attempted to act as a parliament, in the light of an added incubus. The German provisional economic council, originally proposed as an elected economic parliament, of over 300 members, acting by the side of the Reichstag, dwindled down in practice into the nature of a committee ; and the powers of that committee equally dwindled down into a mere power of advising the executive government. In an authoritarian State it may indeed seem possible, and even desirable, to institute an economic parliament by the side of the political ; but in such a State the political parliament is *ex hypothesi* too weak to resent any rivalry, and the executive government too strong to fear any control.

We may conclude that in a democratically governed State the argument of experience would appear to suggest an economic council which is neither, in any sense, a parliament, nor juxtaposed with a parliament, but is rather an advisory or consultative body, and as such attached (and purely attached) to the executive government. An advisory or consultative body need not be, and seldom is, elected : it is generally chosen by the authority which requires advice, according to the nature of its requirements. In the field of economics any system or election of an advisory body is confronted by the additional difficulty that economic groups are not so uniformly and regularly spread through the field, nor so comprehensive and inclusive in their own composition, that they can form satisfactory electorates. We may therefore assume that, at any rate in its initial stages, any economic council likely to be successful will be a body advisory to the executive government ; that, as such, it will be composed of members selected by that government ; and that those members will be selected less as representatives of any ' constituency ' (though that consideration may be partly taken into account) than as experts who are qualified to give the particular advice required.[1] We may possibly envisage a future in which the members of such an economic council, transformed from selected experts into representatives of constituencies, might be selected by economic groups ; but if those groups were general and active bodies (and not mere economic categories designated by the government for this one purpose), the council so formed might be so much composed of delegates instructed by their several groups that it would never cohere enough to give any coherent advice.

We are thus brought back to the system of a consultative council, giving advice when asked, and possibly suffering (so our doubts may suggest) from the disadvantage either of never being asked or of having its advice disregarded when it had actually been asked. This may seem a lame and disappointing result ; and it may appear to present an impotent conclusion to the argument previously advanced in regard to the necessity of planning economic pre-adjustments, planning them betimes, and planning them in proper relation and co-ordination with one another. But there are a number of considerations which may help to remove such doubts and to banish such disappointments.

§ 8   GENERAL CONSIDERATIONS ON THE PLACE OF PLANNING IN
THE DEMOCRATIC STATE

In the first place, so far as the planning of a reconciliation of economic claims and counter-claims is the concern of the State (and we shall see presently that, though the State is always ultimately responsible, and must always act in the last resort, *all* issues of reconciliation need not come to the ultimate

---

[1] See Sir Arthur Salter, *The Framework of an Ordered Society*, Ch. iii. Lord Eustace Percy (*Government in Transition*, pp. 120–124), rejecting any scheme of the election of an economic council by trade unions and employers' federations, suggests that ' a revitalized and reconstituted Privy Council might be given the function of offering advice to the Ministers of the Crown on economic questions '.

authority or be carried to the last resort), we have to remember that the State which plans the general scheme of reconciliation is something broader and greater than any particular planning committee and any particular advisory council which such a committee may employ. Parties, parliaments, and cabinets—acting in their hierarchy, and each respecting and supplementing the others—are the main and final planners on behalf of the general community. It may be desirable that a congested parliament should plan its own time better if it is to play its part properly in planning the life of the community. It may be desirable that a cabinet, harassed by the need of partaking in parliamentary debate and beset by the details of current administration at the same time that it is confronted by the problems of planning the future, should be aided in its embarrassments by planning committees and bodies of expert advisers. But we must not exaggerate these reforms and supplements to the detriment of the bodies themselves which are thus to be reformed or supplemented. Parliament and cabinet—dealing with the plans furnished by political parties (or by political groups of men of goodwill not necessarily aligned in terms of party), and dealing with those plans under the general instructions and according to the general verdict of the electorate—remain the ultimate authorities. No authority can be substituted for them as long as the democratic form of State continues to exist. At the most, auxiliaries and adjuncts can be furnished to them ; but it will depend on them to use those auxiliaries and adjuncts. This is inevitable and unavoidable; and the consequence is that only those adjuncts can be added to parliament and cabinet which agree with their own nature, and which they themselves will therefore agree to use.

In the second place, much of the adjustment of economic claims and counter-claims can be achieved, and should be achieved, at a stage which is prior to the action of the State. The State always stands in reserve to make the final adjustments which cannot be otherwise achieved ; but the world of economics is so far from being a passive world that it is fully competent, in its several spheres and departments, to make adjustments, or to prepare plans for future adjustments, on its own account. In each industry, for example, there is nothing to prevent the institution, by the industry itself, of an organization which will co-ordinate and reconcile conflicts of claims between the different parties and interests engaged in the work of production—between the large concern and the small ; between the interest of large-scale production and low prices, and the interest of small-scale production and higher prices—and which will, in that sense, plan the production of the industry. Self-planning and self-discipline are at least as integral to the economic system as State planning and State discipline. No doubt the State will be vitally concerned, in a number of ways, with every scheme for self-planning and self-discipline in particular industries. It will be concerned, in the first place, with solving the conflicts of claims between different industries and with adjusting the different industrial plans to one another—though even here it is not impossible to imagine a general industrial organization, built on the several organizations of the several industries, and thus built by industry itself at large, which may do something to deal with such conflicts and to bring about such an adjustment. Again, and in the second place, the State will be concerned with each particular scheme of self-planning, in each particular industry, apart from its general interest in the general co-ordination of all the particular schemes. Wherever there are initial difficulties, it will be concerned in stimulating and aiding the formation of an organization which can adjust and plan the production of the industry concerned. Whenever difficulties arise from recalcitrant parties or interests after the organization has been formed, it will be concerned in aiding the organization to overcome these difficulties by the grant of some measure of compulsory power. In every case it will be concerned, and very particularly concerned, in ensuring that schemes of industrial self-planning are compatible with the reasonable claims both of the workers in the industry and of the consumers of its products. Self-planning will be in vain, and even untrue to its own name, if it is planning merely by grouped employers, and if it omits consideration of other claims and other interests (the claim of the worker to reasonable remuneration and a reasonable status, and the interest of the consumer in a reasonable price) which are also vitally engaged. But when all is said, the concern of State is less a concern in actual planning (that is to say, in the actual constructing and operating of plans) than in the constructive and operative criticism of planning. In the field of economics the State is the sovereign *critic*.

The argument, so far as it has gone, is, as an argument, limited to the field of industrial production. It absolves the State, in the main, from the primary duty of planning ; but it charges it always with the duty of the criticism of plans.[1] The same general argument may be applied to other fields of economic activity besides the field of industrial production. The general function of the State, not only in industry, but also in allied spheres (the sphere, for instance, of banking, or the general sphere of investment, with its various agencies), is the function of constructive and operative criticism.[2] If the participation of the State in planning thus consists (generally, or at any rate mainly) in the function of constructive criticism, there is obviously no gulf or incompatibility between

[1] In a number of cases the State will necessarily be a maker rather than a critic of plans. One is the case, already mentioned, of the adjustment of industry to industry—at any rate until such time as there is a general organization of industry to plan such adjustment. A second is the case of an industry (such as agriculture) unable to organize itself, and to plan for itself, because it is managed by a multitude of small producers. (Here, in most European countries, and even outside Europe, the State has necessarily become the organizer and the planner.) A third is the case of those industries which the State is compelled to take over on the g:ound that they are so vital to the public interest that they must be immediately subject to the public authority. Even here, however, to ' take over ' is not necessarily to ' undertake ' ; and the State, after ' taking over ' an industry, may proceed to hand it over again to a managing and planning body, immediately and peculiarly subject to State criticism, but none the less, within the range defined for it, acting on the lines of self-planning.

[2] The Director of the International Labour Office, in his report of 1936 (pp. 45–6), distinguished two current conceptions of the economic activity of the State. The first is the conception of ' directed economy '. This ' implies the co-ordination and direction of the whole sphere of economic activity, or at least of considerable sections of it, by government ' : it seems, by a natural process of extension, to grow and grow ' until it becomes a totalitarian system under which the Government controls the whole economic life of the country '. The other conception is that of ' planning '. This ' is an attempt to allow free competition to continue to function, subject only to certain general limitations : in its application to industry, the initiative is still left to the producers, and the State confines its intervention to legalizing their general will, provided, of course, that it is not inimical to the general interests of the community '.
   On this view it follows that ' planning ' (1) belongs primarily to each several industry, and depends on the formation of a ' general will ' by the producers of each industry, but (2) involves the action of the State in so far as the general will of the industry (*a*) has to be criticized by the State in the light of the general interests of the community, and (*b*), after such criticism, may have to be legalized (i.e. armed with some measure of compulsory power against recalcitrant members) by the State. A speech of the Prime Minister of Czechoslovakia, of June 1936 (quoted in the Director's report, p. 49), states succinctly the idea of ' planning ', which has become a general European idea. ' It is necessary that production and distribution shall be regulated by an autonomous organization under the supervision of the State. In branches of industrial production where competition is shown to be particularly dangerous, it will be indispensable to arrive at compulsory organization.'

democracy and planning. Democracy, whatever else it may fail to provide, can certainly provide criticism ; and where democracy is working healthily the criticism will be constructive as well as critical. Again there is nothing alien to democracy in a system under which each industry first seeks to organize itself, and to deliberate and plan for itself, and then submits its deliberations and its plans to the verdict of the community. But if there is nothing here that is alien to democracy—if on the contrary there is a new opportunity for it—there is also a new demand upon it. It is true that all that is demanded is simply a criticism, a criticism at once sympathetic and impartial, of economic self-planning. But that is a large demand. To bring criticism of that order to bear on *any* plan involves a large equipment in the critic. To criticize a good plan constructively requires the presence of the idea and outline of a better. Otherwise the criticism will be merely negative ; and such negative criticism may well diminish, instead of increasing, the good that is already there. To criticize an *economic* plan requires a grasp, at the very least, of the economic factors involved and their interactions with one another ; and when the State is the critic, it has to remember, in addition, the political factors of which it is the trustee and the guardian.

It is on these grounds that we may desire to see the democratic State armed with auxiliaries and adjuncts for the discharge of a function which, if in no way alien to its nature, makes fresh demands on its powers. We can see too, in the light of these considerations, that the auxiliaries and adjuncts needed may run into even greater detail than we have yet envisaged. The State which is to co-operate in planning, in any instructed way, may need not only a general planning committee and a general advisory economic council : it may also need particular bodies or committees to cope with the particular requirements of particular sets of plans—a committee on industry, for instance, to cope with plans for industrial reorganization ; a similar committee on agriculture ; a banking commission, or an Investment Board, to cope with plans for the organization of banking or investment ; and other similar bodies and committees. If planning is afoot in various ways in the economic world, the State's co-operation in planning (generally critical, sometimes suggestive, and sometimes supplementary) must also be afoot in a number of different ways. But the fact remains, at the end and in the sum of the account, that however important the co-operation of the State in planning may be, and whatever new activities (and new organs for those activities) it may demand from the State, it is always co-operation, and never unilateral activity. It does not involve the conception and the bringing to birth, in a single creative effort, of a ' directed economy ' which begins and ends with the State alone. Planning, in the true and limited sense of the word, suggests a number of self-planning systems—each creative ; all requiring the aid of the State ; but none of them wholly manipulated or wholly directed by it. It is something multitudinous ; a matter of many cells as well as of a single body ; a business of joint co-operation ; an affair of the economic system and its own self-discipline as well as of the political system and the general discipline involved in that system.[1]

There is still a third and final consideration which applies to any economic organs which the State may create in connection with economic planning. It has already been argued that, whatever the economic organs which the State may create, and however valuable they may be, it is the State's political organs—beginning with party and electorate, and culminating in parliament and cabinet—which must bear, and cannot evade, the real and final responsibility. It has also been argued that this real and final responsibility is in the nature of operative and constructive criticism of plans, rather than of actual planning ; that the political organs of the State, with their

---

[1] It may be said that the phrases here used are, in effect, a description of the ideals of Italian Fascism. There is a sense in which this is true. On one of its sides Italian Fascism is part of a general European movement which sets towards planning. From this point of view the ideal behind its system of corporativism has often been expressed as if it were simply an ideal of joint co-operation between the State and the various economic corporations each freely developing a general will within its category. Some of Signor Mussolini's speeches, notably that of January 1934, enunciate such an ideal (see below, pp. 348–51, for some account of these speeches). But the real question is that of the actual practice of Fascism ; and in actual practice it may be said that Italian Fascism is not a matter of planning, in the sense described above, but a matter of a 'directed economy' created and imposed by the State. The speech of the Duce on 23 March 1936, suggesting the nationalization of basic industries for purposes of defence, and proclaiming ' a regulating plan ' based on military exigencies, looks definitely in this direction. A regulating plan imposed by the State, for reasons of State (especially in that form of *raison d'état* which is *raison de guerre*), implies a directed economy as stringent as any in Europe. We may thus say that Italian Fascism has sometimes spoken in terms of planning, and sometimes in terms of a directed economy, but that it has more and more inclined towards the latter of these alternatives.

auxiliary and advisory economic organs, are thus engaged in a joint effort of collaboration with purely economic organizations, for the fusing of State criticism and supervision with plans prepared and proposed by those organizations ; and that the State, far from being the sole planner or director, is therefore only concerned to stimulate, superintend, and supplement self-planning and self-direction. The third and final argument, which is only a corollary of these previous arguments, turns on the relation of the general democratic method to *all* economic planning, whether it is done by State organs, or by purely economic organizations, or by the collaboration of both. The area of planning is not an area exempt from that method. Planning is not a franchise or immunity which lies outside the jurisdiction of free discussion and voluntary compromise. If the State adds to itself economic organs, it does so only in order to achieve a fuller and more informed discussion, and not in order to devolve upon them the burden of decision. If it encourages the leaders, directors, and experts in the various economic fields to do the work of self-planning, it does not remit that work to their unfettered discretion ; it does not abdicate its own duty of criticism and supervision ; nor does it release economic self-planning and self-government (however congenial they may seem to the general spirit of democracy) from their necessary immersion in the general and total flood of political self-government, moving with its whole ' pomp of waters ', and ' moving altogether, if it move at all '. If we accept the basic idea of democracy, we have to believe that all economic planning must be compatible with the liberty of a general society of free minds. However scientifically plans may be elaborated in detail, and whatever the necessary part of the expert in such elaboration, the general review of the whole structure—we may even say, the general planning of the whole structure—remains with the general society. This is the final and general court to which, in the last resort, all plans come ; where they are discussed, compared, and composed ; where they are fitted into a scheme and reduced to a unity.

§ 9. PLANNING COMPLICATED IN THE PRESENT BY THE COMPETITION
OF DIFFERENT AIMS

It is not easy, in these days, to detect the operation of this final and general court. We live in a time of economic disloc-

ation. The old self-acting price-mechanism, which adjusted
production to consumption and supply to demand—which
again, within the area of production, adjusted one producer
to another in terms of their ability to satisfy the conditions
which it imposed, giving success and life to those who could
produce at an automatically determined price, and failure and
extinction to those who could not—is either gone, or fundamentally' disturbed. Active regulation, actively adjusting
production to consumption and producer to. producer, seems
to have taken its place. The problem is vast ; and its very
vastness leads to a further and different dislocation—the
breaking up of the general problem into a number of apparently
separate problems, imposed by the particular exigencies of each
industry. The regulating authority becomes a series of frag-
mentary authorities, each occupied with its particular problem.

A further difficulty then arises. While these authorities
appear to have a common purpose—the creation of an adjustment which no longer creates itself—they may really pursue
very different purposes. It is only a formal or abstract unity
of purpose which is involved in the idea of the creation of an
adjustment. The real nature of the regulation attempted
depends not on the formal or abstract purpose of creating *some*
adjustment, but on the substantial or concrete purpose of
creating *this* or *that* adjustment. Now in any particular adjustment—any adjustment which is definitely this, or definitely
that—there may enter some ulterior purpose, for which an
opportunity is given by the fact of conscious regulation. A
self-acting price-mechanism has no ulterior purpose : it can
only produce its own automatic result. A regulating authority
which takes the place of that mechanism may have, and will
often tend to have, an ulterior purpose. It may seek to. create
an adjustment which serves an ulterior purpose of military
defence or national self-sufficiency (the two may be much the
same) ; or, again, the ulterior purposes which it envisages
may be that of the redistribution of wealth, whether by the
achievement of a greater measure of social justice, or by the
establishment of complete socialism. In an authoritarian State
(fascist or communist) one or other of these ulterior purposes
will triumph. In a democratic State they may co-exist and
struggle together. Some of its members may desire a simple
system of ' self-planning ' in each industry, with no ulterior

purpose, and with the only object of adjusting production to consumption and producer to producer. Others may desire a ' directed economy ' ; and of these some may desire a direction (for instance, in agriculture) towards an ulterior purpose of national self-sufficiency, and others again a direction (for instance, in some industry supposed to be ripe for socialization) towards an ulterior purpose of the different distribution of wealth. At the same time, and in the same State, different desires will thus be urgent. Here, and in one area, there may be simply self-regulation by the organized producers of an industry, with the government criticizing and supervising their self-regulation. There, and in another area, where the government feels compelled to act more positively, there may be definite direction ; and it is even possible that the same government, at the same time, may be using its power of direction in one field of this area towards a purpose of national self-sufficiency, and in another towards a purpose of a totally different character.

It would be foolish to deny the difficulties of our time. But it would also be foolish to demand too great a unity, or too much of a plan, in troubled times. Self-regulation and State direction can, after all, co-exist, according to the measure of the need ; and while the one shades into the other, there is also a place for each separately. Even the different ulterior purposes are not so different as to be antinomies : military defence, national self-sufficiency and the redistribution of wealth may all be simultaneous aims ; and though some one or other of these may be adopted as its characteristic and even exclusive aim by a particular State, all States are concerned with them all. The fundamental question is one of proportion—the proportion between self-regulation and direction ; the proportion again, so far as direction is attempted, between the different aims of direction. On the whole of our previous argument the democratic State is calculated to give the perspective that enables the different causes and claims to be seen and arranged in a due proportion. Democracy can provide the synoptic view and the scientific method which will do ultimate justice to all the factors involved.

It is true that causes and claims are now crowding rapidly on the vision of any democratic State. But temporary conditions (and on a long view the conditions, after all, *are* temporary) should not dictate a permanent pessimism about the competence of democracy.   Nor, again, should the hustle of the time hurry us into the sort of planning, precocious and premature, which imposes the dead hand of the present on the life and growth of the future.   It is necessary to plan for the future ; it is also necessary to leave the future free to plan for itself.   Tom Paine, arguing against Burke's idolization of the tradition of the past, contended that ' each present genera- tion is competent to its own purposes '.   There may also be an idolization of the competence of the present ; and it is also necessary to contend that each future generation is competent to *its* own purposes.   In the life of the State planning must always be piecemeal ;   or, at any rate, it must always be fluid and continuous.   What we do to-day can never absolve the future from doing even more to-morrow ;   and we must never encroach by our planning on its right to plan for itself.

§ 10. THE PLANS OF THE PRESENT, THE RIGHTS OF THE FUTURE,
        AND THE CONNECTING LINK

To argue for the right of the future is not to argue for opportunism in the present.   Past and present and future have each their own rights ;   and each present, just as it is con- ditioned (but not determined) by the past, must also con- dition (but not determine) the future.   In each present we have to act as if everything hung on what we did, and as if we stood, as it were, in an eternal moment (the spring and nerve of our action would be gone if we had not that sense upon us) ;   but while we must plan as if the moment were eternity, it does not follow that we must plan for eternity. There are many presents in the long life of the State :   each demands a serious and considered reply to its demands ;   but each reply must be fresh and spontaneous.   Planning is both a necessity and a danger.   The danger emerges when those who plan have a general doctrine which they wish to carry to victory.   Armed with that doctrine, they glide from planning for the present into dictating to the future[1];   and not content with dictating to the future, and thus stopping development in

[1] An example may be found in those English Socialists who, assuming a socialist plan to have been instituted by a duly elected socialist government, go on to argue that guarantees must be given by the opposition that, even if they are successful and are duly elected to form a government in the future, they will not proceed to modify the plan. See above, p. 182.

the name of progress, they may also assume the character of dictators to the present, refusing to allow it to present itself and its problems as they actually are, and preferring to schematize it in a doctrinaire form of class interests and class war which suits the scheme they wish to dictate to the future. There is a sense, after all, in which we may say that opportunism, as well as planning, is both a necessity and a danger. It is a danger if it means obliviousness of the future ; for the future is always involved in any true calculation of the present. But it is also a necessity, and indeed a virtue, when it signifies awareness of the actual present, as that present actually stands with its actual needs and demands, and not as it is imagined or schematized in the light of a general doctrine. Awareness of the present—the present linked with the past and issuing in the future, but still, when all is said, the present—is a fundamental necessity.

The continuous planning which is based, at each stage, on an awareness of the particular nature, and the unique demands, of each particular and unique present, may not only be continuous when it is viewed as a process : it may also be continuous when it is viewed in the light of the purpose which it carries and fulfils. Besides the explicit plans which we cherish and do our endeavour to fulfil, at each stage of the life of the State, there may also be an immanent plan which we are steadily realizing during all the vicissitudes of the series of particular endeavours ; and this in spite of the fact that the different endeavours may seem, at the time, to be disconnected or even conflicting. To invoke the idea of an immanent plan running through a series of endeavours may seem an easy recourse to mere mysticism. Or again it may seem, at the best, to be an imposition of purpose—an external teleology, readily contrived by the would-be philosopher of history, who can look back after the event and invent an *ex post facto* process ' somehow making for righteousness '. But there is a sense, none the less, in which it may be said that the process of development which may be steadily traced through the succession of parties in office under a democratic system of government proceeds on a plan towards a purpose—or, at any rate, proceeds ' as if ' there had been a plan and a purpose. The plan or programme of one party, confronted and modified, even while that party is in the enjoyment of office, by the

plans and programmes of other parties, is succeeded by the
plan or programme of another, similarly confronted and
modified. Under such conditions there is a general continuity,
and that continuity is more than the progress of an uninter-
rupted stream : it is also the progress of a stream which, in
spite of diversions and windings, is flowing in one direction.
We cannot discover any definite body of persons which plans
or purposes this unity of direction.   But the unity of direction
is none the less there ; and there is, in that sense, a plan.
The plan may not be consciously entertained. But it is implied,
and supplied, by the process from which it emerges ; and it
presents itself to our consciousness in retrospect, even if it was
not originally present there.   The comings and goings of
different parties in office can provide a result which, in review,
is reasonable ; which does justice to different sides and adjusts
conflicting claims ; and which has thus the characteristics of
purpose and of plan.[1] We have to remember, after all, that
there are two modes of planning. There is what may be called
the short-time mode, when, in a given present, at a point of
time, with our eyes on the immediate future, we discuss and
plan the adjustments of which we can see, or forecast, the
imminent necessity. But there is also the long-time mode, by
which planning is spread along a line of time, and the discussion of different possible adjustments proceeds as it were by
successive exposition, rather than by simultaneous debate,
until the final adjustment is eventually attained. It is indolence
and opportunism to relegate issues that require the short-time
mode to the region of the long-time. On the other hand, it is
an impatient and short-sighted policy which would impose the
short-time mode on matters which require the long-time.
There is room for both ; and statesmanship consists in a true
distinction of issues according to the modes they require.
Perhaps we need to-day a great deal of short-time planning.
The more we have the better—provided that it is restricted to its
own proper issues ; that we recognize that the long-time mode
of planning is also, in its way, planning ; and that we reserve
for that mode the great issues which demand its operation.

[1] Cf. A. D. Lindsay, *Essentials of Democracy*, p. 47 : 'in the alternation in power
of political parties there is often worked out in practical dialectic what discussion
could not discover.'   I should prefer to say that there is often worked out in long-
time discussion (one party holding the floor, as it were, for its term of office, and
then another) what short-time discussion could not discover.

PART IV
ALTERNATIVES TO DEMOCRACY
IX
DEMOCRATIC MOVEMENT AND COUNTER-MOVEMENTS

§ 1. THE VOGUE OF DEMOCRACY DOWN TO 1914, AND ITS LIMITS

THE experience of the last few years suggests the idea of a general recession of the vogue of parliamentary democracy. Under the influence of that idea we may be led into a sweeping generalization, and conclude that a century of parliamentary democracy has been rapidly yielding, in our own days, to a new century of leadership and authority. But modes in politics are not unlike the modes of fashion ; and like the modes of fashion they may easily delude us into an impression of the universality and the permanence of novelties which are certainly not universal, and may possibly not be permanent.

The nineteenth century itself was not a century of the general and undisputed vogue of parliamentary democracy. It was indeed a century of democratic movements ; but it is easy to exaggerate both the width and the depth of the permanent results achieved by these movements. It is true that by 1914 there were forms of parliament established from London to St. Petersburg, and from Stockholm to Rome and Athens. But a form of parliament is not the whole of the system of parliamentary democracy. Organized parties, with some historical roots, and a temper which combines the spirit of party zeal with a sense of national responsibility ; an electorate with some education in the use of the franchise and some capacity of discussing the issues on which it casts its vote ; above all, a cabinet at once responsible to parliament and capable of guiding its deliberations and its decisions—all these are also elements. There were few countries in which an integral system of parliamentary democracy could be said to be established in 1914. Even in France—long a united nation, and since 1789 a nation inspired by a great if not always unchallenged tradition of liberty—such a system can only be dated, as a continuous fact, from the year 1871.

Germany and Italy, at the end of the nineteenth century, were newly united countries : national parties, a national electorate, and a national parliament were still novelties ; in Germany, if not in Italy, the organs of constitutionalism were still in the nature of grafts on a parent stock of monarchical absolutism, and the relation of the grafts to the stock had still to be finally determined.   Some of the smaller countries of Western and Northern Europe had indeed established permanent systems of parliamentary government ; but the greater countries of South-Eastern and Eastern Europe—Austria-Hungary and Russia—were still the homes of absolute governments, tempered and qualified (in different degrees) by national or social or liberal movements, but constituting, none the less, the staple bond of cohesion and the general framework of organization.   Any one who had sought, in 1900, to colour a map of Europe according to the political complexion of European governments, marking them as they were absolutist, semi-absolutist, semi-parliamentary, or fully and genuinely parliamentary, would have covered but a small space with the colour which he devoted to the full and genuine parliamentary type.

§ 2.   THE IMMEDIATE AND ULTIMATE EFFECTS OF THE WAR OF
1914–1918 ON THE CAUSE OF DEMOCRACY

Then came the war of 1914–18.   Waged, by one of the two sides, in the name of democracy, it appeared to end, when that side proved victorious, in a great extension of the democratic cause in the name of which it had been waged.   New democratic constitutions—democratic, at any rate, in form and name—sprang up all over Central and Eastern Europe. In Germany, under the Weimar constitution, the graft of constitutionalism triumphed over monarchical absolutism, and became itself the main stock : in Vienna, Prague, and Warsaw new growths of democracy appeared : there was a general epoch of popular constitution-making, which seemed to inaugurate a new period and a new scope of popular government.   It was a turbulent epoch (we may date it, roughly, from the summer of 1918, when Communist Russia gave itself a constitution, to the autumn of 1922, when the Irish Free State adopted a constitution and, as the other side of the picture, Italian Fascism also began its triumphant

career[1]) : it was an epoch in which new and contradictory
ideas, sometimes within the framework of one and the same
constitution, were jostling with one another. There were new
schemes for second chambers, if indeed a second chamber was
retained at all ; there were new forms of elected cabinets,
appointed en bloc by the legislature ; there was a new vogue
of universal suffrage, proportional representation, the use of
the referendum, and the use of electoral initiative for the
purpose of legislation : there were new ideas of federalism
and devolution, and new schemes for economic councils to aid
and to supplement parliaments; there was a new germination
of multiple parties.[2] Theory was in the air ; men spoke of a
new ' democratic rationalization of political power ' : professors
of law and political science were busy. It was all an aftermath
of a great war ; but it was only an immediate aftermath.
There were still other crops to be gathered ; and they soon
began to be gathered.

' War ', Thucydides said, ' is a violent teacher '. The
lessons which it teaches, or the mental results which it produces,
may come in successive waves ; and one wave may contradict,
or at any rate deflect, the trend of its precursor. The first wave
of the lessons of the war, at the end of 1918, trended towards
an extension of democracy. It was not only a matter of the
victory of the side which had professed the democratic cause :
it was also a matter of the human claims of the millions of
men and women who, in every country engaged, had laboured
in the war, and now began to demand a recognition of their
labours. The extension of the suffrage in Great Britain, by
the end of 1918, belongs to the period of this mood. But a
second wave followed, and a third.

First there came, as there was bound to come, the wave of
revisionism. Any great settlement, at the end of a great war,
will inevitably be called in question by those who feel that
they suffer from its terms. This had happened after the
Utrecht settlement of 1713 : it happened again after the
Vienna settlement of 1815 ; and it happened once more after

---

[1] The constitution of the Irish Free State was adopted on 25 October 1922 :
on 29 October the march on Rome had taken place, and Signor Mussolini had
become the head of the Italian government.

[2] See Miss Headlam-Morley, *The New Democratic Constitutions of Europe* (1928);
B. Mirkine-Guetzevitch, *Les Constitutions de l'Europe nouvelle* (1929), especially the
Essai synthétique, pp. 5–56.

the Versailles settlement of 1919. When a general settlement is called in question, and revision is demanded, the attention of the country concerned is diverted from a prior consideration of the internal process of its own life to a prior consideration of its external status in the general system of States. It sees itself as an injured unit or suffering person in that system. The unity of the nation—we may even say, the single personality of the nation—becomes a dominant idea. A democratic system of government, which allows, and even requires, conflicting parties, and entails the permanent presence of differences of opinion and struggle between those differences, seems treason to the unity and the personality of the nation. This mood is already, in a sense, a return to the mood of war. It cherishes the same ideal of closing up the ranks : it is inspired by the same ideas of a menaced national unity and of an injured national personality resolved to vindicate its honour.

Then comes the next wave of reaction, which is the wave of idealized memory of war. The immediate legacy of war is revulsion : the long-time legacy may be an idealization which is almost the opposite of revulsion. Those who were combatants in the war, entering the life of peace-time politics, and annoyed by its rubs and asperities, may hark back in a sort of nostalgia to the comradeship of the trenches. They may construct their ideal for the present from the memories of an idealized past ; they may make the national army their pattern for the permanent government of the nation. *L'esprit d'armeé*, the heroic quality of leadership, the no less heroic virtue of the willing follower—these become the type and example of national life. The community of discussion, which is the democratic ideal— the community, as we may call it in no ignoble sense, of ' the word '—is met and turned back by the community of ' the word of command ', moving with an élan of spontaneous alacrity under the banner of a free but total obedience.

A free and total obedience, rendered by a community of the word of command, is not in itself an ignoble idea, any more than the free and yet critical obedience of a community of the word is ignoble. The community of the word of command requires, and cultivates, peculiar virtues. They are the virtues of the heroic age ; the age of Homer ; the age of the *Völkerwänderung* of the Teutonic peoples. There is a sense in which it may be said that some of the great countries of Europe have reverted to the ideals of an heroic age—ideals curiously associated with modern sophistications and modern complications, but still of the heroic cast. The heroic age is an age of vivid personalities : of an aristocratic or would-be aristocratic society, in which the best are the leaders ; of the heroic-aristocratic virtues—honour, loyalty, mutual faith, and mutual devotion between leader and led. But it is also, by its nature, an age of war. *L'esprit d'armée* always demands an opposing army, or at any rate an enemy, even if the enemy be not organized as an army. The heroic virtues can only be practised in the face of an opposing foe, who gives point and pith to loyalty and devotion. The general conception, and the whole tone, of politics is affected by this necessity. The foe, in the original institution of this latter-day heroic age, may be primarily internal. He may be a political party which has to be negated ; he may be an alien element in the community which has to be eliminated. But he is always conceived as ' foreign ', and he eventually becomes (what is always implied from the first in the logic of this cult of heroism) a definite foreign foe, or set of foreign foes, against whom the border must be defended and the border-warfare, which is the natural activity of an heroic age, must be gallantly waged.

The consequent conception of politics and of the nature of ' the political ' may be seen in a pamphlet published in Germany by Dr. Carl Schmitt in 1932.[1] The writer argues that the essence of politics—the creative factor which brings ' the political ' into being and action—is the antithesis of friend and foe. Just as ethics is based on the antithesis of good and evil, or aesthetics on the antithesis of beauty and its opposite, or economics on the antithesis of gain and loss, so politics is based on the antithesis between the friend or comrade and the foe or stranger. The foe is not the private enemy, but the public : he is not one but many—a fighting group intrinsically opposed, by its very genius, to your own. Essentially, or at any rate ideally, he is a foreign group. It is, in a sense, a corruption of politics when the foe is found internally in an opposed political party, and when the possibility of war, which is always implied in politics, becomes the possibility of

---

[1] *Der Begriff des Politischen*, first printed in a Heidelberg journal in 1927, and then reprinted, in an expanded form, but, as the author notes, with no alteration or extension of the original train of thought, in 1932.

civil war.   But the party struggle, if it is a corruption of politics, is still politics ; and it is still politics because it is based on hostility and may become, at any moment, actual war.   The conception of friend and foe which is essential to politics is thus a polemical or military conception : it always implies struggle : we may go even further and say that ' the conceptions of friend, foe and struggle receive their real sense from the fact that they have, and continue to have, a particular reference to the real possibility of physical killing '.   Not that war is the only goal and aim of politics ; but the fact remains that in politics war is ' the presupposition which is always present as a real possibility ', and that this presupposition constitutes the specific nature of political relations.[1]

The idealized memory of war not only helps to constitute the temper of an heroic age, and to produce a militarization of the conception of the political : under modern conditions of general or nationalized warfare, which engulfs the whole community and is not, after all, left to the heroic class and its body of immediate followers, it also leads to the vogue of a directed economy and the ideal of a self-sufficient and strictly nationalized system of industry.   The memory which survives of past war is that of a nation directed and stimulated by a single scheme of productive effort.   When war, though no longer actually present as a fact, is held to be ' a presupposition which is always present as a real possibility ', this memory of the past will naturally suggest the policy of the present.   The vogue of a directed economy has more than an economic basis, and the ideal of self-sufficiency is more than an economic ideal ; they derive their colour and intention from a political consideration which, in the last analysis, is a consideration of military exigency.   When this colour and intention are dominant, it will not be the presence of economic claims and

[1] War, Schmitt confesses, is now an exception, at any rate in comparison with the past ; but we may still say that ' the exception has a significance which is particularly decisive and reveals the core of things '.   The political motive is thus one which ' affirms, if only as an extreme contingency, war, and also the feeling of war '.
    Led to investigate the ' psychological ' basis of his views, Schmitt argues that the political distinction of friend and foe has its analogy with the theological distinction between those who are in grace and those who are in sin. ' Those who face the facts will not be optimists about human nature and its universal goodness ' ; and Schmitt seems to imply that his type of political theory has ' a methodical connection ' with theology for this reason (p. 52).   But it is very far from clear that there is any parallel or connection between the antithesis friend-foe and the antithesis grace-sin which vexes the inward soul.

conflicts, or any other internal factor of an economic nature, which will finally determine the adjustments to be made and the plan to be imposed. It will be the assumption of the presence of war ' as a real possibility ' which will produce ' a regulatory plan ' and suggest the nationalization of all basic industries which are important for the purposes of national defence. And if the methods of economics are thus controlled by a conception of the political which is essentially military, the same will obviously be true, and still more true, of the methods of government—just because the methods of government are essentially and intrinsically political, and therefore, on this argument, essentially and intrinsically military. A taut and stringent leadership will seem to be an obvious necessity. The violent teacher, War, will teach men that economic competition and political discussion are alike absurdities, and that, if one is more absurd than the other, the greater absurdity is discussion.

§ 3. DEMOCRACY ALSO AFFECTED BY THE SURVIVAL OF AN OLD TRADITION OF EXECUTIVE AUTHORITY, AND BY A NEW INTER-NATIONALIZATION OF POLITICAL PARTIES AND CAUSES

One following wave, or wash, moving in the wake of war, has thus produced an immediate trend toward democratic forms of government—but forms which have sometimes been more formal than substantial. This following wave has then been succeeded, in its turn, by two other waves—first a wave of revision, tending towards an undoing of the results of war and accentuating, in the nations which have felt themselves injured by these results, the sense of corporate national dignity and corporate national prestige ; and then a wave of idealized memory of war, tending to produce the temper of a modern ' heroic age ', to militarize the idea of politics, and to bring economics under the direction of a militarized system of politics. The first wave has been met and turned by the other waves ; and the waters ' stand upon an heap '. But the results of war, however large and however stirring they may have been in the two decades between 1918 and 1939, are only a part of the matter ; and to interpret the state of Europe and the fortunes of liberty exclusively in their light would be to provide a partial and incomplete interpretation. The war of 1914–18 was a shock : it created something in the nature of a break or

a geological fault ; but it was in no sense a complete inter-
ruption of European development, and it left surviving, in
every country, a large legacy from the past. This was one of
the difficulties of the new democratic constitutions which arose
in 1919 and afterwards. Products of the immediate after-
swell of the war, they were not only exposed to later after-
swells which troubled and even contradicted their natural
development : they were also exposed to what may be called
the return of the past—the return of old notions of the rights
and the responsibilities of the executive power, in opposition
to those of the legislative : the return of old notions of the
place of the army in the State ; the return, in a word, of the
general idea of the necessity and the power of administrative
authority. There arose a contradiction between the constitutional form of the present and the active return of the past ;
and the contradiction was often the greater because the constitutional form of democracy—created in a single act rather
than tentatively developed, and created under abnormal conditions which gave an exaggerated temporary power to the
advanced wing of opinion—was itself an exaggerated, or at
any rate an advanced, form.

This contradiction or dualism would in any case have been
acute ; but it was further accentuated by the fact of an
increased connection, and an increased radiation of mutual
influence, between similar bodies of opinion in different
States. Ever since 1789, if not earlier, political causes have
been international as well as national. Legitimism in one
country has appealed to legitimism in others : constitutionalism in one country has found an echo, and sometimes even
a support, in other countries. There is nothing new in the
internationalization of national political causes ; and it is
easy to exaggerate, even to-day, the extent of this internationalization. But it may safely be said that the growth of
new methods of communication, and the increase of their
rapidity, have made each national political cause increasingly
a matter of concern to similar national political causes which
are struggling or triumphing elsewhere. Even if, in each
country, each cause is *sui generis*, because it is penetrated by
the peculiar and incommunicable *genius loci*, the fact remains
that it also receives, and also imparts, suggestion and sympathy, along an electric current which runs outside its

borders. This internationalization of national political issues adds a complication and an obstacle to the democratic process. It is more difficult for parties to join in the give and take of debate, and to develop a system of mutual discussion and compromise, when foreign factors take a hand. A party of the left, which claims to stand for the democratic cause, may feel that it is strengthened by an alliance or understanding with other parties of the left in other countries ; but it may also stand to lose, and to lose in more than one way. It may find itself pushed into a more intransigent attitude by its connection ; it may also find that the party of the right, by which it is confronted, is equally or even more strengthened by foreign connections, and is equally or even more pushed into an intransigent attitude. Nationalism has its defects, and internationalism has its merits. But there is a sense in which it may be said that nationalism (if it be understood to mean the independence and the autonomy of national parties) is a condition of the safe conduct of democratic government, and that internationalism is a difficulty—and even a danger.

Apart from the after-swell of war, there is thus a return of the past, and there is also an increased internationalization of politics, which have both tended to complicate, or even to thwart, the development of parliamentary democracy. But there are still greater factors than these which have to be taken into account. One of them we may call the social factor, though the name is hardly adequate to the thing. Another we may call the economic factor. Mixed with both, and connected with both, there is the factor of the evolution of party.

§ 4. SOCIAL FACTORS : THE GREAT POPULATION AND ITS INFLUENCE ON DEMOCRACY

The social factor is the great population, altered, leavened, and fermenting under the influence of popular education. Little more than a century ago, when James Mill wrote a plea for democracy in his *Essay on Government*, his plea was essentially a plea for the enfranchisement of the middle class, and his defence of democracy culminated in the argument that it meant the government of the middle class. That was *the* political class ; and around it lay the darkness of the non-political classes. We need not deny the narrowness of the notion ; but if we employ the faculty of historical imagination, we can understand how it was that, a hundred years ago, the circle of those who could be described as ' political beings ', even by an ardent democrat, was a limited circle. Rational appeal was still the method of political argument ; and there was a natural limit to those who could be reached by such an appeal. Democracy, under these conditions, was bourgeois : it might even be described, as it is still described by those who use the Victorian terminology of Marx, as capitalistic. But the world has moved ; and it has moved with a remarkable velocity. Not only has the population itself increased at a remarkable rate—a rate, it is true, now arrested, and perhaps even beginning to turn back on its course. The circle of the political class has also increased, until it may be said to be coterminous with the population. Popular education, beginning with us, on any great scale, in 1870 ; the popular Press, following in the wake of popular education, some fifteen or twenty years later ; the film and the broadcast, following in turn on the popular Press, at an interval of some twenty or thirty years—all these have widened the political circle to a new and remarkable extension. A change in the method of political argument has partly helped to widen the circle, and partly resulted from its widening. Taper and Tadpole already knew the value of a ' cry ' when Disraeli was writing his political novels a century ago ; but the technique of the ' cry ', and the general method of psychological manipulation, have grown with the general growth of advertisement. It is a new sea on which democratic governments are sailing to-day— a *mare magnum*, with all the perturbations and oscillations of its magnitude. Men individually are no more emotional than they were a hundred years ago (perhaps less, for the psychological introspection which teaches us to know our emotions also teaches us to control them) ; but the masses in which men necessarily act to-day are greater, and the greater the mass, the greater the possibility that action will proceed in a mood of emotion. The mode of government by discussion, which proceeds on rational assumptions, is thus faced by conditions in which those assumptions may be said to be, if not invalid, at least less valid than they were. The great political circle has a different tone and temper of mental life ; and the adjustment of the democratic process to this tone and temper (if indeed it can be adjusted and still remain itself) is a work of effort and long breath.

The development of the modern nation ; its increased population ; its great political circle ; its mental mobility, and its capacity for being swayed by suggestion ; its self-consciousness, and its consequent tendency to turn inward upon itself with an acute sense of its personal dignity and its proper prestige—all these are social facts of the first order of importance. Particularly important is the fact of national self-consciousness. The great political groups of modern times are aware of themselves, aware of one another, and alive to considerations of their relative standing and prestige, in a new and unprecedented degree. Some of the aliveness and awareness is no doubt the result of war moods, or of post-war moods ; but the general temper has deeper roots.

The sense of the group—nationalism, tribalism, racialism, by whatever name it may be called, and around whatever centre it may cluster—is walking through the world. It is not created by theory, although it may be theorized by its intellectual interpreters. It springs of itself from numbers, from the new physical contacts of numbers produced by a new material civilization, from the new mental filaments of connection between numbers spun by all the new agencies of education. Nor is it, again, the result of an atavism or recurrence, although it sometimes wears the form of recurrence to tribalism and reversion to a sort of pagan philosophy which professes to find the whole significance of life in the service of the tribe. The modern sense of the group is modern ; whatever may be its analogies with the primitive sense of the tribe, it is, in itself, the product of modern achievements and a function of contemporary civilization. Neither a theory nor a recurrence, it is a great contemporary fact. It has its nobility : it demands ardours and devotions : it seeks to inspire a temper of heroism in leader and followers : it suggests a great common venture, in which the little gains of the present may safely and properly be sacrificed to the great cause of the future. But in spite of its nobility, it raises the profoundest problems not only of politics, but also of ethics and religion.

The religious problem is that of the place of Churches, confronted by the presence of a self-conscious national society which is primarily, and may even be exclusively, conscious of

itself and its own claims.   The moral problem, closely connected with the religious, is that of the place of the individual,
and of his individual personality and its individual responsibility, confronted by a presence which tends to vindicate for
itself a major personality and a final responsibility.   The
political problem, which cannot in the last resort be divided
from the religious and the moral, is twofold.   It turns in part
on the international system which regulates, or has been
hitherto supposed to regulate, the relations between different
nations.   If the self-conscious nation persists in its own self-
consciousness, and sets its attention wholly towards the unique
and incommunicable character of its own ideals and its own
conception of itself and its place in the world, it will deny the
very idea of any international system in which it can be
included and by which it can be limited.   In part, again, the
political problem turns on the nature of the internal order in
which the self-conscious society expresses its deep sense of
itself.   If unity is its passion and if it clusters with a burning
intensity about the conception of unity, it will neglect the
groups inside itself, as it neglects the societies outside.   It will
have no room for the dialectic of political parties.   It will be
drawn by the steady pulsation of a constant impulse towards
a single centre : it will move home, in a great and happy
return, towards the idea of the single transcendent group, the
single personal leader, the single party of the élite which
immediately feels the transcendence of the single group and
immediately supports the single person in whom that transcendence is incarnate.   *Venimus larem ad nostrum* will be the
dominant feeling ;   and in a mood of quasi-religious emotion
men may say

> O quid solutis est beatius curis
> Cum mens onus reponit?

§ 5.   ECONOMIC FACTORS : MECHANIZATION, THE IDEA OF
AUTARKY, CLASS DIVISION

The economic factor accompanies, and corroborates, the
operation of the social.   The great population not only becomes
a self-conscious social unit ;   it also becomes a self-conscious
economic concern.   Here, as elsewhere, a difference of degree
tends to pass into a difference of kind.   An increase of the
scale and volume of economic production produces in its turn

a new economic system. The larger the scale of national economy, the more that economy tends to become specifically national. It begins to constitute a linked and inter-connected system, which stands by itself in the magnitude of its dimensions, isolated from other systems, but vitally affecting the self-conscious national society of which it forms the material framework. Larger issues are here concerned than the old and vexed issues of Free Trade and Protection, or even of free competition and socialism. Adam Smith wrote a work on ' The Wealth of Nations ', using a plural word which suggested an international sweep of view, but actually directing his attention (in the main, and apart from some consideration of the needs of national defence) to the wealth of the individual. To-day the problem is that of the wealth of the nation—the nation rather than the individual ; each separate nation rather than all the nations. Each national society, conscious of itself, is equally conscious of the economic structure which the efforts of its members, however unco-ordinated they may have been, have somehow resulted in building. The question before each society is that of the adjustment of this unplanned structure to a conscious conception of the immediate needs and the ultimate ideals of the national life. This is more than a question of the bearing of Free Trade or Protection on individual opulence. Individuals are not in question. It is more than a question of the bearing of individualism or socialism on the distribution of individual happiness. Individuals, again, are not in question. The issue is one, in the strictest sense of the term, of national economy. It involves the relation of the economic structure which the nation has somehow made to the general idea and ideal of itself which it is now beginning to make.

Immediately, and in the perturbations of recent years which were due to maladjustment between the general power of production and the general power of consumption, the aims of national direction and planning have been limited to the adjustment of these two processes to one another. This is conspicuous in agriculture, where the efforts of European governments have been directed to regulating the glut of production and organizing a market within which a diminished product might find an adequate vent. But intervention which begins in adjusting two economic processes to one another will soon tend to become intervention which seeks to adjust both these processes, and indeed the whole process of economics, to a general social objective which transcends economic considerations.   On the one hand the self-conscious national society will desire to draw economics into the range and under the control of its own unity.   On the other hand economic problems and difficulties will impel economic groups to solicit powers for themselves (the power, for example, of controlling the whole of an industry, by determining the amount to be produced and the methods and firms by which it is to be produced), which can be given only by the government of the organized national society, and will be given only on terms which agree with the general objectives of that society.[1]

But the economic factor transcends the immediate perturbations of recent years   The great economic structure, built on the basis of the great population, and made all the greater by all the discoveries of modern technique, raises larger problems, of a longer range.   Some of these are already with us.   One of them is impending in the future.

Greatest among the existing problems is that which is raised by mechanization and the rationalization which is its corollary. However production may be organized—whether on a system of private enterprise and competition, or on a system of collective enterprise and State-organization ; on the model of the U.S.A., or on that of the U.S.S.R.—it confronts us equally with the spectacle of the mechanized life, in which collective bodies of workers are engaged on similar processes, in similar conditions and under similar direction.   The social ' hiving ' of the nation, under the impulse of the sense of the group, has its parallel—we may even say that it has its material basis—in the economic ' hiving ' of the system of production.[2]   The

---

[1] Professor Salazar, who directs the economic destinies of Portugal, argues, very justly, that ' the State, in fostering such an organisation, is not concerned only with the material interests of the enterprises involved.   If the improvement of their conditions is to be justified, it must not only not be injurious to the general interest, but must on the contrary coincide with it '.   Report of the Director of the International Labour Office, 1936, p. 51.

[2] Nay, some I hav seen wil choose a beehive for their sign
and gloss their soul-delusion with a muddled thought,
picturing a skep of straw, the beekeeper's device,
a millowner's workshop, for totem of their tribe ;
Not knowing the high goal of our great endeavour
is spiritual attainment, individual worth,
at all cost to be sought and at all cost pursued,
to be won at all cost and at all cost assured.
                      Bridges , *Testament of Beauty*, II ,200–207.

democratic ideal of the free citizen in the free state has to reckon with both these movements, and not least with the mechanization and rationalization of the economic process— with the growing use of the machine and the growing adjustment of human labour, on what are called 'rational' lines, to the economic requirements of its use. We may argue, as it has been argued in a previous chapter, that the democratic method of politics is the necessary corrective to the mechanization and rationalization of the method of economics,[1] but we must also admit that the inherent logic of the economic process, in itself, runs more towards authoritarianism than towards democracy (otherwise we should never argue for the ' corrective ' of democracy), and we must equally admit that, until its tendency is corrected, the logic of the economic process serves as an ally of political tendencies which move towards the cult of the group and the vogue of leadership. This is not a matter of capitalism supporting fascism. It is a matter which goes beyond these simple categories. A general trend of the economic process tends to support a general trend of the social process which makes for the group and the leader. Even in the communist State the connection may be seen. Mechanization and rationalization can support, and be supported by, the great proletarian society grouped round its leader.

Mechanized and rationalized, the economic structure becomes a definite unit, with all its parts linked and interconnected, which flies the banner of ' autarky '. It is difficult to say how far this ideal of national self-sufficiency is the product of the social development of a self-conscious national society, and how far it is the outcome of the economic development, and the economic needs, of the national structure of production. Perhaps it is foolish to make the distinction ; perhaps it is simplest to say that both factors, hardly distinguishable from one another, have collaborated naturally in producing a common ideal. In any case a long road has been travelled from the mixed internationalism and individualism of Adam Smith's *Wealth of Nations*. The road which goes to autarky is a road which goes far beyond protection, if protection be understood, as the word would naturally suggest, to mean only a policy of covering vulnerable economic points. The aim is no longer protection, at any rate in that sense : it is

---

[1] *Supra*, pp. 243–4.

rather a total exclusion which is also, if we look at it from the other end, a total inclusion. The ideal is *Der geschlossene Staat*— the State which, not merely for reasons of economics, and not merely, therefore, as a *Handelsstaat*, is resolved to include within its borders the whole of the production of its economic necessities, in its own way, and in accordance with its own genius. Temporary necessities (disturbed currencies, or a disturbed state of foreign relations) may serve as the immediate occasion of this development ; but its root cause, and its ultimate philosophy, go beyond these temporary necessities. The shut state, which is being attempted in Germany (where the idea was enunciated by Fichte as long ago as 1800), is something intended for permanence.

Besides the problem of mechanization, and the problem raised by the idea of autarky, economic development has also produced, or accentuated, the problem of class division. To the Marxist this stands in the foreground ; but he would allow on reflection that, at any rate in its modern form, it springs from mechanization, and is a result which follows on factory production and the consequent aggregation both of employers and employed. The problem of divided classes is one which seems to confront, as something totally alien, the problem of rival autarkies. If to the votary of autarky the State appears as an integrated whole, to the Marxist it appears as a house divided against itself—not only riven internally, but also driven externally by the necessity of capturing new markets (so long as the capitalistic section remains triumphant within) into a war of rival imperialisms which makes any idea of a self-contained and self-contented system an idle and vain pretence. But the Marxist is himself, when it comes to the final reckoning, a passionate unitarian. If he emphasizes division, it is only because he has a passion for ending it, and for installing in its stead his own ideal of a unitary and integrated society. He is, indeed, the unitarian *par excellence* ; he would follow to its final conclusion the trend which carries the great population, arrayed in a self-conscious national society, and ' hiving ' in a mechanized and rationalized economic structure, towards the goal of unity. His ideal of a classless and uniform society is in the same vein, after all, as the ideal of autarky. Even if, in the period of struggle, he is an internationalist, and though he would accordingly, in this period, appeal to an international proletariat against an alleged international capitalism (which thus plays, at one and the same time, the two opposite parts of an international system and a system of national imperialism), he ends none the less when the struggle is over (if the Russian example is typical) in an inclusive and shut form of national State.[1] There is a sense in which Marxism flows with the general tide, and, instead of correcting, accelerates the great group movement of modern life. It, too, has the general ideas of the heroic age—ideas of the duty of loyalty and the vocation of leadership ; of the clustering group, the border struggle, the heroic temper, and the heroic virtues.

These are the larger problems of the great economic structure which are already with us and already vexing the present. But there is also a problem impending in the future. The growth of population has been closely connected with the growth of the great economic structure, and has largely helped to produce the problems which we know. It may be that a decrease of population confronts us in the future, and that this decrease, affecting in new ways the existing economic structure, will help to produce new problems which we do not know, but can only guess. Apart from Russia, which is undergoing, at a later date, an economic development and a development of population comparable to that of the period of our own Industrial Revolution, the countries of Europe are tending towards a stationary population, with a prospect of subsequent decline. A declining population will raise grave economic questions. It is comparatively easy for private enterprise to plan for a rising market. It is much more difficult for such enterprise to plan for a falling market. A further difficulty will emerge. The permanent plant of an economic system in which the population is dwindling will be beyond its requirements. That part of the population which has hitherto been concerned with the upkeep and extension of such plant—not the least skilled or the least vigorous part—will be condemned to unemployment, unless it can be transferred to other activities

---

[1] It may be argued that Russia, in her present phase, is erecting a model, and is thus still serving the international cause by showing what a socialized national State can be and can do. It may also be argued that if Russia is, for the time being, an inclusive and shut State, she is such a State against her will, because she is not living in a society or system of like States with which she could freely communicate. But the theory of the model and the plea of isolation still leave us with the fact that, in the present phase and for the time being, socialist Russia is caught in the general tide.

or other areas. In one way or another the action of government will be invoked to plan for a falling market, and to save
an industrial system overburdened with capital equipment. A
declining population may not arrest, but rather accentuate,
unemployment. What has already happened to some areas
of Great Britain, owing to the shrinkage of the general market
of the world on which they so largely depended, may happen in
other European countries, if their population begins to decline,
owing to the shrinkage of their home market.

If numbers are not destiny, they are a part of destiny. The
destiny which falling numbers have in store for us may not
be a destiny of less mechanization (invention obeys its own
laws) ; and it may possibly be a destiny of even greater
autarky, enforced on the ground that a smaller home market
has a smaller need for importation. On the other hand a
decline of numbers may produce a greater solidarity of classes,
sharing a common misfortune, and sharing it, perhaps, more
evenly than they shared the good fortune of previous days ;
and it may also produce, beyond the sphere of economics, a
quieter general temper, less liable to a sudden access of national
zeal and less stirred by a burning sense of national prestige.
But in any case the action of government will tend to be
greater rather than less ; and we may expect, in a falling
market, an increased demand for planning and direction to
ease the fall. The tendencies operative during the present
maladjustment between production and consumption may
grow stronger in an age in which such maladjustment will
seem to be the regular order of the day.

X

THE SYSTEM OF THE SINGLE-PARTY STATE

§ 1. THE ORIGINS, THE DIFFERENT FORMS, AND THE COMMON CHARACTERISTICS, OF THE SYSTEM OF THE SINGLE PARTY

MEANWHILE the present conjuncture of tendencies has already produced, in a number of European countries, the new political phenomenon of the single party.[1] The political party has been torn from its natural context in the system of democratic institutions in which it originated ; it has ceased to be an organ which serves the sovereign purpose of democracy by preparing a 'case' and vindicating it in discussion against other and similar (if also different) 'cases' ; and it has suffered a triple change. It has been adjusted to the new cult of heroism ; it has been turned into the mirror or focus of the new self-consciousness of national society ; it has been made the planner or director of a newly nationalized system of economics. The new style of party (which is the negation of party in the old sense, because it claims to be total, and recognizes no other case than its own) belongs to the present century.[2] We may even go further and say that it has arisen, established itself, and flourished in the period since the war of 1914–18. In its immediate origins—though its ultimate roots go deeper—it is the reflection, or the perpetuation, of the nation at war. Just as the nation at war sends into the field a national army of some two or three millions of men, so, in the time of a troubled peace, some of the nations continued to deploy a national party of some two or three millions of adherents. In Italy and Germany ex-servicemen were active in the formation of such a party. In both countries the party, true to the core of its immediate origins, assumed a form of military uniform : in both the party ultimately became a new sort of militia, standing side by side with the regular army of the nation. The Russian Communist party, it is true, originally showed a different character ; and it did so not only at the time of its triumphant

[1] See above, pp. 88–90.

[2] The Russian Communist party is the oldest ; and it may be said to have begun in 1900, though it did not assume the role of a single party till the end of 1917. The Italian Fascist party began in the spring of 1919, and became a single party after the march on Rome in the autumn of 1922, or, at any rate, after the suppression of any opposition in 1925. The German National Socialist party began in 1920, and became a single party in 1933.

emergence at the end of 1917, but also for a decade, or more, of its subsequent history. It began, not in a mood of war, but in a mood of reaction against war. Nor was it, in its origins, based on a cult or profession of nationalism. On the contrary it acknowledged, and even professed to foster and extend, the rights of national minorities within its borders ; and outside its borders it even sought to become an international party, not limiting its doctrines, or its adherents, to any national soil, but making the world its province and uniting, under its banner, all the workers of the world. The spirit of this original pacificism and this original internationalism is not dead ; but the more Russian Communism has established itself as a particular and peculiar way of Russian national life, which appeals to the proper pride of all who share in that life, and the more it has felt itself confronted by opposition or threats to that peculiar way, the more has the Russian Communist party been drawn into the military and national trend of the analogous single parties in other countries. If it is not a uniformed party, and if it has no party militia, it is a uniform party which can now formally describe itself, in the new Russian constitution of 1936, by the military style of a ' vanguard ' ; and it is a party which needs no party militia only because the regular Red Army (not inherited from any previous régime, but newly constituted to defend the new régime) is itself indoctrinated and imbued with the principles of the party.

The system of the single party is a system which may take different forms. The Russian form is peculiar in more than one respect. In Russia the whole of the political system has been recast and remoulded by the party, and brought into conformity with its doctrines. The party is under no necessity of establishing any relations, or any form of concordat, with old and inherited military and political institutions ; it has no need to claim formal rights in regard to other institutions, and it has no incentive to establish ' paramilitary ' or ' parapolitical ' organizations by their side. In Russia, again, the whole of the social system has been similarly recast and remoulded by the party. The direction and planning of the economic structure is total : there is no grafting of new party ideas of corporativism or autarky on a previous stock : there is simply a totally new economic structure, built by the party, or at any rate built in accordance with the ideas of the party. In Italy and in Germany the eruption of the single party has been more complicated and less engulfing. The single party has supervened on an existing political constitution and an existing social system. It has sought to superimpose itself on the former, while retaining many of its institutions and methods : it has not, as yet, totally altered the latter.

But the analogies of form and character are perhaps greater than the differences. The single party, in each case, is allied with the ideas of the heroic age and the heroic leader. The whole of the party, in each case, professes a ' vocation of leadership ' in the nation, for which it finds the example and the inspiration in the single leader who leads his ' following ' of leaders. The single party, again, professes to be, in each case, the focus and the power-house of the general pulsation of a whole self-conscious society. It centralizes in itself all voluntary social activities (among them the leisure activities of adults, and the activities of youth movements for the training of juvenile life) ; and these voluntary social activities, so centralized, are henceforth coloured by the character of the party, turned by its alchemy into something more than social, and made to assume a quality which is predominantly political. (It is in this sense that the new Russian Constitution of 1936 describes the Communist Party as ' the nucleus of all organizations '.) Finally, in each case, the single party becomes the planner and director of the national economic structure, either (as in Russia) in the light of its own original objectives, or (as in Italy) in the light of objectives which it proceeds to extemporize after its initial triumph. The objectives may range from communism to corporativism ; they may range, again, according to the state and posture of foreign affairs, from ideas of a peace economy, intended to secure some form of internal solidarity, to ideas of a war economy intended to secure external security by State control of production in the interest of national defence. In any case there will be control and direction ; in any case (with martial ideas of the heroic age, and missionary ideas of extending a doctrine, both generally prevalent) there will be a tendency towards the economy of war.

In spite of all these analogies of form and character, it is still possible, and indeed it is tempting, to think of ' a conflict of ideologies' between the different varieties of the single-party State. Each of these single parties has its different single doctrine ; and each of these doctrines (like the doctrines of the religious confessions in earlier days) tends to be pushed to the point of conflict with other doctrines. It is particularly tempting to think of a conflict between the doctrine of Communism and the doctrines (different in themselves, but united in opposition to that doctrine) of the other varieties of the single-party State. But it is also possible, and it is perhaps just, as well as possible, to think of the ' harmony of ideologies ' between all the different varieties. This harmony begins to appear as soon as we reflect on the relation of all the varieties of the single-party State to the form of State in which parties are still plural ; where discussion between the different parties is still practised ; and where parliaments still act as the meeting-ground of parties and the forum of discussion. Divided among themselves by their different doctrines, the single-party States are also divided, as a group, from the form of State which has no single party or doctrine—unless it be the doctrine that there is not, and should not be, in matters political or in any other ' matters of the mind ', a compulsory single doctrine. Not that this deeper division is a division leading more surely to war. On the contrary war, if war should come, is as likely to be war between different single-doctrine States as between a single-doctrine State (or States) and a State (or States) professing no such doctrine.[1]

§ 2. THE SPIRIT OF THE SINGLE PARTY : TOTALITARIANISM AND TRIALISM

The single party is already, in its nature, a supersession of parliament and the general system of parliamentary democracy. It does not, indeed, expressly abolish parliamentary institutions. It simply makes them otiose. In effect, it substitutes a new and vaster parliament—a parliament of millions, the whole body of its adherents —for the old parliament of a few hundreds. The substitution is so simple, and so thorough, that the old parliament may be left in existence as a harmless, if also useless, survival. It is even possible that, as in Russia, the single party may call into existence a new parliament,

---

[1] It will be obvious to the reader that these words were written before 1939. I have left them as they stood.

under the style of the Supreme Council, or again that, as in Italy, it may first add a new council of corporations to the old chamber of parliamentary deputies, and then recast the old chamber by making it a piebald body, partly recruited from the new council and partly from the party itself. The fact remains that the single party is itself the essential parliament. But it is a parliament of a new style. It may conduct some form of discussion within its own ranks, among its own members, under the terms and subject to the limits of its own doctrine. But it is not a true organ of national discussion, and still less is it an organ in a general system of national discussion which includes other organs as well as itself. Unlike an ordinary parliament, it does not conduct a public discussion, open to all the world, which serves as a vent for all trends of opinion and a winnowing fan to separate the chaff from the wheat in each trend. The single party, by its nature, must present an apparent front of unity ; and the discussions within its ranks, when they touch the raw nerve of real difference, will be conducted in secret and fought out in the dark. This constitutes a deep and genuine difference between the State of a single party and the State of a plurality of parties. The one may seem divided, and even distracted : the other seems to be one and undivided. But the division of the one is the public and open division which leaves a central core of unity : the unity of the other is a screen which hides both the secret differences of the single party and the suppressed opinions of the dissidents.

Unlike an ordinary parliament, again, the parliament constituted by the adherents of a single party has no other organ of discussion by its side. If the old parliament is otiose when the new style of parliament appears and grasps the reins, the same is true of the electorate, which ceases to be an organ of discussion and becomes an instrument of registration ; and it may even be said to be true of the cabinet, now no longer actively engaged in a joint formation of policy and its joint defence against the opposition, but swayed by the party leader and merged in the general party. A new system of politics emerges under these conditions. It may be called a system of unitarianism, because it depends on a single party which is not confronted by other parties in parliament or the nation, nor limited by the effective action of a real electorate or a genuine cabinet. It may also be called, and for the same reason, a system of totalitarianism. Any single authority is by its nature total. Having no other authority at its side, with which it must divide the exercise of power, it will equally leave no possible object (or subject) of power untouched : having no partners in power, it will leave no loop-holes and no exemptions from power. It is for this reason that the system of single-party government is led to engulf—to absorb, or at any rate regulate—churches, trade unions, institutions of education, charitable organizations, and every form and phase of the activity of the community's life.

But while this new system of politics may be called a system of unitarianism, or a system of totalitarianism, it may also be called—from another point of view—a system of trialism. If we hold that the party stands at the centre of the common life, reaching out on the one hand into the State (which is the political structure of the army, the civil administration, and the general government), and reaching out on the other into the People or *Volk* (which is the social-economic structure of professions, occupations, and general social groups), then we may say that there are three things in the new system ; but, having said that, we are bound at once to add that the three are one in the central party,·which at once animates the State and inspires the People or *Volk*. This is the view which is expressed by Dr. Carl Schmitt in his pamphlet, published in 1933, on the theme of *Staat, Bewegung, Volk*.[1]

In his view the ' liberal-democratic ' State is essentially a system—or rather an anarchy—of unresolved dualisms. There is the dualism of ' the State and the Individual ', which may also be called, when we take into account the social groups formed (or supposed to be formed) by numbers of individuals, a dualism of ' State and Society '. There is the dualism of legislature and executive, expressed in the idea and practice of a division of powers. There is the dualism of law and politics, which pits a fixed body of static rules—and with it, and behind it, the judges—against the dynamic movement of political life and political exigencies. Particularly important is the dualism of the State and the individual, or, as it is also called, of State and society. In form—but only in form—it opposes the

[1] See especially the second part of the pamphlet, entitled *Die Dreigliederung der politischen Einheit*, pp. 11–22.

' rights ' of the individual, or the ' free play ' of society, to the claims of the State. In reality it creates a gulf between the operation of a paralysed State and the dark activities of vigorous and powerful parties which use the cover of individual rights and social liberty to pursue their own sinister interests. Neither the State nor the individual can flourish under these conditions. The State is threatened, or even captured, by dark and irresponsible powers : the individual is coerced by the drill and discipline of the very forces which profess to be acting in his name. The result is a plurality of irresponsible tyrannies, usurping the prerogatives of the State and defeating the rights of the individual.[1]

To dualism of this order, reduced to such desperate straits, Dr. Schmitt opposes the saving grace of trialism. Under the system of trialism the anarchical multitude of irresponsible parties disappears. A single party, eliminating the rest, assumes an open control. It establishes itself in the centre : it becomes the bridge and the reconciler of State and People : a system of resolved trialism (one may almost say trinitarian-ism) takes the place of a system of unresolved dualism. The division between executive and legislature is ended by the unity of party spirit and the unity of common leadership : the gulf between law and politics is filled by the moving of the party and the doctrines of the party (the doctrine of a common leadership and loyalty, and the doctrine of the common inspiration of a common blood) into the gulf. The essence of the new unity is thus a new system of party : a party con-ceived as an ' order ' or an ' élite ', to distinguish it from the

---

[1] It would take the argument too far afield to discuss, at this point, the justice of Dr. Schmitt's analysis of the working of the Weimar Constitution, as it is here expressed. But it is just to observe that, while he speaks of the liberal-democratic State of the nineteenth century, he is really concerned only with one form of that State, the German, and with that only as it existed in the twentieth century, from 1918 to 1933. (He himself remarks, and remarks very justly, that ' behind the façade of the dualistically interpreted liberal *Verfassungsstaat*, the German State, even in the liberal nineteenth century, remained a State of the army and the official, and therefore a *Verwaltungsstaat* '.) It is perhaps also permissible to add that, so far as party was hypertrophied in the German liberal-democratic State of 1918–33, this was perhaps due to the hypertrophy of the idea of the State, which affected and exaggerated parties. So insistent was the ubiquitous idea of the State that even the party groups, formed in the social area, tended to become States, and to employ the drill and discipline of a State. In England we tend to make the State itself a sort of club, and to extend the methods of the club into the management of the State. In Germany, it may be said, there is a tendency to make even a club into a sort of State, and to extend the methods of the State into the management of clubs.

political parties of the old liberal State : a party which 'carries'
State and People, and which, while it recruits itself from all
sections of the People, is in itself exclusive (or 'shut') and
hierarchically led.[1]

The party, so conceived and so organized, on the one hand
'occupies the key positions in the official organization of the
State', and, on the other, 'penetrates, in a corresponding
manner', the social-economic structure (with its professions and
occupations) in which the People lives its daily life.[2] It constitutes the community typical of the twentieth century—not
only in National Socialist Germany, but also (if in a different
way) in Fascist Italy ; and not only in Germany and Italy, but
also in Soviet Russia, where 'a trialistic system of State,
party, and labour, has been attempted as the total expression
of political and social reality '.[3] The new or triple community
thus constituted by the single party is not only the typical fact
of our times : it also corresponds to the great traditions of
political theory which were established by Hegel.[4] It is the
synthesis which Hegel sought ; and for all its trialism it is the
perfect expression of unity. 'Distinct but not divided, connected but not coagulated, the three great fly-wheels must run
side by side, each according to its own internal law, but all in
the unison of the political whole which is carried by the
movement of the party '.[5]

Unity is thus the transcendent note behind the system of
trialism. The unity of the community, expressed in and vindicated by the single party which carries the community in both
of its manifestations (as a State and as a People), is the essential
thing. This unity is prior to law. Before law can exist as an
actual body of substantive rules (and not merely as a formal
idea), the prior condition is a full assurance of political unity.
Only on the basis of uncontested political decisions (proceeding from the single and uncontested party) can the actual

---

[1] Schmitt, op. cit., p. 13.   [2] Ibid., pp. 17, 20–21.   [3] Ibid., p. 13.

[4] Ibid., p. 13. Later, however (pp. 31–2), Dr. Schmitt argues that 'Hegel
died' on 30 January 1933, when the National Socialist party came into power.
Hegel had been content with a *Beamtenstaat* in which the army and the officials
had taken upon themselves the duty of 'carrying' the State. He had identified
the historic fact of this type of State with the philosophical idea of a realm of
objective reason (p. 29). Hegel was transcended when a party took on its shoulders
the duty of 'carrying' the State—and not only the State, but also the People.

[5] Ibid., p. 32. I find it difficult to see the machine which is here suggested,
but I have done my best to translate the passage literally.

development of substantive law begin to proceed.[1] But law is not only affected by being made secondary to the cause of political unity ; secondary, therefore, to the single party which expresses and vindicates that cause ; secondary, in the last resort, to the single leadership which inspires and controls that party. It is also affected in another way. It loses any specific legislative organ of creation : it loses any independent judicial organ of interpretation. The principle of leadership, which is the essential expression of the cause of unity, abolishes any separation of executive and legislative powers, and vests the executive power with the initiative of all legislation.[2] In Germany, as in Italy and in Russia, the same trialistic type of State involves the same consequence of the repudiation of division of powers. The very judicature must be trained and tuned to unity ; and the man entrusted with the interpretation of the law of his community must be steeped in its particular spirit and penetrated by its particular doctrine.[3] Law is always the law of a particular community ; and its only true interpreter is he who is rooted and grounded in the reality of belonging to his people and his race.[4] ' Every political unity needs a consistent internal logic of its institutions and rules. It needs a unitary idea of form, which shapes every part of the public life without exception or intermission. In this sense there is no normal State which is not total '.[5]

§ 3. PARTY IN SINGLE-PARTY STATES AND PARTY IN STATES OF THE PARLIAMENTARY TYPE

The system of the single-party State, in the form in which it is described and defended by Dr. Schmitt, is a system common to a number of countries. Russia, Italy, and Germany are all agreed in acting through a single party, which in turn acts upon both State and society, and holds them together in a common allegiance to its principles and its control. But there are obvious differences between these countries, as well

---

[1] Schmitt, op. cit., p. 15. It is thus a mistake to substitute justice for political leadership (p. 40) : leadership comes first, and justice adjusts itself to its primacy.

[2] Ibid., pp. 10, 35.   [3] Ibid., p. 44.   [4] Ibid., p. 45.

[5] Ibid., p. 33. The conception of the position of the Church in the community, which Dr. Schmitt is thus led to entertain, is simple. If a Church does not itself raise any totalitarian claim, it may ' find its place in the third sphere '—that of the social-economic structure—under the control of the total claim of the party and the party State.

as a formal agreement. Their agreement is largely negative. They all reject the ideas and the institutions of parliamentary democracy—the idea of discussion, which presupposes the idea of toleration : the institutions (dependent on these ideas) of a party system which embraces more than a single party, of an electorate which chooses between and among several parties, of a parliament which is composed of a number of parties, and of a government or cabinet which is successively constituted by different parties according to the electoral verdict and the parliamentary majority. They reject, again, the system of developed differentiation on which the ideas and institutions of parliamentary democracy are based. As they go back to an earlier heroic age, so they also go back to an earlier age of undifferentiated homogeneity, prior to the present stage of political evolution. They seek to obliterate or to transcend the distinction between State and society, seeking to fuse the two in the common life and the common inspiration of the single party. This is a return to the old Greek city-State, in which State and community were still one and undivided : it is a return, from another point of view, to the thought of the sixteenth century, in which it was assumed, by a similar identification, that the people of a single ' region ' must be a single Church as well as a single State. And just as the distinction between State and society, which is one of the conquests of modern civilization, is thus obliterated or transcended, so the distinctions within the State, which have been gradually achieved in the process of human development, are similarly removed. The legislative and the executive power are blended in a practice, open or implicit, of total leadership : the law of the constitution, like the rest of law, is merged in the merger of the two powers[1]; and even the judge is drawn, like the legislature, in the train of the party and its chief.

In negation, then, the single-party States present a common

---

[1] Russia, however, appears to form an exception, by virtue of her promulgation (alone among single-party States) of a new constitution, in 1936, which can only be amended by a special majority of the legislature, and which guarantees in one of its chapters (Chap. X) the basic rights of citizens. Moreover, if we take the constitution as operative, and as being a fact and not only a statement, we must admit that Russia has not only promulgated a separate law of the constitution : she has also enunciated, in that law, a distinction between the legislative and the executive (under which the former is declared to be ' the supreme organ of State power '), and a distinction between the judicature and the other powers.

front to the States which follow the practice of parliamentary democracy. It is when they begin to affirm that they also begin to diverge. We may consider their affirmations from two different points of view. Some of them turn on matters of method—on the formal position of the party in the State and the social system, or on the formal position of the leader in the party. Others (and they are obviously the more important) turn on matters of end or aim—on the social elements dominant in the different single-party States, and the social and political objectives which the different single parties accordingly use their position of dominance to achieve.

But before we turn to the divergent affirmations of the single-party States, we may pause to consider the general problem of the relation between States of this type and States of the parliamentary type. It may be asked whether the part which is played by party in the two types of States is, after all, fundamentally different. In States of the parliamentary type party may also be regarded as a conduit between society and the State. The party system gathers, at one end, the different currents of social opinion into the definite and recognized channels of party ; and it then releases them, at the other end, to turn the wheels of the State, partly by providing and inspiring the party government which moves the wheels, and partly by providing and inspiring a party opposition which balances the government. In this sense States of the parliamentary type may also be called trialistic. They do not, after all, institute a dualism of State and society ; they provide a channel or conduit between them, which enables the one to act on the other and, more particularly, enables society to act on the State. States of the single-party type are only doing what States of the parliamentary type have already done before ; but they are doing it to a far less extent and with a difference of degree which constitutes, after all, a difference of kind. They begin by blocking up all the channels between State and society except one. The single channel thus left, just because it is single, becomes something more than a channel. It becomes the fountain-head—the original and the only moving power. Instead of responding to social movement and receiving social impulses, it works back on society as a controlling force, which determines what society shall be and what it shall say and do. Instead of carrying social impulses into the State, it carries only itself—or, so far as it carries any social impulse, it carries only the impulse which it has itself determined. It thus stands between State and society not as a mediator, but as a controller. The one channel holds the original and only waters of life, which flow down on either hand into State and society. Society becomes a stagnant uniformity, receiving waters which cannot drain away, and with no original inward springs in itself.[1] The State becomes a single revolving wheel, without compensation or balance— a great mill-wheel, turning in isolation, into which one water incessantly pours from a single 'lead'.

There is thus, when all is said, a difference of kind between the single-party State and the State of the parliamentary type. The fact that there is party in both, and that, in both, party stands related to the State on one side and society on the other, does not obliterate the other and more important fact that party is a very different thing in the one from what it is in the other, and that it stands related to State and society in a very different way. In the one type of State the distinction between society and State remains (though they are kept in connection and interaction) : in the other the distinction between them is blurred or confused by the party, which dominates and controls them both alike. In the one type there is a distinction within the State, not only in the form of division between different powers of government, but also in the form of compensation and balance between the government party and the opposition party : in the other this distinction, in both of its forms, is gone. In the one type toleration, discussion and compromise are involved by the fact of a varied society with many currents of opinion, all flowing freely through the various channels provided by different parties, and all acting within and upon the State into which they flow ; in the other a compulsorily uniform society, flowing perforce in a single channel, issues in a State which is equally uniform.

[1] A fen
Of stagnant waters : altar, . . . pen,
Fireside, the heroic wealth of hall and bower,
Have forfeited their ancient . . . dower
Of *inward* happiness.

The lines of Wordsworth occurred to me after I had written the words 'stagnant uniformity'. Perhaps I read too much into them ; but they have for me a deep significance.

§ 4. DIFFERENCES BETWEEN SINGLE-PARTY STATES IN MATTERS OF
METHOD : THE RELATION OF PARTY AND STATE, AND THE
FACTOR OF LEADERSHIP

But there are also differences among the States of the
single-party type—differences both of method and of aim.
The differences of method are less deep and less characteristic ;
but they have their importance. There are differences, first
of all, in regard to the relation of the single party to the social
system. In Russia the single party has entirely recast society,
introducing an organization (exactly parallel with its own
organization) of trade unions in the sphere of production, and
co-operative societies in the sphere of consumption, which
constitutes a society multiform in appearance if uniform in
spirit.[1]   In Italy the single party has stamped on Italian
society—but stamped less deeply and pervasively—a form of
corporativism which leaves it still largely what it was. In
Germany the single party has been content, in the main, with
introducing its principle of ' leader ' and ' following ' into the
social order, turning the employer into the adventurous
leader and the employed into faithful followers. But the
difference between the attitudes of the different single parties
to the social system is really more than a difference of method :
it involves a difference of aim ; and it can only be properly
considered in connection with aims.

More purely a matter of method is the difference between
the attitudes of the different single parties to the State. In
Russia the Communist party, though it is mentioned in one
of the sections of the constitution of 1936 as the vanguard of the
toilers and the leading nucleus of all their organizations,
stands generally in the background. It is not included in the
constitution of the State as one of its formal elements : it has
no formal rights : whatever it does, it does *de facto*, in virtue
of the influence which it exercises, or through the presence of
its individual members on the governing bodies of the State,
but not in virtue of any *de jure* power with which it is legally

---

[1] It may be said, as it is said by the Webbs, that the Russian community is more
than triple : it is sextuple. Besides the State and the party, there are also four
forms of society—the form composed of the trade unions of wage-earning producers employed by the State : the form composed of unions of agricultural
owner-producers ; the form composed of unions of industrial owner-producers ;
and the form composed of co-operative societies of consumers. In effect, however,
the four forms of society (which is purely and only *economic* society) are only
different expressions of a single uniform scheme.

vested. In Italy the position is different. The party is formally recognized by law, and vested with formal powers by law. Its Grand Council, from 1928 to 1938, had the legal right of presenting the whole list of parliamentary candidates for approbation to the whole of the national electorate ; and since 1938 its National Council (a different body) has been legally included as part of the new Chamber of Fasci and Corporations. More important, the Grand Council has also the legal right of offering advice on all questions of a constitutional character.[1] In Germany the National Socialist party is perhaps more formally connected with the State than the Russian Communist party, but it is certainly less formally connected with it than the Italian Fascist party. It is secured a legal monopoly by a law of July 1933, prohibiting the formation of other parties : under a law of December 1933, for securing the unity of the party and the State, it is vested with the position of a corporate public-law body (analogous, for example, to our English municipal corporations) ; and by the same law the deputy of the party leader, and the chief of staff of the party militia, are made *ex officio* members of the Government. On the whole, however, the National Socialist party in Germany, like the Communist party in Russia, acts *de facto* rather than *de jure* : it is a permeating influence in the State rather than a formal organ of the State. Originally, perhaps, it was less powerful than the Russian single party, in that it had to reckon with an old and surviving army tradition and with the old and surviving tradition of the German civil service ; but even before 1939 the Army had been brought into line with the party, and a Civil Service Act of 1937 had already given the party a large measure of control over the recruitment of the civil service.[2]

Another difference of method between the different States of the single-party type turns on the position of the party leader, and on the importance assigned to the factor of leader-

[1] Under a statute of 1928 (on the constitution and attributes of the Grand Council) the advice of the Grand Council is formally necessary for any constitutional law, along with the approval of the Senate and Deputies ; and a law of 30 December 1930 accordingly enacted a new form for the promulgation of any such law, which records the advice of the Council (and the approval of the Parliament) before proceeding to the Royal sanction.

[2] We may also add that under a law of January 1934, for the ordering of national labour, the head of the National Socialist cell in any industrial enterprise has the legal right to join with the ' leader ' of the enterprise (the employer) in drawing up the list of the members of the Works Council (*Vertrauensrat*).

ship in the constitution of the party and thereby in the constitution of the State. In Germany the factor of leadership is so prominent that it may almost be called the core not only of the constitution of the party, but also of its doctrine. Racialism, or the doctrine of the necessary identity of the community in kind and ' blood ', is indeed another essential doctrine ; but in some presentations of the party belief and practice it is evident that racialism is regarded as a consequence and corollary of leadership. In Dr. Schmitt's view, for example, the primary idea is that of ' the immediate fact and real presence ' of leadership ; and it is on the basis of this idea that there ensues the further idea of racial unity, or identity of kind, uniting the body of followers both to one another and to their leader, and thus providing the leader with the homogeneous and loyal following which he essentially requires.[1] But whether or no we assign a position of logical priority to the idea of leadership, it is evident that the fact of leadership is the primary fact in the National Socialist party and the National Socialist State. ' Leader ' is the essential title of the head of the State : leadership runs through the constitution of the party, the constitution of the State, and the constitution of economic society.

The factor of leadership is less overtly present in Fascist Italy. It is there ; it appears on the very walls, where the word ' Duce ' is ubiquitous ; the leader of the party is the ' head of the government ', and the head of the government dominates every power and every sphere of the action of the State. But leadership here is more of a fact than a doctrine ; and while party is more formally inscribed in the Italian State than it is in the German, the principle of leadership is less formally inscribed as the central and permeating principle of the whole community than it is in Germany. In the State there is still a King as well as a Duce ; and in economic society the general principle is that of corporativism (in the sense of a conjunction of employers and employed in each branch or category of production) rather than that of leadership.

In Russia the principle of leadership is even less formally inscribed than in Italy. This is not to say that leadership is not actually present and active. The memory of autocracy is a long memory in Russia. But the modern autocrat of all the

[1] Dr. Schmitt, op. cit., p. 42.

Russias goes by the simple title of secretary of the party[1]; and the institutions of the State present a plethora of other authorities. There is the elected Supreme Council; there is the Presidium which it elects in turn from its members; there is also the Council of People's Commissars, which the Supreme Council equally ' forms by its choice '. Among these authorities the Supreme Council is defined as ' the supreme organ of State power '; but over and above the Supreme Council, which is only an ' organ ' or agent of power, there stand the soviets of the workers' deputies, to which the essence of power itself is formally and finally ascribed. In the Russian State there is thus a large apparatus of political authorities, professing a democratic character or origin, which surrounds the hidden leader; and Russian society, in its trade unions and other unions of producers, and in its co-operative societies of consumers, presents (or professes to present) a similar apparatus of democratic social authorities. We may add that the Communist party itself, in its own internal constitution, is similarly constituted : it is built up from below by election, and presents (or professes to present) its own apparatus of democratic party authorities, parallel to the similar political and social authorities.

Form and fact often differ in the actual working of political and social systems. The problem of Russia is the problem of discovering the facts of political and social *direction* behind the forms of political and social *election*. There can be no doubt (it is frankly admitted, and indeed asserted, by its own members) that the direction, or ' directives ', of the party determine the action which is actually taken in the institutions of the State and the parallel institutions of society. But though the directives of the party determine the action of the political and social authorities, a doubt may still be raised whether the direction of the secretary determines the directives of the party, and whether a single central leadership is an essential factor of the nature and action of the party.[2] Remembering

---

[1] More exactly, he is the Secretary of the Central Committee of the party (a body of some 70 members) ; and he is also a leading member of the Politbureau, a standing sub-committee of the Central Committee which is the inner core of its activity. (By a recent development the Secretary is now also Premier.)

[2] See the Webbs, *Soviet Communism*, Vol. I, pp. 431-40, where this doubt is discussed. Repudiating the idea that the Secretary is a dictator, they describe him as ' a national leader . . . persistently boosted . . . generally admired . . · and irremovable against his will '.

the deification of the dead Lenin, and the cult of his living successor, we may resolve the doubt in the affirmative. But the fact remains that the actuality of leadership, and even the actual cult of the actual leader for the time being, are something different from the vindication of the 'leader principle' as the pivot of the general life of the community. They are pragmatic facts rather than moving and stirring theories.

§ 5. AGREEMENTS AND DIFFERENCES BETWEEN SINGLE-PARTY STATES IN MATTERS OF SUBSTANCE : COMMON CULTIVATION OF YOUTH ; COMMON RELEASE OF A NATIONAL TREND ; VARIETIES OF SOCIAL BASIS

From differences of method we may turn to differences of substance—differences in the ends or aims pursued by the different single-party States. The ends or aims of a party determine the character and the class of the adherents whom it recruits ; but it is also true, conversely, that the character and the class of the adherents whom it seeks to recruit affect the objects and the programme of a party. In any case our view of the ends and aims of the great single parties may be more concrete, and more living, if we start from the human material on which they draw, and which they seek to attract. A number of factors would appear to be operative in determining the recruitment of these parties. One is the factor of age, or the nature of the age-group and the character of the generation to which appeal is made. Another is the factor of class, or the nature of the social group and the character of the economic aspirations which parties seek to enlist. A third factor, which is concerned not with cross-sections of age or class, but with the long continuous line of national development, is the factor of the national trend and the dominant national longing. The party which can discover and release this trend is at once on the way to become the single party of the nation. An age-group or a social group may be particularly powerful ; but it is always confronted by other age-groups or other social groups. A party which not only appeals to some age-group or some social group, but also discovers and releases a national trend or longing, will soon find itself, or make itself, unhampered by rivalry.

In the matter of age and the generations the different new

single parties are not divided. They all began in revolution ; and the appeal of revolution is always an appeal to youth. Whether we regard the ardours of revolution, or whether we regard its material basis (the capture of power and position from the clinging hands of their old possessors), we come to the same result. The old possessors of power may be attacked on many counts : they may be denounced as unpatriotic or unprogressive, as Jewish or capitalistic, as selfish place-hunters or secret traitors ; but it is always one of the counts, even if it is a hidden count, that they simply block the path of the new and rising generation. All the new single parties—and not least the National Socialist party—have cleared the way for youth.[1] One of their striking features, when once they have established their power, is the organized provision which they proceed to make for the enlisting of youth. In Italy the juvenile auxiliaries of the Fascist party run four deep, from the Young Fascists and the Avanguardisti down to the Balilla and Pre-Balilla : in Russia (where the Communists themselves number at most three millions) there are five millions of young Comsomols, and six millions of younger Pioneers and still younger ' Little Octobrists ' : in Germany the Hitler youth, if less graded and differentiated, is a similar ally of the National Socialist party.

No doubt the appeal to youth, in this form, is the natural policy of a single party, necessarily compelled to make provision for the perpetuation of itself in the unique position which it has achieved. The closed party, not open to every applicant, must train and test the young who, in their day, will be candidates for admission. Nor can the single party, by its very nature, leave the young untutored and undrilled, exposed to educational influences which might imbue them with alien ideas and a foreign tradition. If it is to perpetuate its régime, it must not only isolate its adult opponents in a sort of sanitary detention (as the medieval Church sought to isolate heretics) : it must also indoctrinate the fluid mind of the adolescent with its own orthodoxy. Alike in the interests of its own recruitment and in the interest of the consolidation

---

[1] *Giovenezza* and *Jugend* may almost be said to be key-words in Italy and Germany. But we must also take into account the feeling of national rejuvenation. It is the whole nation, as one body, apart from its members or a section of its members, which is, or rather thinks itself, young. It is a body of *enfants de la patrie*, as the French sang in 1792.

of the régime which it has established, it must bend youth to itself and its needs.

But in bending youth to itself, it is also bending itself to youth. Springing from an *élan* and revolt of youth, it devotes a large measure of its attention to youth. It seeks to satisfy their aspirations, their heroic longings, and their material desires for career and advancement. If the long competition of democracies—the slow selective influence of protracted debate, both within the parties and between the parties—often tends to leave leadership with older statesmen, the single-party State (at any rate apart from its leader) is more ready to renew its youth. It sheds its elder statesmen even before they have become elderly. Perhaps the interest of the leader leads him to prefer younger and newer colleagues less likely to rival his prestige. But apart from any such possible interest there is always a looking to youth and a tendency to bid for the support of the coming generation. In a state of multiple parties each party naturally seeks to attract the vote of the neutrals, and the neutrals are generally men and women of middle years, who have lost youthful ardours and allegiances. In the single-party State there are no neutrals ; and the vote and support which are naturally sought are those of the one residuary factor—the young.[1]

The factor of age, however, hardly serves to differentiate the various forms of the single party and the single-party States. It may be more pronounced in one than another ; but it distinguishes them all, if in different degrees, from States of the multi-party and parliamentary type. It gives them all an impetus towards rapid action ; towards a new-planned future ; toward the cult of a new heroic age and its new heroic virtues ; towards the passionate asseveration of some doctrine, apprehended with the ardour and the insistency of youth. Far more important, when we come to the differences of the single parties, is the factor of social class—the nature of the social group which forms the nucleus of the party, and the character of the social aspirations which inspire its policy.

We need not be believers in the doctrine of class war, or in the philosophy of economic determinism which is associated

---

[1] The passage of time has already produced, in Russia, a new generation which has known nothing but Communism and the teaching of Communism. If time should operate similarly in other single-party States, the factor of age may operate less. But under the conditions of the single-party State it will always be there.

with it, if we recognize the importance of this factor. But we have equally to recognize that it is only one factor among others, with which it is so curiously intertwined that we shall find it difficult or even impossible to disengage it for separate study. We can hardly measure it, therefore, in itself, or estimate its specific and particular influence. The factor of social class will be intertwined, for example, with what may be called the political (or perhaps better the national) factor— with a desire for some greater measure of internal unification, or for some greater share of external prestige and position ; and though this desire may be particularly conscious of itself in a particular class, and be particularly expressed by a particular party connected with that class, it will also be generally present in the general feeling of all classes. Here class runs into the nation, and the nation runs back into class ; and here, too, we touch that third factor—the factor, as it was previously termed, of the national trend and the dominant national longing—which, like the factor of social class with which it is intertwined, can never be treated in entire separation because it is never entirely separate. A national trend and longing obviously lies behind both the Fascist and the National Socialist movement ; and if it is less obvious in the background of the Russian Communist movement, it may still be said that the Russian desire for leadership of a general crusade of all workers is only a new form of that old and general national desire which once made Russia the general champion of all the Orthodox Churches.

Another reflection, which goes even deeper, may also be added. Just as the factor of social class is intertwined with the political factor of the national trend, so it is also intertwined with the intellectual factor of international thought. In other words, the idea of class and the existence of class consciousness tend to be closely connected with the general movement of thought and ideas on that international plane on which thoughts and ideas naturally move. It is difficult, for example, to disengage the factor of general and international Marxist thought from the factor of social class in any consideration of Russia. It may be said, of course, that Marxism would never have been accepted in Russia if there had not been a proletarian class which turned to Marxism. But it may also be said, and that not in a paradox, that there would never have been a proletarian class in Russia—a class conscious of itself, and ready to form a party (and eventually a State) out of itself—unless Marxist thoughts had turned to Russia, diffused itself in Russia, and created a self-conscious proletariat in Russia by virtue of its diffusion.[1] If social class can issue in thought appropriate to itself, it is also true that thought can issue in social class, and may create the consciousness and active operation of class. In the tangled skein of human affairs there is no first origin of everything else ; and as we pick at the knot we are driven to confess that it is tied of a number of strings.

§ 6. THE SOCIAL INTERPRETATION OF THE SINGLE-PARTY SYSTEM, AND THE LIMITS OF SUCH INTERPRETATION

But the factor of social class, even if it is tangled with national and international factors, is none the less a factor of the first order of importance. There was a period—a period which lasted, at any rate in form, down to 1914—in which old dynastic States appeared to determine the destinies of Central and Eastern Europe, alike in Germany, in Russia, and in Austria-Hungary. The monarch, with his army and his staff of civilian officials, seemed to stand above the play of society ; to reconcile and to harmonize its conflicting elements ; to impose the order of his peace. This was the theory of Hegel ; and facts could be held to warrant the theory. It is true that, from 1848 onwards, parliamentary institutions began to appear in the dynastic states ; it is true again that, under the shelter of those institutions, parties also began to appear—some based on a social interest, some on a religious basis, and some on political ideas of national minorities and their proper rights. The dynastic States thus seemed to acquire two centres of gravity—the dynasty itself, with its army and its officials ; and the parliament with its parties. But the dynastic centre (in the broad sense in which it included the army and the civilian officials as well as the monarch himself) remained the real centre, determining the nature of social cohesion, and manipulating parliament and parties to suit its purposes. The war

---

[1] It may be urged in reply that Marx was himself the product and the inevitable voice of a social class and a social interest. But even if it be admitted that the thought of Marx was produced by the social conditions of Western Europe, it still remains true that his thought was one of the factors which helped to produce the idea of class and the existence of class-consciousness in Russia.

then brought the dynastic States, as allies or as enemies, into contact with the democratic States of Western Europe. The dynastic States collapsed. It was the natural, but it was also the illogical, expectation of the victors that the dynastic States would be succeeded by parliamentary States in the image of themselves—States in which the conflicting elements of society would attain a voluntary adjustment by the parliamentary method of discussion and compromise. What the dynastic States had done from above, and as it were transcendentally, would now be done from below, by the immanent power of a national society homogeneous enough to reconcile for itself its conflicting elements, and sufficiently skilled to do so through the organs and by the methods of parliamentary government.

This was a large and, as we now know, an unwarranted expectation. What actually happened was something different. The linchpin had gone ; and in its absence society, which it had held together in some sort of system, fell apart into its different elements. There was not sufficient homogeneity to attain any voluntary adjustment ; and parliaments, which might have been the organs of such an adjustment if homogeneity had only been present, were set an impossible task. The vacuum created by the disappearance of the dynastic State was not and could not be filled by a parliamentary State : it remained a vacuum. The parties which had existed in the old dynastic States were not used to the practice of active co-operation in working a parliamentary system. Never enjoying real power or genuine responsibility, which always sobers and moderates, they had been used to hot conflicts with one another, varied by the manipulations and manoeuvres of a governing authority which stood above them all, but was ready to enlist and use now one and now another of them for its own purposes. When the governing authority was removed, they stood face to face, with no habit of co-operation among themselves, and with no higher authority now present to draw or force them into co-operation with itself. In these conditions national heterogeneity and an acute division of parties were the dominant facts ; and either accentuated the other. A distracted society, which had lost its old centre, made parties still more divided : divided parties, destitute even of the unity once provided for them by the action of the old governing authority, made society still more heterogeneous. Social classes and social interests had a clear field ; and the only way in which a system of social cohesion could be achieved was either a return to the old dynastic State, or a movement forward in the direction of a single party, sustained by a dominant class, which would end the clash by its victory. The third way—the way of the sovereignty of parliament, and of the co-operation of parties in working a parliamentary system —was blocked.

In Germany the vacuum (filled, but filled in vain, by the Weimar Constitution) lasted from the end of 1918 to the beginning of 1933. In Russia the vacuum was of brief duration : the collapse of the dynastic State was followed, after some few months of parliamentarianism, by the rapid triumph of a single party sustained by a single dominant class. In the old Austrian Empire the dynastic State not only collapsed, but also dissolved. In some parts into which it dissolved (such as Czechoslovakia) the sense of a new-found nationality—at any rate among the Czechs—was strong enough to keep the new State together, and to give it, until it was overpowered by external force, the homogeneity which could serve as the basis of parliamentary institutions and the parliamentary method of discussion. In others (such as Austria) parliamentary institutions were tried, but in the absence of social cohesion failed, and were replaced by a modified and moderate form of the system of a single party. Poland, constituted from fragments of all the three dynastic Empires, first tried, and then, under Pilsudski, gradually shed, a parliamentary system ; and in the event, on the eve and under the shadow of war, a virtual system of the single party had already begun to emerge.

Italy followed a line of development peculiar to herself. She had not been the home of a dynastic State : there had been no collapse : a system of parliamentary institutions had been working since the *Statuto* of 1848, and was still in active existence when the dynastic systems crashed. It had weathered the task of war : it had weathered, though more precariously, the task of making peace, but only on terms which failed to satisfy the national sense of sacrifice and the national desire for prestige. The general considerations which apply to the great States of Central and Eastern Europe do not apply to Italy. Here a parliamentary State, with a history at least as long as that of the Third French Republic, converted itself during the years between 1919 and 1922 into a State of the single-party type. The factor of social class, was, no doubt, operative in producing the change. The system of parliamentary government, never strong, and never deeply rooted, was confronted by new claims and new movements of the working classes. They were movements with which it is possible that it might have dealt successfully, if the new and rising party of the Fascists had agreed either to co-operate with the government or to oppose the government on the lines of parliamentary opposition. It did not agree. The very fact that it did not agree, and that it preferred and was allowed to take the line of solitary action by the use of its armed squadrons, proves of itself that independent social factors were emerging, and that the old parliamentary State, if it had not collapsed, was collapsing. Fascism was both a cause and a symptom of that collapse. Whether it was provoked by the new and threatening movements of the working classes, or whether it was in itself no more than one of those movements, which rapidly swung to the other side in the course of its evolution, it attested the dissolution of the old form of State, and it showed that control was passing into the hands of independent social combinations, destined to struggle with one another until one of them became the victor.

The struggle proved to be brief; but it was only brief because the Fascist party depended on something besides the support of a social class or an alliance of social classes. It enlisted and it expressed a political trend and a national longing : it drew the support of all who believed that a more united and a greater Italy mattered more than anything else. The period in which it transcended, or professed to transcend, a policy of reliance on any social class was the period in which it marched to victory. When after its victory it began to take stock, and to construct a philosophy of ends and aims, its philosophy began with the assertion of national unity and national prestige, and it proceeded, on that basis, to the assertion of an ideal of corporativism which aimed at linking together both employees and employers under the aegis and the direction of a highly national State. It may be argued, therefore, that the rise of Fascism, though it began in social struggles and the clash of social factors, was in the last resort, and in the main, due to specifically political factors. One form of State was substituted for another, during a social crisis which might otherwise have been readily surmounted, because the old form had failed to satisfy a national desire which the new form promised to fulfil.

We may thus conclude that the development of Italy, though it shows some similarities to that of Central and Eastern Europe, was in its essence different. There had not been a dissolution of a dynastic régime, followed by a parliamentary régime which failed, for want of the necessary temper, to hold society together on a new basis of mutual self-accommodation, and was therefore forced to yield to the domination of a single party. There had been a long, if never very strong, régime of parliamentary government, which, confronted by a period of social difficulties, proved inadequate to deal with them because they were complicated by political difficulties arising from injured national pride and unsatisfied national desire. The party which expressed this pride and this desire triumphed ; and in its triumph it ejected the régime of parliamentary government, not so much because it had failed to hold society together, as because it had failed to carry the long process of the national *risorgimento* to the expected goal. True, the new party soon developed, and sought to realize, a new doctrine of social cohesion. But it is also true that the new doctrine has some of the marks of an after-thought ; and in any case the goal of political unity and political expansion has determined the essential action of Italian Fascism.

But if a distinction may thus be drawn between the development of Italy and that of Central and Eastern Europe, there is still a close parallel between them—and more especially between the development of Germany and that of Italy. In Germany, too, the political factor, from the end of 1918 onwards, was indissolubly mixed with the social. Whatever the new system of parliamentary government might have achieved if it had been confronted only by social problems (and the odds were perhaps against it even on that assumption), the fact remains that it was also confronted, from the very first, by the political problems of injured national pride and unsatisfied national desire. The National Socialist party has always been national as well as social. Perhaps the only distinction that can safely be drawn between Germany and Italy is that in Germany the social difficulties, even if they were mixed with political problems, were graver than they were in Italy. In Germany a new and untried system of parliamentarianism, succeeding to an older and different system under the dangerous auspices of defeat, had to deal with a society dislocated by a sudden change affecting all its range and the whole of its nature. If, under these conditions, there was social turmoil, and if, out of that turmoil, a social combination emerged which sought to impose its will on society as a new form of peace, the upheaval was not surprising, even if it was aided and hastened by other than social factors. Still less need we be surprised by the upheaval of a new social class in Russian society, which had been still more dislocated by the fall of the old dynastic State, and had even less chance to give any trial to the parliamentary State. If the key of social interpretation cannot unlock all the secrets of the growth of Italian Fascism, it is more powerful in explaining the similar—and yet different—developments which have taken place outside Italy.

But it is nowhere the only key ; and though we must allow that the factor of social class has played a leading part in creating the system of the single party, we must also allow that this part has been played on a peculiar scene, that it has been played in combination with other actors, and that the actor who played the leading part has not always revealed his features clearly. The scene has been peculiar, because social forces and interests have been free to act in a political vacuum caused by the crash of old dynasties or the atrophy of an old parliament. There has been a combination of actors, because the action of social class has been mixed with the action partly of national trends and partly (at any rate so far as Russia is concerned) of international ideas. The features of the social class which has played the part have not always been clearly revealed, partly because, in all countries and at all times, the outlines of social class are never clear-cut or definite, and partly because, in the particular countries and times concerned, the outlines of class have been more than usually blurred by disturbances and dislocations. (In Germany, for example, the effects of deflation and general unrest were shown, during the years immediately succeeding the end of the last war, in a rising and sinking of social position which confused the whole system of classes.) It is difficult, therefore, to describe precisely the social significance and the class basis of the systems of the single party.

But the difficulty of description will not excuse us from recognizing the existence of such significance and such a basis.

In each of the countries concerned the emergence of a single party represents, to a large degree, the uprising and triumph of a social class or combination of classes. That is a feature common to all. But the class or combination of classes emerging varies from country to country ; and to discover the essence of each case we must discover the particular nature of the emergent class or combination of classes. We are thus confronted by the simple question : ' So far as a social class has captured the government and annexed the State, by the formation and the victory of a single party, what has been the nature of that class in each of the three main single-party States ? ' Some answer will be given to that question in the following chapters ; but a summary indication of its lines may serve to conclude the present stage of the argument, and to prepare the way for its future course.

In Russia the emergent class—originally a small minority class, which then proceeded to make itself first a majority and eventually the whole—was the industrial urban proletariat. In Germany no simple answer will meet the case. But it may be said that the National Socialist party, while claiming to be a party of the workers, drew its origin mainly from the ranks of the lower middle class in town and country ; that it was swollen, as it grew, by the adherence of wealthy elements in industry and commerce ; and that it eventually became the vehicle or (as the Germans say) the ' bearer ' of a national trend of Folk-memory and Folk-pride which proved itself to be stronger than class or the sentiment of class. In Italy too no simple answer is possible. But here again it may be said that the Fascist party, while it too claimed in its infancy to be a party of labour, similarly drew its origin mainly from the ranks of a middle class which was frightened by the prospect of loss of social position ; that it similarly became, in its growth, a party of wealthier elements ; and that it also became, above everything else, a party which served as the vehicle or bearer of a national trend towards unification and a national desire for expansion. Both Germany and Italy thus illustrate the mixture or intertwining of factors which we have already had reason to notice. But in both the origin was the eruption of the middle class, and especially, perhaps, the lower middle class (alarmed, but yet ambitious ; bourgeois in its sentiment, but yet professing to be anti-bourgeois and even revolutionary in the new culture which it sought to establish) ; and this original eruption has continued to leave its mark. The new Russia, whatever else it may be or become, can hardly be called middle-class. The new Germany and the new Italy, whatever the glories of blood and State they seek to achieve, retain that character.

The old aristocracy, now banished from the scene in so many countries, had its signal defects. But it had also its merits—a cosmopolitan sense ; a feeling for the values of literature and art, and even for the truths of pure science ; a capacity (at its best) for unselfish public service. The eruption of the middle class in Germany and Italy has left a legacy of what may be called a middle-class temper : an instinct for getting on and making a career ; a tendency towards conformity to type ; a passion for security rather than liberty. It is true that the middle class has come under the influence of a national trend and become the bearer of an ardent nationalism ; but it is also true that this nationalism, if in one sense more powerful than its bearer, has in another sense been subjected to the character and colour of the class by which it is borne. It has become less of a cherished ideal and more of an imposed convention. Revolutionary and anti-bourgeois in its own conception, the new *élite* is none the less resolved to be, and to force others to be, respectable—respectable, indeed, ' from a national point of view ', but still respectable.

XI

THE ALTERNATIVE OF RUSSIAN SOVIET COMMUNISM

§ 1. THE SINGLE PARTY IN RUSSIA : ITS SOCIAL BASIS AND ITS NATIONAL TREND

THE paradox of the victory of the single party in Russia, nearly a quarter of a century ago, lies in the fact—or seems, at first sight, to lie in the fact—that the victorious party was a minority party, resting on a social class which was a small minority of the population. It was the party of the industrial proletariat ; and the industrial proletariat, in 1917, was a thing of recent growth, cantoned in rare urban oases among the vast and uniform expanse of the Russian peasantry. The triumph of this section—or rather, of the intellectuals who led it, inspired it, and (we may even say) made it, in the sense of turning it into a self-conscious and active body—cannot but appear a marvel. It was not a marvel—in Russia.

Russia had been governed, down to 1914, on the lines of a dynastic State, by an old autocracy. That autocracy was in effect a bureaucracy, and a bureaucracy largely recruited from foreign or immigrant elements, mainly German, but in any case separate from the old Russian stock. Parliamentary institutions had been added, as they had been added in other dynastic States, but they had been added at a later date than elsewhere. The Russian Duma, established in 1905, had first met in 1906. It was not to be the seed-bed of a new Russia ; nor were parliamentary ideas, carried across by the winds of thought from the West, destined to germinate in Eastern Europe. When the old autocracy fell in 1917, it carried with it the parliamentary institutions which it had sought to create and to associate with its own working. Native Russia, thrown on itself, and turning away both from an immigrant administration and from Western parliamentarianism, had one native element on which it would depend. This was its own industrial proletariat, with unions which had already been conducting strikes at the end of the nineteenth century, and with leaders who had already elaborated a doctrine by the beginning of the twentieth.[1] Neither autocracy nor parliamentarianism had

---

[1] Strikes were already active, under the guidance of Lenin and others, in 1895. Marxian doctrine began to be actively operative about the same time ; and Lenin's majority (or Bolshevik) programme triumphed at the second congress of the Social Democratic Party in 1903.

any native root : the new class, even if its leaders borrowed the foreign doctrine of Marxianism, was itself indigenous ; and even the borrowed doctrine, as it was gradually interpreted and developed, assumed an indigenous form. The least industrial of European countries thus found its core in its industrial population ; and in the general dislocation this was the social element which emerged, organized itself as a single party, and, as a single party, proceeded to organize the whole community on the basis of its own social aspirations.

We have thus the paradox of the triumph of a minority over the majority—of a small industrial and urban class over the general mass of a country predominantly agricultural and rural. But the paradox is less paradoxical than it seems. There was no other factor which could possibly provide a new scheme for Russian society when the formal and mechanical scheme of the old autocracy had disappeared. Voluntary accommodation, on the lines of parliamentary discussion and compromise, was impossible. The factors to be accommodated were too disparate, and too little acquainted with one another ; parliamentarianism was too recent, and too much of the nature of a stucco insecurely attached to the crumbling walls of autocracy ; the parliamentary tradition, so far as any existed, was carried only by the enlightened members of the landed gentry and the professional classes. An imposed scheme, proceeding from the one social element which, entrenched in the urban centres, could gather itself together and collect and enforce its ideas, was itself imposed by the necessities of the situation. Whatever we may think of the objectives of the scheme imposed, or of the methods (and they too count) by which it has been imposed, we cannot but admit that some scheme had to be imposed, and that the industrial proletariate was, *de facto*, in the best position to impose a scheme.

There was thus a conjuncture in Russia in and after 1917— a conjuncture which united the emergence of a dominant social class (the industrial proletariat) with the triumph of a social doctrine of Marxianism which had at once been built on that class and had helped to build that class This emergence and this triumph were in turn combined with the assertion of a new national trend, making for an independent and self-constituted Russia. The Russian communists might protest against nationalism ; but they were themselves nationalists, and they have become increasingly nationalists. There had long been a deep conviction in Russia that there was a Russian way of life which must find its own expression. Sometimes it had emerged in the political and secular form of Slavophil policy, intended to gather all Slav peoples under the aegis of Russia ; sometimes it had emerged in the religious form of devotion to the Orthodox Church, and in the conception of Moscow as ' the third Rome '.[1] It emerged again and finally in the form of an apostolic communism. This was *the* Russian way of life, found at the long last, after the aberrations of Tsarist Imperialism and obscurantist Orthodoxy. It was a way of life which only Russia could find, and which she would find for herself, escaping from the long years of alien Teutonic administrators and alien Byzantine priests, and speaking and acting at last through her own toilers and workers. Once she had found her way, she would indeed communicate it to the peoples ; her good would also be theirs, and must be given to them for their good. But international communism, at its roots, has a glowing nationalism. The strength of the single party which triumphed in 1917 was not only its social basis : it was also its national basis. And if it appears paradoxical that an imported doctrine of Marxianism should be exported again as a Russian gospel, perhaps it is no more paradoxical than that an imported Orthodoxy should have been similarly exported in an earlier generation.

§2. DEMOCRACY AND DICTATORSHIP, 1917–1936

How far did the action of the proletarian class, which seized the helm in Russia in 1917, proceed on a democratic course in the period prior to the new constitution of 1936? There is an old and natural confusion of the word democratic which renders an answer difficult. We are apt to call action democratic when, apart from its means or method, and simply in its end or aim, it is calculated with a view to the well-being of the whole of the people. But there is another sense of the

---

[1] This devotion still survived, for example, in Dostoievsky. True, he believed, as he wrote in his diary, that the Russian has a feeling for everything human, independent of nationality, blood, and soil : he has a universal human instinct (1861). Thus he could say, ' Every other people lives for itself and in itself only : we will be servants of all, the servants of universal human peace ' (1876). But he also believed in the historic mission of Russia to defend Eastern Orthodoxy and the general cause of Christianity against Mohammedanism and heresy ; and he held that this historic mission involved the Russian conquest of Constantinople.

word—the only sense consonant with its etymology and with a proper use of terms[1]—according to which the means of action is the one and only criterion, and action is called democratic only when it proceeds on a method which enlists the thought, the discussion, and the mental motion of a whole people. In the first use of the term, which is a misuse, we may call the system of Russian Communism democratic, on the ground that its end or aim is, first, to increase the sum of goods available for general distribution among the people by nationalizing the production of goods, and, next, to distribute that sum to the people on a nationalized method of distribution, as evenly and as fairly, and with as great an approach to equality, as the need of efficiency in the production of goods permits. In the same use of the term we may also call the system democratic on the further ground that it tends, in virtue of the nationalization of production and distribution, to abolish the distinctions of class which spring from the private ownership of capital, and to institute a classless society in which all are equally owners and all are equally workers. But in the true use of the term none of these results—the nationalization of production, the revolution of distribution, and the institution of a classless society—are necessarily, or in themselves, democratic. In the true use of the term everything depends on the method or process by which the results are achieved and continue to be maintained.

When we survey the methods by which Russian Communism achieved its results down to 1936 we are bound to notice, at the first glance, a number of features which are not, and cannot be called, democratic. They are in lieu of democracy, or alternatives to democracy, or substitutes for democracy ; but they cannot be called democratic. They may be held to be necessities, inescapable necessities, involved in a long revolutionary crisis, and entailed by a prolonged effort to reconstruct the whole of society. It may be urged in their favour that a society cannot reshape itself, from top to bottom, on the democratic lines of general discussion and the democratic basis of compromise. That may be true. Indeed it will

---

[1] Democracy does not mean the well-being or prosperity of the people, but a method of the *government* of the people ; and a democratic measure is a measure which originates from, or tends to promote, such a method of government—not a measure which tends to increase the amount, or to rectify the distribution, of prosperity or well-being.

certainly be true if the reshaping is intended to be done at the double. But in so far as it is true, and just because it is true, democracy has been dropped, and something has been substituted in lieu of democracy.

In the first place the dictatorship of the proletariat—an industrial and urban proletariat which originally numbered about a tenth of the population—has been a genuine dictatorship. It has assimilated to itself by force the other elements of Russian society : it has expropriated the possessioned or property classes : it has equally collectivized, in its own image, the rural peasantry. In the second place, behind the industrial proletariat, and as the driving force which has set it in motion, there has stood the Communist party, including at its widest about one sixtieth of the population, but itself driven and set in motion by the fraction of itself—the one sixty-thousandth part—which constitutes its leadership. There has been a dictatorship of the single party within the dictatorship of the proletariat ; and there has been a dictatorship of the leaders (or the leader) within the dictatorship of that party. Finally, in the sphere of political organization and the regular action of the State, there was (enunciated in the Constitution of 1924, and expressed in action, down to 1934, by the Ogpu) a general idea of ' revolutionary legality ', and a general conception that conformity to the revolutionary end was a principle superior to that of the rule of law. There was a rejection of the democratic principle and practice of division of power, whether between executive and legislative or between them both and the judicature ; there was also a confusion between the decrees of the party and the ordinances of the State. There was, in a word, a general régime of discretion and a general absence of the rule of law.

On the other hand there were, from the first, democratic elements ; and they have not diminished, even if they have changed. Lenin himself, when he wrote his *State and Revolution* in 1917, was convinced that the explosion of communism was the explosion of a new and larger democracy. Communism would, he believed, provide a substitute or alternative to existing democracy ; but it would do so by providing something still more democratic. Arguing on the lines of Marx's interpretation of the lessons of the Parisian Commune of 1871, Lenin expected and desired a new democracy, which would at the same time be old, and indeed even primitive. This new and yet old democracy would have two features. In the first place it would be as far as possible ' direct '—not a mere indirect democracy of proud and oppressive representatives, but a democracy in which the basis was living bodies of workers meeting in their own Soviets, and in which the representatives were drawn from, and responsible to, these bodies. In the second place it would be an ' omnicompetent ' democracy. Its representatives would not be confined to legislation ; as Marx had said, they would be a working corporation, at once legislative and executive ; as Lenin himself added, they ' must themselves work, must themselves execute their own laws, must themselves verify their results in actual practice '. This conception of a primitive democracy, at once direct and omnicompetent, was expressed, after 1917, in the system of Soviets and of Congresses composed of the representatives of Soviets. It gave a measure of democratic form, and even of democratic feeling, to the dictatorship of the proletariat : it added a factor of ' democratic participation ' to the actual and driving leadership of the Bolshevik party ; and it thus helped to create a system which Lenin called ' democratic centralism '.

No doubt, in the exigencies of revolution and reconstruction, centralism was the substantive fact, and the new democratic institutions of Soviets and Congresses of Soviets (not so new but that they had analogies and sources in the recent Russian past[1]) were adjectival and even formal. But at any rate the idea of democratic participation, even if it was only participation, was always there ; and indeed that idea was inherent in the general conception of Communism, which, appealing to the toiling masses, could not but seek to enlist and to parade the forms of mass-discussion and mass-approbation. True, in the nature of the case, the number of the participants was limited to the one class of the proletariat, and there was thus a large disfranchisement : true, behind the form of participation, there lay the stern fact of a revolutionary autocracy, inheriting some of the instruments, and something of the

---

[1] Soviets—councils of delegates elected by the workers of the different factories in an industrial district—had spontaneously arisen, in the absence of any organized system of Trade Unions, as early as 1905, during the Russo-Japanese War, and had established themselves in a number of Russian cities. Lenin had instantly recognized their importance ; and he built his theory, and his ultimate practice, on their basis.

spirit, of the old autocracy which it had displaced. Democratic centralism meant, in effect, a new autocracy masquerading in a new fashion of democratic dress. . . . And yet not altogether masquerading. Within the limits of the 'general line', and subject to the demand for general conformity to the new orthodoxy, there was a lively play of discussion, which at any rate advertised, if it did not affect, the action of the leaders. By the side of the Communist party, and of the Soviet State inspired and controlled by the party, there also arose a great growth of Trade Unions of workers, inspired and controlled by the party in the same way as the Soviet State, but at any rate distinct from the State, and acting, within their sphere, as the allies and coadjutors of the State ; and there arose, along with them, another great growth of co-operative societies of consumers. In this way, even if there was little or no division of powers within the State, and even if it was alleged to be a new and higher form of democracy that there should be no such division, there was at any rate some division of functions between the State and these other bodies which stood by its side. State, Trade Unions, and Co-operatives might all be inspired and controlled by the Communist party ; but in themselves they still remained distinct and separate organizations.

Russia was thus a mixed (one may almost say a confused) State in the course of its development between 1917 and 1936. It was all along, as indeed it still is, a single-party State ; it had all along no place for a genuine parliament free to discuss real alternatives (the die had been cast, and the one alternative chosen, in 1917) ; but it had some form of representative institutions, and it had some measure of participation by the members of those institutions not only in the sphere of the State, but also in that of the organizations which stood by its side. Nor were these things a poor and jejune salvage from a prior régime of greater liberalism and a more generous self-government. Even if we remember the Duma and its various political parties, in the decade before the triumph of Communism in 1917, we have to confess that they were recent grafts on a stock which remained essentially autocratic and bureaucratic ; and we have equally to confess that the new institutions introduced by the Communists, however imperfect from our Western point of view, were new conquests and new creations, and constituted a first attempt of native elements (even if these elements were only a minority) to construct some sort of native polity. The triumph of Communism in Russia was necessarily different, in its nature and its results, from what the triumph of the same cause would be in any of the States of Western Europe. There it would mean the pulling down of a system based (at any rate in its forms and its intention) on the principle of consent, and the erection of a system based on the right of force. In Russia, Communism could profess to be dethroning force and to be erecting (at least in so far as the industrial proletariat was concerned) the new principle of consent.

§ 3. THE CONSTITUTION OF 1936 AND ITS MOVEMENT TOWARDS
THE FORM OF DEMOCRACY

By 1936 the area of consent had been widened—widened, paradoxically, by compulsion, and by means of the extension, violently and even cruelly achieved, of the ranks of the proletariat until it included, on the one hand the dispossessed owners of capital, and on the other the collectivized mass of the peasantry. ' We are all proletarians now ' was a phrase which could be used, ruefully or gleefully as the case might be, by the vast majority of Russians. Meanwhile another great change had happened, parallel to and not unconnected with the internal transformation of Russian society. In its original phase the ideal of the Russian Communists was not the ideal of a Russian Communist State rooted and grounded in the soil of Russia. If they had a national trend, they were also oecumenical : they were in the mood of quasi-religious belief which demands proselytization and universality : they envisaged a world State of the world proletariat, sweeping like a fire from Russia ; and the Communist International, which stood by the side of the Russian Communist party, was intended to kindle the fire. The hope dwindled when the sparks failed to spread ; and if Communism struck deeper root in Russia, by the extension of the proletariat, it was also confined more obviously within the frontiers of Russia. A Russian State confined to Russia, but so perfected on its native basis that it might serve as a model and an incentive to other States—a State which might spread by the contagion of example and imitation, and not by the conflagration of propaganda and *émeute*—this was the new ideal which now took the place of the old. The nationalism which had always been present assumed a definite prominence.

The Russian constitution of 1936 is the product of this development. It was perhaps intended for foreign consumption as much as for domestic use ; but it is far from being a mere façade which is irrelevant to the interior. Even if it be regarded merely as a theory, it marks a change, or at least a development, in the theory of Communism. Lenin's interpretation of the interpretation put by Marx on the Parisian Commune of 1871 has receded ; and with it there has receded the cult of primitive, direct, and omnicompetent democracy. In place of the ideal of direct or immediate democracy there is substituted the ideal of a parliamentary or representative democracy, with geographical constituencies directly electing their representatives, a regular electorate based on universal and equal suffrage, a formal nomination of candidates, and a system of secret voting. In place of the ideal of omni-competent democracy—unrestrained by any idea either of the rights of man or of the sovereignty of the constitution, unchecked by any division between the legislative and the executive sphere, unimpeded by the presence of an independent judicature, and proceeding freely on the basis of a revolutionary legality determined by its own exigencies and its own will—there is substituted the ideal of a differentiated State, acting differently in different spheres and through different organs of action, acknowledging fundamental rights, and proceeding by constitutional rules.

The Constitution promulgated on 5 December 1936, and alterable only by a two-thirds majority in each of the Chambers of the Supreme Council which forms ' the supreme organ of State power ' under the constitution, is the final rule and the ultimate sovereign of all the activity of the State, determining the sphere and the competence of each organ or authority in the State.[1] Under this constitution, and in its tenth chapter,

---

[1] This leaves the Communist Party intact, as a body outside the State, which may none the less, *de facto*, determine the actual policy pursued by the organs of the State. On the other hand the constitution, in Article 126, recognizes and ensures, for the most active and conscientious citizens, the right of combining in the Communist Party, as a right which is part of (or parallel to) the right of all citizens to combine in public organizations. Recognized in the constitution, and ensured rights under the constitution, the Communist Party may be argued to be (at any rate formally) limited by the constitution. From this point of view

a scheme of fundamental rights of citizens (coupled with fundamental duties, which include universal military service, and the duty of guarding and strengthening the system of public socialized property as the sacred and inviolable basis of the Soviet régime) is proclaimed or declared, and not only declared but guaranteed or ensured.[1] This scheme of rights, as the use of the word 'fundamental' suggests, and as its inclusion in the sovereign constitution involves, must be conceived as binding on all the organs and authorities of the State —at any rate in so far as any declaration of rights, in the absence of a supreme judicial court capable of disallowing laws and acts which contravene the rights declared, can be held to be binding.

Subject to the limits imposed specifically upon it by the constitution (and subject, in some degree, to the rights of citizens declared in the constitution), the supreme organ of the State is the Supreme Council, or Parliament, which corresponds in its form (though it is superior in the extent of its powers) to the Congress of the United States. It is a bicameral body : the members of one house are directly elected by geographical constituencies ; the members of the other are indirectly elected by the legislatures of the States (or Republics) of the Soviet Union.[2] The members who are directly elected are subject to recall by a majority of the electors of their constituency. This is a survival of the idea of direct democracy. Another survival is perhaps to be found in the provision for the use of a referendum, though the origin of the provision (which allows a referendum on the demand of one of the Union Republics) may well be the genius of federalism rather than the idea of direct democracy. Apart

amendment of the constitution might amend the functions of the party. For the present, however, such an argument, and such a point of view, may be said to be purely formal.

[1] A distinction has been drawn by French publicists between the ' declaring ' of rights and the ' guaranteeing ' of rights—the latter being held to be greater. The new Russian constitution first declares a right and then proceeds to state how it is ' ensured '. This statement, however, is not a statement of the remedies provided against violation : it is a statement of those institutions, or methods, of the Soviet régime which may be held to be correlative to the right, and to secure (in their degree) the positive enjoyment of the right. But the language of the tenth chapter is not uniform : sometimes rights are ' ensured ' without being declared ; and sometimes they are said to be ' guaranteed '.

[2] The members of the American Senate were similarly elected by the State legislatures until the passing of the constitutional amendment of 1913, which transferred the right of election to the people of each State.

from these limits,[1] and subject to the ultimate sovereignty of the constitution and its declaration of rights, the Supreme Council remains the immediate ' supreme organ '. But it is only supreme within its own specific sphere. That sphere is large ; but it is definitely a legislative sphere. True, the two chambers of the Supreme Council, sitting in joint session, appoint the executive, or Council of People's Commissars ; true, the executive which they appoint is declared to be responsible to the bodies by which it is appointed. But the distinction between executive and legislative power is none the less acknowledged, and even definitely secured. Just as the Supreme Council, in its capacity of legislature, has no executive power, so the Council of People's Commissars, in its capacity of executive, has no legislative power. It can only issue decisions and orders on the basis of existing laws which have been made, and made exclusively, by the Supreme Council. The principle of division of powers, thus affirmed in regard to the legislative and the executive, is extended also to the judicature. The judges of the High Court are indeed to be elected, for a period of five years, by the Supreme Council ; but they are to be independent of it, and subject only to the law. The independence of the judicature, and the consequent rule of law, may both be less than they are with us ; but at any rate the idea of ' revolutionary legality ', enunciated in the previous constitution of 1924, has disappeared, and the idea of the rule of a standing law, duly made by a standing legislature possessed of exclusive competence, has taken its place.

It seems to follow from this description that the Soviet system, as it has been reconstructed by the Constitution of 1936, is less an alternative to than a new and modified form of parliamentary democracy. There may be said to be three modifications. In the first place, the Soviet system possesses a new organ in the shape of the Presidium, a committee of the two houses appointed by them in joint session, and acting on their behalf, in a variety of ways, as an organ partly parallel

---

[1] It may be argued to be another limit that, in the opening articles of the Constitution, the Soviets of toilers' deputies are declared to be ' the political foundation ' of the Union, and to possess ' all power '. But this is rather a general assertion of the rights of the people (or, as we should say, the electorate) than a diminution of the rights of the Supreme Council. The people are the basis, and they possess ' all power ' ; but they delegate it to their representatives at the apex.

and partly superior to the Council of People's Commissars. In a sense Russia may thus be said to have a dual cabinet : in another sense it may be said to have a third organ (unknown to the West, though not unlike the parliamentary committees of France) intercalated between the legislative and the executive. In any case the Presidium does not vitally affect the character of the Soviet system. A far more important modification in the Russian system of parliamentary democracy is its social and economic basis. The people represented by the Supreme Council is a people of ' toilers ' from which those who do not toil (perhaps one fiftieth of the whole) are necessarily excluded. The economy is an economy predominantly of public ownership, vested in the State or in co-operative farms or other co-operative bodies ; the element of private ownership (though it exists, and though the general economy is to that extent mixed) is a subordinate element. The dictatorship of the proletariat thus remains, though the proletariat has been extended until it is almost the whole of society ; and the socialization of the great mass of property equally remains. There is nothing to prove that democracy may not be democracy when it is conjoined with the general socialization of property, or even (though this is more dubious) when it is conjoined with the temporary disfranchisement of a section of the population and the domination of the rest.

The most important modification, however, in the new Russian system of representative democracy is the existence of only one party and only one set of social and political ideas. This is the crux ; and it is on this ground that the real question arises whether the Russian form of representative democracy established by the Constitution of 1936 is, after all, and when all is said, democratic. If representative democracy involves representation of different currents of opinion, freely ventilated and freely attracting their adherents in the social area, and freely translated and freely acting (by the process of discussion and compromise) in the political area, then it cannot be said that representative democracy exists in Russia. The social area presents a monotonous uniformity like the steppes of Russia, in which only a single current of opinion can exist ; and while that current can be freely translated into the political area, it cannot be freely discussed there—*as an alternative confronted by other alternatives.*   It can only be discussed by and in itself; and what will then be discussed will be merely sub-alternatives within the one permitted choice (or, in other words, niceties and refinements), and never genuine alternatives. Perhaps, in the length of time, the sub-alternatives will grow to the dimensions of genuine alternatives : perhaps real parties may form themselves, and real discussion be engaged, in regard to those alternatives.   For the time being choice is foreclosed, and in the absence of freedom of choice it cannot be said that freedom is present.   It is true that one of the articles of the new constitution grants the right to put forward candidates to ' social organizations and societies of the toilers ' ; but when those organizations are enumerated, they appear to be simply the Communist Party and institutions (such as Trade Unions, Co-operative Societies, and youth organizations) which are controlled by that party.

No doubt a country which has just gone through a sweeping economic revolution must necessarily cry ' Halt ', if only for the sake of a minimum of stability, to theories and parties of revision, which must necessarily appear to be a form of recidivism.   No doubt, in this respect, the position of Russia is fundamentally different from that of an old State, settled in a traditional scheme of life which has weathered the years and is so naturally (even if unconsciously) assumed as a general basis that different plans for its modification—some more and some less progressive—may safely be offered by different parties.   But so long as one general line is demanded, one ideology is prescribed, and one party alone is permitted, the necessary conditions of a democratic State are necessarily absent.   The forms and institutions may exist : there may even be—within the limits of the one party's programme, and in regard to the sub-alternatives which it admits—a vigorous discussion : there may be a genuine attempt to enlist ' democratic participation ' for the realization of the particular scheme which emerges from such discussion ; but all these things added together do not constitute a democracy.   The single-party state remains : opposition, instead of being a part of the system and a merit, is a treason to it and a crime ; and in the absence of room for the movement of an opposition there is an absence of the general process and method which constitute democracy.

§ 4. RUSSIA AT SCHOOL : POLITICAL GRAMMAR : THE PROBLEMS
OF RUSSIAN DEVELOPMENT

There may be times in the lives of nations in which unanimity
is the one thing necessary. It seems to be so in times of war ; it
may also be so in times of turbulent peace, when a nation is
engaged in a rapid and arduous transition from one mode of
life to another. This consideration may serve to justify, in its
measure, the Russian requirement of unanimity—a requirement also made by the other single-party States. But we have
also to remember, in the peculiar case of Russia, that even a
compulsory unanimity, however far it may fall short of an
ideal of the free movement of minds, is better than the vacuity
by which it was preceded. Millions and millions, who before
only followed the daily round of physical life, have been drawn
into the service of an idea and into some comprehension of its
nature. It has been a great piece of schoolmastering, practised (as schoolmastering should not be) upon adults ; but it
may serve as an apprenticeship to eventual independence.
Russia, we may say, is at school, engaged in a *praeparatio*. It is
the time of the headmaster and an enforced curriculum. The
curriculum enforced is scientific, secularist, socialist ; and
there is only one curriculum.[1] It provides a somewhat harsh
and certainly a one-sided introduction to mental life and
mental development ; but it is an introduction none the less.
A community which is at school is not a democratic community, whatever forms of election and whatever modicum of
participation the headmaster may provide. But in the life
of a nation, as in the life of an individual, the school may be a
preparatory stage ; and the age of the learning of what Russia
calls ' political grammar ' (or the Marxian rules) may yield
to an age of free self-direction by the common and original
thought of the whole community.

Meanwhile, Russia remains confronted (in the area of her
own internal life, and apart from the sphere of foreign policy)
by three main problems of future development which are all

[1] It is significant that, in the declaration of liberties (Article 124), freedom of
anti-religious propaganda is recognized on the one side, but only freedom to
perform religious rites (unaccompanied by any mission to the general community,
or any teaching or propagation of faith) is recognized on the other. There is only
one curriculum and only one mission.

closely interconnected. First, there is the political problem of dictatorship or democracy. Since 1936 an actual dictatorship has been acting in combination with a system of formal democracy. What will be the eventual issue of the combination ? It is on the answer to that question that the solution of the other two problems depends. If the answer is in favour of real democracy, and of the fitting of the practice of leadership into the method and spirit of real democracy, the key is at once provided for the solution of the other problems, and the lines of their solution emerge. If the answer goes in the opposite direction, and the decision is given in favour of pure dictatorship, we are left with an unpredictable future which depends on the inclination of a single will.

The other two problems are the economic and what may be called the cultural. The economic problem is double. It is partly, and perhaps mainly, a problem of the relative parts to be played in the area of production by the factors of State economy, co-operative economy, and private economy (which are all present, in their different degrees, in the present system of Russia) : in other words, it is a problem of the building of a ' mixed ' economy, and of the adjustment from time to time of the proportions of the mixture. This is a problem which, as we have seen, democratic States, such as our own, are also compelled to solve, and which, as we have also seen, the democratic method enables them to solve. Partly, again, the economic problem is one of the relative parts to be played in the area of distribution by the two principles of efficiency and equality, the one suggesting different rates of reward for different degrees of productive effort, and the other demanding equal rates of payment to meet equal needs of consumption. This is a problem which vexes Russia, but it is equally a problem which vexes democratic States ; and their method of solution is the only alternative to the method of arbitrary and imposed will.

There remains the last but not the least problem, which is that of the lines of cultural development. For nearly a quarter of a century Russia has opposed a scientific and materialistic secularism not only to her own native religious tradition of Orthodoxy, but also to the West European tradition of freedom —freedom of religious thought and religious propaganda, and, even more generally, freedom of thought at large and the propagation of thought in the whole of its range. She has sought to deposit and harden a single mould of culture. The attempt has been part, and perhaps the core, as we have already noticed, of a general conception of the State as a school engaged in a *praeparatio*. But the State in its nature is not a school. It is an institution of grown men—a university, and more than a university—in which different modes of culture can live and interact. Similarly, it is a place of the mixture and interaction of different factors of economy : similarly, too, it is a place of the co-existence and interplay of different currents of political opinion and different political parties. Politics, economics, culture—the political problem, the economic problem, the cultural problem—all of these raise the same issues, and all these are interconnected.

XII

THE ALTERNATIVE OF ITALIAN FASCISM

§ I. FASCISM : ITS RELATIONS TO COMMUNISM : THE ECLECTICISM
OF ITS DOCTRINE

THE system of Italian Fascism, which celebrated its
triumph in 1922, five years after the victory of the
Communist Party in Russia, professes to be the opposite of
Communism. There are indeed many differences between
Fascism and Communism. But there are also, on a general
view, many similarities ; and the similarities are perhaps as
fundamental as the differences.

The Communist Party in Russia, when it seized the government, had a theory behind it which, if we count from the
Communist manifesto of 1848, was seventy years old ; and it
modelled its tactics of revolution, and its action after the
revolution, upon its theory. The Fascist party, when it came
into power, was an organization which, if it could be said to
have any theory at all, had a new and fluid theory which
depended for its development on the march of circumstances.
It was an *antipartito* rather than a *partito*[1] : in other words its
hand was against the other Italian parties, and according as
one or the other of those parties seemed to threaten its rise
and its victory, it determined the line of its action in this or
in that direction. At one time inclining to syndicalism, and at
a later time to capitalism, it simply acted according to the
exigencies of action : ' la mia dottrina anche in quel periodo ',
as its leader wrote some ten years later, ' era stata la dottrina
dell' azione '.[2] ' Action will furnish belief ', wrote one of our
English poets. (He also added, ' but will that belief be the
true one ? '). The action of the years between 1919 and 1922
resulted ultimately in a pragmatic belief. The original ' points,
anticipations, accents . . . liberated by the inevitable march of
contingencies . . . developed into a series of doctrinal positions '.[3] The author and leader of the development might say,
again with our English poet,

What one wants, I suppose, is to predetermine the action,
So as to make it entail, not the chance belief, but the true one[4] ;

---

[1] ' Non fu partito, ma, nei primi due anni, antipartito e movimento '. Mussolini,
La Dottrina del fascismo, II, §1.

[2] Ibid., II, §1.   [3] Ibid., II, §1 (a sublime definition of opportunism).

[4] Clough, *Amours de Voyage*, Canto V, ii.

and he might claim that there had been such predetermination. The fact remains that the whole development, and the consequent doctrine, was involved in chance and contingency. That is not necessarily an argument against the development or the doctrine. Our own English development, and the doctrine in which it has issued, has been fundamentally pragmatic—though with this difference from the Italian that it has been a long-time development. But the course of Fascism has at any rate run differently from that of Communism : it has been less planned, less continuous, and more opportunist ; and this difference of development is one of the differences between Italian Fascism and Russian Communism.

Another and a more fundamental difference emerges when we turn to consider what was the eventual enemy against which the Fascist *antipartito* directed its attack, and what, in consequence, became the burden and core of its doctrine. Along the 'march of contingencies' the Fascist party, with its original mixture of ex-service men and syndicalists, and its corresponding oscillations between a militant nationalism and a radical policy of social and economic reconstruction, came eventually to grips with socialism of the communist type. It found, or at any rate posited, the enemy ; and it constructed the antithesis to his thesis. But the antithesis, as we shall see, was also a synthesis ; and the new doctrine soon developed a character of eclecticism which made it a sort of portmanteau, stuffed with a large variety of somewhat incongruous novelties.

Primarily, however, Fascism was (and is) a synthesis of the negations or contradictions of Communism. To the original internationalism of Communism there was opposed a doctrine of nationalism (a doctrine of the ' sacred egoism ' of the nation and the transcendency of the national organism over all individuals and groups), which had already found expression in Italy at least as early as the Tripolitan war of 1910. To the secularism of Communism there was opposed the cause of religion ; and this later issued in the concordat and treaty with the Head of the Catholic Church in 1929. To the system of public ownership and public enterprise advocated and established by the Communist there was opposed the cause of private property and private enterprise ; and Fascism thus found a basis, or an ally, in capitalism.

But these three elements of anti-Communism were not the whole of the synthesis. If it included negations of communism, Fascism also included negations of liberalism and democracy— regarded indeed as things incompatible with one another (for in the Fascist view liberalism meant an escape from the necessary control of the State, and democracy, on the contrary, meant the assertion of absolute State-control by mere mass of numbers and quantity), but regarded none the less as equally inimical to the new party, which had thus to vindicate itself against the Liberal and the Democrat as well as against the Communist. To the Liberal cult (or alleged cult) of *laissez-faire* there was therefore opposed a new theory of regulation, which modified or qualified pure private property and pure private enterprise; and to the democratic cult of electorate, constituencies, and parliament there was opposed a new idea of the true nature of national representation.

Here one of the early phases of the party furnished an anticipation or ' accent '. The party had passed through an original phase of syndicalism, during which it toyed with the idea of the right of each syndicate, or Trade Union, of workers to take over and to manage production within the particular field of its own economic activity. From 1926 onwards, or even earlier, during a phase of evolution which ended in the law of 1934, on ' the formation and functions of corporations ', it proceeded to turn its original syndicalism into the new form of corporativism. It now proclaimed the doctrine that in each determinate branch or ' category ' of production a corporation should be established, which would be a tamed or domesticated version of syndicalism. This corporation would have two features. In the first place, and in point of form or structure, it would not be composed of a syndicate of workers only : it would include, and it would combine, both the syndicate (or Trade Union) of workers and the syndicate (or association) of employers concerned with its branch of production. In the second place, and in point of function, it would not take over and manage production, within its branch, to the exclusion of private property and private enterprise : it would simply ' regulate ' the working of private property and the conduct of private enterprise, and it would do so ' under the aegis of the State ' and as ' an organ of the State '. This was an answer to Liberalism and its doctrine of the free competition of individuals : it was also an answer to Communism and its doctrine of the warring classes of workers and capitalists.

This, however, was not the whole of corporativism. It was only its economic side. There was also, or there was held to be, a political side. The Fascist party accordingly enunciated the doctrine that the corporation, in some way or other (either in the way of proposing candidates to the national electorate, or in the way of serving itself as an electorate and electing the members itself[1]), was the proper basis for any system of national representation. This was their answer to the Democrat, who thus saw his cherished system of quantitative representation on a territorial basis displaced by a new and so-called 'qualitative' system, which professed to elicit the best elements of the nation through the sieve of a vocational method of choice.

The doctrine thus constructed may not unjustly be termed eclectic, not only because it is a double synthesis of negations (partly the anti-communist, but partly also the anti-liberal and the anti-democratic), but also because it adds, in order to sustain these negations, a double or triple synthesis of affirmations. There is the affirmation, which we have just noticed, of a transformed and extended syndicalism : there is the affirmation, which we have also noticed, of a strained and rarified nationalism, which consorts somewhat curiously with syndicalism : there is the affirmation of the cause of catholicism and the Catholic Church, which, if it seems, or can be made to seem, to possess some congruity with the cause of syndicalism, has little congruity with the cause of a rarified nationalism. But the doctrine, however large and however eclectic, is not the real essence. It is an epiphenomenon ; and the phenomenon itself is simply the party— whatever the doctrine it holds or the theory it professes, and whatever the institutions which it constructs in virtue of its theory or of its exigencies. The leader of the Fascist party has written that ' a party which governs a nation totalitarianally is a new fact in history '.[2] That is, for him, the essence. But

[1] From 1928 to 1939 the first method was pursued ; and functional or corporative bodies, composed of employers and employed, proposed a list of parliamentary candidates which, after revision by the Grand Council of the Fascist Party, was submitted to the vote of the national electorate. After 1939 the second method was pursued ; and the corporations directly provided the great majority of the members in the new chamber of Fasci and Corporations which took the place of the old Chamber of Deputies.

[2] *La* Mussolini, *Dottrina del Fascismo*, II. §9.

this essence did not begin with the Fascist party, or in 1922 :
it began with the Communist party, and it began in 1917.
Here, on this fundamental ground, there is no antithesis. The
Communist and the Fascist parties are both single parties,
which tolerate no other. They may differ in their social
recruitment : they may differ in their social and political
aims : they may differ in the social and political institutions
with which they surround themselves. In themselves, and as a
phenomenon of history, they belong to the same *genus*. They
are both of them close and exclusive parties dominating
everything within their area, and therefore ' governing
totalitarianally ' in that area according to the factor (or
factors) dominant in themselves.

§ 2. THE DOMINANT FACTORS IN THE FASCIST PARTY : THE CAUSE
OF SOCIAL SECURITY AND THE CAUSE OF POLITICAL UNITY

What is the factor dominant in the Italian Fascist party ?
Different answers may be given. To one who looks at the
Italian stage as a spectator, and remembers the great actors
who have trod that stage in history as dominant personalities,
the answer readily occurs that the dominant factor in the
drama played by the party is the personality of the protagonist. He has bestridden the Italian world, undisputed, for
more than half a generation : he has enjoyed a continuity
of power unparalleled elsewhere under any similar system of
leadership : he has been vested by law with special powers :
above all, the people has ' recognized ' its leader, as the
preamble to the *Statuto* of the party declares, ' by the marks of
his will, his force, and his work '. But it may also be said, as it
is said in the Italian Charter of Labour of 1927, that the
dominant factor in the party—a factor which stands above
the leader, if it is also incarnate in the leader—is the conception
or creed of the national organism, transcending all individuals
and combinations of individuals, but ' integrally realized in
the Fascist State ' and thus realized also in the Fascist party
which constitutes and carries that State. Or again it may be
said, on a lower and more realistic level of interpretation, that
the dominant factor in the Fascist party is the social interest,
or group of interests, which it represents, and the social strata
by which it is sustained.

Perhaps all these things—leader, nationalistic creed, and

social interest—interact. The prophet who founds, or extemporises, or simply borrows, a creed must draw his recruits not only from those who follow him for himself, or who follow, for its own sake, the creed which he professes, but also from those who are impelled by social interest to march behind a new banner in the hope of bettering their position. The prophet and his creed will work upon these followers, but they will also react upon the prophet and his creed ; and the ultimate result will depend on ' the march of contingencies '. In Italy the Fascist leader and his embryonic creed attracted a mixture of elements ; but a dominant element, by the end of 1921, was already drawn from the independent or professional classes—industrialists, men of business, landowners, and students. That element, even if it is now being outnumbered by the annual intake from the youth organizations ancillary to the party, which include the general youth of Italy, is still predominant. Seniority of membership and service counts heavily in the party ; and the old element of middle class interest is still perhaps the strongest.[1]

A ' frightened bourgeoisie ' (the phrase is that of a Fascist historian of the movement) was originally led by its fear of ruin and the breaking down of laws towards the programme of a single front of order. Whether the fear was warranted by the actual ' excesses ' of the proletariat, or whether it was induced and created by the ' retaliations ' of Fascist bodies which swiftly visited any appearance of such excesses, is a matter which need not be debated. Fear is fear, however it arises. Fear fed the idea that the State must be a non-party or super-party State, which meant, in effect, that it should be a single-party State. (It is impossible to banish the factor of party combination from the modern State, with all its facilities for communication and therefore for combination ; and those who profess to banish such combination, or to erect something superior to it, only banish combinations other than their own,

---

[1] The nature of the social interest behind a party has to be deduced (1) from the record, if there is any, of the occupations and professions from which its members are drawn, (2) from the account, again if there is any, of the sources from which its funds are provided, and (3) from the tendency and direction of the social policy which, if it attains power, it seeks to pursue. Under (1) there is the record given by the Secretary of the Party at the Congress of 1921 (quoted by Finer in *Mussolini's Italy*, p. 143) ; under (2) there are the facts and quotations given by Salvemini in his work *Under the Axe of Fascism*, pp. 22–4 ; under (3) there are the acts and decrees of the government, and the pronouncements of the party, which furnish more certain and cogent evidence.

and only erect the superiority of their own combination over others). Fear, again, fed the idea that the State must be non-class or super-class, which equally meant, in effect, that it must be one-class, and must necessarily promote one particular social interest. (For here again it may be contended that it is impossible to banish the fact of class and of social interest from the modern State, with all its rich differentiation of classes and interests; and it may thus be argued that those who would banish social interests, or erect something superior to them, only banish interests other than their own, and only erect the superiority of their own interest over others). A foundation of fear thus led to the building of a single party devoted to a single interest. A single front was constituted in the name of Italian unity; but under that stirring name there lay the desires and the interests of a class, or combination of classes, alarmed by the movement of other classes and dissatisfied with the place which it occupied itself in the Italian scheme.

Yet there were other and nobler elements in the policy of the single front. Side by side with social dissatisfaction, and even, perhaps, superior to it, there also went the dissatisfaction of a body of political opinion—a body of opinion not confined to a social class or limited to a single group—with the place and status of Italy in the system of Europe. That dissatisfaction, whether or no it was warranted by the facts of Italian effort and achievement, was natural in the general state of Italian feeling. Italy had grown into a united Italy between 1815 and 1870: national unification had left a legacy of nationalism which demanded, and expected, the growth of united Italy into a greater and imperial Italy. There was the memory of ancient Rome: there was the analogy of the colonial growth of other powers: and when little seemed to have been accomplished, even by the sacrifices of the war of 1914–18, there was a sense of defeated expectation and of baulked ability. Who or what was to blame? Immediately, it could be said, the other powers which blocked the way and thwarted the growth of Italy. Ultimately, it might be argued, the government of Italy itself (the local particularisms, the conflicting parties in the legislature, the overgrowth of the legislature at the expense of the executive, the whole system of combination of local autonomies with an overgrown and party-ridden parliament at the centre) which weakened the national strength and played into the hands of the national adversaries.

There was thus a mixture of the political and the social in the revolution in Italian life which followed the war of 1914–18 and ended, for the time being, with the march on Rome in the autumn of 1922. There was the political motive of desire for the final unification, to be followed by the triumphant expansion, of Italy ; there was the social motive of a desire, strong among threatened classes and interests, for a super-party or super-class State in which they could be at rest. It is difficult to estimate the relative weight of the two motives : it is sufficient to notice that they readily fused. The integration of the Italian polity and the salvation of Italian society could easily be identified. The same interests which demanded social security were those which could be enlisted in the cause of national unity and power. No doubt the cause of national unity and power attracted its own adherents—a mixed company of poets, philosophers of the Hegelian type, and militarists ; no doubt, again, there were those in the camp of social security who were just content to be secure, and had little political interest. But on the whole there was unity of adherence to a mixed cause of unity which was at once political and social. The defence of a ' frightened bourgeoisie ' and the advancement of its interest could march in step with the vindication of the name and fame of Italy. They both demanded a new deal and a national recovery.

The dominant factor in the Fascist party, which itself was, and still is, the dominant factor and the essential phenomenon in the development of Italian politics and economics, was thus a mixture of desire for social security, in some of the social elements, with a desire for political unity, and consequent national power, which was active partly in the same social elements, but partly also in nationalist sections (active as early as 1910) that lay outside their range. The revolution would not have begun without the first of these desires : it might not have triumphed without the second, which secured the benevolent neutrality of the army and thus paralysed opposition. Political unification, achieved by drastic purges and sweeping changes, was the first fruit ; and a new political system of totalitarianism was accordingly constructed by the end of 1929. The new system not only unified Italy under a single and totalitarian direction which absorbed local particularisms, eliminated political parties (other than one), regulated parliament, and enthroned the executive over the legislative.   It also, in the same act and by the same means, supplied an external framework which would guarantee social security.   But the framework of social security began to be widened into something which professed to be more than an external framework and vindicated the character of an internal reconstruction of Italian society.   This was the new social system of corporativism—the new bridge between capital and labour, which were thus not merely to be kept in their old positions by an iron framework of security, but to be spanned and joined and united by a new and busily frequented way of communication and cooperation.   Political unification, establishing in its stride the cause of social security, seemed accordingly to pass into social transformation. . . . But has there really been any change ?   Or is the single party still the single party, and is the corporative system (with its repercussions on parliament and its reconstruction of parliament) simply a new expression of the dominance of the single party ?

§ 3. POLITICAL UNIFICATION : THE TOTALITARIAN GOVERNMENT
    OF THE SINGLE PARTY : ITS METHODS AND ITS RESULTS

We may first consider the system of political unification, or, as it may also be called, of totalitarian government.   The unification achieved in the period between 1922 and 1929 consisted primarily in the enthroning of the one party and its one leader as the single directive force of Italian political life. In the enthroning of the party there was one peculiarity, which distinguishes the régime of the single party in Italy from similar régimes elsewhere.   Generally the single party is content with a *de facto* supremacy secured by the proscription of other parties.   In Italy the Fascist party has been secured in a *de jure* supremacy.   By an act of 1928 it was vested with the legal right of making the final list of parliamentary candidates to be submitted, in one block, to the national electorate.[1]   By a further act passed at the end of the same year

---

[1] This position, as has already been noticed, was altered by the reconstitution of the Italian Chamber of Deputies in 1939.   The new Chamber of Fasci and Corporations now contains 150 members drawn directly from the party, and 500 drawn from a National Council of Corporations which is, in effect, the creation and the creature of the party.

it was declared to be the supreme organ which co-ordinates and integrates the whole activity of the régime issuing from the revolution of October 1922 ; and it was vested, as such, with the right of giving advice on all constitutional questions, and with the further right of keeping a list of the names of persons who were qualified to be submitted to the Crown for the office of Prime Minister, or were fitted to hold a post in the government. . . . Within the party, thus formally enthroned, the leader, in turn, was secured in final supremacy. He presides over and summons at his discretion the meetings of the Grand Council of the party : he appoints the general officials and the general executive of the party : he controls its general policy and inspires its general action, by virtue of formal right (partly under the *statuto* of the party itself, and partly under act of parliament[1]) as well as by virtue of actual power.

Apart from the political unification involved in the position of the party and the position of the leader within the party, a further unification—outside the party, and in the sphere of institutions of government other than the party—has been achieved by a general extension of the power of the whole of the executive side of government.[2] In the first place, the prime minister or head of the government (who is identical with the leader of the party) is permanent and continuous : so far as he is responsible, he is responsible to the king and not to parliament ; and instead of the old system of one parliament living through several ministries, there is a system of one minister living through several parliaments. In the second place, in virtue of the absence of other parties, he is immune from opposition ; and he is also specially protected, by a new version of the law of treason, against any attempt on his life or liberty and any offence to his reputation either by word or by deed. In the third place, he has been exalted, in his capacity of chief executive officer, above the legislature. The

[1] The preamble of the *Statuto* (as approved by a decree of the State of 20 December 1929) declares that ' the people must receive light and leading from above, where there is the full vision of the attributes to be given and the tasks to be assigned, of function and of desert '. The act of parliament passed at the end of 1928 (' on the constitution and powers of the Grand Council of the party ') formally confers on the leader, in his capacity of head of the government, the general control of the party.

[2] This extension was mainly achieved by the law of 24 December 1925, on the attributes and prerogatives of the head of the government, also called first minister and secretary of State.

old Italian parliamentary system, in which the legislature tended *de facto* to sway the executive (unless the executive could manage it sufficiently to carry its own policy), has been superseded by a new system in which the executive *de jure* sways or supersedes the legislative. By a law of 24 December 1925, no proposal can be placed on the agenda of the Chamber without the consent of the head of the government ; and he can insist that a proposal rejected by the Chamber shall be re-submitted, after an interval of three months, to a new vote taken in secret session without any further discussion. Nor do the new powers of the head of the executive stop at control of the action of the legislature. They also include the right of direct action in lieu of the legislature. By a law of 31 January 1926, 'juridical rules' may be issued in the form of royal decrees, after deliberation by the Council of Ministers (which means, in effect, upon the decision of the head of the executive), in regard to the execution of laws, the use of the powers belonging to the executive, and the organization and functioning of the general administration. By the same law 'dispositions having the force of law' may be made by the same procedure in regard to any matter whatsoever, 'whenever urgent and absolute necessity requires'—subject, however, in such case, to subsequent confirmation by the legislature.[1]

This enthroning of the party and its leader, and this simultaneous and connected exaltation of the executive at the expense of parliament, were the main elements in the new system of political unification. But they did not stand alone ; and they were accompanied by other elements marked by the same general trend. A law of 4 February 1926, amplified and

[1] The English Act of Proclamations of 1539 generally enabled the King, with the advice of his council, to issue proclamations having the force of an act of parliament. But this act provided that the common law, statute law, and rights of property were not to be affected by such proclamations ; and in any case it was repealed in 1547. The modern English practice of 'delegated legislation' depends on a particular enabling of a particular minister by virtue of a particular act, in relation to the matters, and subject to the conditions, stated in that act. The Italian law of 1926 has thus no proper English parallel, either in the sixteenth or in the twentieth century. A closer analogy is afforded by the German law of 23 March 1933 (the 'enabling law'), which lays it down that for a period of four years—since extended—the laws of the Reich may be issued by the government of the Reich as well as by the Reichstag. But the German law, which enables the government to issue laws going outside the provisions of the constitution, is *sui generis*. Italian Fascism has respected the constitutional *Statuto* of 1848 more than German National Socialism has respected the Weimar Constitution (more recent and far more disputed) of 1919.

extended by later decrees, introduced nominated podestás and advisory bodies, in place of elected mayors and councils, into the Italian local communes (as the Emperor Frederic Barbarossa had sought to do in the twelfth century) ; and generally local government, already centralized through the office of prefect in the ninety-two provinces, and now further centralized through the office of podestá in the 7,000 communes, was drawn more tightly under the control of the central executive, and loosed from the participation of local elected bodies.[1] Simultaneously the prefect of the province, always a powerful official in the Italian system, and similar to the préfet in France, was exalted still further. He has become the general and totalitarian head of his province, in tune with the central development of the national executive ; and like the central executive he has been vested with the power of acting on his own motion in case of necessity or urgency. Local particularism has thus been curbed on the circumference, as the legislature and its parties have been curbed at the centre. Like the local or territorial groups, voluntary groups or associations have also been drawn into the general surge of the central trend. Apart from and prior to the later phase of corporativism (which is, in effect, a simple and logical extension of the central trend particularly designed to secure a central control of economic groups and associations), this engulfing and regulating of groups was already evident in the early legislation of the Fascist State. A law of 26 November 1925 required associations to communicate to the authority for public security the terms of their articles of association and the names of their officers and members. A further law, of 31 December of the same year, empowered the Government to modify the rules of the law of public security ; and a voluminous decree of 6 November 1926 accordingly issued orders relating (among a number of other subjects) to the control of public meetings and associations.

The general system of political unification and political

---

[1] Local elected bodies have now generally yielded to local *advisory* bodies of a *nominated* character. The law of 4 February 1926 instituted a system of councils nominated for each commune by the prefect of the province, one-third directly, and the other two-thirds (by a method which is one of the early hints of corporativism) on the recommendation of local economic groups. Provincial councils similarly composed (advising the prefect in the same way as the communal council advises the podestá) have also been instituted, since 1931, in lieu of the old elected provincial councils, which were suspended in 1927.

security thus instituted laid an acute accent on the action of the State—the State in the sense of the government; the government, again, in the sense of the central executive, and more especially of its head, the *capo del governo*. The liberties and rights of citizens faded before the exigencies and brilliance of the State. There could be no list of the basic rights and freedoms of citizens (such as communistic Russia recites in the Russian constitution of 1936) : there could be no declaration, in the old French style, of ' les droits de l'homme et du citoyen '; the old idea that there were any ' fundamentals ' which the State was bound to respect disappeared before the idea that the State itself was the one fundamental. The conception of voluntary society, and of a social sphere in which freely associated groups could voluntarily operate, similarly disappeared in a lunar eclipse : all light was in the sun of the State, and all light came from that sun. There could therefore be no distinction between society and State : there could be no idea that trade unions, and other and similar associations, were able to build collectively a system of society which had its own voluntary life and activities, and might continue to live that life and pursue those activities side by side with the State. Even the conception of the nation, which had been inherited from the old nationalists and had been placed in the forefront of the Charter of Labour of 1927, proved to be secondary to that of the State. When ' The Doctrine of Fascism ' was published in 1931, the nation had ceased to be a transcendent organism, which had integrally realized itself in the State : it had become an artifact created by the State. ' The higher personality is only a nation in so far as it is a State. The nation does not exist to generate the State . . . the nation is created by the State, which gives to a people, conscious of its own moral unity, a will, and thereby an effective existence '.[1] ' All is in the State, and nothing that is human or spiritual exists, far less has value, apart from the State. In that sense Fascism is totalitarian, and the Fascist State, the synthesis and unity of all values, interprets and develops and energizes *all* the life of the people '.[2]

---

[1] *La Dottrina*, I, § 10 ; cf. *supra*, p. 160.

[2] Ibid., I, § 7. The quotations here made, from the first part of *La Dottrina* entitled *Idee Fundamentali*), are perhaps from the pen of the philosopher Gentile. It is true that the whole of *La Dottrina* is ascribed to Signor Mussolini, the philosophic and abstract Part I as well as the lively and concrete Part II, which is

§4. THE CORPORATIVE SYSTEM OF SOCIAL ORDER AND THE STAGES OF ITS DEVELOPMENT

The political legislation enacted and the political measures taken down to the end of 1929 had guaranteed the cause of political unity against all menace ; and the final proclamation of that unity might well seem to have been made when 'The Doctrine of Fascism' was published in 1931. But the cause of political unity, generally termed by the name of totalitarianism, is not the only cause espoused by Italian Fascism. There is also the cause of social transformation, generally styled by the name of *il corporativismo*. This is a cause which, in its origins, is independent of the nationalist trend of thought expressed in the cult of political unity and the ideal of totalitarianism. But the fundamental question which is raised by corporativism is not a question of origins. It is rather the question whether, regarded in its subsequent development and in its present practice, corporativism has retained any trace of the independence which it may have originally possessed. If the doctrine of the Duce—that 'for full, complete, integral, and revolutionary corporativism it is necessary to have only one political party and a totalitarian state'[1]—be accepted as final, the answer to that question is necessarily an answer in the negative. Before, however, that answer can be definitely given some account of the historical development of the idea and practice of corporativism must be attempted.

That development would seem to have passed through three main stages. In the first stage we have the simple idea— the French idea—of syndicalism. Syndicalism, like Marxianism, is a doctrine inimical to the bourgeois or capitalistic State ; but while Marxianism erects a whole class, called the proletariat, as the enemy of the bourgeois State, and proposes

entitled *Dottrina Politica e Sociale*. But (1) the style of Part I is different from that of Part II ; (2) Part I is specially fortified by notes referring to speeches and utterances of the Duce, as if to prove that it is really drawn from or consonant with his ideas ; and (3) above all, the autograph of *La Dottrina* in the Duce's handwriting, exhibited in the Fascist exhibition in Rome in 1934, *began* with Part II and did not include Part I. It follows that the quotations made in the text are not necessarily official, but only expressions of the philosophic views of Gentile—endorsed, indeed, and adopted by the Duce, but proceeding immediately from Gentile's pen. (The writer was informed in Rome that this *was* the fact, in 1934.)

[1] *Scritti e Discorsi di Benito Mussolini*, VIII, p. 272. Strictly speaking, three conditions are stated to be necessary : (1) a single party, (2) the totalitarian State, and (3) a period of the highest ideal tension. The last condition appears to make corporativism a temporary thing, connected with emergency and emotion.

to build on that class, in its hour of triumphant explosion, a new State representing the dictatorship of the proletariat, syndicalism, has evolved a different system of tactics. It erects as the enemy of the bourgeois State the various and separate ' syndicates ' or unions of the workers—each acting on the basis of its own industry or occupation ; each proceeding by its own method of the industrial or occupational strike ; but all conceivably, and even ideally, combining their separate strikes, by a sort of spontaneous parallelism, into one simultaneous or ' general ' strike. It then proposes to build, on the basis of these various and separate unions, in the hour of their joint and yet several triumph, a State which is hardly a State at all (far less a dictatorial State), but rather an economic federation which is to be doubly federal. It will be federal, in the first place, in its strong localism. Unions of workers have always had strong local organizations ; and these must continue to be strong, and even sovereign within their areas, under the new dispensation. It will be federal, again, in its loose central bond. That bond will merely consist, on the logic of syndicalism, in a confederation of separate and almost autonomous national unions.[1]

Syndicalism, as it was preached in France at the beginning of the present century, had thus a number of peculiar features. It left little room for the State, whether bourgeois or proletarian. It left a good deal of room for local life and local autonomy, though it confined that life and that autonomy to local organizations of workers. It made economic groups its basis, both locally and at the centre ; but the only economic groups which entered into its theory were the syndicates or unions of workers. The syndicates of the employers, if they entered at all, entered only to be ejected, and destroyed, by the explosive force of the strike.

Syndicalism, as an alternative to Marxianism, found students and sympathizers in Italy both before and after the war. Among them was Signor Mussolini, the founder of the Fascist party. It may seem *prima facie* a curious thing that syndicalism, the enemy of the State and the opponent of the ideas of national unity and political centralization, should come to be

---

[1] It should be explained that the *local* organizations of workers were to be inter-occupational, acting as ' the organs of class solidarity ' somewhat on the basis of our English Trades Councils ; while the *national* unions were to be uni-occupational, acting as ' the organs of professional solidarity ' for each occupation.

connected with the *étatisme*, the nationalism, and the passion
for political unification, which lay at the core of Fascism.
Perhaps the solution of the puzzle lies in the fact that syndicalism, the enemy of the State, was particularly the enemy of
the democratic State. Arising in France, it had directed its
attacks against the democratic system of France—the geographical constituencies, the political parliament, the political
parties. This negative side of syndicalism—in contradistinction
to its ultimate and positive goal—had a natural appeal to
those Italians who, on other grounds and with a different
goal in view, were attacking the same institutions in their own
country. But the ultimate and positive goal of syndicalism—
its general idea of a social order based on the management of
each industry or occupation by its own syndicate—could also
be adopted. True, it would have to be supplemented, and even
transformed, before it could be adopted. In other words, the
syndicates or associations of employers would have to be
added to the syndicates or unions of workers in order to
constitute a dual management of each industry or occupation ;
and the single syndicalism of the French model would have to
be transformed into the dual syndicalism of the Italian. But
the addition could be made, and the transformation could be
effected, as soon as a single party, prepared to inspire both
associations of employers and unions of workers, and able to
hold them together in the bands of a common·allegiance to
itself, was firmly established in the saddle.

Here we enter upon the second stage of the development.
It began even before the triumph of the single party, though
not before the party had begun to organize its own Fascist
unions of workers which would provide it with the *point
d'appui* for its policy. As early as ‘January 1922 the idea of
the dual or ‘ mixed ’ syndicate—or, as it was also called, the
‘ corporation ’—uniting both the employers and the employed
in each of a number of economic units, was already proclaimed
in a Fascist syndical convention held at Bologna.[1] But the party
had to consolidate its general hold, and above all it had to
make sure that the unions and associations to be ‘ mixed ’
were inspired by itself and loyal to its creed, before it could

---

[1] Even earlier, in 1920, Signor Rocco had suggested that ‘ the workers’ unions
and the employers’ associations should be unified, trade by trade, into one mixed
syndicate ’. (G. Salvemini, *op. cit.*, p. 106.)

proceed to realize the idea in actual practice. A period of twelve years thus elapsed between the proclamation of the mixed syndicate in January 1922 and the final passage of the law of February 1934 ('on the formation and functions of corporations') which actually established the Italian system of dual or domesticated syndicalism, and inaugurated the third and last stage of development.

The twelve years between 1922 and 1934 are years of transition.[1] During them Italy is moving from a previous phase of syndicalism pure and simple, through an intervening phase of 'mixed' (but very imperfectly mixed) syndicalism, toward the phase of corporativism at last established by the law of 1934. The twelve years are far from idle ; but they are full of paradox. Corporations are in the air, and the corporative State becomes a term of official use ; but there are nc corporations. They are mentioned, indeed, by name in a decree of 1 July 1926 : a Ministry of Corporations is established on 2 July of the same year ; but there are no corporations. The Charter of Labour promulgated by the Grand Council of the Fascist party in 1927 is eloquent about corporations : a central council of corporations is actually established in 1930 ; but there are still no corporations—no actual bodies uniting employers and employed in any actual branch or category of production.[2] What was actually happening behind all these expressions of theory, and under all this use of nomenclature ?

Two things. In the first place, the negative side of syndicalism—its aversion from geographical constituencies, political parties, and parliaments—was applied to the reconstitution, or rather the attenuation, of the old Italian system of parliamentary democracy. This was not exactly corporativism ; but it might be described as such, and there was some justification for such a description. When, in 1927, the Italian Chamber of Deputies began to be elected not by geographical constituencies but by the whole national electorate, and when the candidates thus elected were proposed, in the first instance, not by political parties but by confederations of employers and confederations of employed, it could be argued that the Chamber

---

[1] The political system of totalitarianism was established, in the main, during the quadrennium 1925-29. The social system of corporativism was a slower growth.

[2] The one corporation actually in existence before 1934 was, curiously enough, a 'corporation of the stage', established in 1930.

became a corporative body, in the sense that it drew together representatives from half a dozen great occupational groups of employers and the same number of parallel groups of employed. When again, in 1930, the Council of Corporations was similarly constituted from confederations both of employers and of employed, and placed by the side of the Chamber of Deputies with the purpose of formulating rules for the general co-ordination of the national economy, it could be contended that here was a definitely corporative body with a specifically economic purpose. But what had actually happened, on a realistic view, was not the actual institution of a corporative State ; and this for the simple reason that there were not, as yet, any actual corporations. It was simply the attenuation of the Italian parliament, first by its own reconstitution on an economic basis, which deprived it of the life-blood of political representation, and secondly by the constitution of a new economic council by its side, which provided it with a rival, and a possible supersessor, even in the economic field to which it now seemed to be relegated by the nature of its composition. Reconstruction, from the point of view of parliamentary democracy, had been in effect destruction. Syndicalism, in its new dual or ' mixed ' or ' corporative ' form, had thrown up nothing new in the actual conduct of national economy and the actual social order : it had only shown a negative and cutting edge in the sphere of political institutions and at the expense of parliament. Even the new Council of Corporations was mainly negative. It could be pitted against parliament. But it did little itself.

The second thing which was happening between 1922 and 1934 was the establishment of the control of the Fascist party and of the Fascist government over the syndicates of the workers in order that they might be brought into harmony with the syndicates of employers. This, after all, was a necessary preliminary to any corporative system : it would be idle to unite the workers with their employers in a system of dual syndicalism unless there was some cement. The old trade unions or syndicates of the Italian workers were accordingly transformed. Under the legislation of 1926 and its subsequent development they lost the right to strike—the right which was the very core of the doctrine of French syndicalism, as it is also the essential weapon of ordinary trade unionism. A system of legal recognition was introduced.[1] Under this system only a legally recognized union could henceforth negotiate or make agreements, and only such a union could thus become a partner in any subsequent corporative structure. To be legally recognized a trade union need contain only 10 per cent of the workers in its branch, who must, however, be 'of good moral and political conduct from a national point of view'. Only one trade union could be recognized in each branch; but the workers in any branch, whether or no they belonged to the recognized union in their branch, were bound to subscribe to it, and bound by any agreement which it made with an association of employers. The Fascist government, in giving legal recognition, which it could also withdraw, naturally determined its price. The price was the soundness of the membership, and also of the leadership,[2] of the recognized union: it was also, and further, the control by the government of the general rules (*statuti*), the budgets, and the acts of the union.

When the unions of the workers had thus been brought under the control of the party and the government, it was possible to proceed to the third and last phase of the development, and to bring them into combination (as hydrogen is combined with oxygen) with the associations of employers—themselves already, on their side, in touch with the party and the government. (What the nature of that touch was, and how far the associations of employers were originally controlling or controlled, it would be difficult to say; but whatever was the nature of their relation to the party and the government, it was close enough to allow them to be brought without any alarm into combination with the unions of workers.) The system of combination instituted early in 1934 established twenty-two corporations—'joint standing industrial councils', as they might be called in our English terms—in twenty-two branches or categories of economic life.[3] The councils of these corporations include representatives drawn,

---

[1] This system was not compulsory, and unrecognized or *de facto* unions might still continue (legally) to exist. But there was little point in the continued existence of such unions, or in the continued payment of subscriptions to them, when their members were bound, in any case, to pay subscriptions to the recognized unions.

[2] The officials of the recognized unions, according to the writer's observations, are rather professional and party figures (often of the legal type) than genuine representatives thrown up by the workers themselves.

[3] The arrangements and rearrangements of Italian economic groups are somewhat confusing. (*a*) In 1926 six national confederations of employers were

in equal proportions, from the unions of workers and the associations of employers, with the addition of an expert element and with the further addition of representatives of the government and of members of the Fascist party ; their powers include, particularly and especially, the formulation of rules for the collective regulation of economic relations and for the unitarian regulation of production.[1]

§ 5. THE NATURE OF THE CORPORATIONS : ORGANS OF STATE, OR ORGANS OF *AUTODISCIPLINA* ?

The corporativism established in 1934 is an actual corporativism ; at the long last there are actually corporations. It embraces the general sweep of Italian economic life : it enlists representatives of trade unions along with representatives of employers in a joint discussion of the methods by which their mutual relations, and their common productive effort, are to be regulated and rationalized. But the fundamental question involved, if we are to speak of this development as a social transformation or a new scheme of social order, is the question of the autonomy and the spontaneity of the corporations. If the new organs are ' organs of State ', and act by its motion and under its impulse, they will involve political subjection, and not social reconstruction : they will mean the bringing of the economic process into and under the mechanism of the State, and not the development of new initiatives and a new

established in six great *spheres* (industry, banking, commerce, agriculture, and two different spheres of transport), and six parallel confederations of employees were established by their side. These were the groups which made nominations for the Chamber of Deputies under the law of 1927, and formed the basis of the Council of Corporations under the law of 1930. (*b*) Within the sphere of each of the national confederations there were also national federations, for each of the various *trades* which it included. (*c*) In 1934 twenty-two corporations were created in twenty-two newly demarcated economic *categories* (*e.g.* the category of wool), each category containing the agriculturalists or producers of the raw material concerned, the manufacturers of that material, and the merchants concerned in the sale both of raw material and of finished product. The members of these corporations are drawn from the national federations of the trades belonging to the category, in so far as they belong to the category. . . . There are thus (*a*) the ' spheres ' of the confederations, (*b*) the ' trades ' of the federations within each sphere, and (*c*) the ' categories ' of the corporations. The ' category ', by its nature, cuts across the ' sphere ', because it includes bits of several ' spheres ' (*e.g.* agriculture, industry, and commerce) ; and the ' trade ' enters both into the ' sphere ' and into the ' corporation '.

[1] The first subject of ' rules ' is thus the relations of capital and labour : the second subject is the rationalization of production (in its broadest sense) throughout each category. The important subject, for the representatives of the unions of workers, would appear to be the second, which gives them a concern in the process of rationalization.

self-discipline within the process itself. They will not be a development, or a modification, or even a domestication, of syndicalism : they will be its very opposite. Instead of liberating economics from politics, they will have completed the political control of all economic groups and units.

Already in its first adumbration, and before it actually existed, the corporation was defined, in 1926, as an organ of the administration of the State.[1] The definition was repeated in the Charter of Labour : ' the corporations are recognized by law as organs of the State '.[2] The definition is important. The corporation is not the result of a voluntary marriage between voluntary trade unions of workers and voluntary associations of employers. It is a State-created cramp ; and the unions and associations which it binds together, in its branch of economic life, are themselves ' legally recognized ' unions and associations, which have paid the price for their legal recognition and are subject to the control of the Fascist party and the Fascist government. The conception of the State-created cramp, which, as such, is a part of the machinery of the State and acts in the name and by the authority of the State, has been emphasized both by Italian jurists and by official declarations. The Council of Corporations defined the corporation in November 1933, as ' the instrument which, under the aegis of the State, effects the integral, organic, and unitary discipline of productive forces with a view to the development of the wealth, the political power, and the well-being of the Italian people '. Instrument, aegis, integral discipline, political power—the words are all eloquent.

The speeches of the Duce at the end of 1933 and in the course of 1934 elaborated a general view of the new corporations and corporativism which, though it oscillates, never departs from the fundamental elements of this definition. In a speech of 14 November 1933,[3] delivered before the National Council of Corporations, he stated that the corporations were on the economic ground what the Grand Council of the party and its militia were on the political, and that corporativism was a disciplined and therefore a controlled economy. Raising the question whether it could be applied in other countries, he

---

[1] Law of 3 April 1926, as applied by the Royal Decree of 1 July 1926, § 43 : ' the corporation does not possess juridical personality, but is an organ of the administration of the State '.

[2] *Carta del Lavoro*, § vi.　　　　　　*Scritti e Discorsi*, Vol. VIII, pp. 258 sqq.

replied that a full, complete, integral, and revolutionary corporativism depended on the presence of peculiar conditions—
a single party, which added political to economic discipline
and, transcending the opposition of interests, formed a cramp
(*un vincolo*) that bound all men together in a common faith :
a totalitarian State which absorbed in itself all the energies,
interests, and hopes of the people ; and, finally, a period and
an epoch of the highest ideal tension. Here the cause of corporativism was linked indissolubly with that of the single
party and a totalitarian government, and with their temper
and colour : it became a part and an article of the political
régime. In a speech delivered before the Senate on 13 January
1934[1] he altered the note and the accent. Corporativism had
now become a part, and indeed the consummation, of the
general movement of the world's economy. It was a happy
balance of individuals, groups, and the State. It left to
individuals private property and individual initiative : it left
to associated groups the right of self-discipline (*autodisciplina*)
in their several categories ; it left to the State the right to
intervene, in the name of the anonymous mass of consumers,
when the associated groups in a category failed to find the way
of agreement and equilibrium. Here corporativism seems to
assume an independent existence, or at any rate to vindicate
a greater measure of freedom. It is a thing, we are told, which
is not to be overburdened by bureaucracy, though any human
organization will need a minimum of bureaucracy : it is
something which is primarily a matter of self-discipline, with
the State standing generally in reserve—not so much in the
name of the single party, or in the cause of a totalitarian
system, as on behalf of the consuming masses.

In a later speech of 6 October of the same year (1934), delivered to the workmen of Milan,[2] the note is altered again.
The part and the share of the worker in the system of corporativism is now the theme. Repudiating State control of the
economy of the nation, and arguing for the self-discipline of a
system of production entrusted to the producers generally
(employed as well as employers), the Duce proclaimed that the
aim of that system was a higher social justice for the whole of
the Italian people. That higher social justice meant a higher
standard of living, with guaranteed work, a fair wage, and a

[1] Ibid., IX, pp. 13 ff.　　　　[2] Ibid., pp. 127 sqq.

decent house : it also meant, and it meant even more, the participation of the workers both in knowledge of the process of production and in the determination of its necessary discipline. But there was also, he added, another aspect of corporativism. If it looked to peace and social justice, it also looked to war and to national efficiency ; and in this second aspect it was a means of producing a contented body of workers which would in turn produce the necessary return in the hour of need and show the high morale which that hour might require. This double aspect of corporativism—the internal or social, and the external or military—was further elucidated in a speech of 10 November, delivered to the assembly general of the Corporations.[1] Internally, the aim of corporativism was again defined as a higher social justice. This social justice was in turn defined as consisting in a new equality (the social equality of all before the duty and the right of labour), which the new Fascist century had added to the old nineteenth century ideal of formal equality of all before the law ; but even in the assertion of this new equality a caveat was added, and it was insisted that the new equality, far from excluding, really .involved the principle of hierarchy—or in other words, of inequality—in respect of functions, merits, and responsibility. Externally, the aim of corporativism again assumed a political, and even a military, character. It became the aim of augmenting steadily the total power of the nation for the purposes of its expansion in the world. Created by the State (*create dallo Stato*), the corporations are accordingly made to appear, in the last resort, not as the servants of a higher social justice or a new equality, but as the ministers of their creator.

Corporativism can thus be made to mean many things in the course of a year. It is peculiarly Italian, but it is also part of the development of the world's economy : it is national power, but it is also social justice ; it is a State creation and a system of State control, but it is also self-discipline : it is peace, but it is also war : it is a new equality, but it is also hierarchy. If we turn from speeches to facts, and inquire what the corporations have actually done, there is no very clear lesson to be learnt. More than half of the twenty-two corporations met in the course of 1935 : they concerned themselves mainly— with war impending, and by the end of the year actually

[1] *Scritti e discorsi*, Vol. IX, pp. 143 ff.

engaged—in advising the government on the economic problems which were arising, under these conditions, in their
particular fields. The workers' representatives, joining with
those of the employers in the deliberations which preceded
this advice, were educated in the conditions and problems of
their industry ; but no serious attempt was made by the
corporations to deal with that half of their duties which con-
cerns the regulation of the relations between capital and
labour. The effects of the war in Abyssinia, and of the generally disturbed state of Europe, ran contrary to any development of self-discipline. The idea of State control of national
economy (*statizzare tutta l'economia della Nazione*) which the
Duce had repudiated at Milan in October 1934, in favour of
corporative self-discipline, had gained ground by the spring
of 1936, when the nationalization of the credit system and of
all basic industries important for national defence was already
proclaimed. On the whole the corporations, so far as they
have acted, have acted for the State as advisory bodies concerned with its needs and seeking to regulate production with
a view to their satisfaction ; and since 1936 any action of the
corporations seems to have steadily receded before the advance
of the State.

§ 6. THE THREE CLAIMS MADE FOR THE ITALIAN SYSTEM OF
CORPORATIVISM

Three claims have been made for the Italian system of
corporativism. The first is that it provides a new conception
of the function of the State, superior both to the *laissez-faire* of
liberal individualism and to the State-control of socialism—
a conception which reconciles the State and the individual to
one another by reconciling them both to the corporation,
where individuals find their expression and conciliate their
differences, and the State, at the same time, stands by them
and aids them in their task. The second claim is that corporativism is, or can be, distinct from any particular political
régime, and that although it may be wedded, under Italian
conditions, to the totalitarian form of State, it is in its nature
independent of that form and can in its nature co-exist with
other forms. The third claim—somewhat incompatible with
the second—is that corporativism provides a new conception
of the form and structure of the State ; that it inaugurates the

new and true democracy of the twentieth century ; that besides introducing a new self-discipline of all the factors concerned in the field of economics, it introduces also, in the field of politics, a new basis of representation, and constitutes a representative body which depends not on divided geographical constituencies and quarrelling political parties, but on the essential national *cadres* and their complementary interests.

So far as the first claim is concerned—the claim of a new conception of the function of the State—there are two things which may be said. In the first place, and so far as regards the general idea of the reconciling group in which not only employers and employed, but also the State and its agents, join amicable hands, history records its like, and cannot admit its novelty. The *collegia* of the later Roman Empire (for example, that of the shippers or *navicularii*) are already examples of corporations acting under a discipline which increasingly ceased to be self-discipline and became more and more a discipline imposed by the pressing requirements and the stern authority of the State. The guilds of the Elizabethan period of our English history, regulated by the Statute of Artificers of 1563, are equally examples of corporations in which the State sought to classify and regiment the productive factors of the community, so that it should know what they were doing and where they were to be found. An anxious government, particularly in a period of change and development, is glad to have its *cadres* fixed and to be concerned in their working. In the second place, and so far as regards the particular idea of the association of employers and employed in a common industrial council for the common regulation of their branch of production, contemporary history records a general movement which has touched England as well as Italy. The system of joint standing industrial councils was inaugurated in England in 1917, and it still continues to exist. It is a system independent of the State ; indeed the State is so far from controlling it that it may even be said to have admitted its control, in so far as it has erected such councils in the sphere of its own employing activity and in connection with its own employees. If the system is not corporativism, that is only because corporativism involves something more than the association of employers and employed in the common regulation of their common activities.

We are thus led to the second claim which is made for corporativism—that it is, or can be, independent of a political régime, and is not necessarily connected with a totalitarian State. This is a claim which has been made by English admirers of Italian corporativism ; but it is not generally made by Italian theorists or statesmen. To them the corporation is, as it was already stated to be as long ago as 1926, ' an organ of the administration of the State ' : to them it is connected with the régime ; in their eyes it has a specific, an Italian, a Fascist quality. Signor Mussolini may have spoken, on occasion, as if corporativism were a part of the general development of the world's economy : he has also said that a genuine corporativism requires the system of the single party and the totalitarian State. If corporativism be really an organ of State—an instrument by which the State expresses its will and realizes its policy in the sphere of economics—we are bound to accept the second of his sayings. Corporativism always includes, and includes first and foremost, the ' third partner ' of the State ; and because it does so it is dependent upon, and connected with, the conception and practice of the totalitarian State which, by its nature, must enter and penetrate the sphere of economics equally with other spheres. Any form of corporativism which does not include the State—or, if it includes it, includes it not as the managing partner, but only as a minister or servant rendering the *subsidarium officium*[1] of help and advice—is not in the Fascist view a true form of corporativism. Such a form is envisaged in the papal encyclical of 1931, *Quadragesimo Anno*. It is envisaged in contrast with, and in opposition to, the Italian form. It is envisaged as a voluntary form of order, freely imposed on themselves by the social factors concerned.[2] Different things need different names ;

[1] It is argued in *Quadragesimo Anno* (II § 5) that it is a disturbance of the right order if the great society of the State withdraws from lesser societies functions which they could perform, since its true natural function is to give help (*subsidium*) to the members of the body social, but never to destroy or absorb them. On this basis there emerges the *principium subsidarii officii*, and with it a criticism of any scheme which substitutes regimentation of smaller societies for the true and natural function of help. There are those who fear, the argument continues (with an implicit reference to the Italian system of corporativism), ' ne respublica, cui satis esse deberet ut necessarium et sufficiens auxilium praestaret, liberae activitati se substitueret '.

[2] The true rule for ' colleges ' or corporations based on occupations, it is argued in the same context, is the same as the rule laid down by Leo XIII in regard to the form of political government—' integrum esse hominibus quam maluerint formam eligere '.

and the papal programme cannot be called by the name of corporativism in the Fascist sense of the word. The Italian form of corporativism belongs, and belongs only, to Fascist Italy and its political régime. The Catholic form of corporativism, if it can be called corporativism at all, is an entirely different thing.

The third claim made for Italian corporativism—that it is, or rather that it makes possible, a new and better democracy—is a claim which can hardly be pressed, whether we regard democracy on its economic or on its political side. Economically the corporation, as we have already had reason to notice, is not based on a firm foundation of the freedom of trade unions. Nor is it free in itself and its own internal system. It is determined and controlled by the State (as indeed, if it be an organ of the State, must necessarily be the case), alike in its composition and in its exercise of its allotted functions. Such a system provides no pattern of industrial democracy. Politically, again, the system of State-created and State-controlled corporations provides no basis for a democratic form of State. A controlled corporation, acting as an organ of the State, cannot be a source of popular representation. The ' representative ' institutions in which it issues—whether they take the form of a national council of corporations, or that of a quasi-corporative chamber of deputies, or that of both chamber and council uneasily joined and imperfectly cemented—will not represent the free currents of popular opinion. They will represent, and they will share, the directed flow of a made and official opinion.

But even if the corporations were free, it does not follow that they would produce a free or effective system of representation. Representation based on economic groups, however autonomous they may be, will be representation of different and divergent interests : indeed, the more they are autonomous, the more it will bear that character. A representative body so constituted, and therefore so divided, cannot be a powerful factor in the political system. It will need a cement to hold it together if it is to act as a factor at all ; and that cement will necessarily be found in the permanent executive. A corporative parliament is a corollary, but in no sense a control, of the management of the State by an enthroned executive chief. There may be a fascination in the notion

of a new type of parliament, transcending the alleged
artificiality and the supposed particularism of geographical
electorates ; and the idea of a parliament based on natural
social groups may possibly appeal to the theoretic mind. In
actual fact, the ' natural social group ' is itself an artificial and
particularist construction, even more than the geographical
electorate. It has the artificiality of an economic abstraction ;
it has the particularism of a single interest. A local constituency, after all, is an all-sorts-and-conditions group which
is a microcosm of the nation. The people, if it speaks at all,
will speak best in areas of neighbourhood. If it does so, it will
speak with an informed voice : it will speak after listening to,
and after choosing among, the alternatives presented to it, in
such areas, by different political parties. The difficulty of a
corporative parliament, over and above the absence of local
constituencies, is the absence of political parties, which cannot
dwell in the rarified air of pure economic units. That is a
reason why the corporative parliament may well appeal to
those who are adverse to the existence of the party system.
It is also a reason why such a parliament finds its home in the
single-party State. But a parliament which is not only destitute
of homogeneity of interest and any internal cement, but also
destitute of local roots, and destitute too of the stimulus to
choice presented by the alternatives of party, is a parliament
destitute of so many things that it hardly remains a parliament.

We may thus conclude that the system of corporativism does
not offer an alternative to parliamentary democracy which can
itself be termed a new style and form of democracy. Considered in itself, and apart from its marriage with totalitarianism, the system of corporativism does not represent, and
it is not based upon, the general body of the people. It is a
system of sections within the range of economic society. If
these sections freely arose within that range, they might well
be of the greatest value for the purposes of that society. They
might be the basis of an order which not only kept the peace
between capital and labour, but also increased the efficiency
and the productivity of every branch of production. Even so,
they would not be the basis of a political order which brought
the people into the government and kept the government
responsive and responsible to the movement of popular
thought. Sections acting in the one field of economics cannot

be a substitute for the whole body of the people acting in the whole area of general political life. They may serve as auxiliaries : they may act, if they are gathered together in an economic council, as an advisory organ; but auxiliary functions and advisory organs can never be a substitute for the essential function and the decisive organs of representative democracy. The whole philosophy of ' corporations ', or *ordines*, or *Stände*, even at its best and highest, is a philosophy of society, and of the economic aspect of society, but not a philosophy of the State. This is not to assume any clean or clear-cut distinction between economic society and the State. Either must act on the other and be intertwined with the other. Political parliaments and other political organs are vitally concerned with economics : economic groups and other economic organs are vitally interested in politics. But either sphere, however much it may be concerned with or interested in the other, remains itself, and needs its own structure and methods for its own work. The structure and methods of the economic sphere, whether they be corporative or of any other pattern, cannot be transported into the political sphere and substituted for its structure and methods.

§ 7. THE GENERAL RELATION OF THE ITALIAN CORPORATIVE
SYSTEM TO TOTALITARIANISM AND THE NEW CAESARISM

But Italian corporativism can hardly be called a projection of economics into politics. It is rather the reverse. Instead of being a spontaneous development of the economic sphere, which has surged over into the political, it is an incursion of the political régime into economics. It is intended to be a recasting of economic life by the State, partly to bring it into conformity with itself, and partly to produce for itself new organs calculated to serve its own political needs. Corporativism in Italy cannot therefore be considered in itself. It must be considered along with the features of the régime from which it proceeds and which it is intended to serve. When it is so considered, we see at once that it cannot provide any organ of political discussion, for the simple reason that it is interlocked with political factors which eliminate such discussion. It is interlocked with, and dominated by, the ' representative ' leader who is held to resume in himself alone the general thought and will of the nation. It is interlocked with, and overshadowed by, the single party which, under the guidance of the leader, expresses and represents the whole purpose of the State. It belongs to a system in which local self-government, and the liberties of communes and provinces, have been subordinated to the exigencies of the central executive : it belongs to a system in which ' the rights of the man and the citizen ', whether he be acting individually or in association with his fellows, are declared to be subject to the higher being, the higher ends, and the higher means of a national organism which is integrally realized in the single party and its leader.

A comparison of the *form* of the corporative-totalitarian State in Italy with the *form* of the communist State in Russia suggests that Italy has a tighter binding of the lictorial rods of executive authority than Russia.[1] Russia has, in form, a democratic parliament side by side with free trade unions of producers and free associations of consumers ; and if in fact the communist party permeates alike all three—the parliament, the trade unions, and the associations of consumers—the form remains and may, in time, acquire some substance. The Italian corporations, dominated by the party, have to serve, as one institution, all the purposes of the triple organization of Russia. In form, again, Russia has a federal scheme, a recognition of autonomous Republics, a profession of the rights and liberties of its contained nationalities ; Italy leaves no room for federation, or for autonomy, or for anything but a single dominant nationalism. Finally, in form the Russian constitution of 1936 ends with a declaration of the ' freedoms ' or rights of individual citizens : Italian Fascism leaves no place for any such declaration, except in so far as its Charter of Labour of 1927 enunciates the rights and duties of corporations within the ambit, and under the interlocked system, of the Fascist State.

Form is not everything : indeed it may be only a veil and a delusion. The Russian form of a diversity of democratic organs and institutions has proved itself compatible with a rigorous uniformity and an arbitrary proscription of real or imagined enemies of the régime. The Italian form, however

---

[1] It should perhaps be said that this passage was written before the entry of Russia (and, for that matter, before the entry of Italy) into the present war, and that it has not been modified since.

tightly unified, has no such drastic record of trials and executions. But in the domain of the State, with its organized life and its regular procedural operation, form still counts ; and the Italian form can only be described, in the final issue, as definitely, and indeed of set purpose, anti-democratic. The corporative element in that form introduces no new phase or manifestation of democracy—so far, at least, as the political sphere is concerned. At the best it introduces, in the economic sphere and that sphere only, some opportunity for chosen members from the working classes, who are acceptable to the régime, to observe at first hand, and even possibly to influence, the working of the industrial system in their particular branch. In the political sphere the corporative element is something extraneous—something passive and inoperative, except in so far as, by being substituted for a political parliament which might be effective, it operates, by its mere presence, adversely to democracy.

There is thus no dyarchy between the dictator and the corporation ; no balancing of the representative leader by a new form of representation, based on the economic group, which stands solidly by his side. This is not to say that the whole system has no representative basis at all. The representative leader and his party *have* a representative quality —a quality neither decreased nor diminished by corporativism, which is simply another expression of the leader and the party. Just as a Roman Emperor could claim a representative character, voluntarily conferred by the Roman people through a *lex* by which he was invested with *imperium et potestas*, so the Duce can claim a similar character in virtue of a general sanction, by the Italian people, of his party and his position—a sanction formally given by the vote of the national electorate which has elected Fascist parliaments, or conferred more really, if more informally, by the simple fact of acceptance and acquiescence. Ancient Rome is still eloquent in modern Italy ; and modern Rome has seen the renewal, in a new form, of the recurrent historical fact of the *renovatio imperii Romani*. Napoleon, one of the many heirs of Rome, could claim that, four times approved by a national *plébiscite*, he was ' the first representative of the nation '. The Duce, who has added to the armoury of Napoleon the new modern fact of the single party passionately devoted to his leadership,

can claim that he and his party are the *only* representatives
of the nation. This is not democracy. It is the abnegation
and resignation of democracy. But the abnegation and resignation may themselves be argued to be democratic acts. In
ancient Rome the resignation of the people was made in the
name of order after many years of civil war. In modern Italy
it has been made in the name of national unity, held to be still
imperfect, and in the cause of national liberty (the liberty
of the national Ego and its *sacro egoismo*), held to be also
imperfect so long as internal disunity prevented the nation
from playing its role on the international stage. So in the
name of liberty itself, and by an act which could be regarded
as formally democratic (even if force and coercion marked the
beginning and course of the movement), an imperfect and
troubled democratic state was moved to surrender the keys to
the representative leader, who could claim that in himself,
and in those whom he gathered round him, there was now
expressed the desire and the purpose of the people. This is
not corporative democracy. It is simply a new would-be
Caesarism, wearing a new democratico-corporative disguise.

§ 8. THE CATHOLIC DOCTRINE OF CORPORATIVISM : THE PORTU-
GUESE SYSTEM AND ITS AFFINITIES : THE AUSTRIAN CHRISTIAN
STATE *AUF STÄNDISCHER GRUNDLAGE*

The corporative idea has hitherto been discussed, except for
one passing reference to the papal Encyclical of 1931, with
exclusive reference to Italy. But it is an idea which belongs to
the general Catholic world ; and as part of the philosophy of
that world it was applied in Austria, under the constitution of
1934, and it is being applied in Portugal. It may therefore be
pertinent, in conclusion, to devote some attention to the
Catholic idea of ' a guild social order ', as it is sometimes called,
and to study briefly the States in which the idea has been
partially or temporarily applied.

The Catholic doctrine of corporativism is naturally influenced by a desire to retain a place for the Catholic Church,
as a substantive group existing in its own right along with
other groups in face of the growth of the modern State.
Starting from the conception of natural law (which is also
divine law), and from the assumption of a natural order (which
is also a divine order) based on this law, Catholic thought

develops a philosophy of the various groups designed and intended by the divine order of nature. There is the elementary group of the family, based on the bond of blood : there is the local group of the township or *municipium*, based on the bond of neighbourhood : there are the economic groups (*collegia seu corpora*), based on the common practice of a trade or occupation : there is the political group of the State, based on the common interest of all its members in a common good. All these groups alike have their basis in natural law ; all are alike assigned their place by that law ; and the place or function of the State is to support and aid, but never to destroy or absorb, the other groups which exist by its side. The general tenets of this philosophy, based on the natural order prescribed by natural law, are buttressed by an appeal to the past of history. There was once, it is argued in the Encyclical *Quadragesimo Anno*, a rich social life which had developed itself in a system of associations of different kinds. It has been impaired and almost extinguished, and we are left with virtually nothing but individuals and the State. The old rich social life has to be rebuilt : particularly, in the economic sphere, a system of groups has to be reconstructed to meet the needs of modern conditions. What then are the groups—or, in other words, the natural societies belonging to the natural order based upon natural law—which are needed in the sphere of economics, and needed in just the same way as family, township, and State are needed in other spheres ? They are the groups to which each man belongs, not according to his position (as employer or employed) in the labour market, but according to the social function which (whether he be employer or employed) he joins with others in fulfilling by virtue of the trade or occupation which he practises in common with them. There is needed, therefore, a vocational group for each vocation which performs a social function : there is needed, in that group, the conjunction of employers and employed, who work together in the vocation : there is needed, finally, the collaboration of each group with the other groups, because all the groups are labouring together to discharge their specific social functions for the common benefit of all.

The general natural order therefore demands, as its expression in each branch of production which constitutes a social function, a particular order which takes the form of a vocational group (a *collegium seu corpus*, or, as we say, a corporation), jointly composed of the employers and employed who work together in the branch and discharge the function together. On the principle of economy of effort which belongs to any complex order—a principle which leaves each part of the order free to discharge its specific function—these vocational groups will be left by the State to constitute themselves and to conduct their operations for themselves ; and the State, so far as it is concerned with them, will be concerned in giving them aid (*subsidarium officium*) rather than in imposing control. It will be their coadjutor and not their master ; and they in their turn will be natural-law societies, with their own basis, and not ' organs of the State ' (*Status instrumenta atque instituta*).[1] It follows, as the Encyclical states, that the members of any vocational group will be free to choose the form which they prefer for the organization of their group. It also follows, if we look at the two sides of each group (that of the employers and that of the employed), that either of them will have a free faculty of instituting its own association (or associations), and of determining its rules and regulations. Workers will be free to form and manage their own trade unions or syndicates : employers will also be equally free. *Libertas consociationes instituendi*—that is the general principle.

The free family, the free *municipium*, the free vocational group—all these are linked together by the one general principle. In the Encyclical of 1931 this principle of group liberty is especially emphasized, in regard to vocational groups, by the drawing of a contrast between the system which it involves and another peculiar system (*singularis ratio*) which has been recently planned. (The reference to the Fascist system of corporations is plain, though it is never mentioned by name.) In this peculiar system it is the civil power which constitutes recognized associations of employers and employed ; and these recognized associations have the right of exacting subscriptions from all (whether members or not) who are occupied in their branch of production, and equally of imposing on all (again whether members or not) the provisions of any agreements they make. In this system, moreover, the corporations,

---

[1] The phrase appears to be an exact repetition of the Fascist definition of the corporation which has already been quoted.

formed from representatives of such recognized associations, are ' organs of State' which direct and co-ordinate the activities of the associations. Good, it is admitted, may result from such a system. It may, in particular, diminish the chances of class war. But it is a system which also raises grave doubts and excites real fears. May not the State, which ought to be content with giving aid, substitute itself for free activity ? May not this new type of associations and corporations assume an excessively bureaucratic and political character ? May it not be used to serve particular political aims rather than to promote a better social order ?

We may turn from this summary sketch of the Catholic ideal of the free corporative group to an equally summary account of contemporary or recent systems in which an attempt has been made to translate it into effect. In the Portuguese system of corporations the Catholic ideal seems to predominate ; but it would also appear to be mixed with Fascist elements. In Portugal, as in Italy, there is a single party ; in Portugal, too, there is a single, if far less prominent, leader ; in Portugal, as in Italy, the system of corporations is combined with a prohibition of strikes and lock-outs. But the Portuguese system generally is closer to Catholic ideas, as it is also further removed from the ideas and the institutions of the totalitarian State. Professor Salazar has specifically rejected the totalitarian State, as ' essentially pagan and naturally incompatible with the temper of our Christian civilization '. In the Portuguese constitution of 1933 a National Assembly, elected by direct suffrage, is an essential part. Since the National Assembly meets concurrently with the corporative chamber, no man can simultaneously be a member of both bodies ; and the corporative chamber is definitely limited to examining and reporting on measures submitted to the Assembly. The first part of the constitution contains a system of fundamental guarantees ; and these guarantees include not only the rights of individual citizens, but also those of the family and of churches. This is already an approximation to Catholic ideas ; and that approximation also appears, and appears more evidently, in the general conceptions of corporations. The corporative organizations of Portugal are not only economic : they also include intellectual and moral organizations, which exist for purposes of science and art or of charity and relief. Nor is this all. The chamber of corporations not only includes representatives of ' social interests ' in a broad and general sense which embraces cultural and moral as well as economic interests : it also includes representatives of local autonomous bodies based on the bond of neighbourhood, and it thus recognizes the principle of contiguity as well as the ' interest ' principle. If, therefore, the Portuguese State is corporative, its corporations are spiritual as well as material ; and it adds, moreover, a recognition of the importance of local life (and also, it may be added, of the life of the family) to its recognition of the importance of groups based upon social interests. There is here a general attempt at synthesis in the Catholic sense—synthesis of individual rights and their guarantees with the life of societies ; synthesis of the family and local society with the various societies of the corporative type. This involves the recognition of a general system of natural order, with its subordinate and included ' orders ' ; and that in turn involves the recognition of a sovereign natural law, in terms of which the State, and the other groups forming with it the system of natural order, all move and have their being. This, once more, means a rejection of the idea and practice of the totalitarian State. The State is not total ; it is a *part* of a natural order based upon natural law. The constitution of 1933 emphasizes, in its first section, the duty of the State ; it emphasizes especially its duty to establish order by determining and enforcing respect for the rights and guarantees derived from morals, equity, and law. This is to enthrone, in the last resort, the sovereignty of natural law.

It is not necessary to idealize the actuality which lies behind the general theory of the contemporary Portuguese State. We must confess that if it is not totalitarian, it is certainly authoritarian. We must also confess that if it is not a copy of Fascist Italy, it has many analogies, and even some imitations. Besides the system of a single party, and besides the regimentation of economics by the prohibition of strikes and lock-outs, there is also a general statute of National Labour, enacted in 1933, which corresponds to the Italian Charter of Labour of 1927. On the other hand it is only fair to say that the actual working of the Portuguese system of economic regulation, under the guidance of Professor Salazar, has been marked by an honest attempt to combine the improvement of production with amelioration of the working conditions and the general life of the working classes.[1] If there is a system of recognized trade unions of workers and recognized federations of employers, as in Italy, and if, as in Italy, the agreements made between such recognized bodies bind all alike, whether or no they are members, the actual fruits of the system seem better than the system.

The corporative system of Austria had a brief life of less than four years, from the May-day which inaugurated the constitution of 1934 to the beginning of 1938. During that brief period Austria sought to become ' the pattern State of *Quadragesimo Anno* '. The constitution was proclaimed in the name of God, the source of all law ; it was proclaimed for a Christian federal State resting on a corporative basis (*auf ständischer Grundlage*). It would be a work of supererogation to examine the details of a system which has already passed, and which, even during its short life, existed mainly on paper. The Austria of this brief period was authoritarian, but without effective authority : it was based on a single Christian social party, and yet it was vexed by party divisions. The corporativism on which it rested, or professed to rest, was part of a general unreality. It was struggling into existence, but it did not effectively exist. Its unit was the *Berufstand*—an institution (or a term) which married the medieval idea of the Estate to the modern idea of the occupation. There were seven of these bodies (compared with the three estates of the Middle Ages and the twenty-two corporations of the modern Italian age); and each of them, wherever it was possible (it was not easy, for example, in the occupational group composed of the free professions), had a representative body drawn from both employers and employed. It can hardly be said that this representative body was based on a system of equality ; nor can it be said that the occupational groups themselves either emerged spontaneously or exercised any real power of self-government. They were State creations, if they were not ' organs of State ' ; indeed in the early stage of corporative development through which Austria was passing nothing could have emerged, or acted, without the incentive and direction of the State.[2]

---

[1] Cf. *supra*, p. 279, n. 1.

[2] It should be added that the United Trade Union, which was the basis of each *Berufstand* on the workers' side, was itself set up by the government in the

On the other hand, though the *Berufstand* was an artificial construction, State created and State controlled (and in that sense contrary to Catholic theory), it was conjoined in Austria with other units which seemed to strengthen its life and redeem it from total subordination to the State. This conjunction appeared in a curious form. The constitution of 1934 drew a distinction between 'probouleutic organs', which prepared legislative proposals, and a federal diet which acted as the actual legislature. One of the probouleutic organs was a federal economic council composed of representatives drawn from each of the seven *Berufstände*. (This economic council was thus a body like, and yet, in virtue of its preparatory and probouleutic position, unlike, the Italian council of corporations and the Portuguese corporative chamber.) By the side of this federal economic council there were other federal councils based upon different grounds, but holding a similar probouleutic position. There was a federal council of culture, composed of representatives drawn from religious societies, from educational institutions, and from the fields of science and art. There was again a federal council of the provinces, based on the territorial principle of neighbourhood, and composed of representatives drawn from each of the provinces. The federal diet itself was composed of representatives drawn from these various councils (and from a fourth body called the Council of State, whose members, mainly administrators, were nominated by the federal president[1]) ; and it was thus a curious mosaic of the members of four different groups—the economic, the cultural, the provincial, and the administrative—without any substantive basis or title of its own.

The whole was a peculiar Catholic construction, like and yet unlike the Portuguese system. It might claim to be a construction based upon the divine order of natural law : indeed the constitution, in its very designation, runs 'im Namen Gottes, des Allmächtigen, von dem alles Recht ausgeht'. It might also claim to be a construction which respected the

spring of 1934, after the struggle with the socialists and the dissolution of the old trade union system of organization. It should also be added that this body, on the Italian model, had authority over, and might claim subscriptions from, non-members.

[1] The members of this *Staatsrat* were to be *verdiente charaktervolle Bundesbürger*, including persons actively engaged in the service of the State. They sat for ten years ; and it would seem that they were intended to represent administrative experience.

rights of individuals : its second section is devoted to a recital of the general rights of all citizens. The whole system was closely joined with a Concordat made with the Holy See in the June of 1933. This Concordat was declared and recited, along with the constitution, at the time of its promulgation on the May-day of 1934 ; and by it the rights of the Catholic Church (in education and in other spheres) were specifically and liberally recognized. But the general system had grave defects. It was an imperfect combination of a weak authoritarianism and a weak single party (weak because it only appealed to a minority of the country) with the Catholic doctrine of natural law, the natural rights of individuals, and the natural order of groups. It differed from the Portuguese system in the weakness of its authoritarianism and the weakness of its single party : it also differed in the fact that its organization of groups was at once more complicated and less effective—more tortuously intertwined, but with less of a basis in real life. The seven *Berufstände* might march in procession on the May-day of 1934[1] ; but their feet were never established on the actual ground. The complicated system of four proboul-eutic councils and a federal diet drawn from their members was in any case too complicated ; and it existed mainly on paper. A struggling authority, moving in the circle of Catholic doctrine but unable to realize its ideas—this was the essence ; and the essence, weak within and beset without, was destitute of the substance necessary for continued existence. But the memory of the Austria that struggled to be the pattern State of *Quadragesimo Anno* is still a touching and poignant memory to any man who watched its struggles.

[1] It was an unforgettable day and an unforgettable sight. Dollfuss sat and watched and smiled gaily in the afternoon sunshine. The writer, a Cambridge Professor, sat in the crowd on a platform opposite, and watched his brother professors marching in their *Berufstand*.

XIII

THE ALTERNATIVE OF GERMAN NATIONAL SOCIALISM

§ 1. PRUSSIANISM AND ROMANTICISM AS PERMANENT FACTORS IN GERMAN LIFE

THE alternative to democracy which has been propounded in Germany by the National Socialist party, and developed and enforced since its triumph in 1933, is the most thoroughgoing and the most drastic of our times. It is all the more drastic because the democratic system of the Weimar Republic, which was constructed in 1919 and began to collapse in 1930, was itself a drastic and doctrinaire system, which had little root in the German past and little hold on the abiding sentiments and the permanent ideas of Germany.

From the beginning of the nineteenth century, if not earlier, Prussianism and Romanticism may be said to have been the two steady factors in German life. Prussianism meant the system of a transcendent State, uniting a congeries of territories—a State expressed in the directing will of a monarch or leader who was supported, on one side, by the army and the army officers whom he had gathered round him, and, on the other, by a trained and disciplined staff of administrative officials, loyal to their employer and versed in all the technique of running and arranging smoothly the various wheels of his business. In the ideal of Prussianism the people, in the sense of the gathered and welded body of the inhabitants of the congeries of territories, is a managed multitude, content with its management. The State is not immanent in the people, and it does not spring from the thought and the will of the people. It is rather a transcendent being—a being resident in the director and his double staff—which regulates the life of the people from its own height. That height is solitary and stern. It has a Spartan quality of asceticism. The director himself is pledged to a life of service as 'the first servant of the Republic': the members of his double staff are equally, under his impulse, an austere body of servants. The spirit which animates the higher being is discipline, alike for itself and the people whom it transcends and whose life it regulates. The two great virtues are *Ehre* and *Pflicht*. These are the ideal chains which all may well be proud to wear. Wearing them in the service of the higher being, which pre-eminently wears them itself, men may feel that they have the perfect freedom of obedience to something above themselves, which yet guides them to the stern satisfaction of a realization of themselves.

The factor of Romanticism, which was already powerful in German thought by 1800, may appear at first sight the antithesis of Prussianism. The Romantic conception, in its application to the problems of the nature of community and the character of the common life, starts, as we have seen, from the idea of the *Volk*—the ' folk ' or people or nation. In the Romantic view, there *is*, after all, something immanent in the people. There is a life which acts and creates, as well as a stuff which is disciplined. The folk, in the general sphere of culture, is a maker of folk-music, folk-tales, and folk-ballads : it is also, in the juridical sphere, a maker of law, which in the last resort expresses the folk-sense of what is right and may therefore be defined as ' the organ of folk-right '. If it is thus a maker, in these different spheres, the folk must have a mind (otherwise there would be nothing to do the making) ; and we must therefore accept the existence of a folk-mind or *Volksgeist*. We may go even farther, if we seek to discover the ultimate origin and basis of the folk-mind, and we may say that a folk-mind is an incarnation of the eternal mind of God, as He works in space and time. It has a divinity, and its works are right. Working and creating freely, in its time and for its space, it realizes the purposes of God.

Different as this Romantic conception of the Folk may appear to be from the Prussian conception of the State, it proved, in effect, to be its complement and corroboration. The transcendent State, which shapes the people from above, can readily make its peace with the immanent mind of the Folk. Prussianism can be combined with Romanticism ; and Prussianism wins in the combination. This is the tendency which German political thought has generally followed. Granted that the folk has its own inherent and immanent mind, it may still be argued that it needs an organ of expression—at any rate in the sphere of politics and law. It needs an uttering voice to proclaim its thought and elucidate its will. The transcendent State is at hand to serve as organ and to act as voice. Indeed the director himself, pure and simple, in his physical personality, is ready to perform these functions.

The unity of the people, Hegel could say, must be incorporated 'in an actual individual, in the will of a decreeing individual'. The being immanent in Folk thus becomes compatible with the transcendent higher being of the authoritarian State. Romanticism can romanticize Prussianism ; and Prussianism can find an ally, or rather a basis, and not a rival or an antithesis, in the theory of Romanticism.

§ 2. THE GERMAN EXPERIENCE OF CONSTITUTIONALISM AND
LIBERALISM

We have here the ultimate roots of the National Socialist doctrines of the Leader and the Folk which he leads and expresses. But in the course of the nineteenth century new factors entered into the development of Germany, which have impinged on the combination of Romanticism and Prussianism, and have eventually produced its present form and its contemporary balance.

The chief of these new factors was Western constitutionalism and Western liberalism—the idea of the State as acting under a constitution formed, or at any rate ratified, by the people : the idea of the State as acting through a liberal system of government which included an electorate, parties, a parliament, and some form of parliamentary executive. Constitutionalism and liberalism were Western, from the German point of view, in the sense that they were trans-Rhenane, and that they expressed, as a whole, the genius of France. They were imports and not indigenous products. Moreover what was imported—in Prussia under the constitution of 1848–9, and in united Germany under the constitution of 1871—was formal rather than substantive. The essence of the old dominant State remained. There was never, in any real sense, a true form of parliamentary executive before the Weimar constitution of 1919. The real executive, and the real bearer of the authority of the State, was always the monarch and his military and civil staff : electorate, parliament, and parties were outworks, or even a façade. The strongest part of the outworks, and the part of the façade which was most substantial, was the system of parties—doctrinaire parties each marked by the German genius for a synthetic philosophy of life (*Weltanschauung*), but all acting by way of criticism, rather than of construction, because the keys of power (which alone would have unlocked the doors for construction) were with-held from their grasp by the very nature of the dominant State. It was the paradox of Germany in the nineteenth century, and down to the outbreak of the war of 1914-18, that it developed, above all the other elements of Western liberalism, the element of party—and that in the peculiar form of the totalitarian party, engaged in pursuing some particular philosophy of life to its logical consequences, and therefore engaged in a general criticism alike of other philosophies and of the central executive round the monarch which actually conducted the government.

That executive, under Bismarck and his successors, con-ducted transactions with the parties (Liberal, Clerical, Con-servative, and Socialist), or with some combination of parties, and thus bowed and bent the State into some sort of accom-modation with the new and hardly digested fact of a party system. With the end of the war of 1914-18, and with the temporary collapse of the old German system of the trans-cendent State, there ensued a new period of transaction—not between the Government and the parties, but between the parties themselves. The Weimar constitution of 1919 was itself the fruit of such a transaction. It was a tesse-lated pavement—partly Liberal, partly Clerical, and partly Socialist. In form it represented a complete victory of Western constitutionalism and Western liberalism. There was a written constitution, professing to proceed from the German people, and containing (in its second part) a long declaration of the fundamental principles on which a State must act, a declara-tion which followed the general analogy of the French declara-tion of the Rights of Man in 1789, but was expressed in the different form (and the form itself is significant) of the funda-mental Rights and Duties of Germans. There was a uni-cameral parliament, based on exact proportional representat-ion of parties, and buttressed (or weakened) by provisions for popular initiative and referendum. But the whole system, created by a transaction of parties, depended for its continuance on a continuing transaction of parties. A permanent trans-action of parties could not be achieved. Each was too set in itself : each had its own exclusive and total philosophy of life ; each tended to provide itself with a whole apparatus for its followers which made it a State within the State. As in the period before 1914, so (if in a different form and to a greater degree) in the period after 1919, the fact of parties—multiple parties—was the dominant expression of the democratic or liberal idea in Germany. Multiple parties, thrown on their own, without the old iron framework of the dominant State, and without the interior and natural cohesion of a pervading sense of the homogeneity of the nation, failed to work. As early as 1930, it was found necessary to use a provision (or an interpretation of a provision), in the mosaic of the Weimar constitution, which enabled the president to govern through presidential cabinets appointed by and responsible to himself, and allowed these cabinets to legislate by way of decrees, which thus took the place of parliamentary statutes. This was a return of the old dominant State, now incarnate in the president. It was also the harbinger of the more complete return which came with the final victory of the National Socialist party in 1933.

The form in which the transcendent or Prussian State returned in 1930 was obviously temporary, and could not last. It was based on a provision of the constitution intended for an exceptional and transitory period in which public security and order were seriously imperilled ; and no permanent system of government could be built on such a provision. Some new system had to be found which went to the root of the difficulty ; which faced the problem of multiple parties acting in an environment that provided neither an iron framework of unity nor a national sentiment of cohesion ; which gave, or tried to give, some form of unity to German life. That new system, in the logic of the internecine struggle of parties and of party philosophies of life, was bound to be some single party which enthroned itself and its philosophy. The core and content of that system, after long years' of what could now be held to be 'foiled and circuitous wandering' away from the old traditions of Prussianism and Romanticism, was bound to be a return to those traditions.

The German experience of constitutionalism and liberalism had indeed been tragic. In its first phase, down to 1914, it had been an experience of a formal and even illusory liberalism, acting under the shadow and control of an authoritarian State. In its second phase, from 1919 to 1930, it had been an experience of liberalism mixed with socialism and clericalism—

mixed, too, with constitutional provisions which on the one hand tended to a presidential autocracy, and on the other hand made for the primary democracy of initiative and referendum. The Weimar constitution was a cento rather than a constitution. More tragic still, in the history of this second experience, was the fact that it had been begun under the shadow of defeat, and that it trailed clouds of the memories of defeat throughout its course. Liberalism thus seemed an imported, and even an imposed thing—imported from the West in homage to the ascendancy of the victor : imposed by the West in order to secure a cowed and congruous neighbour. When this was the mood, and when this was the interpretation of constitutionalism and the parliamentary State, the old German past—the past before such things had entered and confused the German soul—could not but appear in bright and glowing colours.

§ 3. THE ORIGINS AND BASES OF NATIONAL SOCIALISM

The eventual reconstruction, from 1933 onwards, was thus a restoration ; but it was also, like most restorations, a revolution. It was a restoration in that it went back to the old idea of the directing Leader and the old idea of the united Folk. It was a revolution in that the Leader was of a new type, and allied, after all, with the new fact of party (Germany had not undergone for nothing her experience of party) ; it was also a revolution in that the Folk too was of a new type, and allied with a new idea of race and racial purity.

The National Socialist party began its life in the party struggles after 1919, and it bore, and continues to bear, the marks of those struggles. It began and it has continued its life as an exclusive party, with a general doctrine or ' philosophy of life ', and with what may be called a general ' apparatus of life ' (uniforms, rallies, recreation, relief, and a general direction of activities) for all its members. So far as party formation is part of the democratic State, the National Socialist party bears the traces of that State. But in so far as the party is a single and exclusive party, which has eliminated all others, it has shed the very genius and spirit of democracy. From this point of view it marks a return of the old Prussian State, but a return ' on a higher level ', or at any rate in a different form. If we interpret its development in the terms of Hegelian dialectic, we may say that the thesis of the unity of the Prussian State, and the antithesis of the party division of the democratic State, have now been joined in the synthesis of a single and exclusive party, which still carries on the old Prussian State, but carries it on with a new power (and, in that sense, on a higher level) because the directing leader has now the support and the basis of a body of followers—a body such as surrounded the old Teutonic chieftains of primitive German antiquity in ages long anterior to the birth of modern Prussia. The Prussian State has thus become immanent as well as transcendent—immanent in a party which supports and sustains the political activity of the State, as it also supports and sustains the social activities of the Folk. We may add that if the old Prussian king could wed the State and the Folk, because he could be regarded not only as the king but also as the Folk-leader, the new leader-chancellor of Germany can wed them even more intimately, because he is the core of a great and general party which acts in and upon the State at the same time that it acts in and upon the Folk.

In its origins the party mixed an old Nationalism with a new non-proletarian Socialism. So far as it was National, it drew its adherents from all, of whatever rank, who desired a national renaissance ; so far as it was Socialist, it appealed particularly, at any rate in its origins, to the elements less regarded by the orthodox social democrats—the peasantry, the small shopkeeper, and the lower middle class. Like all new parties, it particularly appealed to the young ; but as a nationalist party it particularly appealed to those of the young who had seen war service, and wished to preserve the best of what they had learnt in the war by cultivating the virtues of fellowship and heroism. From its first beginnings the party called itself German (The German Workers' Party) ; and whatever elements it gathered—youth or age, the lower middle class or the great industrialists—it remained essentially and fundamentally German. It thus wedded itself to the idea of the Folk and of *Volkstum* ; it proceeded from that to the idea of eradicating ' foreign ' elements from the body of the Folk ; it ended by conceiving the Folk as a native and natural race, which must above all things preserve its racial purity, enhance its racial vigour, and expand to its racial limits. The romantic conception of the Folk as a spirit (or *Geist*) might seem to suffer a sad change when it became the National Socialist conception of the Folk as a race or blood ; but when race was held to be knit to spirit, and when it was argued that only the pure race could possess and transmit the true spirit, men might well think, and they came to believe, that the old conception had only been set on a firmer and deeper foundation.

Like the Fascist party in Italy, the National Socialist party was originally an *antipartito*, with its hand against all other parties, but particularly against the Communist party. Like the Fascist party, again, it started with a conglomerate of ideas and social elements. But unlike the Fascist party, it had attained a doctrine before it attained to power ; and it attained this doctrine because there were permanent German traditions on which it could draw, and by drawing on which it could gain the *élan* of a positive party and the unity of a single creed. The two central principles of this creed have been described by Carl Schmitt as the principle of ' Leadership ' (*Führung*) and the principle of ' Identity of Kind ' (*Artgleichheit*). We may study the nature of the National Socialist system, and examine how far it presents a new scheme of popular government (whether or no we regard that scheme as in any real sense democratic), if we study the operations and effects of these two principles.

§ 4. THE PRINCIPLE OF LEADERSHIP AND ITS RELATION TO THE IDEA OF REPRESENTATION

The principle of leadership, in its modern conjunction with the fact of a great single party of followers, is a restatement and a recasting of the old Prussian principle. Instead of the hereditarily imposed monarch of the early Prussian system, in the period before 1848, there is now the freely emergent leader who has come from the people and is sustained by the people. Instead of the qualified monarchy of the second Prussian system, between 1848 and 1914, with the monarch standing behind a façade of constitutionalism and governing by means of transactions with the parties which filled that façade, there is now the unqualified hegemony of a leader standing behind no façade and acting in a living harmony with a single and congruous popular party. There is an obvious sense in which the new leader, emerging from the people and linked with a great popular party, may be called representative.

If we argue, as it is argued in modern Germany, that 'true representation is the personification of the will of the people in a representative who feels himself to be one with the people', we shall conclude that the new system of leadership is a system (and indeed the only possible system) of true representation. But before we can accept that conclusion, we must look a little more closely at the conceptions both of leadership and of party, and we must examine somewhat more deeply the nature of representation.

Leadership is a Protean thing in the literature of National Socialism. If it is sometimes depicted as representative, or popular, or even democratic, it sometimes appears as aristocratic, and sometimes as autocratic. Hitler himself speaks of the aristocratic principle which gives leadership and supreme influence to the best heads, and thereby pays respect to the idea of personality and not to that of majority.[1] The title of the leader thus rests in himself and his personal right, and not in his representative capacity. Carl Schmitt, when he seeks to describe the essence of leadership, is driven into theological terms. 'Our conception of leadership neither needs nor admits any mediating image or representative metaphor : it is a conception of immediate or real presence.'[2] Leadership is thus a fact which is *sui generis* ; which represents nothing, but is simply itself ; which acts, and has rights of action, simply because it is. Here the aristocratic principle becomes autocratic. The only limitation on leadership is the fact that by its definition it requires a body of followers. But if the leader, by the magnetic quality of his own nature, inevitably attracts a body of followers, even that limitation ceases to be a limit. It will be a necessity of nature, and not the consent of man, which provides him with a following. It will be a matter of grace, and not of constitutional duty, that he seeks any formal approbation for his acts—that he retains an elected Reichstag, that he receives at its hands a grant of plenary powers authorizing the cabinet which he controls to issue laws, that he conducts a referendum or plebiscite for the ratification of his policies. Leadership, when it is made a principle, transcends and overpowers representation. *De facto*, the leader may be representative. *De jure*, it is sufficient that he should be the emergent leader existing in real presence. The circle of ideas

---

[1] *Mein Kampf*, p. 493.   [2] *Staat, Bewegung, Volk*, p. 42.

which ripples outwards from the principle of leadership is a new circle, entirely distinct from the circle which starts from representation. It is a circle of leader-decisions. It is a circle of leader-choice of counsellors and associates. It is a circle of leader-attraction, issuing in consequent duties of fidelity to the leader.

Just as the leader is *sui generis*, even while he renews and recasts old elements of the Prussian past, so too the National Socialist party may be termed unique, even though it was born among other parties and in competition with them. It is not a body open to the adherence of all recruits, like the parties of the democratic State : it is rather an ' order ', or an *élite*, whose members have a particular capacity and vocation.[1] Drawn into the general circle of ideas which moves around the idea of leadership, the party, however broadly it may be recruited from the various strata of the people, is confined to those who are inspired by 'the spirit of fidelity ; and it is controlled by a hierarchical system of leadership which ensures the operation of that spirit. Because it is firmly led, it can be in turn a leader—a body of leading (*Führungskörper*) which stands above both the organs of the State and the groups within the Folk, and pours its energy and fidelity into those organs and groups.

This is something different from the old conception of party —different, and yet like. It is something different in the sense that party is here adjusted to a final and central leadership which is above it, shapes it, and moves it. Party has ceased to be a spontaneous body which freely discusses and precipitates a programme, freely recruits adherents to the programme, and freely moves in a spirit of joint endeavour towards its realization. The new party is a *Gefolgschaft* rather than a *Genossenschaft* ; it is filings drawn to a magnet, and clustering round the magnet, rather than a free society. On the other hand the new party is, in one great respect, like the old German parties. It inherits and accentuates their ' total ' tradition. Like them, it has a general philosophy of life, which is an exclusive philosophy. Like them, it seeks to pour that total philosophy both into the administration of the State and into

---

[1] Schmitt, *op. cit.*, p. 13. In this respect the Nationalist Socialist party is like the Russian Communist or the Italian Fascist party. All are *élites*, with a special vocation.

the activities of the Folk, shaping and staffing the former in accordance with its ideas, and drawing the latter, in all their manifestations (cultural or economic), under its direction and in its train. In this aspect the subject and following party is also a sovereign and a leader. But of these two aspects the newest, and also the strongest, is the aspect of party which makes it a following body of fidelity.

If we consider the dominance of the idea of leadership, and the subordination of the single party itself to the dominance of this idea, we shall see that the idea of representation, in any ordinary sense of the term, is necessarily submerged. The leader may indeed be termed ' the representative of the will of the people ' ; but the term ' representative ' is here being used in a new and strained sense. The will which he represents, or rather incarnates, is a will which he inspires, and which would not exist without his inspiration. He represents a will projected from himself and reflected back upon himself. Immediate representation of the people by a single leader can never be representation of the original will of the people. The people never forms a single original will which can be reflected or represented in the mirror of another single will. When it acts originally, in a form which can be immediately represented, the people acts in a variety of ways of thinking and feeling ; and it can only be represented by a variety of representatives. That variety of representatives may subsequently, by process of parliamentary discussion and parliamentary compromise, achieve a single will, which in turn is accepted by the people and becomes the will of the people. But the process by which a single will of the people emerges is a long process ; and if the people is to have any say in it, the process must involve in its course a stage of multiple representation by a variety of different parties. The single representative immediately representing an original will of the people is a short cut which lies outside the complexity and delicacy of actual political life and actual representation.

To deny a representative character to the present German system is not to deny the existence of a willing body of followers, or even the fact that this willing body may be almost as broad as the whole of the people. But however large and however willing the body of followers may be, it is still a following. The fundamental fact is the fact that this following represents

or reflects the will of the leader, and not that the leader represents or reflects the will of the following. If there is representation, it is inverse representation, proceeding downwards from
the leader. The party represents the leader : the people, so
far as it takes its colour from the party, equally represents and
reflects the direction of the leader. Not only the party and the
people, but also (by the law of 20 January 1934) the whole
system of industry, becomes a reflection and representation of
the principle of leadership.[1] In each undertaking the employer
becomes the leader, and the employed the following. The
employer, in his capacity of leader, decides, though in the
same capacity he must also concern himself with the well-being
of the employed in their capacity of followers ; the followers,
on their side, owe fidelity to the leader. Industry, like other
ranges of the national life, thus comes within the circle of a
new feudalism and the notions of fealty which it involves.
Feudalism—an idealized and modernized feudalism—is indeed
the essence. Under this new system of feudalism the lord
represents and carries his men—though he may, and will,
gather them round him to ensure their confidence and to hear
their counsel.[2] Representative institutions thus undergo a
medieval change into a feudal court gathered round its lord.
In the same way the law and judges are also carried back,
along with representative institutions, into an idealized
medievalism. They must take account of fidelity and honour
as well as of legality and the performance of legal duty. In
industry there are accordingly instituted courts of honour : in
the general sphere of law ' the obligations of honour which are
a vital necessity for the law of a *Führerstaat* ' (the phrase is that
of Carl Schmitt) are incorporated in, or added to, the old
obligations of law. Leadership not only affects the political
system. It affects equally, and consequentially, the legal
system. If the leader moves into the political centre, in lieu
of a representative legislature, the modes of action required by
fidelity to the principle which he represents will equally move
into the legal or judicial centre, in lieu of (or at any rate in
addition to) the modes of action required by legal enactment
and judicial rule.

[1] Gesetz zur Ordnung der nationalen Arbeit, Erster Abschnitt, pp. 1-2.
[2] In the system of industry, accordingly, there is in each undertaking a council
of confidence—' dem Führer des Betriebes . . . traten aus der Gefolgschaft
Vertrauensmänner beratend zur Seite ' ; ibid., § 5.

§ 5. THE PRINCIPLE OF RACE, OR IDENTITY OF KIND, AND THE
IDEA OF THE *REICH*

The other great principle of national socialism is that
which we have called ' identity of kind '. Just as the principle
of leadership is a modernized (and also, for that matter,
medievalized) version of Prussianism, so the principle of
identity of kind, or *Artgleichheit*, is also a modernized version
(which is archaic, or primitive, as well as modern) of the old
Romanticism. The two old colleagues are still colleagues in
their modern dress and their new manifestation. It has been
argued by Carl Schmitt that the two principles are essentially
necessary complements.[1] The ' real presence ' of the leader
requires for its residence a people identical in itself and identical
with him. If there were not identity of kind between leader
and following, there could not exist between them a continuous
contact and a mutual confidence ; the rule of the leader might
become a tyranny foreign to his following. If, again, there
were not identity of kind between all the members of the
people, the impulse and the inspiration of the leader would
fail to achieve their proper result. They would move one
part of the people, and leave another part unmoved.

It is possible to connect the doctrine of race with the doctrine of leadership by this subtle logic. It is also possible, and
it is tempting, to establish the connection in a simpler way,
and to say that the doctrine of race is connected with that of
leadership for the plain and pragmatic reason that the actual
leader who has emerged in Germany has proclaimed his
belief in the doctrine of race. But that is not the whole of the
matter. The leader himself, in proclaiming his belief, has
linked the doctrine of race with that of leadership by the
logic of an inner connection. Hitler not only believes in race
as the fundamental and determining element which makes men
what they are and causes them to do what they do. He also
believes that one race is superior to others and the natural
leader of others. He proceeds from that to the further belief
that if there is leadership between race and race, we are
logically bound to accept the view that there must also be
leadership within the leading race. ' A philosophy of life which
attempts, in reaction against the democratic idea of number,
to give this earth to the best people, and therefore to the best

[1] *Staat, Bewegung, Volk*, p. 42.

men, must logically obey the same aristocratic principle in the interior life of that people, and assign the leadership and the supreme influence in that people to the best heads.'[1] In the view of Hitler the doctrine of race thus leads to that of leadership, as conversely, in the view of Carl Schmitt, the doctrine of leadership leads to that of race. In either case an inner connection between the two is vindicated, or at any rate assumed.

Considered in itself, and apart from the doctrine of leadership, the doctrine of race involves a fundamental rejection of the general axioms and bases of democratic thought. On this doctrine the individual is coloured by his race in the whole of his being. He is determined by this one fact ; he is swung towards the racial centre in all his goings and all his thinking. There cannot be different currents of social thought expressing themselves in different programmes and parties which meet in the process of discussion and compromise : there can only be the One—the Folk which is also a race, and which is a' Folk in virtue of being a race. Before this centripetal impetus all divergencies disappear. First, the divergency of local particularisms, expressed in the form of the old dynastic States before 1914, and in that of the modified *Länder* during the period between 1919 and 1933, is swept away. Next, the divergency of political parties, allied (in the new view) with those local particularisms, and finding its especial basis in the opportunity thus provided,[2] is equally swept away. Finally, the divergency of social formations, such as the old German Trade Unions (in their Socialist, Clerical or other forms), equally disappears. Only the Churches remain ; and the Churches, face to face with the centripetal doctrine of race (and the no less centripetal doctrine of leadership), have to make their account, as best they can, with the compelling force of the total unity of the Folk.

The varied ground of local self-government, of political

---

[1] *Mein Kampf*, p. 493. The same idea also occurs on p. 421 : 'if a State is fundamentally directed to the racial principle, and does homage to nature's aristocratic principle, the people will recognize not only the different value of races, but also the different value of individuals '. This is the *Herren* principle of National Socialism. Not only is there a *Herrenvolk*. There is also a *Herrenschicht* within the *Herrenvolk*. The *Arbeiterpartei* is also an aristocratic party.

[2] In a speech of 1 September 1933, Hitler spoke of party egoists deliberately uniting their perverse party interests with the particularist *Länder* traditions, and thus seeking to imperil the unity of the *Reich*. Cf. *supra*, p. 144.

parties, and of free social formations, which is the basis of democratic thought and practice, has thus been cleared. Other postulates of democratic thought and practice have equally gone into oblivion.   One is the simple postulate of civic equality—that in the eyes of the State, and before its law, one man counts equally with another.   In the matter of the Jew, a distinction has been drawn between the full citizen, who fully belongs to the Folk regarded as also a race, and the imperfect citizen, with imperfect rights, who has no full membership.   That is a denial of an old principle (which is not merely democratic, though it is recognized in all democratic States) that any man once accepted as a member or the legal association of the State is a member on the same terms, and under the same conditions, as other men.   Indeed it is a denial not only of that principle, but also of the whole modern conception of the State as a legal association, which is transmuted, by reversion, into a conception that makes it a kin group or blood connection.   But the racial principle goes still further in the direction of inequality. It not only involves purity of the blood, and a consequent depression (or even elimination) of the impure.   It also involves the soundness, health, and vigour of the blood ; and on this it follows that blood which is not sound, or healthy, or vigorous, possesses a less claim, and must enjoy inferior rights, in comparison with blood which possesses these qualities.   Accordingly a law of sterilization, which came into effect on 1 January 1934, has denied the right of having offspring to persons who are afflicted with transmissible defects. Race, after all, is a physical idea ; and when it is made the main and the sovereign idea, it issues in a legal differentiation of human beings according to their physical value.

But the idea of racial unity has a still further, and a final, manifestation.   Under its pressure the liberty of a varied ground of human life has gone. Under its pressure the equality of the members of the political association has gone : indeed the idea of political association has itself disappeared. There remains in its place the fraternity of race. But the fraternity of race is not only an internal idea or an internal force. It is also an external influence, acting as a solvent and corrosive on the legal boundaries of States. Claiming to be something greater than law, or legality, it seeks to transcend externally the legal system of States (struggling to be an association or league under a common law of the nations) in the same way as it seeks to transcend internally the conception of the State which makes it a legal association. Now there is a sense in which this external transcendence of the legal system of States is so far from being alien to democratic principles, that it can even plead those principles on its behalf. The race reclaiming its members who live in other States can plead not only their consent, but also their active wish ; and it can accordingly use the democratic principle of self-determination as an argument in its favour. This is a formidable argument, all the more because it may rest on substantial grounds of fact. But it still remains an argument which is borrowed and extrinsic. The fundamental argument of racialism is the command of the leader and the compulsion of the blood. That the command is followed and the compulsion accepted—that consent is added, and an active wish supervenes—is a consequence rather than a premiss of argument. In this sense, and from this point of view, it may be said that fraternity of race is really a compelling and determining material fact—a fact of the physical order, even though it also trends to its inevitable spiritual consequences of emotion stirring in the blood and volition tingling along the veins—and that the self-determination alleged in its favour is really a naturally imposed necessity. Man does not choose his blood : his blood chooses, or determines, man. Self-determination is not an act of the free volition of individuals consciously choosing among alternatives : it is an act of the total and necessary volition of the whole kind or race, choosing the one alternative permitted to its choice.

It follows upon this view that any part of the race cannot choose its destiny for itself, or by itself. Being only a part, it is carried into the whole (as Austria was carried in 1938) for the act of choice ; it chooses, along with the rest of the race, by a choice which is the choice of the whole and not of the separate part. Not only, therefore, is the ' must ' of race an ineluctable ' must ' in the sense that it necessarily proceeds from the compulsion of physical fact : it is also a ' must ' in the further sense that is imposed on the part (though *ex hypothesi* the part is already being impelled in the same direction by its own internal compulsion) through the action of the whole. If this is self-determination, it is self-determination in

a new and subtle sense. We may almost say that just as
the idea of leadership and following, if it is in any sense
representation, is an inverted form of representation, so the
idea of race and identity of kind, if it is in any sense a
form of self-determination, is also an inverted form. It is not
men who, upon this doctrine, are self-determining. It is something which, if it is in them, is also above them, and which
determines and moves itself in determining and moving them.

The joint movement of the two doctrines of leadership and
race (the contemporary forms, as has already been said, of the
old ideas of Prussianism and Romanticism) has its grandeur
and its majesty. It is adding a new and twentieth-century
chapter to that history of German unity which began to be
written in the nineteenth century. It inaugurates a new
' heroic age ' : it is a free revision and a national rewriting of
a European settlement which left nothing settled for German
sentiment. It is an ingathering or homing of the lost elements
of the people, scattered and dispersed by the iniquities of the
historical process, but now hearing and following the call

> Post longa regredi tandem exilia.

Here we touch the deep and ancient historic memories which
lie behind the modern movement of Germany. They are
memories as old as the Middle Ages, and older still. If there
is one word in which those memories are enshrined it is the
word ' Reich '. That untranslatable word (so like and so
unlike our word ' Empire ') has become, especially in the form
of the ' third ' or millennial or final Reich, the universal
synthesis. It includes and connotes unification, heroism,
revisionism, and ingathering—in a word, all hopes and aspirations. It not only includes them : it also gives them a sanctification. The sanctification is partly that of memory and
ancient glory—the memory and the glory of the Holy Roman
Empire of the German people : it is partly that of expectation
and future perfection—the expectation and the perfection of a
final grace in a final and millennial *Endreich*. The ' Kingdom ',
if one may use that word to suggest some of the associations
which cluster round the idea of the Reich, is a kingdom which
was, but is also to come : it is a kingdom of Heaven, in the
sense that it is, or is to become, a community in the acknowledgment and realization of ' values ',[1] as well as a kingdom

[1] Moeller van den Bruck, *Das dritte Reich*, pp. 229-45.

on earth. The *Reich* stands behind, or above, the unity of the race. The leader is the prophet of the Reich. Secular human society becomes something more than secular in the light of this conception. If the Reich can hardly be called a church, it leaves little room for a church.

When we thus introduce the idea of the Reich, especially in its millennial form of the kingdom to come, which is a state of final grace, we add to leadership its goal, and to race its destiny. Leader and followers are marching to a consummation : race bears on its shoulders a peculiar orb of fate. The conceptions of the goal and the destiny—the consummation and the fate—bring us into a kingdom of ends and a world of values. But it is a solitary kingdom and a lonely world— solitary and lonely in the sense that it belongs to a single people, which stands in the light among surrounding clouds. Germany, one of its writers has said, is one great ' Mark '—a great frontier region on every side, with the frontier tradition of internal intimacy, but also with the frontier feeling of the dividing line and the entrenched boundary.[1] Its ends and its values are not common ends and values : they are enclosed and defended by the frontier. The ideas of leadership, race, and Reich have all a quality of isolation.

§ 6. THE IDEA OF SOCIAL FRATERNITY, AND ITS ECONOMIC AND OTHER MANIFESTATIONS

The internal intimacy and the warm fraternity developed behind the frontier are singularly evident in many spheres. They are evident, first of all, in the economic sphere. Autarky is a prevalent idea ; and in the pursuit of the idea of autarky, or, as it may also be called, the self-sufficiency of the brotherhood, leaders of enterprises and their followers must labour together in a common obligation of honour for the exclusive profit of people and State. The conflict of interests and classes is superseded : a single ' Labour Front ' (the term is significant) includes some 26,000,000 of Germans, employers as well as employed. The unity of the single Labour Front distinguishes the unitary economic system of Germany from the corporative economic system of Italy. In both countries, it is true, there

---

[1] The land frontiers of Germany touch (or touched in January 1938) eleven other different States ; and the frontiers are mainly frontiers. France touches five other States ; but France has also large frontiers on the open sea.

is the same attempt to combine labour and capital together, and to obliterate their difference : the same idea of the 'cramp' which holds the two sides closely united in its firm grasp. But Italy has retained trade unions, both of employers and employed ; and the cramp which she has applied is the multiple cramp of over a score of corporations. In Germany the trade unions, whether of employers or employed, have gone ; and the cramp applied is the single cramp of the single Labour Front, which is the one national organization both of employers and employed.[1] It is a further difference between the two countries that in Italy the multiple cramp of the corporations is State created, and acts as an 'organ of State' : in Germany the single cramp of the Labour Front is not a department or organ of government, but is rather conceived as a spontaneous body, though it is closely connected with the National Socialist party (the Leader of the party is also the Leader of the Front), and may thus be ranked as a part or an offshoot of the party. On the other hand a feature of similarity between Germany and Italy recurs in the elimination of the strike from the economic life of the nation. In both countries the strike or the lock-out is inconceivable : it would be treason to national unity and a lapse into civil war.

The internal intimacy and general fraternity of the economic life of Germany, as conceived in the new order of things, are not only shown in the Labour Front of the whole nation : they are also shown in the organization of each undertaking (*Betrieb*). We have already seen that the employer in each undertaking is linked with the employed by the nexus of leader and following ; we have seen that representatives of the 'following' form a confidential council (*Vertrauensrat*) which gathers round the leader for the purpose of joint deliberation. Here, in this confidential council in each undertaking (in the

---

[1] There are however some organizations of a 'corporative' character in Germany. One is the Reichsstand for agricultural production, which includes all associations or groups connected with agriculture ; but this is rather a sum composed of all bodies concerned with agriculture (co-operative societies, trading groups, and the like) than a two-sided combination of employers and employed. (On the other hand it is like an Italian corporation in so far as it is of the nature of an agricultural guild, devoted, as the Italian corporations in one of their main aspects are, to the 'unitarian regulation of production' in the national interest.) Another German organization of a corporative character is the Reich Chamber of Culture, with its seven sections dealing with different aspects of German cultural life (such as the theatre), and including professional organizations in the whole of Germany.

constitution of which the head or leader of the National Socialist 'cell' in the undertaking plays his part, and is consulted by the employer), there is the essential nucleus of the National Socialist organization of industry. The confidential council is formally like the Workers' Council instituted for each undertaking under one of the articles of the Weimar constitution of 1919 : it is also fundamentally unlike the old Workers' Council, in that it has the employer for its president or leader, and in that it has for its inspiration the philosophy of mutual confidence and mutual loyalty between the two sides. Here the confidential council has its analogy with the Italian corporation, which equally professes to link the two sides together ; but the Italian corporation differs from its German parallel not only in its sweep, which covers the whole of a national branch of production, but also in its character, which is that of an institution of State and an organ of public administration. The German confidential council seeks to bear the impress of a homely intimacy, imprinted indeed by a law of the State and imprinted with the aid of the single party which stands behind the State, but none the less inspired by the idea of a spirit of loyalty and fraternity assumed to be naturally inherent in each and every undertaking.

Behind the confidential council there stands, in the general system inaugurated by the Labour Law of 1934, the Labour Trustee (*Treuhänder*). The *Treuhänder der Arbeit* is an officer of the State who stands behind the confidential councils of his area in the name of trust and faith, and in the cause of industrial peace. He has a council of experts at his side, which he consults on all general or fundamental issues ; it is his function to stand in reserve as an impartial instance, to which appeal can be made by a majority of the confidential council. He is linked with another institution, which is also part of the general system of the Labour Law of 1934—the institution of the Court of Honour (*Ehrengericht*). There is such a court in the area of each Labour Trustee : it deals with offences against the social obligations involved in the membership of an undertaking, whether they have been committed by the leader or the general following or the members of the confidential council : it is set in motion, after he has made an investigation, by the Labour Trustee of the area. The three institutions of the Confidential Council, the Labour Trustee, and the Court of Honour form a cycle of complementary ideas—the idea of *Vertrauen*, the idea of *Treue*, and the idea of *Ehre*. The ideas, as we have already said, are those of an idealized and modernized feudalism. They emphasize the feudal or chivalrous virtues of fidelity, loyalty, honour and mutual trust. They have their analogies with the ideas of Disraeli's ' Young England ' period, when he was enamoured of a new feudalism, or the period of Carlyle's ' Past and Present ', when he celebrated the captains of industry who recovered, or might recover, the temper and faith of the Middle Ages. In any case, and whatever its analogies, the new German cycle of ideas cherishes the ideal of social fraternity ; and if it keeps the ideal of leadership and hierarchy, it seeks to temper that ideal, in the domain of industry, by a doctrine of social obligation, and by institutions and sanctions designed to enforce that doctrine.

It may be contended that if fraternity is the note of the new organization of industry, and if there is also (both in the Labour Front and in the system of works councils) some respect for equality, liberty has been entirely banished. It is true that the liberty of workers and employers to form trade unions is gone : it is true that the right of the two sides of industry to bargain freely, and in the last resort to employ the strike or the lock-out, is gone. The system of ' private war ' in industry is regarded by National Socialist Germany as a form of medievalism which was diseased in its own day and is impossible to-day. The liberty of forming trade unions has accordingly given place to the liberty (which in practice is a necessity) of joining the united Labour Front of employers and employed : the right of bargaining freely, and of employing the weapon of the cessation of labour, has given place to the system of rights contained in the Labour Law of 1934. Those rights are associated with virtues or ideals other than that of liberty. But it cannot be said that the ideal of liberty has entirely disappeared ; and the ideal of equality may even be said to have acquired a new emphasis. Along with the leadership of the employer there goes his inclusion along with the employed in common membership of the Labour Front : there goes his duty of co-operation with the employed in the activity of the confidential council, which may inquire into the accounts and the general conduct of an undertaking : there goes the common submission of employer and employed to the appellate powers

of the Labour Trustee. All this may be an enforced equality :
it is none the less a form of equality. Liberty is less evident ;
but in so far as workers can play their part in the works
council, and in so far as, through appeals to the Labour Trustee
and through their membership of the Labour Front, they can
influence the local officials of the State and the central ministers
who are in charge of industrial legislation, they may be said
to enjoy some measure of liberty in determining the policy of
their factory, the rulings of the *Treuhänder*, and the legislation
of the Ministers.

In other institutions the simple idea of social fraternity is
more apparent. The system of Labour Service finally enacted
in the summer of 1935 cuts through all social divisions ; it
draws all young men together, irrespective of the district from
which they come or the class to which they belong, for six
months of common life in a common effort addressed to the
reclamation and improvement of the soil of Germany. The
national system for the better employment and enjoyment of
leisure, which goes by the name of *Kraft durch Freude*, addresses
itself to the ideal of ' joy in widest commonalty spread '. It
is intended for those members of the Labour Front (of which it
forms a section) who receive a lower rate of remuneration : it
provides them, in return for the contributions which they make
from their savings, with facilities for enjoying holidays, music,
drama, and sport on the same footing and at the same level as
the well-to-do. It is an instrument for the equalization of play,
in matters both of the mind and the body, through the whole
of life—just as the system of labour service, for its six months'
span, is an instrument for the equalization of work. National
Socialism in Germany may justly be said to be marked more
strongly by Nationalism than it is by Socialism. But in the
institutions of Labour Service and of *Kraft durch Freude* it has
made a genuine attempt to wed the two factors equally together. It has sought to socialize national enjoyment : it has
sought—at any rate for one period of a man's life, and in the
one sphere of land reclamation and land improvement—to
socialize national work.

These things may seem to be only fringes or details in the
general scheme of National Socialism, with no intimate bearing
on its central purpose and its cardinal method. But they must
necessarily be taken into account in any impartial appraise-

ment, which has to weigh good at least as heavily as evil ; and they are also integral and essential elements in the general scheme. They flow from the general philosophy of ' identity of kind ' : they are the other side of a scutcheon which also shows that philosophy producing more dubious consequences— the consequence of internment or persecution of elements held to be unassimilable to the kind ; the consequence of hostility to religious societies not based upon the kind and the idea of the kind ; the consequence of violent reclamation of elements of the kind belonging to other allegiances. The ' Kind ' (the Folk, the Race, the *Gemeinschaft*, whatever it may be called) has a double face. If the face which looks outward is severe, that which looks inward on its own members has a benevolent aspect.

Benevolent, and yet authoritative. The principle of the identity of kind can never be divorced, in any part of the field of social and economic policy, from the principle of leadership. The circle which starts from leadership must always return on itself. It may have passed, in the course of its sweep round the kind, through regions of social fraternity, of some degree of social equality, and even of some appearance of social liberty : it ends where it began, in the drive and the impulse of the single leader of the single party which inspires and co-ordinates *Staat* and *Volk*. The party, and the leader of the party, run through the whole of the industrial organization of the community, in so far as it is not determined by the legislation of the State ; and since the legislation of the State may not only assign specific legal powers to the party,[1] but is also itself determined by the leader of the party, the exception is hardly an exception. The Labour Front, however profoundly it may differ from the old Trade Unions which it has superseded, is like them, and even goes beyond them, in its connection with party. They were connected with different parties, according to their sympathies : it is connected with the one surviving and only possible party, and its connection is the stronger in proportion as a single party is stronger than each of a number of parties. It may therefore be said that the German system of industrial organization, no less than the

---

[1] Under Section 9, 1, of the *Arbeitsgesetz* of 20 January 1934, the composition of the confidential council in each factory is determined by the agreement of the leader of the factory and the head of the factory cell of the National Socialist party.

Italian corporative system, depends for its working on the
presence of ' a single party and a totalitarian state '[1]—a single
party running, by means of its ' cells ' and its general connection with the Labour Front, through the whole of industry :
a totalitarian State, dominated by that party, which includes
in the total scope of its action the regulation of economics
equally with the regulation of all other departments of human
life.

§ 7.   THE *WELTANSCHAUUNG* OF NATIONAL SOCIALISM : THE SHUT
STATE, OR THE COMMON TRADITION OF EUROPE ?

The general conclusion, and the general philosophy, presented by National Socialism is something unique in Europe.
National Socialism has indeed some elements which are
common with other régimes. It has the element of the single
party which is common both with Communist Russia and
with Fascist Italy : it has some elements of social economic
policy which are common with Italian Fascism : it has the
same emphasis on the power and the responsibility of the
executive, in comparison with the legislature, which also
appears in Italy. But National Socialism is fundamentally
unique. It is devoted to the ideal of a ' closed ' society, which
is based on a peculiar and individual genius of soil and stock.
It issues in a peculiar polity, expressive of that peculiar genius :
it issues in a peculiar and self-contained economy which is
similarly expressive. This is what differentiates National
Socialism not only from the democratic pattern of State, but
also from the Communist and the Fascist. The democratic
pattern, in spite of national differences (which are like differences of colour in a web), has a common thread and a common
design. Communist Russia, in both of its phases, has based
itself on some idea of ' the common '. When it aimed at the
international revolution of the proletariat, it emphasized the
common interest of the proletariat in all countries : when it
seeks, as it now appears to be seeking, to construct a model
Communist scheme within its own borders, it cherishes the
hope that the model may gain a common acceptance, and
it uses a common form (even if it be only a form) of constitutional method in the construction of the model. Fascist Italy
has varied, sometimes professing to be unique, and sometimes

---

[1] Cf. *supra*, pp. 341, 349.

claiming to be a contributor to the common stock ; but on the whole it has tended to proclaim that its doctrine, and in particular its doctrine and its practice of corporativism, has a general value, can be generally advocated, and may be generally adopted. In a word, both Communism and Fascism are general alternatives : they are presented to the world at large ; and if in the Italian view Fascism is an alternative produced by the Italian genius and peculiarly connected with Italy, it is none the less an alternative presented to the common choice.

What Germany presents to Europe is simply Germany—the ' kind ' itself, in its own identity ; leadership of the kind, in its own peculiarity. It is something autochthonous and indigenous—something springing from earth itself ; something of native birth. There is nothing here which presents an alternative to other countries for their own internal choice. There is no general alternative to democracy (or to any other form of government) which can be weighed as such in the balance and pondered in other countries. There is simply the fact of Germany, shaping itself from within by its own philosophy of life. The German kind has its own destiny : we may even say that it *is* its own destiny. In the international sphere it is a fact which does not adjust itself to other facts and to other States—for it can only obey its own inner commands, and thus be the fact that is—but simply requires from them the adjustment which the presence of a fact must always require. In its own internal life it does not follow any *general* rules, or standards, of constitutional structure or constitutional procedure : the word ' general ' has no application, and any rules will be necessarily the particular rules of the particular people. It follow that general principles, whether of the ' rights of individuals ' against the State or of the ' division of powers ' within the State, can have no validity. The particular self-determining people will be the beginning and end of political wisdom.

It is of course possible that the particular self-determining people, which stands by itself, and neither presents alternatives to the common stock nor accepts them from it, may none the less act on lines which are parallel, or even similar, to those of other peoples. It may reject general constitutional rules ; but it may still enact and obey particular constitutional rules which are valid within its area. It may reject the general form of democracy ; but it may still create and cherish its own particular form. We are thus led to inquire whether the close society of the ' kind ' has its own fixed constitutional rules, and whether it acts, as a self-determining society, in obedience to such rules, If the German ' kind ' obeys no rule of life which is general, or common to other States, has it a rule of its own, and does it obey the standard of its own rule ?

A simple answer can be given. The will of the kind is a dynamic will which perpetually maintains a fresh and integral initiative, and cannot and does not sink into static rules which would destroy, or at the least impede, that initiative. Again, the will is a will which in form has been transferred (at any rate for the time being) to the leader of the kind,[1] and in substance is held to be permanently expressed and crystallized (whether or no there has been any form of legal transference) in the dynamic will of that leader. He too cannot be static : he must always retain a fresh initiative. Fundamentally the only rule or constitutional standard is the absence of any rule or constitutional standard. The principle of German life is the principle of a free subjectivity, or egoism, engaged in the process of ' becoming ' and in the perpetual unfolding of itself. Whatever we may hold the Subject behind this subjectivity, and the Ego behind this egoism, to be—whether it is the whole *Volk*, or the *élite* which constitutes the party of the *Volk*, or simply the leader of the party—the essential thing is that this Subject or Ego is always *sui generis*, always dynamically free, always freely engaged in growing and acting according to its own kind.

' According to its own kind '. This phrase may seem to contain or involve, after all, some notion of limit ; some idea, if not of a constitution, at any rate of a control ; some conception of something objective, something normative, which imposes a sovereign standard on the play of will. From this point of view it may be argued that the fact of kind, or in other words the factor of race, is a hard and an irreducible core which the play of the Subject or Ego cannot escape. People, party, and leader are all tied and bound by race :

---

[1] The enabling law of April 1933 vested full powers in the Chancellor (who by a later law of August 1934 became Leader for life as well as Chancellor) until 1937 ; and this law has since been renewed for a further period.

Germany can do nothing, externally or internally, which cannot be justified by the ultimate standard of race. If this were so, and if race were an objective fact, we should all know where we stood : we should see the limits ordained for outward, and also for inward, growth. But when we examine the fact of race, we find that it is not objective, or a fact : it is nothing more than an idea entertained by the Subject. Race is whatever the people, who regard themselves as a race, think race to be : it is a set of ideas, clustering round a central idea, but the whole complex remains an idea. This idea, or set of ideas, can always be interpreted in any way that the people and its leader like, or on any basis convenient to the contingency of the hour. *Rasse* can turn into *Reich*, and become an historic memory instead of a physical fact, as it did when Bohemia was ' reclaimed ' in the spring of 1939. *Reich*, by another change, can turn into *Raum*, and base itself on the economic plea of life-space instead of historic memory, as it has done in the course of 1940. The one thing which is always constant (apart from the letter R) is a German idea, or complex of ideas, which Germany alone entertains, Germany alone interprets, and Germany alone, by the method of unilateral action, translates into fact and act.

The current German name for such a complex of ideas is *Weltanschauung*. A *Weltanschauung* is an intuitive total apprehension—a mystical insight, proceeding not from reflection, but from contemplation (*Anschauung*)—by virtue of which a light is shed on the general significance of the world and human life in the world, and corresponding modes of behaviour are indicated for human beings. Different cues may give the signal which leads to such an intuitive apprehension : for instance, the cue for the contemplation of the German Marxist is matter, material production, and class ; the cue for the contemplation of the German National Socialist is organic life, the reproduction of species, and race. Different cues thus produce different (and possibly conflicting) apprehensions of the world. What has happened in Germany is the victory of one such apprehension—the racial apprehension—over all others. From this point of view we may say that the ultimate control of German life, and the sovereignty of Germany, is vested to-day in this dominant *Weltanschauung*. In other words, it is vested in a philosophy of life and the universe—or, more exactly, it is vested in a mystical and contemplation-created faith (which is something different from a philosophy) about the significance of the life and the universe.

How shall we judge the sovereignty of a *Weltanschauung*? One thing may be said at once : it does not impair the freedom, or hamper the play, of subjectivity. On the contrary the enthroning of a *Weltanschauung* is also the enthroning of the principle of free subjectivity. The *Weltanschauung* is a product not of the intellect, which speaks a common language, but of particular ' contemplation ', starting from a particular cue, and proceeding along a particular line. It is a product which by its nature is never expressed in any authoritative common form. Religion has its scriptures ; but a *Weltanschauung*, though it may have a great book, or more than one great book, depends essentially upon a continuing intuition. All mysticisms remain fluid ; if they acquired a fixed form and a regular liturgy, they would cease to be mysticisms. The mysticism of the National Socialist *Weltanschauung* does not run into a legal system, or indeed into any system of known and certain standards.

There is a double reason which prevents such a consummation. It is not only the subjectivity of the *Weltanschauung* which prevents it from taking a fixed and permanent form of legal embodiment that might create, alike for the German people and its neighbours, the security of a regulated and therefore ' expectable ' life. It is also the totality which is inherent in the nature of a general and all-inclusive *Weltanschauung*. A legal system cannot be based on the idea of totality ; nor can it attempt to cover and regulate *every* aspect of life. Any legal system must deal with a definite and specific area— the definite and specific area of external relations and conduct, which can be brought (and which alone can be brought) under certain and fixed legal rules capable of certain and fixed legal enforcement. This is a limited area, as all experience proves. It is an area which excludes the play of social taste, the movement of the inward conscience, the general march of the mind, and the general building of culture. These are all things which escape legal rule and legal compulsion, for the simple reason that they possess the quality of quicksilver. The *Weltanschauung* which is vowed to totality will seek to escape the limitation of area inherent in the nature of law ; but in the very act of seeking to reform and ' totalize ' law it will deform what it touches, and it will abolish all the precision and certainty of law. German jurists, pleading that law must be a mirror and a manifestation of the whole of the new *Weltanschauung*, and seeking therefore to extend its scope to many areas of life (social, moral, and intellectual) which law has not hitherto entered, have been led so to modify the notion of law that it has ceased to be a legal notion. They still speak of law, but it is ' a law for life and not formal law ' : it is a *Werdendes Recht* which moves with the movement of the new *Weltanschauung* : it is biological, or organic, or dynamic : it is anything which is the opposite of the fixed and constant. Totality, by its own confession, brings us back once more to fluidity. A total law may profess to be law, but it is a new sort of law (living, becoming, dynamic, changing) which demands, as its own prophets confess, a new form of juridical thought.

The combination of subjectivity and totality which characterizes the idea of the *Weltanschauung*—at any rate in its particular contemporary form of racialism—thus ends in the reign of fluidity, which is also the reign of the arbitrary. ' What helps the people is right '—right at any given moment, and in any sphere of life, in which it is thought right by those who express, or claim to express, the thought of the people about its life and the requirements of its life. The principle of this dictum may be carried, and has been carried, even further. It has been argued that when a man has the intention of helping the people, his intention is the primary and sovereign consideration, irrespective of the act done. By the side of the subjectivity of the general conception of law there is thus enthroned the subjectivity of the individual agent. Intention is made, if not everything, at any rate the main thing ; ' the motives and aims of offenders ', as Hitler said in a speech of March 1933, ' are to be taken into account as much as possible '. It is not the act—as the infraction of a scheme of law and order, and to the extent to which it is an infraction of that scheme— that primarily matters : it is rather the intention, considered as an intention either harmonious or dissonant with the general intention of the life of the people, and to the extent of its harmony or dissonance. This is the general principle of the new Penal Code, submitted by a commission at the end of 1936.

A new conception of the office and duty of the judge is entailed by this principle. If a judge is to understand the intention of the life of the people, and to measure the intention of the offender by that criterion, he must himself be steeped in that life, and he must primarily think and essentially act as a member of the people (*Volksgenosse*). He must ask himself, when he sits in the seat of judgment, ' How would the leader, who embodies the intention of the people's life, judge in my place ? ' The subjectivity of the judge is thus enlisted in the general service of the subjective. Dr. Carl Schmitt, arguing that law is essentially the law of an identical kind, logically concludes that the kind and type of the judge is the crucial matter. (' So hängt eben alles von der Art und dem Typus unserer Richter ab.'[1])   ' The essential substance of his personality must be assured ; and that substance consists in the solidarity with their people, and the identity with their kind, of all who are entrusted with the exposition, interpretation, and application of German law '.

People, offender, judge—all are thus beckoned into a new reign of subjectivity, in which the common values and the common norms of humanity disappear.   In this reign of subjectivity (or, as it has been justly called, this ' revolution of nihilism ') values are the creation of the kind, and peculiar to the kind.   In it the only norm, if we may properly speak of a norm, is the consciousness of the kind, and the demand which that consciousness makes for what helps its own integrity. ' All Right is the Right of a particular People '.[2]   This is the old tenet of German Romanticism, revived (but also secularized) by a new racial interpretation.   Once more, but with a new intensity, it results in what a Greek might have called a ' daedal ' world, in which ' living human existence is filled with organic, biological, and racial (*völkisch*) varieties '.[3]   The motto of the world may be said to be ' Ourselves and our own kind '.   What is the meaning of the motto ?   What is its truth, and what is the truth which it omits ?

Möller van den Bruck regarded each community as ' a community of values '.   If we adopt his term, we are faced by the question what values are, and whether their nature is such that they differ from community to community.   In the German view, there is such a difference.   Values are what

---

[1] *Staat, Bewegung, Volk*, p. 44.   [2] Ibid., p. 45.   [3] Ibid.

each community considers them to be, and one community creates a different set of values from another. It does not follow necessarily from this view that one set of values is better than another *sub specie aeternitatis* : it only follows that, for any community, its set is the only set which it can accept as its own and by which it can guide itself. But this result is sufficient to produce a reign of relativity, with as many sets of values as there are communities of men, and with each set purely relative to its own particular community. Can the mind acquiesce in a reign of pure relativity ? Even if we are content to regard values as mental inventions— human inventions constituted and enthroned by the minds of men, and not objective characters of an absolute reality which is reflected in our minds—we are none the less compelled to inquire into the nature and the range of the society of minds which constitutes and enthrones values. What is the area of that society ? What is the area of the ' collective mind ' which discovers and constitutes values ; or, more exactly (since the idea of the ' collective mind ' is apt to suggest the more dubious idea of a ' group mind ' independent of individual minds) what is the area of ' that co-operation and conflict of many minds which produces standards of approval or disapproval ' ?[1] There is no good reason for saying that this area is the area of a particular national or racial society. There has been, and there is, a European area of the co-operation and conflict of many minds in producing standards of approval or disapproval. We may even say to-day that there is an oecumenical area ; but in any case, and at the least, we are entitled to say that there has been, in all the great ages of Europe (the Middle Ages, the Age of Renaissance and Reformation, the Age of Enlightenment) a collective mind of Europe, engaged in maintaining and extending European standards of value. No doubt each nation has always given its own colour to the common : no doubt at times (as in France under Louis XIV, or again in the years after 1789) a particular nation may almost seem to have annexed the common as its own particular prerogative. But any just view of the European past must recognize that Europe has steadily constituted a single area of values, even if there have always been different

---

[1] The words are those of Professor Alexander, in *Space, Time and Deity*, II, p. 240.

provinces or regions within that area, and even though this or that province may sometimes have claimed to be the whole. To study the tradition of Natural Law in Europe is to study one great manifestation of the common European. It is only one of many manifestations ; but it is sufficient to answer the contention that ' all right is the right of a particular people '. In every department of man's activities in which he has sought to find standards and to discover values (in music or in literature, in science or in painting and architecture, as well as in law and politics), the common is always there. It is only an ignorance, or an ignoring, of the whole process of the building of our system of standards which can result in the nationalization of values.

XIV

THE CHOICES AND THE DECISION

§ I. CHALLENGES AND RESPONSES

IN the myth which comes at the end of Plato's *Republic*, an
Interpreter marshals in order the souls which are standing
on the brink, about to plunge into a new cycle of existence.
Mounted on a high platform, he speaks. ' Souls of a day, here
shall begin a new round of earthly life. . . . No guardian spirit
will cast lots for you, but you shall choose your own destiny.
. . . The blame is his who chooses : Heaven is blameless '.[1]

οὐχ ὑμᾶς δαίμων λήξεται, ἀλλ' ὑμεῖς δαίμονα αἱρήσεσθε. Mankind is confronted to-day, as perhaps it has never been
confronted before in its history, by the problem of a deliberate
and conscious choice of destiny. Men are gathered together,
' multitudes, multitudes in the valley of decision ' ; and in the
old and original sense of the Greek word ' crisis ' they are
asked, first to discriminate among, and then to decide between,
the alternatives by which they are confronted. On the one
hand stands the cause of civil and political liberty, with all
its corollaries and consequences. It is not an easy cause, nor
does it promise a soft and easy destiny. ' Heaven knows how to
put a proper price upon its goods ; and it would be strange
indeed if so celestial an article as freedom should not be highly
rated '.[2] On the other hand stand the alternatives to freedom
which we have sought in the preceding chapters to distinguish
and describe. None of them presents an altogether easy
cause ; nor are the destinies which they offer alluring, or
even intended to be alluring. They offer, indeed, security,
but they offer it at the price of liberty ; and the promise of
the gift is accompanied by a demand for a drilled and arduous
obedience.

Three main movements of human life have brought men to
the moment of crisis in which they stand. One of these movements sets towards the division of each community into
opposed and conflicting social groups, based on opposed and
conflicting social interests. It is a movement within the
internal life of the community : it makes, at any rate in its
immediate trend, for disintegration ; but it also tends, in its

---

[1] The translation is that of F. M. Cornford (Oxford, 1941).
[2] From the beginning of the first number of Paine's *American Crisis*, 1776.

ultimate effects, towards some new form of reintegration, whether achieved by mutual compromise or by the enthronement of one of the groups and the interest which it embodies. Simultaneous with this first movement, but flowing, apparently, in an opposite direction, there is a second movement, which tends towards the ideal of autarky, and makes for the sealing up of each national community in its own closed system of life. Each great national economy, as we have already had reason to notice, becomes an end in itself and folds itself back on itself.[1] Immediately a movement of integration, this second movement is also, in its larger and broader effects, a movement of disintegration ; and if it seals and solders the national community of production, it also dissolves the international community of intercourse and exchange, for which it seeks to substitute the separation of rival autarkies. Behind both of these movements, and closely connected with both, there is the general movement of mechanization. It is a movement which helps to divide the community into those who manipulate and those who serve the machine : it is also a movement which helps to turn the community into something which itself is of the nature of a machine, so nicely interlocked and so intricately complete that it stands in the isolation of a solitary mechanism.

We have already seen the general response which the democratic State, in its nature, can offer to the challenge of these three movements. So far as there is division and variety of interests within the community (and in any living and growing community there must always be variety and a consequent measure of division), it sets the various interests to state their cases and adjust their claims by a reasonable method—which may also be properly called scientific—of discussion and compromise. So far as each community, in its relation to others, claims the right to follow the ideal of a rounded and independent self-sufficiency, the democratic State will adopt externally the same general tactic which it has already adopted internally : it will set itself, and it will invite and expect every other State to set itself equally, to state its case and adjust its claims in terms of international discussion and international compromise : it will believe, and it will act on the belief, that no national community can ever be an

[1] *Supra*, pp. 278–81.

isolated whole, and that each, being only a part or ' interest ' within the general society of mankind, must submit its case and its claims to the general arbitrament of that society. Finally, in so far as mechanization is concerned, democracy, while it accepts the fact, in the economic sphere to which the fact belongs, will not be subjugated or dominated by it in its own political sphere. It will maintain the integrity of its free process of thought and discussion, not only for the sake of its own inherent value, but also in order to provide a necessary corrective or compensation to the automatism of the economic machine ; and it may even seek to carry its process into the economic field, and to encourage the voluntary adjustment of claims, in each branch of economic activity, by the interests and agents engaged in the branch.

The response which is offered to challenge by the alternatives to democracy follows a different line. It is not a uniform response ; but it shows a large measure of similarity. In Russia the division of social interests and social groups is met by a policy which, enthroning one of the groups in the position of dictator, compulsorily assimilates the rest to its character and ideas by a process of coercive adjustment. The trend towards autarky and the institution of a closed economy is accepted and obeyed ; but it is obeyed in the name and the cause of another and higher ideal (the ideal of a socialist system, which is conceived as necessarily differentiating and separating the Russian union of socialist republics from all other States) ; and it is obeyed only for the time being, until the workers of all countries have united in a common cause which will merge the temporary autarky of a solitary socialism in the open system of a socialist world. The movement towards mechanization is obeyed with less qualification : indeed it may even be said to be obeyed with a pathetic faith. Believing in scientific materialism, Russia puts her trust in the triumphs of applied science : she can accept, and even worship, the machine as the most wonderful of those triumphs. Mechanization seems to run easily through the uniformity of the Russian plain ; and though there may be some counter-ideal of demo-cratic participation—some passion for popular education, especially in the truths of science, and some scheme of a scientific constitution, which, as such, will include democratic organs and institutions—it is the pattern of the machine, rather than the free movement of minds, which tends to be the dominant ideal.

In Italy the division of social groups and their interests has been met by the answer of a State system of corporativism, which supplies a State cramp, or a score of State cramps, to hold society together by the iron bands of ' organs of administration '. The old elective parliament has accordingly become a corporative parliament, a part of the general system of cramps ; and if a grace and a flourish have been added to the system by the leisure activities of the *Dopolavoro* organization, intended to draw intellectual and manual workers together in the common employment of their free time, the system of cramps is greater than the added grace and flourish. Meanwhile, in a country less naturally self-sufficient than any other country of its size, the trend to autarky is not only accepted, but also artificially fostered ; nor is the view of the Italian Fascist, like that of the Russian Communist, directed to any future in which autarky will have become an old and discarded garment. Mechanization, perhaps naturally alien to the Italian genius, and hardly congruous with the nature of the Italian soil, has made less progress than in Russia ; but a grandiose cult of the mechanical is one of the marks of the Fascist régime, and the Fascist system of government, directed more to the mechanism of administration than to any idea of democratic participation, is itself an example rather than a corrective of the victory of mechanism. Germany, resolved to be boldly abreast or ahead of all modern movements, has gone further to meet and to answer their challenge than any other country. She has met the division of groups and interests within the community by a comprehensive affirmation of unity—the unity of the single leader ; the unity or identity of the kind which follows the leader ; the unity of a single Labour Front, of a single system of labour service, and of a single organization for the common enjoyment of leisure. She has equally met the trend towards autarky with a comprehensive and total affirmation of the principle of the closed State—the State which is spiritually as well as materially shut and folded upon itself, and which, if it opens at all, opens only in the cause of its own ' life-space ' and in order to engulf by conquest the soil and the human instruments needed for its own independence. In Germany, as in Italy, the ideal of the closed and self-sufficient State is regarded as a permanent ideal. In both countries, too, and especially in Germany, the mechanization of life has been accepted as the order of the day, and even as the order of all time. It is true that physical machinery (except for the armoured and panoplied machinery of war) has won less adoration in Germany than it has in Russia : it is less of a novelty, and it cannot offer so many new triumphs over the reluctance of nature. It is also true that the National Socialism of Germany has sought to infuse new psychological motives of loyalty and honour into the mechanics of the industrial process. But it is equally true, or even more true, that in a broad and general sense mechanization has won its supreme triumph in Germany. It has triumphed in the realm of the mind. That is a greater triumph than any of its victories in the realm of matter.

§ 2. THE OLD BATTLES AND THE NEW

It may be contended, with some show of reason, that the alternatives to democracy which are presented by three of the great States of Europe have at any rate one merit in comparison with States of the democratic type. They have faced, it may be argued, the challenges offered by the movement of contemporary life, and they have given them some sort of answer ; while the democratic State has stood in the ancient ways, and confronted the challenges of the present with the doctrines of the past. But it may also be contended, with at least as much show of reason, that these States have not so much answered the challenge of contemporary movements as simply succumbed to their impact ; while the democratic State, instead of simply succumbing, still offers the answer of ideas and ideals which still remain true and still have a lesson to teach even in the face of new challenges. To acknowledge division of groups and interests to the extent of accepting and enthroning one of those groups and interests : to acknowledge the trend of national States towards autarky (a trend not necessarily good) to the extent of instituting a closed and exclusive system of national economics : to acknowledge the growth of mechanization (a growth, again, not necessarily good) to the extent of turning the community itself into a mechanism—all this is to admit defeat rather than to offer an answer to challenge. On the other hand it would also be a defeat, or at any rate a failure to answer challenge, if the democratic State simply met the trends and movements of contemporary life with an unmoved and unbending affirmation of ancient principles and methods, however true and however good. There *is* a new challenge; and an answer which contained nothing new—no new principle or method, and even no new extension of old principles and old methods— would hardly be an answer at all.

But before we address ourselves to that final and fundamental issue, it will be wise to examine more fully the nature of the general challenge which the cause of liberty now has to face, and to do so in the light of old challenges already faced and old answers already given. It is not a single challenge which confronts the democratic State to-day. It is a double, or even a triple, challenge. There is not only the challenge offered, directly and immediately, by the movements of human life which are running through all European communities. There is also the challenge offered, less directly but even more obviously, by the alternatives to the democratic State—the alternatives of Communism, Fascism, and National Socialism—which have made themselves the subjects and the vehicles of these movements. There is also a third challenge, the more dangerous and the more subtle because it is an internal challenge, proceeding from the central core of the democratic State itself. The core of that State is the system of parties which prepares and presents to the people the issues of general discussion. In the natural course of affairs these parties are national parties, operating in the general framework and true to the general principles of the national community. But a new internationalization of politics and parties, as we have already had reason to notice,[1] has injected into the democratic system of parties new factors of an international type. Communist and Fascist parties, of different sorts and degrees, have established themselves by the side of the old national parties. The challenge of the alternatives to the democratic State thus becomes not only an external but also an internal challenge, which is active in the very vitals of the State. It may not, in this form, assume any great dimensions; but it is the more insidious because it can claim, with some show of logic, the benefit of the democratic temper of tolerance

[1] *Supra*, p. 273–4.

and fair play. It can hardly be met, or it can only be met with difficulty, by a policy of frank rejection and suppression : the democratic State would seem to be false to itself if it adopted such a policy towards any body of men who could claim to represent some section of popular opinion. Yet a party owing a foreign allegiance, and only acting in the democratic system in order to overthrow the system, can hardly in justice claim the benefit of the system.

The battle for the cause of liberty is an old battle ; and the fight which the democratic States have been waging in this century (a fight which proceeds on its way in times of uneasy peace no less than in times of open war) is a chapter in a long history. At one time in its long course the battle turned on the issue of religious liberty. That issue was eventually decided, or seemed to be decided, in favour of a doctrine and practice of toleration which gave freedom equally to all Churches and all confessions. At another time the battle turned on the issue of civil liberty, or the liberty of the subject. That issue, again, was eventually decided, or seemed to be decided, in favour of a doctrine and practice of common civic rights appertaining to all men alike, and duly declared, duly guaranteed, and duly furnished with sanctions and remedies by the substance and procedure of civil law. At still another time the battle turned on the issue of political liberty, or the liberty of the active citizen. That issue, too, was eventually decided, or seemed to be decided, in favour of a doctrine and practice of parliamentary democracy, under which every citizen was vested with a voice and a vote in the determination of the common affairs of the community. But though the issues seemed to be decided, they still remained, as we are now discovering, potential issues ; and to-day we are engaged in a struggle which is a struggle for all the three old liberties in one. Liberty, we find, is not an achievement, but a process : and because it is a process, immersed in the continuous flow of history and subject to historic vicissitudes, it has no end and no final achievement, but a continuous life of effort and a continuous struggle of readjustment to the demands of time.

Authority—if that be not too good a name to give to the principle which challenges liberty—has asserted itself again with vehemence and vigour. The new authoritarianism of our days, as we have already had reason to notice, has its analogies in the past ; but it is essentially an authoritarianism of a new and more drastic type. It is the vehicle of modern movements ; it is affected by the movements which it carries ; and it is strengthened by their strength. In particular, it commands the forces and resources of a great mechanical civilization, which enable it to make itself immune from attack, and even from criticism, to a degree unprecedented in history. The older authoritarianism which emerged in the sixteenth century might equally claim that it was imposing unity on a divided society and its different interests—though the division with which it was confronted was a division affecting only, or at any rate affecting mainly, the upper or feudal layer of society, and not, as to-day, a division affecting the whole of society from top to bottom. Similarly the old authoritarianism might equally claim that it was fostering, by the policy which was then called mercantilism, the same trend of national development which now goes by the name of autarky—though here, again, the trend of the past did not run so deeply into the very nature of national society, and was not so drastically directed towards the one aim of a closed system of national economics. It is peculiarly its command of the power and the instruments of a new mechanical civilization—and (we may also add) its own mechanical character—which differentiates the new authoritarianism from the old, and makes it peculiarly vigorous with a novel and drastic vigour.

But the new authoritarianism has not only a new power of mechanism. It has also taken to itself new powers in the realm of the spirit—new powers which are closely connected with the growth of the great population and the new methods provided by science for swaying that population. There is the power, for example, of personalism : the power which comes from ' the eruption of the personal ', where a magnetic leader, emerging from the depths and claiming to be the incarnation of his community, demands and receives a mass devotion greater than any that an hereditary dynast could ever command. This is a power which can be manufactured, and given a fictitious grandeur, by the art of propaganda ; but it can also be a power which is innate in the leader and congenial to the temper of the masses whom he leads. There is again the power (fundamentally connected with the power of personalism, though it seems at first sight to belong to another dimension) which springs from the sense of the group and flows from the eruption of group-feeling and group-worship. This, too, can be manufactured ; but this too can also be an indigenous and instinctive feeling, which induces a great population to translate its clustering and interconnected life into terms of a transcendent group-being superior to individual existence. Finally there is the power which stands behind both these powers—the power which may sometimes seem to be their servant, but sometimes also their master—the power of publicity, of propaganda, of the exhibition of perpetual drama, and the staging of perpetual tension. Life is reduced, or exalted, to terms of a life of the nerves : men are taught that their days are cast in times of ideal tension : authority adds to itself the great armoury of excitement. These are all powers of the lower and subliminal reaches of man's mind. But they are powers which arm a new Leviathan not with the frigid calculations which Hobbes sought to accumulate, but with the headier and more provocative stimulus of emotions and exultations.

It is not only a new and far more heavily armoured authoritarianism—of a magnitude that would have amazed, and might have terrified, Hobbes himself—that confronts the principle and the practice of the democratic State. Besides the recurrence of authoritarianism, in a new form and new dimensions, there is also another recurrence. This is the recurrence of what may be called secession from the State. The State is the necessary condition of any organized human life : the necessary condition of justice : the necessary condition, as it develops its nature and learns its duties, of liberty as well as justice. But men have been tempted, from time to time, to revolt against the condition and to secede from the State and the loyalties which it claims to some other society and some other system of loyalties. In such times the State has been compelled, whatever its form and whatever its method of government, to fight a battle against new and distracting loyalties : to vindicate its own independent title to existence ; and to claim, in the name of the values which it serves, the right to continue to exercise its office and its ministration. Whatever may be our view of the relations of Church and State, we cannot but admit that there have been times when the State was not wrong in challenging the claims of Churches. When Churches sought to become States, and to establish a theocracy, they were inviting a secession which would have wrecked the existence of States. They might be acting in the name of a divine justice, founded on divine revelation, which they held to be greater than human justice : they might be acting in the name of a religious liberty, or ' spiritual independence ', which they held to be greater than political liberty or civic independence ; but they were, in effect, seeking to secede from the justice and liberty of the State into another world of justice and liberty. Whether the challenge came from the Right or from the Left—from Catholic Rome or Calvinist Geneva—it had to be met and answered. The ' majestic lord who broke the bonds of Rome ' was after all breaking bonds, even if he was also imposing new and heavy bonds of his own. The great Protector and his Puritan colleagues, who sought to break the bonds of kings, were also seeking, in the name of ' Reformation ',[1] to establish a new bond of the rule of the saints which irked the political instinct of their countrymen ; and if the bonds they had broken were to remain broken, the bond they also imposed had also itself to be broken—as indeed it rapidly was. The State has its own title to existence, and its own right to do its own duty. Cromwell might believe that the essence of the people of England was ' the people of God ', or communion of true believers, which lay at its heart and must be free to move its life ; but the general people of England still clung to their ancient State and its ancient system of liberty.

In our own days it is not the religious, but the economic group—the whole class of the workers, or their several and separate occupations—which tends towards secession into a new loyalty to a new society. It is a new form of an old trend, with economic justice and economic liberty taking the place of the old cause of religious justice and religious liberty. Twice in Roman history there was a secession of the Roman *plebs* from the city of Rome to a hill which came to be called the *Mons Sacer*. On each occasion the secession was rapidly ended by the victory of the general good sense ; and the city of Rome

---

[1] ' It is a thing I am confident all liberty and prosperity depend upon— Reformation. Make it a sin to see men bold in sin and profaneness, and God will bless you. . . . Truly, these things do respect the souls of men, and the spirits—which *are* the men.' (Oliver Cromwell's speech to Parliament, on 17 September 1656.)

remained a single city, which still contained the *plebs* but gave it due recognition. Our own city, which we call the State, is always with us, and will always be with us ; and it will always be its duty to resist, but even more to avoid and avert, the threat of secession to any *Mons Sacer*—whether it be the *Mons Sacer* of the religious confession, or that of the economic occupation or class. Resistance by the State which is mere resistance, and ends in its pure domination, is the natural policy of authoritarianism ; and indeed the need of State resistance to threats of social secession is a cause which has helped to produce, and has certainly been alleged to justify, the modern growth of authoritarian government. Here secession has not been ended, as it was in ancient Rome, by any victory of general good sense, but by a policy of suppression and violent re-integration. This is a policy which a democratic government is prevented by its nature from pursuing. Faced by the menace of secession, it is constrained indeed to resist and to defend the integrity of the State ; but it is also and equally constrained to examine frankly the justice of the case which is pleaded on behalf of secession, and to achieve re-integration, so far as it possibly can, by the way of persuasion and just concession. It is a difficult task, which demands a nice balance of different duties and a delicate equilibrium of policy ; and it is a task which becomes even more complicated, as we have already had reason to notice, when secession assumes an inter-national character, and the secessionists of one country are linked with the governments or parties of others. But the task is not a new task in the long history of the State ; and even the complication is old. As long ago as 1579, when the problem of secession was a religious problem, the author of the *Vindiciae contra Tyrannos* was already examining, in the last section of his argument, the question whether one government might help the struggling subjects of another when they were afflicted in the cause of true religion and seeking a refuge from affliction. We need not pause to consider the answer which he gives to the question. But we may justly find comfort in the reflection that these problems, and even their complications, have arisen before our times ; that solutions have been eventually found ; and that they are still to be found for the seeking.

§ 3. THE WORKS OF JUSTIFICATION NOW CONFRONTING
DEMOCRACY

The mass movements of our times ; the emergence, largely in answer to them, of a new authoritarianism, armed with new physical powers and appealing to new mental forces ; the re-emergence, in a new form, of old threats of secession from the body politic—all these things may inspire grave doubts, and even serious fears, about the future of government and the fortunes of the State. Doubts and fears may well be intensified by the catastrophe of a world war—the second, as we are apt to say, in our generation, but in a truer and deeper sense the first—which has involved alike all the great and most of the smaller States, and may seem to have been produced by their existence and their rivalries. But States and governments are not necessarily condemned by their connection with war. They conduct it rather than create it : they canalize a turbid flow, rising in the deep springs of human jealousies and rancours, which, if it were not so canalized, might produce a general deluge overwhelming all civilization. War so conducted and canalized is at any rate better than chaos ; and it may even serve as a test and a trial of the value of the States and the forms of government which do the work of conducting and canalizing. The saying of Thucydides, that war is a violent schoolmaster, is a hard saying. But there is a sense in which the ordeal of war tries the metal and the value of each combatant, and teaches the general world the lesson of their worth.

Tried by the ordeal of war, the democratic form of government has not hitherto—in the course of the present century, and so far as the conflict has yet run its course—failed to stand the ultimate test. It is indeed a form which has its defects for the purposes of war. It shows a defect—if it be a defect— during the time of preparation for war. In that interim, ' like a phantasma or a hideous dream ', which comes between the action of war and the first motion leading towards it, the democratic State, by its nature, is engaged in hesitation and parley. It essays the way of compromise with its potential enemy, and attempts to appease his ambitions : it divides its internal councils, and falls into opposing parties of armaments and conciliation, The defect of the period of preparation prolongs itself into the period, and may prolong itself far into the period, of actual hostilities. Unprepared ; still hoping to agree with the adversary quickly : reluctant to divert the whole life of the community from ways of peace to the one way of war—the democratic State begins, and may long continue, with a series of reverses. Its advantages only begin to tell if it can face reverses stoutly ; gain for itself the benefit of time ; and begin to devote itself with a tenacious unanimity to the delayed task of preparation. Then it may show its mettle ; and then the initial reverses, if they have been safely endured, may become the parents of hope and unconquerable resolution. The issue, at the worst, will not be defeat : at the best it will be total victory, and the prestige of total victory.

But the prestige of victory, however great, can never establish the cause of democracy on irrefragable foundations. Victory in war will be an argument for democracy ; but it is not the greatest or the most enduring of arguments. The prestige of victory passes and perishes ; and indeed no prestige, however earned, will long endure unless it is being constantly earned afresh. Victory may sweep away the new authoritarianism ; and the dictators who have loomed so large and so titanically on the European stage may pass, along with their systems, as dictators have passed before (in South America[1] as well as in Europe), into the limbo of history. But the passing of authoritarian governments may still leave us confronted by the powers which they have evoked or enlisted in their service—the powers of personalism, of group-feeling and worship, of publicity, propaganda, drama, and constant tension. It will certainly still leave us confronted by the great movements of human life which have found their vehicles or exponents in authoritarian governments—the division of social groups and the demand for their integration in some scheme of unity : the trend towards autarky and the demand for its satisfaction or limitation : the movement of mechanization and the demand for its completion or correction. In particular, we shall still be confronted by the idea of secession from the State—an idea which is closely connected with the division of social groups.

It has been said by a leading Swiss writer on matters of

---

[1] Dr. Francia, the dictator of Paraguay, who has been called the prototype of the dictators of the modern world, exercised an absolute authority for the space of twenty-six years (1814–40). He was a great name in the time of our great-grandfathers. How few of us remember him now !

politics, who is a man of affairs as well as a scholar, that while dictatorship must justify its existence by its accomplishments, democracy owes its main accomplishments to its very existence.[1] It is a true saying, and it lays a just emphasis on the fact that the very process of democracy, in virtue of the demands which it makes on the minds and wills of its members, is in itself, and apart from any other results which it may achieve, a high and great achievement of the faculties of man. But it may also be observed, as indeed the writer himself proceeds to observe, that there are accomplishments which must be achieved by democracy if it is to ensure its own continuous and prosperous existence. It is justified as a faith ; but it must also be justified by works. It remains to inquire, in the conclusion and cadence of the argument, into the nature of the ' justification by works ' which remains to be achieved by democracy in that next and immediate stage of its life which is all that we can foresee.

Democracy must enlist the thought of the whole community in a process of discussion ; but it must also produce a government capable of conducting the affairs of war and peace. The production of a capable government, ready to initiate policies and able to maintain itself in power for a sufficient length of time to translate its policies into effect, is no easy matter. The tendency of many of the European States which have adopted democratic institutions has run towards the exaltation of party and the magnification of the legislative body in which parties wage their struggles and weave their combinations. The result has been a depression of the factor of executive government, and a subjugation of cabinets to the interests of parties (or combinations of parties) and to the self-importance of legislatures. It is true that cabinets must be dependent on parties, and responsible to legislatures ; but it is also true, as we have already had reason to argue, that the factor of cabinets stands by the side of the other factors of the democratic system (which includes both cabinet and the electorate as well as parties and the legislature) in a position of equal importance and equal independence. In the delicate balance of the democratic system cabinets have to command, as well as to obey, the organization of party : they have to guide, as well as follow, the opinion of the legislature ;

[1] Professor Rappard, in *The Crisis of Democracy*, p. 252.

they have to maintain their touch with the electorate, as well as with party and the legislature ; and it may be their duty to draw from the electorate an independent strength which enables them to confront with authority the other factors with which they are linked. It would be an error of policy to exalt the cabinet unduly at the expense of the legislature ; but it is perhaps a still greater, and it has certainly been a more widespread error, to exalt the legislature unduly at the expense of cabinet. A system and centre of leadership is necessary in any form of government ; and if governments of the authoritarian form have exaggerated this necessity into the *unum necessarium*, they can at any rate plead in their own defence that there was a large substance of truth behind the exaggeration.

The strengthening of executive government, and an adequate provision of leadership, is thus a work of justification which democracy has to achieve. It is not a paradox, but rather a truism, to add that the provision of a united and commanding executive must be accompanied by the provision of a united and challenging opposition. A cabinet is strengthened rather than weakened by the presence of an organized anti-cabinet ; and the general need for the ready provision of leadership is most likely to be satisfied when there is a coherent group of alternative leaders prepared to supply an alternative guidance as soon as it is required. It has been the absence of an organized and coherent opposition, no less than the absence of stable cabinets, which has weakened the cause of democratic government in a number of European countries. But the provision of an organized and coherent opposition, like the provision of a united and commanding executive, is not a thing which can be done by itself, or without other and allied accompaniments. An effective cabinet and an effective anti-cabinet both require a system of national parties which will make them possible ; and such a system of national parties demands, in turn, an organization of the electorate, and of its constituencies and methods of voting, which will be congruous with its existence. To achieve the reforms which democracy needs if it is to produce an effective government, balanced and strengthened by an effective opposition, will involve a large overhauling of democratic machinery. It will also involve the shedding of many old prejudices and presuppositions, and, above all, a purging and purification of the zeal of party, and a thinning and pruning of the self-importance of legislatures. Parties are not ends in themselves ; and parliaments are not enough to constitute the whole of democracy.

A second and an even greater work of justification is the strengthening of the power of discussion—the broadening of civic intelligence and the extension of civic knowledge. While democracy must, like all other forms of government, produce an effective government, it must above all, if it is to be true to its own peculiar nature, enlist the effective thought of the whole community in the operation of discussion. This is its essence ; and these are, for it, the *articuli cadentis ant stantis reipublicae.* Here we begin to see a large work of education adding itself to the work of political reconstruction and the overhauling and strengthening of government. Such work is particularly congenial and necessary to democracy, which itself is a mode and an instrument of the education of man and the development of human faculties. It is a work which may well proceed simultaneously in a series of ascending degrees and stages. In the first stage the elementary rights of freedom of speech, freedom of the Press, freedom of meeting and freedom of association—the necessary conditions and bases of any system of government by discussion—will have to be cleared from the clogs and impediments which have accumulated in the times of war and trouble. This, in itself, is a negative stage ; but it naturally leads to a second stage of a more clearly positive character. In that stage it will be necessary to enlist and develop, in the service of democracy, the new means of communication and discussion which have been provided by the achievements of scientific invention. Wireless communication, for instance, which has largely been used to amplify the voice of authority, may be used, by a juster application of its powers,. to disseminate the different voices of the different bodies of social opinion : and it may thus provide a new organ and instrument of discussion (as indeed it has already begun to do) which will draw together the great population in a common mental effort. But discussion proceeds at its best in more limited and intimate circles, as any teacher who has ever conducted a discussion class well knows ; and whatever may be the triumphs that broadcasting ultimately achieves, there will always be needed a number of small discussion groups (which may be based indifferently and equally on political parties, on religious societies concerned to discuss and present the bearing of religious views upon social issues, on social or ' community ' centres, and on educational associations) for the purpose of ventilating and formulating ' new notions and ideas, wherewith to present, as with their homage and fealty ', the broad general forum of national discussion.

We are thus carried forward to a third stage in the work of the educational justification of democracy.   This is a stage which involves a general and national system of adult education.   One of the lessons which we are gradually learning—and it is a lesson essential to the proper conduct of a true democracy—is that we cannot achieve an educated democracy merely, or even mainly, by the education of youth.   The mind is a vessel which constantly needs to be filled : or rather, to speak more justly, it is a living thing which needs to be constantly exercised and breathed.   In a moving world the movement of politics, of economics, of natural science, of literature and art, and of all the products and achievements of human thought, is in constant need of survey if we are to understand where we stand and what we ought to be doing ; and no adult can safely dispense with the continuance of education which is involved in such a survey.[1]   The modesty of the disciple who knows that he has still to learn, and is willing to act in the light of that knowledge, is a modesty that befits the citizen of a democratic State.   It is useless to belong to a political society which depends for its very existence on the active participation of the minds of all its members, unless you are willing to throw in your mind and to throw it in properly equipped.   It is useless, too, to live in an age of great scientific developments—an age in which the cool calm temper of science can lay a healing hand on fevers and distempers of the mind—unless you are willing to seek to understand something of those developments and, above all, of that temper.   We

[1] It has been the experience of the writer, for some little time past, to be connected with courses for the training of men of an average age of nearly 40—some of them men of affairs, more versed and experienced than he can claim to be, and some of them scholars of an equipment equal, at least, to his own.   It has been a moving experience.   We all learned, both those who were nominally teachers and those who were nominally students.   But above all, we all learned that we needed to learn, and that we still had the faculty of learning and a zest for the use of our faculty.

should all be wise to go to school at the feet of the true man of science, to whom his science is a method and not a dogma, and who can teach us, if we are willing to learn, the sovereign sanity of his method. We should all be especially wise to do so when we are citizens of a democracy ; and this for the simple reason that the temper of true science and the temper of true democracy are congenial and allied.[1]

The work of the educational justification of democracy will arm us against those emotional powers—powers of the lower and subliminal reaches of man's mind—which have been enlisted in the service of the new authoritarianism. It will enable us, without forfeiting or abandoning the leadership which we need, to reduce personalism to its due limits : it will enable us, without neglecting or forfeiting the mental unity and the common purpose which we require, to prick the bubble of the transcendent group and to discipline group-feeling and worship into a sober sense of co-operative fraternity : it will enable us, without relinquishing the high appeal of reason to reason and the high and noble excitement of mental effort, to chasten the power of propaganda and the dramatization of tension. But when the educational justification has been achieved, or while it is being achieved, there still remains another work of justification to be done. We may call it, if we will, a work of *social* justification. It is a work which has to be done to meet the threat of secession. In a more general sense, it is a work which has to be done to meet the great movements of contemporary human life. Democracy has to face the division of social interests and groups. It has to face the trend which sets towards autarky. It has to face the movement which makes for the mechanization of life. These are its greatest tasks : and it is by the extent to which it discharges these tasks that it will be mainly justified.

No policy of non-intervention, and nothing in the nature of *laissez-faire*, will solve the problems by which we are confronted. But we shall be misconceiving the very name and the whole of the nature of democracy if we connect it with non-intervention or a policy of *laissez-faire*. A system of government which proceeds by the method of discussion—which begins by the statement and recording of all claims, and proceeds to their reconciliation on a working hypothesis that

[1] *Supra*, pp. 226–31.

takes them all into account—must always intervene, and can leave no claim unregarded. The threat of secession is only a threat when an urgent claim is left unregarded, either because the governing authority washes its hands of all claims indifferently (a thing which no government, and certainly no democratic government, has ever done or even attempted to do), or because, animated by a social prejudice, it shuts its eyes to social claims which run counter to its prejudice. We may admit that the government of a democracy is liable to social prejudice. That is an inevitable result of the system of parties ; and it necessarily flows from the fact that different parties have a different social complexion and a different set of social presuppositions. But the social prejudice of one party will be corrected by that of another ; and the succession of parties in office will normally secure the succession and balance of prejudices. There is a compensating mechanism inherent in democracy.

It would be a folly, however, to trust to the operation of a compensating mechanism. If we did, we should still be putting our faith in ' the leading of an invisible hand ' which will reconcile different interests and promote the common good apart from our own intention and without our co-operation. It is not enough that different parties should represent different outlooks, and that the succession of parties in office should secure the successive representation of those outlooks. Democracy will always require, over and above the divergency and difference of different opinions and parties, a common fund of national opinion in which all parties share alike and of which all parties alike are agents. The problem before us, therefore, is the problem of so augmenting and enriching this common fund that we can all face the future with a common social philosophy, which reckons with the movements of contemporary life, and a common social policy which will enable us to guide and control them. We may think of two main conceptions which are needed for the enrichment of the common fund of national opinion. One of them is a new and broader conception of equality. The other is a new and broader conception of fraternity.

If democracy is wedded to liberty, liberty, in its turn, is wedded to equality. If men share a common liberty of thought and action, they are already, in that respect, the equals of one another. But the equal possession of liberty of thought and action is not the whole of equality. It is, in itself, and if nothing more be added to it, a bare equality. Equality in liberty of thought, if it is to have substance and content, must mean a large measure of equality in the education of mental capacity. Equality in liberty of action, if it too is to have substance and content, must mean some measure of equality in the possession of what we call ' means ', and this for the obvious reason that ' means ' are the means and conditions of action, and that inadequate ' means ' prevent free and liberal activity in the pursuit of ends. The equalization of education and ' means '—perhaps it would be better to say the steady reduction of the existing inequalities of education and ' means ' —is not an easy policy to pursue. If equality is wedded to liberty, the marriage must be equal, and liberty must not be dominated or diminished by equality. The compulsory institution of a system of pure equality would freeze the springs of initiative and reduce the variety of a living society to a static and dead uniformity. If a new and broader conception of equality is needed, it must not be purchased at the cost of surrendering our old conception of liberty. Each new approach to equality must be made by the methods of liberty, and it must also be consistent with the retention of liberty. But even in the name and the cause of liberty there is much that still waits to be done which would increase the scope and the general enjoyment of equality. Liberty in the sphere of industry—liberty which made employees as well as employers free partners, with a common status in a co-operative society where all had a voice about the conditions of production, and all enjoyed some ownership of its means—such liberty would disseminate a new and generous equality at the point, and in the range, where inequality is most irksome. To liberalize industry is also to equalize the human agents of industry.

We may thus hope to see the cause of equality advanced not only by the direct method of equalization of education and means, but also by the less direct, but perhaps even more fruitful, method of the extension of liberty into the conduct of production and the organization of industry. There remains the cause of fraternity. How can we add to the common fund of national opinion a new and broader conception of the nature of fraternity ? Fraternity is an old and vague term, which may almost seem to have been given vogue in 1789 for the simple purpose of rounding a triad. But it is possible to find a sense for the term which gives it a large and substantive value. Fraternity is the general sense of co-operation in a national society which impels its members to create, in the spirit of a family, the common framework or equipment, both material and mental, which is the necessary condition of the good life of the society and of each and all of its members. Here we may notice the word 'equipment'. It was the belief of Aristotle, and it was a just and well-founded belief, that the goodness of the individual required an adequate equipment, or, as he called it, 'choregia', composed of external goods. It was also his belief, and it was equally a just and well-founded belief, that the goodness of a political society similarly required an adequate equipment similarly composed. The political society of our days, no less than the political society of Aristotle's day, requires a common equipment, open equally to the enjoyment of all, which has to be created, in a spirit of fraternity, by a common effort of co-operation. It is an equipment both material and mental. On the material side it runs through a whole ascending gamut, from the provision of roads for the movement of the community to the promotion of its health, the development of its soil, and the preservation of all its amenities ; and in the length of time it may go further still, until it approaches the consummation which the ardent socialist desires to see immediately attained. On the mental side it begins with the provision of schools ; it has already proceeded to the provision of galleries, museums, libraries, and a system of national broadcasting : it may proceed to the provision of national theatres, concert-halls, and opera-houses (in the old Athenian manner of the theatre of Dionysus and the Odeum of Pericles) ; and who shall say where the national provision of a national equipment of culture may end ? This is the true and progressive socialism, which leads a nation to endow its life with an ever-growing equipment for the common enjoyment and profit. It is also the broad high-road to a new and larger equality, which invites all men to share equally in the riches of a common store. One of our poets has spoken of ' joy in widest commonalty spread '. Humanity desires comfort as well as joy, and joy as the crown of comfort. The State of the future has to bring us tidings of both—'tidings of comfort and joy'—comfort and joy both spread in commonalty, and both provided, by a common equipment, for all alike and all equally. Nothing, indeed, will ever absolve each man from the duty of providing, for himself, and by his own effort, the equipment which he needs for his own individual life. That is the way in which men try themselves out and prove what they are. But our descendants may none the less marvel that we spent so much time in storing private treasures, and neglected so long the building and storing of the common treasure-house.

Fraternity of this order, serving to provide a common stock and equal facilities for a common and equal enjoyment, and thus allying itself readily with a new and broader conception of equality, will enable the democratic State to meet and direct the movements impinging on its life. It will bring a new sense of unity into the division of social groups and interests. It will raise to a higher plane the movement which makes for autarky, lifting the nation above the pursuit of mere economic self-sufficiency to the ideal of a general equipment, mental as well as material, of the whole of the national life. It will correct and complement the movement of mechanization, adding to the triumphs of the machine a new triumph of the spirit, and setting by the side of the factory the facilities and institutions for the exercise of the mind.

But above and beyond the building of a broader national fraternity, in each democratic State, there lies the work of building an international fraternity, equipped with its own resources, which can serve as the shelter and shield of the building of national fraternity. It is vain to think of the expansion of a generous national life except in the shelter and under the protection of an organized system of international peace. But the more each nation is moved to expand its internal life towards a broader equality and a broader and deeper fraternity, the more will it move towards an international system.

January 1942

INDEX